The V

M
coasta

1 2 MAY 2000

3 0 APR 2002

1 2 APR 2005

i

The Wet Grassland Guide

Managing floodplain and coastal wet grasslands for wildlife

Written by
Phil Benstead, Martin Drake, Paul José,
Owen Mountford, Chris Newbold and Jo Treweek

Edited by
Jo Treweek, Paul José and Phil Benstead

Citation
For bibliographic purposes this book should be referred to as *The Wet Grassland Guide:*
Managing floodplain and coastal wet grasslands for wildlife;
under the authorship of RSPB, EN and ITE

The techniques described or referred to in this book do not necessarily reflect the policies
of the partner organisations or individuals involved in its production. A great deal of the
information presented originated from the experiences of individual grassland managers
and must therefore be considered on a site-specific basis.

No responsibility can be accepted for any loss, damage or unsatisfactory results arising
from the implementation of any of the recommendations within this book.

The use of proprietary and commercial trade names in this guidebook does not necessarily
imply endorsement of the product by the partner organisations.

Published by
The Royal Society for the Protection of Birds,
The Lodge, Sandy, Beds SG19 2DL

Design by
Philip Cottier

Typesetting and page design by
Harry Scott, Pica Design

Figures by
Rob and Rhoda Burns, Drawing Attention

Printed by
Portland Print Ltd.

RSPB Ref: 24/1010/98-9

ISBN No: 0 903138 86 7

Cover photographs:
Wet grassland: M W Richards (RSPB)
Snake's-head fritillary: A Parcell (Bruce Coleman Ltd)
Broad-bodied chaser: A Hay (RSPB)
Black-tailed godwit: F V Blackburn (RSPB)

Endorsements

The following organisations have endorsed the production of this guide:

 Ministry of Agriculture Fisheries and Food

 ENVIRONMENT AGENCY

 ada

 RIVERS Agency

Cranfield UNIVERSITY

COUNTRYSIDE COMMISSION

 WWT

 FWAG

 THE wildlife TRUSTS

 SAC

 THE NATIONAL TRUST

 SEPA

EUROSITE

Contents

Part 5 Survey and Monitoring of Flora and Fauna of Wet Grassland

Part 6 Case Studies

Appendices

References

Index

Acknowledgments

The Royal Society for the Protection of Birds, English Nature and the Institute of Terrestrial Ecology acknowledge that the production of this book was only made possible by the input from many people and organisations, who so willingly gave of their time and information.

The book was edited by Jo Treweek, Paul José (Project Manager) and Phil Benstead (Project Officer). Sylvia Sullivan was production editor. Special thanks go to the members of the RSPB Internal Steering Group: Roger Buisson, Sarah Fowler, Carl Hawke, Les Street and Jim Glover. John Leece spent his sabbatical visiting four case study sites and drafting reports for them. Carl Hawke also drafted several of the case studies. The ITE internal steering group also provided valuable advice and thanks are due to Prof. Mike Roberts, Prof. John Sheail and Richard Caldow.

General acknowledgments

We are grateful to the following who provided contributions or comments on parts or all of the text:
Malcolm Ausden (RSPB), Hannah Bartram (RSPB), Dave Beaumont (RSPB), Phil Boon (SNH), James Cadbury (RSPB), Tim Callaway (RSPB), Julianne Evans (RSPB), David Gowing (Silsoe College), Mike Hann (Silsoe College), Michael Harrison (MAFF), John Harvey (National Trust), Nigel Holmes (Alconbury Environmental Consultants), Doug Ireland (RSPB), Rob Jarman (NT), Richard Jefferson (EN), Debbie Jones (EA), Chris Joyce (Loughborough University), Richard Knight (FWAG), Alison Lea (RSPB), Jane Mackintosh (SNH), Sarah Manchester (ITE), Stuart McFadzean (Environment Agency), David Noble (ADA), Mark O'Brien (RSPB), Paul Raven (EA), Prof. Mike Roberts (ITE), Steve Sankey (RSPB), Matt Self (RSPB), Prof. John Sheail (ITE), Jude Smith (WWT), Ken Smith (RSPB), Prof. Gordon Spoor (Silsoe College), Dr David Stevens (CCW), Vicki Swales (RSPB), Andy Swash (MAFF) and Mark Whiteman (EA).

Management and case study information and time was provided by the following:
Clive Barber (E Allman & Co Ltd), Dave Barrett (RSPB), Mike Bell (Stirling University), Mike Blackburn (RSPB), Keith Blomerley (RSPB), Jane Brookhouse (RSPB), Tim Callaway (RSPB), Cliff Carson (RSPB), Danny Cavanagh (RSPB), Joan Childs (RSPB), John Courtney (DANI), Pete Cranswick (WWT), Russell Cryer (RSPB), Jonathan Curtoys (RSPB), Jim Dixon (RSPB), Tim Dixon (EN), Alistair Driver (EA), Vicki Emerson, Ceri Evans (RSPB), Julia Fairey (RSPB), David Gilvear (Stirling University), Dick Greenaway (EA), Bob Gomes (RSPB), Mike Harding (SWT), Ron Harold (EN), Andy Hay (RSPB), Andrew Henderson, Graham Hirons (RSPB), Julian Jones (EN), Roger Key, Francis Kirkham (ADAS), Charlie Kitchin (RSPB), Albert Knot (EN), Neil Lambert (RSPB), Roy Lambourne, Sandra Lambton (RSPB), John Leece (RSPB), Peter Mayhew (RSPB), Andrew Mayled (National Trust), Godfrey McRoberts (DANI), Clive Mellon (RSPB), Alistair Moralee (RSPB), Joe Nicholson (DANI), Sarah Niemann (RSPB), Alan Parker (RSPB), Kevin Peberdy (WWT), Mike Prosser (Ecological Surveys), Dave Rees (RSPB), Nick Sanderson (SWT), Chris Sargeant (RSPB), Graham Scholey (EA), David Sexton (RSPB), David Sheppard (EN), Anne Skinner (EA), Les Street (RSPB), Iain Sturdy (EA), Rick Southwood (EN), Jerry Tallowin (IGER), Jon Taylor (RSPB), Chris Tyas (RSPB), Hilary Wallace (Ecological Surveys) and Jan Williams (Environment Agency).

Finally, thanks and apologies to any individuals or organisations who contributed in any way but whom we have inadvertently failed to acknowledge.

Foreword

Wet grasslands are very much a part of a diverse countryside. They epitomise the way in which traditional livestock farming supports abundant and varied wildlife, including flower-rich meadows with breeding snipe and lapwing. They also act as flood storage areas and buffer zones, protecting more vulnerable land from flooding and improving water quality in our rivers.

In England and Wales, recent initiatives such as Water level Management Plans and Local Environment Agency Plans should make it possible to balance the occasionally conflicting interests of water management, conservation and agriculture. The Government's Biodiversity Action Plan process provides the framework for such action on our wet grasslands, setting out clear targets for protecting existing habitats and for restoring others. A good example has been set by the provision of specific incentives within Environmentally Sensitive Areas made by Schemes such as Countryside Stewardship which have enabled real benefits to be realised.

I am pleased to be associated with this new management guide and sincerely hope that it will encourage and enhance the conservation of wet grassland throughout the UK.

The Lord De Ramsey

INTRODUCTION

Background

This guide is a practical handbook to techniques of wet grassland management that integrate the requirements of wildlife with sustainable low-intensity agriculture. The publication of this guide is timely for a number of reasons:

■ Recognition both by government agencies and conservation organisations of the benefits of taking a systematic approach to biodiversity conservation. This is reflected in the biodiversity action planning process which through clear objectives and measurable targets for species and habitats aims to safeguard existing, and restore degraded, floodplain and coastal wet grassland habitat (HMSO 1995).

■ Increased public awareness of environmental and agricultural issues, particularly as a result of losses of wildlife throughout the country.

■ The acknowledgment that wet grassland management has to be addressed in an integrated manner taking account of wider water management issues. Recognition of the value of wet grasslands as flood storage areas and buffer zones providing flood defence and water quality benefits has been critical to realising their environmental value. The development of the catchment management planning process (now through Local Environment Agency Plans) and Water Level Management Plans should enable key players to balance agricultural, wildlife and water management interests in an integrated manner.

■ Significant changes in agricultural policy have led to the development of several schemes which provide funding for low-intensity/sensitive wet grassland management (eg Environmentally Sensitive Areas, Countryside Stewardship, and the Wildlife Enhancement Scheme).

■ It fills the current information gap, collating 'state of the art' prescriptive guidance on best practice management options. These should prove invaluable for land managers who wish to enter agri-environment schemes for the first time or those who wish to 'refine' their management approach to further benefit wildlife.

■ It discusses alternative management options for the habitat and should help when addressing the potential impact of BSE, which could threaten the very existence of our wet grasslands as a result of lack of grazing.

The guide is aimed at all land managers who have the desire to sustainably manage wet grassland for the benefit of wildlife. The guide provides managers with a range of information on wet grassland management in a readable, yet authoritative format.

Structure of the guide

The text is separated into six parts.
Part 1 defines wet grassland and highlights its importance for conserving a range of plants and animals. This section also considers the other values of wet grassland and outlines the threats, causes of damage and loss. Finally, opportunities for the future and potential funding mechanisms are discussed.

Part 2 of the guide highlights the importance of planning for management and creation. This section considers what should be done once the potential to rehabilitate a site or create new wet grassland has been recognised. It explains how to evaluate a site and examines the range of physical, chemical, wildlife and legal factors that may influence management decisions.

Part 3 considers the ecological requirements of wet grassland plants and animals, including plant communities, aquatic plants of drainage channels and ponds, terrestrial and aquatic invertebrates and birds which make use of wet grassland.

Part 4 describes wet grassland management and rehabilitation techniques and gives examples of best practice for relevant site conditions. Sub-divisions outline the management of water, drainage channels, grassland and its associated habitats. The water management section explains how the water regime of a site can be influenced by environmental factors and by management. Problems associated with water quality and soil type are discussed and practical solutions proposed. Techniques for water level control such as bunds, sluices and dams are described. The importance of drainage channels for wildlife is highlighted and provides guidance on best practice for their management. The grassland management section looks in detail at the two main management techniques – mowing and grazing. Other aspects of grassland management are also covered such as the use of fire and herbicides. Grassland restoration looks at available restoration techniques, such as natural regeneration, species introduction and seeding techniques. The advantages and disadvantages of different techniques are discussed. Management of associated habitats deals with the management of the important habitats often found alongside wet grassland, such as pollards and springs and seepages. Part 4 is completed with a section on Managing for Multiple Objectives, which attempts to bring together information from Parts 3 and 4 to produce general management prescriptions for wet grasslands with wintering and breeding birds.

Part 5 briefly examines techniques available for surveying and monitoring a range of plants and animals, as well as discussing the monitoring of water levels. Using plants as indicators of water quality is also described.

The general text is supported by cross-referencing to **Part 6**, which consists of 17 case studies, each illustrating one or more of the management techniques described in the guide. The order of these case studies parallels the structure of Parts 1–5. The management case studies are concluded by a look at the overall management of West Sedgemoor RSPB Nature Reserve, to show how a range of management techniques can be successfully integrated.

The appendices consist largely of detailed information on the requirements of wetland plant communities and species, as well as providing useful addresses, and details of funding mechanisms.

Part 1
WET GRASSLAND

Contents

1.1 Introduction

Wet grasslands in the UK provide valuable habitat for indigenous plants, birds and invertebrates, particularly in the lowlands where wildlife habitats are so limited. They develop on land which is periodically flooded or waterlogged by fresh water and where management for agriculture (grazing, mowing or a combination of the two) promotes vegetation dominated by lower growing grasses, sedges and rushes (Figure 1.1). They do not include reed-dominated habitats.

Wet grassland encompasses a broad continuum of wetland types. These include:

- semi-natural floodplain grassland

- washland

- water meadows

- wet grasslands with intensive water level management on drained soils

- lakeside wet grassland.

Figure 1.1 Major wet grassland areas in the UK; many of these have ditch systems of conservation importance. Sites in bold include areas designated as Environmentally Sensitive Areas (ESAs).

1.1.1 Semi-natural floodplain grassland

This occurs where floodplains are subjected to a semi-natural hydrological regime (Plates 1 & 2). These range from the Insh Marshes (a floodplain mire on the River Spey – Case Study 1) to areas of seasonally inundated flood meadows (eg the Lower Derwent Valley – Case Study 12).

Naturally functioning floodplains are rare in the UK where most rivers are intensively engineered and regulated. The rich biodiversity of active floodplain systems, such as the Insh Marshes, where past attempts to embank the river have proved largely ineffective, demonstrates the importance of natural processes in wet grassland systems.

(RSPB)

Plate 1
Insh Marshes (River Spey, Scotland), the most natural remaining floodplain in the UK, where low-intensity grassland management is carried out for the benefit of wildlife.

(RSPB)

Plate 2
The River Avon (Hampshire) has a semi-natural flooding regime and maintains wet grassland wildlife interest.

1.1.2 Washland

Washlands are embanked areas created for the purpose of flood storage. Unlike floodplain grassland (described above), which generally experience gradual rises in water levels above the surface, washland may be subject to sudden inundation, often of longer duration. The Ouse Washes were constructed between 1630 and 1653 by Dutchman Cornelius Vermuyden in order to drain the East Anglian Fens. This artificial flood storage area now forms the largest washland in the UK. Winter-flooded washlands often support large populations of wintering birds (Case Studies 2 and 11, Plate 3). Characteristic plant communities tolerant of extended periods of inundation have developed in these areas (section 3.2.2).

(RSPB)

Plate 3
Artificial washlands (eg the Ouse Washes), regularly inundated each winter, prevent adjacent low-lying areas from flooding and provide habitat for thousands of wintering birds.

1.1.3 Water meadows

In some areas, deliberate controlled flooding was used to boost fertility and raise hay yields. Such water meadows were a particular feature of many of the southern chalkland valleys in the 17th and 18th centuries. Some were also constructed in the Midlands (Taylor 1975). They were generally flooded in February to provide spring grazing for ewes and lambs; then again to irrigate the hay crop in June. These were complex systems to maintain and declined with changing farming practices by the beginning of the 20th century. Few remain in working order (Case Study 3).

1.1.4 Wet grassland with intensive water level management on drained soils

Plate 4 West Sedgemoor, situated on drained peat within the Somerset Levels and Moors is managed for low-intensity agriculture. Shallow flooded fields with abundant rushes support one of Europe's largest regular wintering flocks of teal.

(RSPB)

Many wetland areas on both peat and alluvial soils have been converted to productive agricultural grassland (eg the Somerset Levels and Moors and areas of the Norfolk Broads). By the 19th century the present-day landscape of pasture with drainage channels had evolved (Plate 4). Further agricultural improvements occurred in many of these areas after the Second World War when flood alleviation works, and the introduction of artificial fertilisers and herbicides increased their productivity. These areas now have artificial highly regulated water regimes. The grass composition is frequently improved as a result of re-seeding with rye-grass mixtures and other fast-growing species. However, some areas still contain significant botanical interest within field areas and in the drainage channels (eg West Sedgemoor – Case Study 15).

Plate 5 Coastal grazing marshes (eg Elmley RSPB nature reserve) support characteristic plant and animal communities, as a result of salt water influence.

(RSPB)

In the UK the term coastal grazing marsh has been used traditionally to refer to those areas of land reclaimed from the sea (eg saltmarsh areas) behind sea walls (eg Elmley, Kent – Plate 5). Such areas are referred to as polders in Europe and have highly regulated water regimes. Truly natural coastal grasslands, as found in other parts of Europe (eg the Baltic), are rare in the UK.

1.1.5 Pond and lakeside wet grassland

These are areas of wet grassland around the margins of lakes and ponds which may be temporarily inundated owing to seasonal water level increases (eg Lough Beg in Northern Ireland – Plate 6).

(RSPB)

**Plate 6
Lakeside wet grassland is an important feature of many wetland areas in Northern Ireland and Scotland.**

1.1.6 Drainage channels

Drainage channels, as well as grasslands themselves, play an important part in supporting wildlife. There are an estimated 128,000 km of drainage channel in England and Wales (Marshall *et al* 1978). These include natural creeks and man-made drainage channels which provide an important aquatic habitat on wet grassland sites (Plate 7). They are variously referred to as dykes, drains, ditches, lanes, rheens or rhynes. The network of drains may also include shallower, surface drainage channels (grips or foot drains). Areas with extensive networks of drainage channels include the predominantly arable Fenland basin and also the Broads and the Somerset Levels and Moors where there is more grassland. The greatest diversity of drainage channel species and communities occurs in these grassland areas, particularly in the grazing marshes. In some cases the flora and fauna of drainage channels may be relicts from earlier wetland ecosystems. This is believed to be the case for some drainage channel systems in the Somerset Levels, the Broads, and Romney Marsh in Kent.

(Malcolm Ausden)

**Plate 7
Grazing marsh drainage channels often support a wealth of wildlife, including rare plants and invertebrates. This ditch system at Castle Marshes (Suffolk) supports a population of a rare dragonfly, the Norfolk hawker.**

1.2 Value of wet grassland

1.2.1 Value for wildlife

Wet grasslands have high nature conservation interest and support a wide range of indigenous plant, bird and invertebrate species (Ratcliffe 1977, Fuller 1982), many of which are rare and or declining.

Plants

Approximately 500 species of vascular plants have been recorded from wet grassland and associated drainage channels (Thomas *et al* 1995). Drainage channels support some 130 of Britain's 170 species of brackish and freshwater vascular plants. A 20-m stretch in a good drainage channel can hold more than 15 aquatic plant species. Some rare species, such as rootless duckweed (Britain's smallest flowering plant), sharp-leaved pondweed and water-soldier, are seldom found in other types of water-body (Table 3.5).

The plant communities of wet grassland consist of grasses and wild flowers, rushes and sedges. The National Vegetation Classification (Rodwell 1991, 1992, 1995) lists 18 plant communities associated with wet grassland (Table 1.1). Some of these communities have become very restricted in extent (Table 1.2). Of particular conservation importance, in a European context, is the MG4 meadow foxtail and great burnet flood meadow, which is included in Annex 1 of the Council Directive on the Conservation of Natural Habitats and Wild Flora and Fauna (The Habitats Directive – 92/43/EEC). Although few Red Data Book (RDB) and nationally scarce plants are restricted to wet grassland habitats, they make a valuable contribution to the conservation of those species (Table 1.3).

Table 1.1: National Vegetation Classification (NVC) of wet grassland and associated communities.

Typical wet grassland		
MG4	–	Flood meadows – meadow foxtail and great burnet grassland
MG5	–	Old grazed hay meadows – crested dog's-tail and common knapweed grassland
* MG6	–	Dairy and fatting pastures – perennial rye-grass and crested dog's-tail pasture
* MG7	–	Improved and sown swards – perennial rye-grass leys and related grasslands
MG8	–	Water meadows – crested dog's-tail and marsh-marigold grassland
* MG9	–	Tussocky wet meadows – Yorkshire-fog and tufted hair-grass grassland
* MG10	–	Ordinary damp meadows – Yorkshire-fog and soft-rush rush-pasture
MG11	–	Inundation grassland – red fescue, creeping bent and silverweed grassland
MG12	–	Upper saltmarsh ungrazed swards – tall fescue grassland
MG13	–	Inundation grassland – creeping bent and marsh foxtail grassland
Mire		
M22	–	Rich fen-meadows – blunt-flowered rush and marsh thistle fen-meadow
M23	–	Western fen-meadows – soft/sharp-flowered rush and marsh-bedstraw rush-pasture
M24	–	Litter and wet Culm grassland – purple moor-grass and meadow thistle fen-meadow
M25	–	Purple moor-grass grassland – purple moor-grass and tormentil mire
Swamp		
S5	–	Washland – reed sweet-grass swamp
S6	–	Tall sedge-meadows – great pond-sedge swamp
S7	–	Tall sedge meadows – lesser pond-sedge swamp
S22	–	Floating sweet-grass hollows – floating sweet-grass water margin vegetation

Most of these communities are semi-natural, with the exception of those marked with a *, which are considered to be agriculturally improved.
Source: Rodwell (1991, 1992, 1995)

Table 1.2: Estimated areas of the scarcer, botanically interesting, typical wet grassland plant communities in England.

NVC community type		Area (ha)
MG4	– Flood meadows	<1,500
MG5	– Old grazed hay meadows	<5,000
MG8	– Water meadows	<500
MG11	– Inundation grassland	<1,000?
MG13	– Inundation grassland	<2,000?

Source: Jefferson and Robertson (1996)

Invertebrates

Wet grassland supports very large numbers of invertebrate species (Drake 1988a, b). Many species, particularly some of the less common ones, are associated with the drainage channels and saturated ground rather than with the grass sward itself. Over a thousand nationally notable species have been recorded on wet grasslands, about a quarter of which are listed in Red Data Books (Drake in press a). One of these, the marsh fritillary, has an internationally important population in the UK (ie >20% of the western European population). Although the majority of invertebrates found on wet grassland can also be found in other wetland situations, wet grasslands are the stronghold for species like the hairy dragonfly, variable damselfly and the great silver water beetle. Brackish marshes are the stronghold for many coastal water beetles. Appendix 1

Table 1.3: Red Data Book and nationally scarce plants of wet grassland

Species	NVC community that it occurs in*
Red Data Book	
Downy-fruited sedge	MG4
Tuberous thistle	MG5
Greater yellow-rattle	MG5
Creeping marshwort	MG13
Nationally scarce	
Marsh-mallow	
Slender hare's-ear	
Divided sedge	
Elongated sedge	
Narrow-leaved water-dropwort	MG4
Sea clover	
Snake's-head fritillary	MG4, MG5
Dwarf mouse-ear	MG5
Sulphur clover	MG5
Sea barley	MG6
Milk-parsley	M22, M24
Wavy St John's-wort	M24
Cambridge milk-parsley	M24

* see Table 1.1 for full names of NVC communities.

lists nationally scarce and rare species that are widespread on wet grasslands. It does not include, however, species such as the water beetle *Hydaticus transversalis* and the lesser silver water beetle that have very restricted ranges.

Table 1.4: Birds of conservation concern that use wet grassland

Season	Red list species – high conservation concern ie those whose population or range is rapidly declining – either recently or historically – and those of global conservation concern.	Amber list species – medium conservation concern ie those whose population is in moderate decline, rare breeders, internationally important and localised species and those of unfavourable conservation status in Europe.
Winter	Hen harrier, merlin, twite	**Bewick's swan**, whooper swan, **bean goose**, pink-footed goose, white-fronted goose, barnacle goose, brent goose, wigeon, **shoveler**, gadwall, pintail, peregrine, golden plover, common gull, short-eared owl, fieldfare, redwing, starling
Summer	Quail, corncrake, **black-tailed godwit**	**Garganey**, pintail, **spotted crake**, **ruff**, oystercatcher, **whimbrel** (on passage), curlew, redshank
All year	Grey partridge, skylark, tree sparrow, linnet	Teal, shoveler, pochard, kestrel, lapwing, ruff, snipe, barn owl, kingfisher, goldfinch.

Species in bold are those where over 40% of their UK population uses the habitat during the time period.

Table 1.5: Examples of important wet grassland sites for birds in the UK.

Site	Maxima of wintering waterfowl 1993/94	Wintering species of conservation concern occurring in internationally important numbers	Breeding species of conservation concern
Ouse Washes	54,381 ■ wildfowl 49,779 ■ waders 4,602	Bewick's swan, whooper swan, teal, wigeon, gadwall, pintail, shoveler and black-tailed godwit.	Garganey, shoveler, pochard, black-tailed godwit, ruff, lapwing, snipe, redshank, spotted crake, quail and barn owl.
Somerset Levels and Moors	61,107 ■ wildfowl 29,833 ■ waders 31,274	Bewick's swan, teal and lapwing.	Garganey, black-tailed godwit, curlew, snipe, redshank, lapwing and quail.
Elmley RSPB Nature Reserve	48,483 ■ wildfowl 26,005 ■ waders 22,478	European white-fronted goose, wigeon and black-tailed godwit.	Gadwall, shoveler, pochard, grey partridge, oystercatcher, lapwing, snipe, black-tailed godwit, avocet, ringed plover and redshank.
Lower Derwent Valley	32,312 ■ wildfowl 26,356 ■ waders 5,956	Teal.	Garganey, pintail, shoveler, black-tailed godwit, ruff, lapwing, snipe, redshank, spotted crake, quail and barn owl.
Nene Washes	25,491 ■ wildfowl 19,989 ■ waders 5,502	Bewick's swan and pintail.	Garganey, gadwall, shoveler, black-tailed godwit, ruff, lapwing, snipe and redshank.

Sites such as these, which regularly support over 20,000 wintering waterfowl, are considered to be internationally important.
Source: Winter count data from Cranswick et al *(1995).*

Birds

Over 40 bird species of conservation concern are dependent or partly dependent on the UK's remaining wet grasslands, most are winter visitors (Table 1.4). A number of species, eg black-tailed godwit, are declining across much of their range.

Wet grassland provides breeding or wintering habitat for a number of species, particularly waders and wildfowl. Several wet grassland sites in the UK attract internationally important concentrations of wintering wildfowl and waders (Table 1.5, Case Studies 2 and 15). These sites are safeguarded as Special Protection Areas (SPAs) under the EC Directive on the Conservation of Wild Birds (The Birds Directive – 79/409/EEC). Additionally, the UK government has ratified The Convention on Wetlands of International Importance especially as Waterfowl Habitat (drafted in Ramsar, Iran). A total of 27 UK wet grassland sites are designated as SPA/'Ramsar' sites in recognition of their international importance for wintering birds.

Large concentrations of wintering waterfowl may attract predatory birds, such as peregrines, merlins and hen harriers. Resident birds of prey include kestrels and barn owls, which mainly specialise in catching small mammals. More widespread species may also rely on wet grassland. Skylark, and to a lesser extent meadow pipit, use the habitat for breeding, whilst wintering flocks of starling, thrushes, crows and gulls feed in large numbers on invertebrates linked with short grass swards. Seed-eating birds, principally finches, buntings and sparrows, feed on the fruiting bodies of many grassland plants.

Fish

Drainage channels and open water areas of wet grassland support a number of fish species, including pike, roach, bream, rudd, stickleback and eel. The more diverse the habitat, in terms of structure, extent and depth, the more species are likely to be present. Eels are an important prey item for grey heron and otter, while smaller species, such as the stickleback, are important for kingfishers and grass snakes.

Amphibians and reptiles

The drainage channels and ponds of wet grassland are utilised by five of the six native species of amphibians. Although they are not restricted to wet grassland, these species have declined over the last 100 years with the reduction of suitable habitat in the lowlands. The only amphibian with a marked association with wet grassland is the introduced marsh frog, which is found primarily in grazing marsh drainage channels in south-east England.

Few reptiles are encountered in wet grassland. The exception is the grass snake, which is largely aquatic and feeds on frogs, newts, fish, large invertebrates, small mammals and birds.

Mammals

Wet grassland is also important for a small number of threatened (or declining) mammals:

■ Otters will use drainage channels close to suitable rivers. Water quality is important. Organo-chlorine poisoning is one of the factors that has led to declines this century (Jeffries 1996). Unfortunately, modern-day threats may continue to cause problems, especially exposure to polychlorinated bi-phenyls (a by-product of the manufacture of electrical components) and acidification of waterways. Artificial holts can be constructed to encourage otters in suitable areas (RSPB *et al* 1994).

■ Water voles also occur along drainage channels in wet grassland. The UK population appears to be in a steep decline. For example, Strachan (1996) recorded a 75% decline during a study of the Thames Valley between 1990 and 1995. This is probably associated both with an increase in the populations of introduced mink and habitat destruction. A similar decline has been noted on RSPB nature reserves, coincident with the arrival of mink (Cadbury and Lambton 1994).

■ Wet grasslands are also important feeding areas for bats. They provide prey-rich feeding areas for species such as pipistrelles and noctules, especially when they form a part of a matrix of other habitats, including woodland edge and open water.

1.2.2 Wetland values

Wet grassland maintenance, restoration and creation can not only enhance nature conservation values, but also provide wider benefits such as:

■ floodwater and sediment storage in floodplain/washland areas

■ improvements in water quality through natural purification functions

■ improvements in water quality by reducing the area of land under intensive agricultural management

■ water resource benefits, such as improved aquifer recharge and fewer associated problems with low river flows.

1.3 Threats to wet grassland

Historically there have been substantial losses in the area and quality of wet grassland in the UK and a consequent decline in populations of dependent flora and fauna. This has been brought about by:

- changes in agricultural practices including:
  - increased land drainage
  - increase in fertiliser use
  - change from hay cutting to silage
  - degradation by neglect (in some areas)
  - re-seeding
  - herbicide use
  - conversion to arable.

- land drainage/flood defence leading to:
  - modification of natural floodplain regimes
  - isolation of floodplains from river flows
  - early fall in water-table levels in spring
  - rapid evacuation of winter floods
  - maintenance of low drainage channel levels in winter to increase floodwater storage capacity
  - use of aquatic herbicides.

- abstraction (Plate 8) leading to:
  - lowered river flows and water levels
  - lowered water levels in wetlands
  - exacerbation of drought-related problems.

- eutrophication leading to:
  - changes in grassland sward/communities
  - increased sward vigour, which allows higher stocking densities.

- sea-level rise leading to:
  - loss of coastal grazing marsh.

- built development on floodplains leading to:
  - restrictions on future flooding regimes
  - increased flooding of remaining washlands.

- site fragmentation leading to:
  - isolation of sites making specialist species vulnerable to extinction
  - problems with water-level control and agricultural management.

Plate 8
Water abstraction for agriculture and particularly for domestic supply continues to pressurise a scarce resource.

(Environment Agency)

Plate 9
Channelisation of rivers has resulted in seasonal declines in water-tables throughout the UK, particularly during the spring. This has had a serious impact on wildlife habitats.

(RSPB)

The driving force behind many losses of wet grassland in the past was UK and EC agricultural policies which promoted increased agricultural production above other considerations, including wildlife conservation. Conversion of grazed grassland to arable crops and the more intensive utilisation of remaining grassland was facilitated by the introduction of improved drainage infrastructure and an increase in drainage efficiency, which reduced the conservation interest of many wetland sites (Plate 9). The introduction of the Agri-environment Regulations has done a lot to curb the damage by providing financial incentives for positive management but poor water quality, increased abstraction and the impact of historic, or former, flood defence activities continue to have deleterious effects.

1.4 Extent, distribution and loss of wet grassland

Wet grassland is distributed throughout the UK with notable concentrations in the lowland floodplains of England and, to a lesser extent, Wales, Scotland and Northern Ireland (Figure 1.1).

Table 1.6: Examples of the loss of wet grassland this century

England
Around 28,000 ha lost since the 1930s in the Greater Thames estuary:

- 69% converted to arable

- the remainder lost to industry and housing developments

- the grassland areas that remain are very fragmented.

Wales
All the wet grassland sites that held substantial numbers of breeding or wintering waterfowl have been drained, leaving none of international importance in Wales. There have been substantial but unquantified declines in waders in the post-war years. Recent surveys of lapwing, snipe and curlew between 1981/82 and 1988/89, and of redshank at six coastal marshes between 1985 and 1991 revealed the following declines (Tyler 1992):

- snipe 60%

- redshank 58%

- lapwing 54%

- curlew 13%.

Northern Ireland
Some 3,500 ha of the River Blackwater catchment, in Northern Ireland, was drained in the early 1980s. This resulted in declines of:

- 52% in the number of pairs of breeding wader

- 78% in curlew numbers

- 69% in lapwing numbers.

Scotland
There is little information on wet grassland loss or decline in Scotland. Declines are evident in waders breeding in wet grassland in the Outer Hebrides and Orkney. But other populations are stable and even increasing.

Land drainage and agricultural intensification have caused marked declines in many of the plant and bird species of wet grasslands (Table 1.6, Figure 1.2). It has been estimated that the area of wet grassland has decreased by 40% between the 1930s and 1980s primarily as a result of drainage and agricultural improvements (Williams and Hall 1987, Williams *et al* 1983). During this period more wet grassland has been lost than any other type of grassland (Figures 1.3 and 1.4).

Figure 1.2 Maximum count of wintering wildfowl at Pulborough Brooks, before and after major river engineering work (embankments)

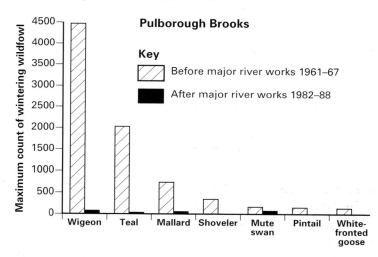

Figure 1.3
Decline in the extent of coastal grassland in four areas of south-east England (Williams and Bowers 1987)

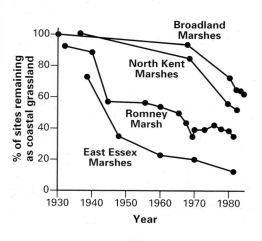

Figure 1.4 Loss and fragmentation of grazing marsh in North Kent, 1935–82 (Williams *et al* 1983)

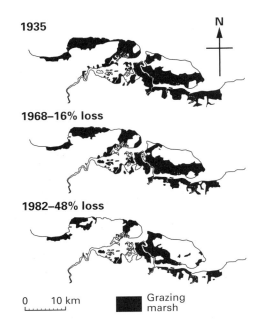

1935

1968–16% loss

1982–48% loss

0   10 km

■ Grazing marsh

Only 220,000 ha of wet grassland remain in England and Wales from a historical resource of 1,200,000 ha. Much of this remaining wet grassland has been agriculturally improved and is of reduced value for wildlife. The widespread disappearance of extensively managed hay meadows and pastures has been reflected in a marked decline in many plant species, even those like the cowslip and meadow buttercup which were once common (Mountford 1994, Wells *et al* 1989). Only 109,000 ha currently support breeding waders and a mere 20,000 ha are thought to be agriculturally unimproved wet grassland of high conservation value (Thomas *et al* 1995). By 1984, the extent of unimproved lowland grassland in England and Wales was estimated to be 3% of its extent in 1938 (Fuller 1987).

The loss of wet grassland in the lowlands has had demonstrable effects on breeding wader populations. A survey of wet grassland sites in England and Wales in 1982/83 found that one-third of all breeding waders were concentrated on just five sites (Smith 1983). The breeding range of the snipe for example had contracted markedly since the national survey of 1968–1972, with its disappearance from many southern counties of England (Gibbons *et al* 1993). A third of the remaining snipe in 1982/83 were recorded on the washlands of the Ouse and Nene. Follow-up work in 1989 (O'Brien and Smith 1992) found further declines for the lapwing (37%) and snipe (12%), although the population of the redshank remained stable. The status of the snipe in England and Wales is particularly worrying, as the species continues to decline and is now almost restricted to nature reserves (Smith 1991).

1.5 Opportunities for the future

A number of incentive schemes and grants are now available for conservation and restoration of wet grasslands (Appendix 2). Although these have limitations, they undoubtedly have a part to play in conserving and enhancing the existing wet grassland resource. It is equally important, however, that such schemes be used to restore areas of wet grassland. Restoration should ideally be aimed at areas adjacent to existing grassland or where fragmented sites can be linked in order to maximise colonisation opportunities and to establish appropriate management (Jefferson and Grice in press).

The Environmentally Sensitive Areas (ESA) Scheme, administered by the Government Agriculture Departments, is one of a range of environmental land management schemes which have been developed by the UK government and its agencies to implement the European Union (EU) Agri-Environment Regulation (No. 2078/92). Under this Regulation, Member States must endeavour to adopt 'agricultural production methods compatible with the requirements of the protection of the environment and the maintenance of the countryside'. There are, at present, 42 designated ESAs, which cover 3.5 million hectares of agricultural land (Plate 10). Several ESAs include significant areas of wet grassland, ranging from seasonally inundated meadows and pastures in the floodplains of rivers such as the Thames and the Spey, to the large areas of grazing marsh found in the Somerset Levels and Moors (Case Studies 5 and 15), and the Broads. There are also large areas of coastal grazing marsh in the North Kent Marshes (Case Study 16) and Essex Coast ESAs. Under the ESA scheme, farmers are offered incentives both to conserve existing valued countryside 'areas, features and resources' and to enhance and restore them where possible. On seven of the nine ESAs with wet grassland, incentives are offered to raise or restore water levels, as well as to maintain or return to extensive farming methods.

(Owen Mountford)

Plate 10 ESA schemes aim to preserve agricultural landscapes dependent on low-intensity agricultural management (eg Southlake Moor in the Somerset Levels and Moors).

The Countryside Stewardship Scheme provides important opportunities for conservation and restoration of wet grasslands outside designated ESAs in England. Payments are made for changes in farming and land management practices which produce conservation benefits or improve access and enjoyment of the countryside. 'Waterside landscapes' (which includes wet grassland) is one of the categories identified for support under the Habitats Option of the Countryside Stewardship Scheme (Case Study 3).

English Nature has recently developed a number of Wildlife Enhancement Schemes (WES) for groups of Sites of Special Scientific Interest (SSSI) in particular areas, under which payments are provided for positive management. Wet grasslands rely heavily on continued management, and a number are represented in the WES developed to date. The following areas are currently included in the pilot scheme: the Culm grasslands of Devon and Cornwall, Vales of Yorkshire wet grasslands (Case Study 12) and the Avon Levels and Moors. This scheme may eventually be extended to cover all SSSIs.

The achievement of conservation objectives for wet grassland as outlined in the Biodiversity Action Plan (HMSO 1995) is affected by European and Government policies and plans formulated by relevant organisations (eg MAFF and the Environment Agency). Water Level Management Plans are an opportunity to ensure a water supply to areas of wildlife interest (section 2.2.7).

The Environment Agency is preparing Local Environment Agency Plans (LEAPs – formerly known as Catchment Management Plans) for some 163 catchments in England and Wales. These are framework documents for decision-making at the catchment level and could provide the vehicle by which creation and enhancement opportunities can be carried forward (section 2.2.7).

Scope for restoration of wet grassland has been identified in many areas, including the Fens of East Anglia, (where the infrastructure of the old, drained and now cultivated washlands are still in place, together with adequate water supplies in adjacent rivers) and in the inland catchments of rivers like the Thames and Severn and their tributaries, the lower Trent, the Hampshire Avon, the Arun and the Lower Derwent Valley. There are also numerous candidate sites in the Broads, the Somerset and Pevensey Levels and in the Suffolk, Essex and Kent coastal marshes (Thomas *et al* 1995).

Partnership between landowners, statutory and voluntary conservation organisations and water management agencies is essential to address conservation and flood defence priorities in a catchment framework. This will enable wet grasslands, especially in floodplains, to carry out their natural flood storage and buffer zone functions, while also providing conservation benefits.

Newson (1991) estimated that there were 1.5 million ha of land in the UK with potential to become, or be restored to, wet grassland. To realise just some of this potential, it is important that the requirements of the wildlife species associated with wet grassland should be clearly understood, so that appropriate management can be implemented.

Key references

Crofts, A and Jefferson, R G (Eds) (1994) *The Lowland Grassland Management Handbook*. English Nature/The Wildlife Trusts.

Purseglove, J (1988) *Taming the Flood*. Oxford University Press, Oxford.

RSPB (1993) *Wet grasslands – what future?* RSPB, Sandy.

Thomas, G, José, P and Hirons, G (1995) Wet grassland in the millennium. *Enact* 3 (1): 4–6.

Part 2
SITE EVALUATION AND MANAGEMENT PLANNING

Contents

2.1 Introduction – setting goals and how to achieve them

This section considers how to identify the potential for enhancing or restoring wildlife value and then how to ensure that appropriate management decisions are taken. The existing and potential wildlife value of the site must be known so that appropriate management objectives can be defined. Whatever the ultimate goal for a site, making the most of any opportunity requires careful consideration and planning.

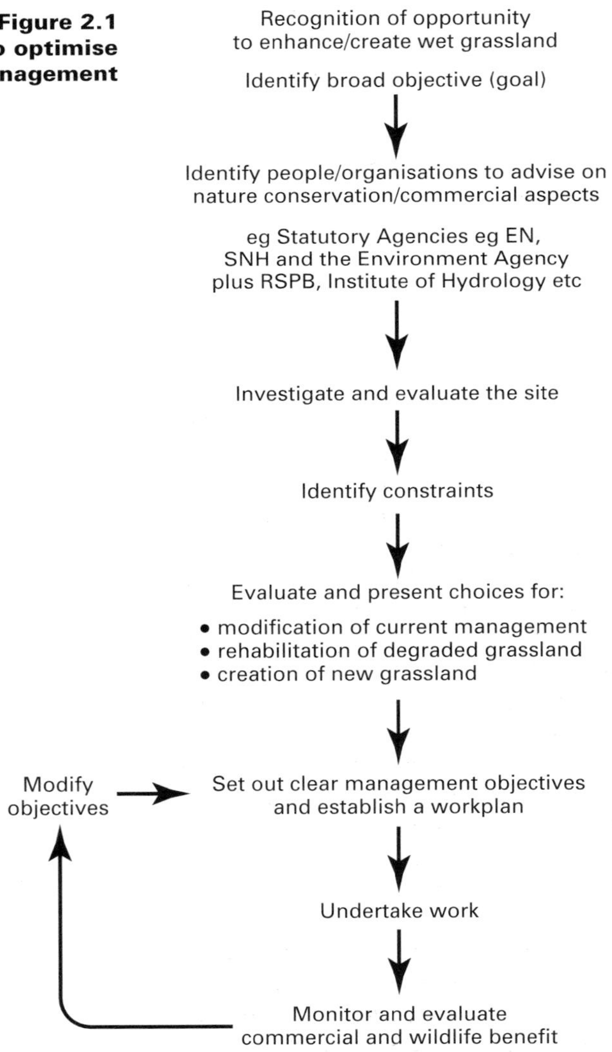

The steps in Figure 2.1 should be followed to make the best use of management and creation opportunities. Some sites will have greater potential than others, depending on the factors, outlined in Table 2.1.

Site evaluation is important to determine current wildlife interest and identify potential for enhancement. It is also necessary to identify any legal, technical and financial factors which might constrain management options. The ability to modify management in the light of results from monitoring is essential if any unforeseen, undesirable changes are to be reversed.

**Figure 2.1
Steps to optimise
management**

Recognition of opportunity
to enhance/create wet grassland

Identify broad objective (goal)

Identify people/organisations to advise on
nature conservation/commercial aspects

eg Statutory Agencies eg EN,
SNH and the Environment Agency
plus RSPB, Institute of Hydrology etc

Investigate and evaluate the site

Identify constraints

Evaluate and present choices for:

• modification of current management
• rehabilitation of degraded grassland
• creation of new grassland

Modify objectives → Set out clear management objectives
and establish a workplan

Undertake work

Monitor and evaluate
commercial and wildlife benefit

Table 2.1: Points to consider when setting objectives for wet grassland management

Evaluate status/ownership
- Site designations (eg SSSI, county designations, local Wildlife Trusts)
- Past and current management
- An existing management agreement (eg ESA or Stewardship agreement) and management criteria laid down within the agreement
- Scope for enhancement of wildlife value

Site characteristics
- Size
- Past wildlife interest
- Existing and potential wildlife value
- Vulnerable communities and species present
- Proximity to other wet grasslands
- Surrounding land use/management
- Soil type
- Water supplies and infrastructure

Legal constraints
- Discuss any proposals with statutory water management and conservation agencies
- Discuss any planning considerations with local authorities and other stake-holders

Management constraints
- Availability of resources/labour/equipment/skills
- Availability of grants
- Availability of stock for grazing management
- Potential problems with water excess, shortage or quality

2.2 Planning for management and creation

2.2.1 Conservation status and ownership

The starting point for any site assessment should be to ascertain its conservation status. If the site is designated (eg SSSI/ASSI), it is always necessary to contact the appropriate statutory conservation agency and options for management will already be set. For such sites the Wildlife and Countryside Act 1981 and the equivalent Northern Ireland legislation include specific legal requirements, which must be considered. The landowner/occupier of a SSSI/ASSI is provided, by the statutory conservation body, with a list of 'potentially damaging operations' (PDOs) thought likely to harm the interest of the site. PDOs are now called 'Operations likely to Damage' (OLD) by English Nature. These might include drainage work, variation of grazing, and spraying of pesticides, and are specific to individual sites (though drawn from a standard list). The landowner/occupier must consult with the statutory conservation agency before carrying out a PDO. The agency then has four months to consult with the landowner, during which time the landholder is constrained from proceeding with the operation. Even if a proposed activity is not identified as a PDO, it is good practice to consult the statutory conservation agency.

If a site has no existing conservation interest, options for management will be less constrained.

2.2.2 Wildlife value

It is vitally important to establish the current value of a site for wildlife, so as to ensure that any proposed changes in management will safeguard important species, communities or habitats present. Again the statutory conservation agencies may be able to provide valuable information about the site's wildlife value and past/present management practices. County and local wildlife trusts (Appendix 3) could also be contacted. Previous landowners and managers may also be able to provide valuable information on past site management. County Biological Records Centres and local museums may hold relevant information on species records and historical management respectively. For information about birds, contact the County Bird Recorder and gain access to national survey data, such as the Wetland Bird Survey.

All possible sources should be tapped, but few sites are really well recorded and it can be difficult to assess the quality of information collected from different sources for different purposes. It is always advisable to complement existing information with field surveys to assess the current status of habitats and species on a site and this should be budgeted for. For species which are less apparent (more often invertebrates, but also some plants), it is easy to inflict inadvertent damage. Specialist help in identifying the less well known species groups may be sought through the statutory conservation agencies, County Wildlife Trusts or from individual experts.

For sites already supporting a diverse assemblage of wildlife and rare and threatened species, changes in management should be considered very carefully.

Determine whether such sites are stable under their existing management or whether they are deteriorating and merit remedial action. If the existing management regime has led to the development of valued communities, it should be retained if possible. If, on the other hand, there is evidence that existing management is leading to a decline in interest, action can be taken to halt the decline. As a general rule, changes should be implemented gradually and only over a proportion of the site. Sudden changes, even when undertaken with the best intentions, can sometimes lead to the wholesale loss of species.

Exhaustive surveys are expensive but it is important to determine the presence of rare and vulnerable species. It is also useful to focus on species known to be vulnerable to changes in water levels, for example, or which might indicate deterioration in site quality (eg competitive pasture species like perennial rye-grass, or algal blooms in drainage channels). Such surveys should also be designed to act as a suitable baseline for follow-up surveys and monitoring. Wherever possible, quantitative estimates such as species cover and population size should be obtained using standard, agreed, methods, so that surveys can be repeated in future (Part 5).

2.2.3 Site size and location

Options for management are greater on larger sites, where a range of habitats and species can be supported. On small sites, characteristic species and communities are more vulnerable to the detrimental effects of external influences (edge effects).

The location of a site has implications not only for its management, but also the likelihood that species will colonise it spontaneously and establish viable populations. Even where large areas of wet grassland remain, they have often become increasingly isolated from potential sources of colonising species through habitat loss and fragmentation. Their isolation means that many target species may be slow to colonise, even when management has created appropriate conditions for them.

For less mobile species (plants and many invertebrates), deliberate introductions or re-introductions may be necessary. Introduction projects should only be

considered as a last resort and should be well researched and totally justifiable. Permission must be sought from the relevant statutory conservation agency for introductions on SSSI/ASSIs. For plants this might mean transplanting species onto a site rather than relying on natural regeneration. When considering transplanting species the impact on the donor site should be evaluated.

It is also important to ensure that management caters for species and communities appropriate to a site's geographic location. Not all conservation objectives are applicable in all parts of the UK. Species distributions show inherent regional variation. Species should not be introduced outside their natural ranges. Introduction of species or genotypes from other parts of the country can also have an adverse effect on the genetic viability of native populations.

2.2.4 Site hydrology

Rehabilitation and creation of wet grassland often hinges on deliberate raising of water levels, so availability of water is a crucial factor. Even on wet grasslands with existing high wildlife value, maintaining water supplies of a suitable quality can be a major challenge.

Liaison with staff responsible for water resources and flood defence in the appropriate water management agency may be sufficient to give a general indication of water availability. However, more detailed assessment of a site's water balance and the calculation of water budgets is essential for major schemes (Plate 1). It will be necessary to estimate inputs (eg rainfall or in-flows from rivers) and losses (including evapotranspiration and seepage). Advice from the Institute of Hydrology, universities and colleges with expertise in this area should be considered. Advice should also be sought from the Environment Agency, Scottish Environmental Protection Agency (SEPA) or Department of Agriculture Northern Ireland (DANI) or from the local Internal Drainage Board (IDB), where appropriate. Addresses of potentially useful contacts are included in Appendix 3. The factors which should be considered when determining water requirements and water management options are summarised in Appendix 4.

Obviously, it is also vital to understand the water requirements of target habitats and species. These are considered in Part 3. It is especially important to make contingency arrangements for unusually wet or dry conditions. For example, methods for holding and manipulating water levels are examined in Part 4 of the guide and are also described in Case Studies 5 and 15.

Table 2.2 shows the range of factors which may be investigated, depending upon the scale of a project and the resources available, before determining options for water management. A description of the site, including location of low-lying areas, patterns of water flow and soil types is useful as a first step in characterising hydrological conditions (Case Studies 3, 4 and 5). The need for detailed topographic survey (Plate 1) may be reduced if it is possible to observe the sequence of flooding on a site and make a photographic record (Case Study 6).

(Dave Rees)

**Plate 1
Levelling surveys
provide detailed
topographic
information and aid
the understanding
of site hydrology.**

Table 2.2: Possible approaches to hydrological assessment

What to assess	Sources of information	Implications for water management
Catchment area	Ordnance Survey Maps, aerial photographs.	Indicates sources of water, likely directions of flow and location of low-lying areas.
Soils	Soil Survey Maps, field investigations (soil pits, augers).	Soil type influences type of hydrological regime which can be sustained. Grasslands on clay soils can be managed by surface flooding and do not require control over drainage channel water levels. Those on peat require control of drainage channel water levels to be kept wet.
Topography	Levelling survey. Observe extent of flooding (take photographs and examine old photographs).	Large-scale topography determines design of hydrological control system. Assists in siting of sluices, etc.
	Observe patterns of flow.	Small-scale topography determines extent of field flooding at given water levels.
Climate/weather (especially rainfall and evapotranspiration)	Meteorological Office Records.	Influences likely availability of water, rates of evapotranspiration, etc.
	Weather station records on-site.	Important for calculation of water budgets and estimation of need for winter storage to supplement summer deficits.
Water sources: river/ drainage channel levels and seasonal regime	Gauge boards on-site. Consult with the appropriate water management agency.	Sluice construction or pumping may be required where water levels in supply are below field surface.
	Check for level of water in river/stream/ drainage channel relative to field surface and soil water-table.	Information on water quantity and quality is required to determine if target hydrological regimes can be implemented.
	Check with water management agencies for information on availability of surface water and water quality, pollution records, etc.	
	Investigate groundwater supplies. Establish seasonality of seepage/spring flows.	Groundwater can be a source of high quality/ low nutrient level water, but can also be polluted (particularly in Eastern England).
	Measure water-table heights using simple, low-cost dipwells.	If carried out regularly, should indicate problem periods of low soil water levels.
		Caution: detailed assessment of groundwater (other than simple water-table measurements) is notoriously difficult: seek expert advice.
Requirements of other water users in catchment	Consult any Catchment Management Plans and Water Level Management Plans.	Water needs may have to be balanced with those of other users. This is particularly important in low rainfall/highly populated areas.
	Consult with water management agencies for details of abstractions.	
Water management infrastructure	Establish condition of any existing drainage infrastructure (including sub-surface drainage) and water control structures.	New water management infrastructure may be required. Major, expensive engineering works may be necessary.
	Check for leakage in bunds, check sluices are operational, etc.	
	Liaise with water management agencies.	
Other factors	Potentially adverse impacts on adjacent land, liaise at earliest opportunity with water management agencies.	Protective mechanisms such as bunding, secondary ditching may be required to protect adjacent land from flooding/raised water levels.

2.2.5 Legal and planning considerations

A range of legal and planning
considerations may need to be taken into
account when certain management
improvements or restoration activities are
proposed. Table 2.3 provides a checklist of
factors which should be considered.

Table 2.3: Legal and planning considerations

Issue	Action required
Water management Water is required from a river, stream or groundwater source.	Consult water management agency* to discuss need for abstraction licence.
Proposals involve retaining water above original ground level or raising water levels above surrounding land.	Bunds and dams constructed to impound water may need licensing. Dams impounding more than 25,000 m³ above the surrounding land (eg to construct a 1-ha lake 2.5 m deep) require a licence. Major constructions require supervision by a civil engineer.
Proposals affect drainage of neighbouring land, or alter existing flow regime.	Land drainage consent may be required. Consult water management agencies to discuss licensing requirements. Their staff may be able to give informal advice on sluice, dam design, etc. See Table 4.7 on drainage channel management responsibilities. In determining all works that need approval, the EA, IDB and LAs must consider whether the proposals conserve and enhance the natural environment.
Surplus water to be discharged into a water course.	Usually acceptable without discharge consent unless it results in a marked deterioration in water quality. Liaise with the water management agencies.
Wildlife interest The site is designated (eg SSSI, ASSI).	Consult the relevant statutory conservation agency. For sites of local interest contact local/County Wildlife Trusts.
The site is a Special Protection Area (SPA) or a Special Area of Conservation (SAC).	These sites have additional safeguards, again consult the relevant statutory conservation agency.
The site supports protected species.	Consult statutory conservation agency.
Public rights of way Proposals may divert or block existing public right of way, eg footpath, bridleway.	Consult County Council.
Planning Proposal affects landscape/drainage of area.	Discuss with local planning authority (essential for AONBs). For ESAs, consult relevant Agriculture Ministry or Department. For National Parks consult the relevant National Parks Authority.
Is location on/near aircraft flight paths or airfields.	Discuss with local planning authority and, if necessary, the MOD and/or Civil Aviation Authority (CAA).
Material (eg spoil) to be transported on/off site via public highway.	Consult local planning authority. If excavated material is to be sold, also consult with the mineral planning authority.
The site includes a Scheduled Ancient Monument (SAM).	Consult the relevant statutory country agency regarding any change in management (eg English Heritage).
Is there any other archaeological interest on the site?	Consult local planning authority, before undertaking any engineering works, eg scrape building, car parks or new ditches.

* See Appendix 3 to obtain addresses for the water management agencies.

2.2.6 Resource constraints

From the outset, the resource implications of management proposals should be considered. The costs of feasibility studies, any necessary engineering works and subsequent management should all be examined. The following costs should be considered:

- design and feasibility studies, eg
  - hydrological survey
  - wildlife survey
  - archeological survey (important on peatlands such as the Somerset Levels)

- one-off capital items, for example for:
  - land-forming, eg bund and drainage channel construction
  - installation of water control structures
  - machinery purchase

- ongoing management
  - labour/staff costs to undertake grassland management
  - servicing/maintenance of machinery
  - animal husbandry

- ongoing survey and monitoring.

2.2.7 Project proposals and management plans

Whatever the proposals for a site, it is often useful to put the background and reasons for any work in writing. This can take the form of a short project proposal or a comprehensive management plan. Ideally, both should contain the following sections:

- site description

- site evaluation

- rationale behind site proposals and objectives

- prescriptions to achieve objectives including monitoring

- work plans.

Such a framework can assist with long-term planning of resources, labour and monitoring programmes, enabling constraints and any conflicting objectives to be identified (Case Study 4). Much information can be collated in the form of maps and diagrams. Detailed guidance on the management planning process is available in Alexander (1996). Appendix 5 sets out the categories in the nationally promoted Countryside Management System (CMS) which can be adopted where a detailed management plan is required (Alexander 1996). An additional benefit of producing a management plan is that the necessary work for a five-year period can

be agreed with the statutory conservation agency and the provision of financial assistance may be facilitated. A recent MAFF initiative to develop Water Level Management Plans (WLMPs) for wetland SSSIs has helped to formalise this planning process of defining the water level requirements for a range of activities in a particular area (MAFF 1994).

Water Level Management Plans

The Water Level Management Planning process (in England and Wales only) attempts to balance all user interests within a defined hydrological area or unit, thereby giving some surety of water supply to sites of acknowledged wildlife interest. The production of WLMPs will be led by the operating authority for the area (usually EA or IDB), but will involve all those interested parties who may be affected by water management within the area covered by the plan. It is essential that conservation objectives are properly integrated into the WLMP. They will be available from the operating authorities or from MAFF's Regional Engineers.

Initially, WLMPs are to be drawn up for all SSSIs where an operating authority (the Environment Agency or an Internal Drainage Board) is able, through its flood defence or drainage activities, to control water levels. The highest priority has been given to internationally important sites, especially SSSIs that qualify as SACs, SPAs or Ramsar sites, and World Heritage Sites. WLMPs for SSSIs will be agreed between the operating authority and English Nature or the Countryside Council for Wales, although endorsement by others should also be encouraged.

A Plan can contain proposals to maintain existing management, or to enhance or restore water levels. Any Plan has to include an agreed conservation statement and to specify the water levels necessary to sustain that interest. Where the alteration of water levels might have adverse effects on neighbouring agricultural land, the operating authority has to balance the desired conservation aim against other interests. The Plan process for SSSIs is timetabled for completion in 1998, after which WLMPs for other high wildlife interest sites will follow. However non-SSSI sites are not excluded from the WLMP process up to 1998. If there is a strong case to be made and there are resources available to advance a Plan then an operating authority is able to take it forward (MAFF 1994).

Table 2.4 outlines key elements for inclusion in WLMPs.

Catchment Management Plans/Local Environment Agency Plans

When it was formed on 1 April 1996, the Environment Agency inherited Catchment Management Plans (CMPs) from the National Rivers Authority (NRA). Plans produced after this date are referred to as Local Environment Agency Plans (LEAPs). These plans cover river corridors throughout much of England and Wales and consider a range of topics including water quality, water resources, flood defence and the conservation of fisheries and wetland wildlife, as well as landscape and cultural assets.

CMPs/LEAPs should help site managers to understand how the management, and wider use, of water in a catchment may affect a wet grassland site. They should classify the quality of water in monitored rivers, and state long-term objectives for water quality. They should also catalogue the number and type of river and groundwater abstractions. Flood defence activities should be outlined; the most comprehensive plans may classify land uses in floodplains and indicate a standard of service appropriate to those uses (expressed as a flood return frequency). Higher standards apply to built-up or intensively farmed land than apply to areas of permanent grassland.

Table 2.4: Key elements for inclusion in Water Level Management Plans

- Statement summarising purpose of plan and the individual/office responsible for it.
- Map showing site boundary, watercourses, water management structures, normal flow directions, designated conservation areas and other features of interest.
- List of individuals and organisations consulted, with brief summary of their main interests.
- Summary of the interests of the area (eg conservation, agriculture, forestry, commercial, flood defence, transport, recreation).
- Objectives for the site (and for its different parts).
- Required operating procedures such as target water levels, seasonal requirements, pumping cycles, minimum flows and maintenance operations.
- Outline programme for changes required to drainage infrastructure.
- Identification of any problems with water availability.
- Summary of any unresolved differences with outline of proposed means for overcoming them.
- Outline of agreed contingency measures to cope with exceptional floods, drought, etc.
- Outline of agreed recording/monitoring procedures (both hydrological and biological).
- Agreed period of review for the plan and who will be responsible for it.

Source: MAFF (1994).

CMPs/LEAPs should identify designated sites particularly if they have wetland interest, and outline how the management of the catchment may affect these sites. CMPs/LEAPs should also identify issues where the status of a site may be threatened by current or future use of land and water in the catchment.

The Environment Agency will continue to develop LEAPs, which will accommodate the wider responsibilities of the Agency for air quality, waste management, and the regulation of the use and disposal of radioactive materials. By 1998 the whole of England and Wales should be covered by a CMP or a LEAP.

2.3 Making choices

Wildlife conservation involves making choices. Limits to what can be achieved will be imposed by cost, practicality, legal constraints and personal interest. Some species or communities will be more important than others. It is rarely the case that the most worthwhile wildlife management is also the cheapest to undertake.

The first stage in decision-making involves evaluating survey results to identify the most important parts of a site. Species or communities that are internationally or nationally important should have first priority for conservation management. In some cases priorities for species conservation will have already been set out in policy frameworks or in local or regional strategies for biodiversity, eg Local Biodiversity Action Plans. Priorities are likely to be ranked as follows:

1. **Species/communities of international importance** eg marsh fritillary and corncrake

2. **Species/communities of national importance** eg black-tailed godwit

3. **Species/communities of county/regional importance** eg small pockets of breeding waders and associated semi-improved wet grassland habitat

4. **Species/communities of local importance** eg ponds and drainage channels, pollards and associated flora and fauna.

In many situations, it may be useful to distinguish between management for the restoration of wildlife interest where it has declined and management intended to maintain or enhance existing value. When considering a restoration project the desired end-point should be identified from historic records and/or investigation of remnant flora and fauna on the site. In extremely neglected sites, restorative management may have to be introduced piecemeal to parts of the site, so that there is a gradual change in the vegetation,

allowing less mobile animals to migrate and adapt to the altered conditions. Once restorative management has begun to take effect, the implementation of a maintenance management regime can be considered. The time taken for restoration to be successful obviously depends on the condition of the site at the outset and the objectives that have been set.

Table 2.5 gives examples of starting points and possible strategies and options for wet grassland management. The management techniques that may be employed on wet grassland sites are considered in more depth in Part 4 of this guide. It should be remembered, however, that each site is unique and while guidance can be given as to the range of management techniques available, management decisions must be closely tailored to the specific needs of individual sites based on the experience of the wet grassland manager and the interests of other stake-holders.

A number of financial incentive schemes are available for the creation of wet grassland (Section 1.5 and Appendix 2). Where these schemes are discretionary, land managers are advised to ensure that their projects fit into Local Agenda 21 and Local Biodiversity Action Plans visions and priorities.

Key references

Alexander, M (Ed) (1996) *A guide to the production of management plans for nature reserves and potential areas.* Countryside Council for Wales, Bangor.

MAFF (1994) *Water Level Management Plans: a procedural guide for operating authorities.* HMSO, London.

NCC (1988) *Site management plans for nature conservation – a working guide.* NCC, Peterborough.

Table 2.5: Making choices: management strategies and options

Management strategy	Management options
Area with high wildlife interest Maintain existing regime	Water management: ■ Identify existing regime by talking to previous land managers. ■ Maintain water control infrastructure and implement appropriate drainage channel maintenance regime. Grassland management: ■ Identify existing regime by talking to previous land managers. ■ Maintain grazing regime, especially in respect to type of grazing animal and stocking density used.
Area with moderate wildlife interest and potential for enhancement Improve/modify existing management	Water management: ■ Check operation of water control structures to ensure water level prescriptions can be met. ■ Install new low-cost structures (eg flexi-pipe sluices) to improve water management. ■ Implement appropriate drainage channel management regime to improve flows while enhancing drainage channel wildlife value. Grassland management: ■ Ensure cutting is delayed until July. ■ Consider cutting followed by aftermath grazing. ■ Optimise grazing regime: consider type and density of stock and timing and duration of grazing. ■ Reduce/stop fertiliser and herbicide applications.
Area with limited wildlife interest (eg pump-drained grassland cut repeatedly for silage with wildlife restricted to drainage channels) Implement programme of rehabilitation	Water management: ■ Consider options for reinstating water levels by repairing existing or installing new water management structures (eg dropboard and flexi-pipe sluices and windpumps). ■ Reprofile and re-excavate existing drainage channels. Dig new ones as necessary. ■ Consider need for winter water storage, eg by reservoir construction or using natural fleets. Grassland management: ■ Extensify management. ■ Reduce/eliminate applications of fertilisers, herbicides and pesticides. ■ Consider options for grazing. ■ Consider reintroduction of herbaceous species (eg slot-seeding, transplants).
Area with negligible or no wildlife interest (eg land drained and under arable for many years) Implement restoration/creation programme	Water management (in addition to measures listed for rehabilitation): ■ Consider need for sub-irrigation/removal of under-drainage. ■ Consider scope for setting back/removing floodbanks (requires consent from EA/MAFF/local planning authority/neighbouring landowners etc). Grassland establishment: ■ Assess/estimate condition of soil seed bank. ■ Assess proximity to other sources of grassland species. ■ Consider soil remediation (eg nutrient stripping, topsoil removal). ■ Consider spraying to eliminate competitive weeds. ■ Rely on natural regeneration on sites under arable for relatively short periods which are near suitable seed sources. ■ Otherwise select and sow appropriate seed mix. ■ Consider subsequent transplanting of herbaceous perennials. ■ Remember to consider follow-up management.

Part 3
ECOLOGICAL REQUIREMENTS

Contents

3.1 Introduction

Knowledge of the requirements of wet grassland species is important in order to implement appropriate management. However, the requirements of many species are poorly understood, particularly invertebrates and, to a lesser extent, plants.

Wet grassland has two main components:

■ the grassland itself, which supports largely terrestrial species

■ water-bodies and drainage channels which support predominantly aquatic species.

It is not always straightforward to distinguish terrestrial and aquatic components. Wet grassland ecosystems are highly dynamic and one area can be subject to a range of hydrological conditions, for example with flooding in winter and spring followed by drier conditions in the summer, or with floods in one spring and drought in another. Although some species are totally restricted either to grassland or to water-bodies, others (particularly birds and some invertebrates) may use a variety of areas.

Wet grasslands rarely exist in isolation and are usually found in association with other wetland habitats, eg saltmarsh, reedbed, fen or open water, and many species rely on a mosaic or continuum of wetland habitats. Wet grasslands may also include features such as bankside vegetation, droves, isolated trees and hedges, earth banks and sea walls which diversify the range of habitats available.

The ecological requirements of wet grassland vegetation, invertebrates and birds are considered in the following pages.

3.2 Plant community / species requirements

3.2.1 Introduction

When managing wet grassland for its botanical interest, the needs of both individual species and communities (characteristic assemblages of species) must be considered. In some circumstances, management may be targeted to promote one rare or threatened species. In others, the intention might be to maintain a number of vegetation communities. Wet grassland vegetation forms an important part of the habitats of invertebrates and birds and it is often necessary to consider their needs when managing vegetation (see sections 3.4 and 3.5). Vegetation structure and composition are important to both groups of species and are strongly influenced by management.

3.2.2 Wet grassland plant communities

Very few natural grasslands occur in the UK. Most grasslands have been influenced in some way by management, usually for farming. Semi-natural grasslands, which developed under traditional, low-intensity farming have become vital for the conservation of native wildlife (Plate 1). Semi-natural grasslands retain most of the species which would occur naturally, but their composition and structure is determined by human use and management. Many have become degraded or lost in recent decades as a result of agricultural intensification. Under intensive agricultural management, species-poor swards develop, which are of reduced value to wildlife (Plate 2, sections 1.3 and 1.4).

Grasslands which are managed predominantly by grazing are called *pastures*, and those managed by regular mowing, *meadows*. There have been many attempts to describe and classify the UK's semi-natural grasslands in terms of their botanical composition (Ratcliffe 1977, and Tansley 1939). Nowadays, the National Vegetation Classification (NVC) (Rodwell 1991, 1992, 1995) is the most widely used classification system in Great Britain. The NVC has helped to clarify the circumstances under which the main vegetation types occur and the management with which they tend to be associated.

The NVC plant communities which occur in wet grassland (Table 1.1), together with their characteristic species and requirements, are listed in Appendices 6, 7 and 8. Background material is given in Appendix 9 which lists the more important plants of wet grassland, including information on the requirements of these species in terms of soils, water regime, salinity and management.

**Plate 1
Semi-natural
grasslands (eg
North Meadow,
Cricklade - Case
Study 14), are
valuable for the
conservation of
wet grassland
flora.**

**Plate 2
Intensive
agricultural use
converts herb-rich
grassland
communities to
species-poor
swards, often
dominated by
perennial rye-
grass.**

(Owen Mountford)

(Owen Mountford)

The NVC describes three broad categories of vegetation, which are generally referred to as wet grassland communities:

■ **typical wet grasslands** are dominated by a mixture of grasses, wild flowers, soft-rush and hard rush. Sedges and jointed rushes, such as sharp-flowered and blunt-flowered rush are uncommon. They include NVC mesotrophic grassland types **MG4–MG13** (Plate 3).

■ **mire grasslands** are similar in general appearance, but with more low-growing sedges and a variety of rushes present. They include NVC mire types **M22–M25** (Plate 4).

■ **swamps and sedge-beds** are species-poor vegetation stands usually dominated by a single coarse grass or sedge. They include NVC swamp types **S5-S7** and **S22** (Plate 5). S6 and S7 are sedge-beds, rather than grasslands, but are included here because they tend to be managed as grasslands.

Typical wet grasslands

Typical wet grasslands may be dominated by any one, or a combination, of 10–15 grass species. Red fescue, crested dog's-tail, creeping bent, perennial rye-grass, Yorkshire-fog and sweet vernal grass are usually the most abundant. These typically occur alongside wild flowers such as white clover, common mouse-ear, red clover, common sorrel and buttercups (especially meadow buttercup). Species richness varies from >20 species per 4 m² for MG4 to <11 for MG7. Table 3.1 highlights the differences between the communities of typical wet grassland. The significance of perennial rye-grass derives from its use as an agricultural pasture species, and its relative dominance often reflects the degree of agricultural improvement of these grasslands.

Mire grasslands

Mire grasslands may include grasses (notably Yorkshire-fog) which are common in the typical wet grasslands, but they have more low sedges, rushes and mosses. The wild flowers present are also different. Clovers and buttercups found in typical wet grasslands are likely to be replaced to a great extent by greater bird's-foot-trefoil

(Owen Mountford)

Plate 3
Typical wet grasslands are dominated by a mixture of grasses, herbs and soft and hard rush.

(Owen Mountford)

Plate 4
Mire grasslands, eg M24 purple moor-grass and meadow thistle fen-meadow, are similar in appearance to typical wet grasslands but have more low-growing sedges and a variety of rushes.

(James Cadbury)

Plate 5
Swamp communities, eg S5 reed sweet-grass swamp, are usually monospecific stands of grasses/sedges and are very species-poor.

Table 3.1: Typical wet grassland communities classified according to percentage composition of perennial rye-grass and average height of vegetation

Perennial rye-grass rare (always <10% of the sward and usually < 5%)		
MG4	Flood meadows	Species-rich and tall
MG5	Old grazed hay meadows	Species-rich and short
MG8 MG9 MG12	Water meadows Tussock wet meadows Upper saltmarsh swards	Moderately species-rich and tall
MG10	Ordinary damp meadows	Species-poor, rushy and tall
MG11	Inundation grasslands	Species-poor, rushes rare, sward short
MG13	Inundation grasslands	Very species-poor, often in depressions
Perennial rye-grass common (always >5% of the sward and often >20%)		
MG6	Dairy and fatting pastures	Species-poor with crested dog's-tail
MG7	Improved and sown swards	Very species-poor, without crested dog's-tail

[Total species within a 4 m² sample: Rich >20 spp.; Moderate 16–20 spp.; Poor 11–15 spp.; Very poor <11 spp.]

Source: Rodwell (1992)

and thistles in mire grasslands. In practice, the distinction between mire grasslands and typical wet grasslands can appear vague. Intermediates may be found between water meadows (MG8) and rich-fen meadows (M22), and between ordinary damp meadows (MG10) and western fen-meadows (M23).

Mire grasslands are nearly always species-rich (>20 species per 4 m² sample) and can be distinguished as follows:

■ blunt-flowered rush frequent: rich fen-meadows (M22)

■ blunt-flowered rush usually absent, other rushes common: western fen-meadows (M23)

■ purple moor-grass dominant: litter and wet Culm grasslands (M24) and purple moor-grass grassland (M25).

Swamps and sedge-beds

Swamps and sedge-beds occur within wet grasslands, and in composition are very similar, even identical, to the lush emergent vegetation that may dominate adjacent drainage channels and ponds. They are typically species-poor with one clear dominant and are often found as rank

patches in depressions in fields, though locally (as in washland) they can form extensive stands. The four kinds considered here are readily recognised by their characteristic dominant species:

■ reed sweet-grass (S5)

■ greater pond-sedge (S6)

■ lesser pond-sedge (S7)

■ floating sweet-grass (S22).

Figure 3.1 (a-e) illustrates characteristic plant communities that may typically be found in the continuum of wet grassland sites in the UK (section 1.1)

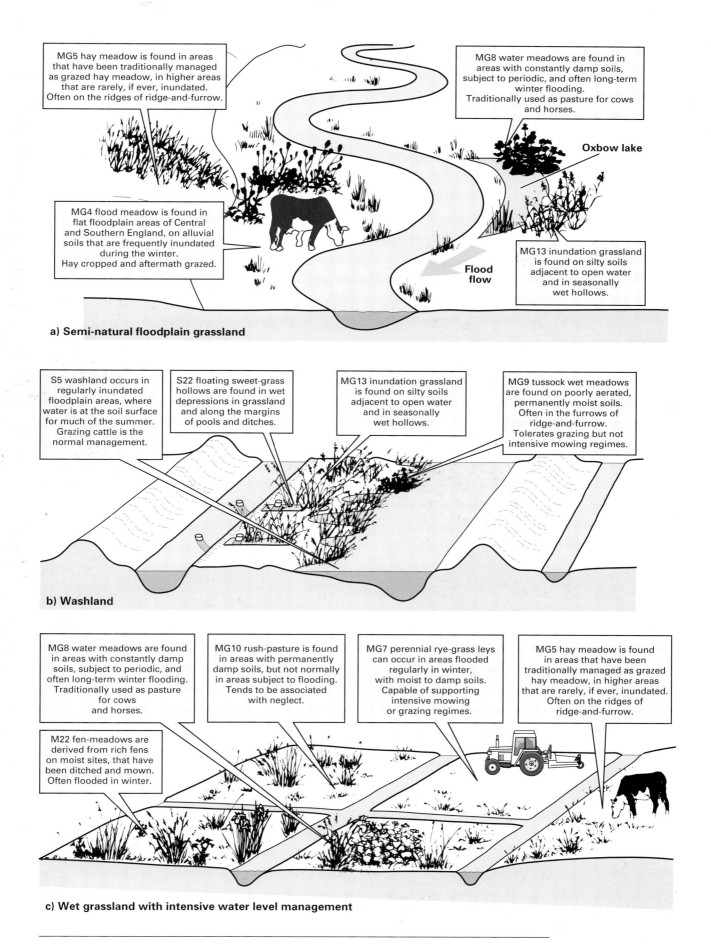

MG5 hay meadow is found in areas that have been traditionally managed as grazed hay meadow, in higher areas that are rarely, if ever, inundated. Often on the ridges of ridge-and-furrow.

MG8 water meadows are found in areas with constantly damp soils, subject to periodic, and often long-term winter flooding. Traditionally used as pasture for cows and horses.

Oxbow lake

MG4 flood meadow is found in flat floodplain areas of Central and Southern England, on alluvial soils that are frequently inundated during the winter. Hay cropped and aftermath grazed.

MG13 inundation grassland is found on silty soils adjacent to open water and in seasonally wet hollows.

Flood flow

a) Semi-natural floodplain grassland

S5 washland occurs in regularly inundated floodplain areas, where water is at the soil surface for much of the summer. Grazing cattle is the normal management.

S22 floating sweet-grass hollows are found in wet depressions in grassland and along the margins of pools and ditches.

MG13 inundation grassland is found on silty soils adjacent to open water and in seasonally wet hollows.

MG9 tussock wet meadows are found on poorly aerated, permanently moist soils. Often in the furrows of ridge-and-furrow. Tolerates grazing but not intensive mowing regimes.

b) Washland

MG8 water meadows are found in areas with constantly damp soils, subject to periodic, and often long-term winter flooding. Traditionally used as pasture for cows and horses.

MG10 rush-pasture is found in areas with permanently damp soils, but not normally in areas subject to flooding. Tends to be associated with neglect.

MG7 perennial rye-grass leys can occur in areas flooded regularly in winter, with moist to damp soils. Capable of supporting intensive mowing or grazing regimes.

MG5 hay meadow is found in areas that have been traditionally managed as grazed hay meadow, in higher areas that are rarely, if ever, inundated. Often on the ridges of ridge-and-furrow.

M22 fen-meadows are derived from rich fens on moist sites, that have been ditched and mown. Often flooded in winter.

c) Wet grassland with intensive water level management

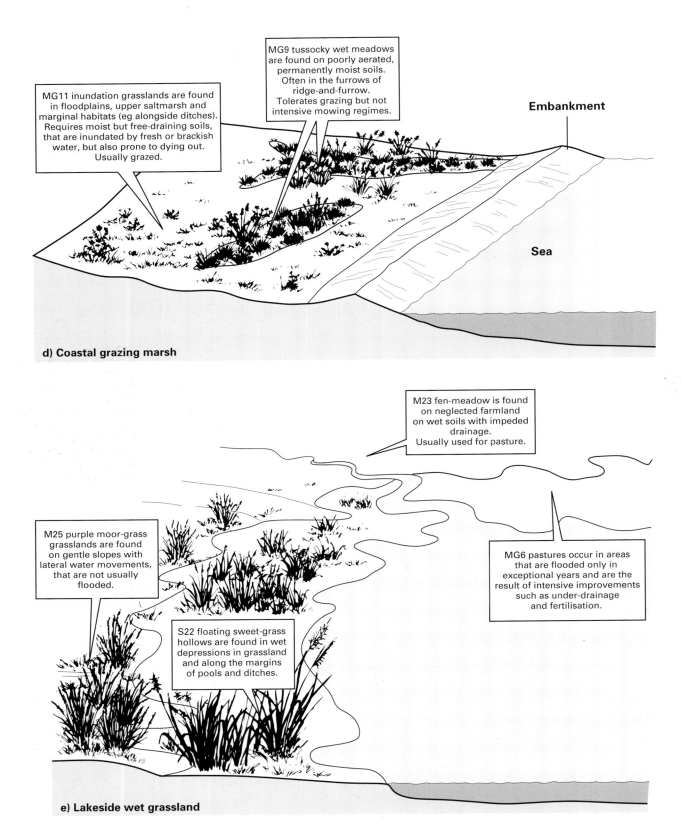

MG11 inundation grasslands are found in floodplains, upper saltmarsh and marginal habitats (eg alongside ditches). Requires moist but free-draining soils, that are inundated by fresh or brackish water, but also prone to drying out. Usually grazed.

MG9 tussocky wet meadows are found on poorly aerated, permanently moist soils. Often in the furrows of ridge-and-furrow. Tolerates grazing but not intensive mowing regimes.

Embankment

Sea

d) Coastal grazing marsh

M23 fen-meadow is found on neglected farmland on wet soils with impeded drainage. Usually used for pasture.

M25 purple moor-grass grasslands are found on gentle slopes with lateral water movements, that are not usually flooded.

S22 floating sweet-grass hollows are found in wet depressions in grassland and along the margins of pools and ditches.

MG6 pastures occur in areas that are flooded only in exceptional years and are the result of intensive improvements such as under-drainage and fertilisation.

e) Lakeside wet grassland

Figure 3.1(a-e) Wet grassland types include: a) semi-natural floodplain grassland; b) washlands; c) wet grasslands with intensive water level management; d) coastal grazing marsh; e) lakeside wet grassland

3.2.3 Soil and water requirements of wet grassland plant communities/ species

Soil type is an important influence on the plant species composition of wet grasslands. Soil types on which the different wet grassland plant communities are usually found are shown in Appendices 6, 7 and 8. Figure 3.2 shows how different pasture (eg MG6) and rush-dominated communities (eg MG10) are associated with variation in the base-richness of soils and their drainage.

Most wet grasslands occur on neutral to mildly acid soils. However, flood and water meadows (MG4 and MG8) and rich fen-meadows (M22) are more common where the water is slightly alkaline. Where wet grasslands are washed by brackish water (eg coastal grasslands), or subject to salt spray, the swards may contain halophytes, and many of the usual dominant grasses will be excluded. Shoreline swards (MG11) and upper saltmarsh ungrazed swards (MG12) can occur in such situations.

Most wet grassland communities of conservation importance are associated with low soil-nutrient availability. In more nutrient-rich soils, agricultural grass species out-compete wild flowers and other grasses, and become dominant. There is clear evidence to indicate that even very low applications of inorganic fertiliser can damage botanical interest, causing changes in species composition which can persist for many years (Mountford *et al* 1994a). Eutrophic winter floodwater can also affect the plant species composition of grassland vegetation. At the Ouse Washes, for example, eutrophication of the water supply has resulted in reversion to swamp vegetation dominated by reed sweet-grass (Burgess *et al* 1990).

Figure 3.2 Distribution of wet grassland plant communities on a hypothetical lowland floodplain managed for hay with aftermath grazing, in relation to soil type and water regime

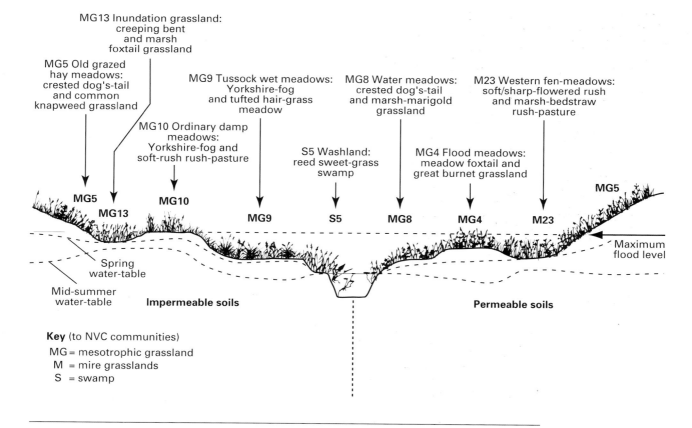

Plant growth and distribution is significantly influenced by water regime (Spoor *et al* in press), ie the depth and variation of the water-table throughout the year:

■ The composition of a plant community may be radically altered by minor shifts in water regime (Gowing *et al* in press).

■ The timing of variations in availability of both water and oxygen in the root zone with respect to key life-stages is the critical factor; for example, plants may tolerate waterlogging in December but not in March/April, when it may result in a grass kill.

■ On larger sites it may be possible to cater for a wide range of species, exploiting even minor natural topographic variation to create a variety of wetness regimes under the same water management.

Some species are adapted to survive in situations where the soils have little or no available oxygen, due to high water-tables. Plants such as the marsh-marigold have a system of air-conducting tissue (aerenchyma) which can supply roots in waterlogged soils with atmospheric oxygen via the aerial parts of the plant. In contrast, many of the agricultural grasses are

relatively intolerant of very high water-tables. Soil wetness can have a considerable influence on the competitive balance between species, depending on their relative tolerances.

Plants can be ranked very broadly in terms of their preference for a particular soil moisture content (Mountford and Chapman 1993). Ellenberg (1988) assigned indicator values to different plants on the basis of their tolerance to wetness (Table 3.2). However, it must be noted that it is not possible to define the water regime requirements of grassland vegetation by reference to a single water level, as water-tables fluctuate seasonally.

A recently developed method calculates the length of time during the year in which either the water-table is so low it restricts the amount of water available for evaporation from the surface (drought stress), or so high that it restricts the diffusion of oxygen into the root zone (aeration stress). A procedure for setting these thresholds and a database of the resultant tolerance bands for wet grassland species has been devised (Gowing and Spoor in press).

Table 3.2: Plants as indicators of water regime

Water value (F)	Description of occurrence	Examples
3	Dry site indicators, more often found on dry ground than moist; not found on damp soil.	Changing forget-me-not
5	Moist-site indicators, mainly on soils of average dampness, absent from both wet ground and places which may dry out.	Common knapweed, crested dog's-tail and tufted vetch
7	Damp-site indicators, mainly on constantly damp, but not wet, soils.	Carnation sedge, creeping buttercup and hard rush
9	Wet-site indicators; often in water-saturated, badly aerated soils.	Common marsh-bedstraw, floating sweet-grass and greater pond-sedge
10	Indicators of sites occasionally flooded but free from surface water for long periods.	Reed sweet-grass and yellow iris
11	Plants rooting under water but at least for a time exposed above or floating on the surface.	Amphibious bistort
12	Submerged plants, permanently or almost constantly underwater.	Fennel pondweed and fen pondweed

The water (F) values of Ellenberg (1988) define the water tolerances of plants in relation to the gradient from dry shallow soil on rocky slopes to marshy ground, shallow and then deep water. Care should be exercised when applying F values to UK plants as the data set derives from Central Europe. Some species do not show clear relationships with water-table depth.

3.2.4 Vegetation management requirements of wet grassland plant communities

Vegetation management (mowing, grazing and, exceptionally, burning) is important for conserving semi-natural grassland communities because it:

■ removes plant material containing nutrients

■ prevents succession to coarser grassland types and eventually scrub/woodland

■ favours less competitive species, allowing more of the slower-growing perennials and species of smaller stature to survive.

Traditional management techniques, such as hay making and aftermath grazing, can create exceptionally diverse swards. Careful consideration should be given to altering a management regime where a long-term tradition of management is established.

Plants differ in their ability to withstand the effects of grazing or mowing, depending on their ability to recover:

■ Grasses have growing points which are close to ground level. Some plants readily produce new shoots from the base of the plant in response to grazing, a process known as tillering. This allows plants to colonise new habitat as it becomes available, as for example, where bare ground is created by trampling. The dominance of grasses over wild flowers in grassland is largely due to their ability to tiller (Table 3.3).

■ Wild flowers have growing points at their tips and the most common adaptation to escape defoliation is to adopt a flattened form. Some of the taller herbaceous species are able to assume a rosette form under close cropping (the knapweeds and ragworts for example). Those unable to adapt in this way are generally inhibited by grazing and are confined to mown grasslands (eg great burnet and many umbellifers), and may

be thought of as meadow specialists. Some species, notably the plantains, are adapted to trampling and can exploit the areas that receive the most traffic, around drinking troughs and gateways, and on footpaths.

Although grasses can tiller at any time, they are stimulated by mowing or grazing and the resulting higher light intensities near ground level. Tillering is thus especially associated with the frequent defoliation which occurs under grazing, but where grazing is too intense, growing points can be destroyed, reducing the capacity of the plants to respond. At a point during the year (characteristic to each species) resources are diverted from the production of new leafy tillers (vegetative growth) towards the production of culms (stems supporting flowers and later seeds). The creation of new tillers is suppressed until the culm is removed or dies, a process that may be accelerated by heavy grazing. Continuous grazing therefore tends to delay or inhibit flowering and generally results in a denser, more leafy sward.

Timing of management regimes with respect to key life-stages is important. For example, grazing or mowing can prevent the flowering and/or seeding of some species, thereby reducing their ability to persist in the community. Knowledge of plant regeneration strategies is therefore necessary when trying to conserve important plant communities.

Table 3.3: Tillering capacity of common meadow and pasture grasses. Species which produce many tillers are those likely to invade bare areas left after flooding or by poaching

Species producing many tillers	Species producing few tillers
Common bent	Meadow foxtail
Creeping bent	Sweet vernal grass
Red fescue	False oat-grass
Perennial rye-grass	Crested dog's-tail
	Yellow oat-grass

Source: Crofts and Jefferson (1994).

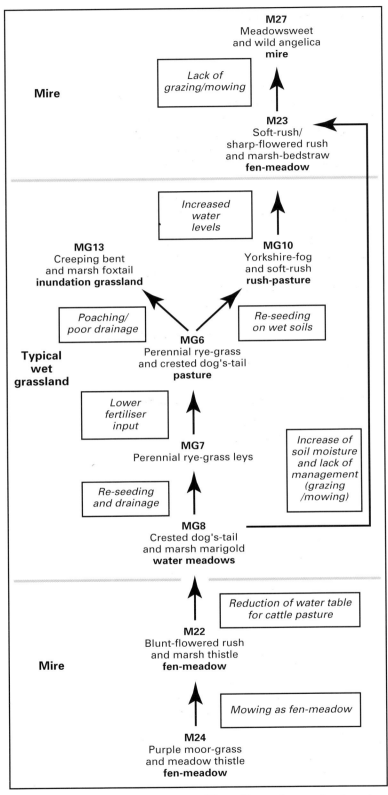

Figure 3.3 The effect of grassland and water management on grassland communities, based on data collected at a peat site in the south-west; West Sedgemoor (Prosser and Wallace 1992)

Community structure and composition is influenced by management regime. Some communities are promoted by frequent and quite intensive management, others are associated with agricultural neglect or dereliction. Tussock wet meadows (MG9), ordinary damp meadows (MG10) and the closely related western fen-meadows (M23), for example, are all more common in economically marginal farming areas, particularly in the north and west. Figure 3.3 illustrates some of the plant community changes that can occur through altered management (eg improvement or neglect) and water regime.

Grazing can favour some species by opening up the sward to light and creating bare patches in which seedlings can germinate.

Many of the most important wet grassland communities have evolved under a regime of hay cutting followed by aftermath grazing. These include:

- flood meadows (MG4)
- old grazed hay meadows (MG5)
- water meadows (MG8)
- rich fen-meadows (M22)
- litter and wet Culm grasslands (M24)

Relatively late hay cuts allow plants to flower and set seed. Grazing of the aftermath (usually in the late summer onward) is an important diversifying influence. It helps to create regeneration niches and also causes variable defoliation, which promotes diversity of both species composition and structure (also important for invertebrates and birds). Grass crops do not have to be taken every year but possibly on a one-in-three year rotation.

3.2.5 Agricultural management practices

A number of techniques have evolved to boost the agricultural productivity of grasslands, namely the application of:

■ inorganic fertiliser

■ farmyard manure and other organic fertiliser

■ lime

■ herbicides.

All the above are damaging to grasslands of high botanical interest and their effects are considered below.

Inorganic fertilisers

For grasslands generally, there is ample evidence that the use of nitrogen fertiliser or compounds of nitrogen, potassium and phosphorous (NPK) leads to a reduction in species richness and diversity. For wet grasslands in particular, recent detailed studies at Tadham Moor in Somerset have shown that even very low rates of nitrogen application (in agricultural terms – eg 25 kg N/ha/yr) can significantly reduce species richness. Phosphorus and potassium also cause marked reductions in species richness. There is growing evidence that phosphorus is the most significant element in affecting botanical composition (Mountford *et al* 1994b).

The inescapable conclusion is that no fertilisers should be used where conservation of botanical diversity is an objective. Sites can take many years to recover from the effects of fertilisers. At Tadham, after only four years of using 25, 50, 100 and 200 kg N/ha/yr, it was predicted that 3, 5, 7 and 9 years respectively will be required for the grassland to return to a composition approaching that found without fertiliser (Mountford *et al* 1996). Longer periods are likely to be needed for grasslands with a longer history of fertiliser application.

The more uniform and lush vegetation which develops when fertilisers are used is also generally less suitable for invertebrates

and most breeding waders and wildfowl. More intensive grazing or cutting to control the increased growth creates an additional problem. However, overwintering grazing geese can benefit from the effects of fertilisers in boosting sward production.

High rates of nitrogen fertiliser result in replacement of old grazed hay meadows (MG5), water meadows (MG8) and fen-meadows (M22 and M23) by dairy and fatting pastures (MG6) and improved swards (MG7). Very similar changes occur following drainage, with wet grasslands becoming replaced by more species-poor mesotrophic types. Also biological drying can be caused by fertiliser use, as the more productive vegetation has an increased evapotranspiration rate.

Farmyard manure and other organic fertilisers

There are four main categories of organic fertiliser:

■ slurry

■ farmyard manure (FYM)

■ sewage sludge

■ others (including dried blood, guano, hoof-, horn- and fish-meal, seaweed and wool shoddy).

The impact of organic fertilisers is similar to that of inorganic fertilisers. For the same reasons, their use in grasslands managed for high existing botanical interest is inadvisable. However, it is important to recognise that making hay without using FYM (or some other fertiliser) is likely to be agriculturally uneconomic. Hay cropping removes phosphate and potash from the soil; hay at 85% dry matter removes 7 kg of P_2O_5/tonne of hay and 21 kg of K_2O/tonne of hay. As buying in hay is undesirable because of the risk of importing weeds and nutrients and hay making is an intrinsic part of the traditional management that has maintained desirable floras, there may be both an economic and conservation argument for the continued use of some FYM on some sites (Simpson and Jefferson 1996).

Where appropriate, well-rotted FYM should be used; for example, cattle dung mixed with straw that has been stored for at least four months. Small quantities are recommended, eg a single dressing of <20 t/ha every 3–5 years, provided that there is clear evidence of traditional usage. FYM should always be spread outside the breeding season where there are ground-nesting birds, and care should be taken to ensure that it is well distributed. Applications of FYM are most appropriate in flood meadow (MG4), old grazed hay meadow (MG5), and inundation grassland (MG11, MG13) communities.

More extensive guidance on the use of FYM on semi-natural (meadow) grassland can be found in Simpson and Jefferson (1996).

Lime

In some wet grasslands there is a long tradition of lime application to offset losses by leaching and cropping and to prevent excessive acidification. Acidification can reduce the diversity of plant communities. It can therefore be advisable to lime occasionally, for example every 5–10 years, on sites with a tradition of use. Dressings should not exceed 3 t/ha of calcium oxide (or equivalent) and should always be made outside the bird breeding season (ie 16 July – 14 March).

The practice of liming should be avoided in semi-natural grasslands with no clear tradition of use (see Crofts and Jefferson 1994). Liming can make phosphorus both more available to growing plants and more likely to leach into drainage channels where it may damage distinctive plant and animal communities.

Herbicides

Herbicides are used to eliminate or control undesirable plant species. Many species of conservation interest are physiologically similar to target species, and are therefore also vulnerable. Such agrochemicals should therefore be used selectively (eg by weed-wiping – see section 4.4.6) or very sparingly, if at all, on semi-natural wet grasslands.

3.3 Plants of drainage channels and ponds

3.3.1 Introduction

Drainage channels and other water-bodies found in wet grasslands provide aquatic habitat for many plants and are also important in providing bankside and marginal habitat (Plate 6).

The vascular plants of aquatic habitats are often referred to as macrophytes (ie large plants) to distinguish them from microscopic algae. Although stoneworts and other multicellular algae may be referred to as macrophytes, it is common to use the term only for flowering plants, horsetails and ferns. A summary of the habitat requirements of the more important aquatic and swamp plants found in the drainage channels and other water-bodies

(*Owen Mountford*)

**Plate 6
The drainage channels of wet grassland, their banksides and margins, can provide habitat for a number of aquatic and riparian plants.**

associated with wet grassland is given in Appendix 10. This section summarises the requirements of aquatic macrophytes with respect to water quality, water level (or depth) and management.

3.3.2 Marginal and aquatic plants

Several attempts have been made to classify the plant communities of drainage channels, and to relate these communities to water depth and quality and management factors. This has proved difficult because some species are mobile (free-floating) and may not remain in the same place with particular companion species. Drainage channel vegetation also shows very rapid growth and succession.

The NVC separates the swamp component (emergents) from the truly aquatic, both floating and submerged (Rodwell 1995), whereas a more integrated approach has been taken in the Broads (Doarks and Leach 1990) and other grazing marshes. Results of a survey of over 600 drainage channels in three English grazing marshes (Mountford *et al* in press) were used to designate provisional vegetation types and their characteristics tabulated in terms of species richness (of all components – floating, submerged and emergent), prevalent management and mean water

depth. Table 3.4 arranges these working vegetation types in order, from those most typical of deep water, to those occurring in drainage channels that are dry for much of the year. Such studies strongly suggest that species and communities have a characteristic range of tolerance of water depth, and that this pattern is influenced and sometimes determined by management factors. For example, deep water results from regular or recent cleaning operations, whereas drainage channels dominated by tall emergents (eg reed), are normally not grazed along their margin.

Structurally aquatic and marginal vegetation can broadly be divided into three categories (Figure 3.4):

- *Emergent* species root in the sediments of the drainage channel and grow up through the water to emerge as aerial shoots. They include the tall dominants of reedbeds and related communities

Table 3.4: Water depth and drainage channel management regimes affecting aquatic plant community distribution

Vegetation type by depth (m)	Mean number of species/20 m			Management, percentage of sites that have been:		
	Emergent	Floating	Submerged	unmanaged	grazed	cleaned in year before survey
>1.0 m						
Sea club-rush – fennel pondweed	7.1	3.0	2.5	7	69	55
Horned pondweed – Canadian waterweed	4.3	2.6	2.6	0	42	75
0.75–0.99 m						
Greater duckweed – reed sweet-grass – rigid hornwort	7.0	3.7	1.7	5	46	58
Common reed – marsh foxtail – starwort	3.6	2.1	1.0	36	36	43
Frogbit – tubular water-dropwort	10.8	4.3	1.3	9	62	12
0.5–0.74 m						
Duckweed – common reed	5.7	2.7	0.7	35	42	4
Common reed – bindweed	5.1	1.5	0.1	67	3	0
Duckweed – Nuttall's waterweed	3.9	2.9	1.4	12	6	65
0.25–0.49 m						
Duckweed – branched bur-reed – fine-leaved water-dropwort	8.3	2.2	0.1	31	42	0
Duckweed – fool's water-cress – starwort	5.3	1.5	0.9	27	27	20
Reed sweet-grass – reed canary-grass	5.5	0.9	0.4	55	18	16
Rush – creeping bent	7.3	0.5	0.8	25	14	36
0–0.24 m						
Branched bur-reed – water-parsnip	6.0	0.4	0.4	55	18	0
Floating sweet-grass – creeping buttercup – hard rush	7.7	0.7	0.3	33	44	4
Creeping bent – marsh foxtail	6.5	0.4	0.05	33	31	13
Bittersweet – creeping buttercup – common nettle	4.4	0.2	0	92	0	0

Source: Mountford et al in press.

**Plate 7
Greater pond-sedge is a typical emergent species of drainage channels.**

(James Cadbury)

(common reed, reed sweet-grass, pond-sedges and bur-reeds), as well as lower-growing species such as floating sweet-grass, creeping bent, marsh foxtail, common spike-rush, lesser water-parsnip and water-plantain (Plate 7).

■ *Floating* species bear their leaves on the surface of the water. This group includes plants rooted in the sediment, which may also have some submerged leaves, such as common water-starwort, some pondweed species and water-lilies and also free-floating plants that form carpets, eg duckweeds and frogbit (Plate 8).

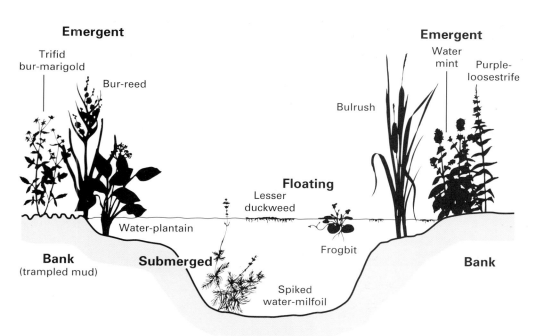

Figure 3.4 Drainage channel profile illustrating the different growth forms and habitats of aquatic and bankside plants (after Evans 1991)

■ *Submerged* (wholly aquatic) plants have all their leaves under the water, and although some species are free-floating (hornworts), the majority are rooted, for example water-milfoils and many species of pondweed (Plate 9).

These three layers may not necessarily all be present and they are not static. Characteristic or typical alliances do form between layers of particular species composition, but they are not exclusive. In addition, some plants, for example arrowhead, branched bur-reed, bulrush and water-violet, can contribute to all three layers, depending on the prevailing depth and flow of the water.

Compared with the fields themselves, the drainage channels of grazing marshes and other wet grasslands are far more important for nationally rare and scarce plant species (Table 3.5). To a great extent, this reflects the small amount of unpolluted freshwater habitat remaining in the lowlands. The role of drainage channels as a refuge for aquatic plants makes it especially important to bear in mind the secondary impacts of grassland management practices such as fertiliser application.

The bare margins of drainage channels, ponds and water-bodies, which occur

Plate 8 Floating species, such as frogbit and water-soldier, bear their leaves on the surface of the water.

(Malcolm Ausden)

Plate 9 Submerged species, such as spiked water-milfoil, have all their leaves under water.

J. A. L. Cooke (Oxford Scientific Films)

where water levels are allowed to fluctuate without deliberate regulation (particularly in mid-late summer), can also support a number of rare species. In particular, the poached margins that develop where stock have access to drainage channels or ponds for drinking enable a very distinctive community of annual plants and dwarf perennials to develop (Plate 10). The frequent filling-in of ponds, their replacement with troughs, the closer

Table 3.5: Rare, scarce and restricted-range plants of drainage channels, ponds and other water-bodies on wet grassland

AQUATIC PLANTS
Red Data Book Ribbon-leaved water-plantain Sharp-leaved pondweed
Nationally Scarce Whorled water-milfoil Fringed water-lily Floating-leaved water-plantain Tasteless water-pepper Fen pondweed Grass-wrack pondweed Hairlike pondweed Water-soldier Rootless duckweed Spiral tasselweed Greater water-parsnip
Western European endemic, restricted range outside British Isles. River water-dropwort

EMERGENT/BANKSIDE
Red Data Book Creeping marshwort Cut-grass
Nationally Scarce Cowbane Milk-parsley Borrer's saltmarsh-grass Stiff saltmarsh-grass Narrow-leaved water-dropwort Marsh sow-thistle Saltmarsh goosefoot

Red Data Book (RDB) species are also referred to as nationally rare and occur in only 1–15 10-km grid squares in England, Scotland and Wales. Nationally scarce species are found in 16–100 10-km squares.

(James Cadbury)

Plate 10 Nodding bur-marigold is one of the species adapted to colonise bare mud.

regulation of water levels, and the fencing of drainage channels, can all eliminate such communities. These temporary bare margin habitats transform gradually from truly aquatic to terrestrial conditions. The plant species adapted to them include several that have suffered a severe decline in range and abundance over the past 150 years (Mountford 1994). Many are now nationally scarce or rare, including brown galingale, cut-grass, tasteless water-pepper and pennyroyal.

Variation in aquatic plant communities arises from differences in soil type, water depth, trophic status (concentrations of dissolved nutrients) and pH as outlined in the following sections.

3.3.3 Water requirements of drainage channel plants

Many species have exacting water quality requirements. Factors like pH, salinity, the presence of specific cations and trace elements, and concentrations of oxygen, and especially nitrogen and phosphorus all influence the suitability of water for different species. These factors may be influenced by the source of the water supply, (including inputs from rainwater), soils, geology and land use within a catchment. The quality of groundwater is an important consideration on sites which rely on it for a surety of supply during the summer, and may be influenced by geological factors. For example, at Amberley Wild Brooks in Sussex, acid greensand water intrudes from springs in peat soils to allow acid plant communities

to survive alongside the alkaline plant communities associated with alluvial and eutrophic inputs from the River Arun.

The potential productivity of the water is related to its trophic state. This is defined using measurements of inorganic nitrogen and total phosphorus, pH or alkalinity (calcium carbonate concentration). The four main trophic states are defined in Table 3.6. In reality there is a continuum, with productivity straddling these artificial boundaries. Nevertheless, such a classification can be very useful in defining the potential productivity of water and soil and therefore its suitability for different species or communities.

Table 3.6: The trophic states of water

Nutrient status	mg/litre of nutrients			pH	Other characteristics
	Total Phosphorus	Inorganic Nitrogen (NO_3–N)	Calcium carbonate		
Oligotrophic to Mesotrophic	0.005–0.01	0.2–0.4	10–30	c. 6	Moderate productivity. Slightly green algal colouration in summer.
Mesotrophic to Eutrophic	0.01–0.03	0.3–0.65	c. 30	6–7	High productivity for algae and macrophytes. Often discoloured by algae.
Eutrophic to Hypertrophic	0.03–0.1	0.5–1.5	>30	>7	Discolouration noticeable due to high algal productivity. Macrophyte productivity variable.
Hypertrophic	>0.1	>1.5	>30		Algal productivity extremely high. Few macrophyte species able to compete with algae.

Source: Newbold and Palmer (1979)

Most important areas of wet grassland in lowland England and Wales are irrigated with relatively base-rich water which drains from surrounding chalk, limestone and calcareous clay uplands. In such situations, the pH of the water is normally between 7.0 and 9.0. Prior to the large-scale intensification of agriculture and increased urban population, the trophic conditions in these drainage channels would usually have been mesotrophic. Although significant areas of mesotrophic water survive, especially lower down the drainage hierarchy in field drainage channels, there has been a marked eutrophication of the main arterial channels.

Examination of Appendix 10 shows that the vast majority of plant species typically associated with wet grassland drainage channels prefer mesotrophic-eutrophic conditions (Table 3.7) and a neutral or mildly acidic pH. Consequently, the richest

Table 3.7: Some of the plants associated with base-rich drainage channels

Aquatic	Emergent/bank
Opposite-leaved pondweed	Lesser water-parsnip
Spiked water-milfoil	Marsh pennywort
Fen pondweed	Blunt-flowered rush
River water-dropwort	Water-cress
Fan-leaved water-crowfoot	Marsh stitchwort

(Owen Mountford)

(James Cadbury)

assemblages of macrophytes occur where conditions are mesotrophic or only slightly richer. Where the grassland occurs on nutrient-poor peat, the water may tend towards an oligotrophic state. In such circumstances, a very distinctive community of floating club-rush and alternate water-milfoil may occur in drainage channels. In contrast, where the drainage water becomes enriched with nutrients derived from sewage, fertiliser or slurry, conditions may tend toward hypertrophic, in which case domination by algae and duckweeds is likely (Plate 11), with small amounts of a few more tolerant macrophytes such as mare's-tail, hornworts and fennel pondweed. The brackish drainage channels of coastal grazing marshes have a specialised, low diversity flora (Table 3.8, Plate 12).

Hypertrophic standing water in drainage channels in summer is likely to suffer from low oxygen levels. Similar effects may be observed in other stable aquatic systems such as permanent pools. Where stagnant water remains for long periods, algae, duckweeds and other floating species such as water fern are able to complete their life-cycles rapidly and may exclude other species.

In all cases where aquatic macrophyte communities are present, it is suggested that any excessive floating plant growth be removed selectively. However, all of the above possible effects caused by stagnant water can be reduced by artificially creating flow. During summer there may be insufficient water to have inflows and outflows through a site, but simply creating water movement will help.

Plate 11 (top) Algal domination often occurs in response to increased nutrient inputs, from slurry or fertiliser run-off for example.

Plate 12 (bottom) Brackish water-crowfoot is adapted to live in brackish conditions and often forms part of the restricted flora found in coastal grazing marsh drainage channels.

Table 3.8: Some of the drainage channel plants associated with brackish water

Aquatic	Emergent/bank
Soft hornwort*	Marsh-mallow*
Spiked water-milfoil	Sea club-rush*
Fennel pondweed	Grey club-rush*
Brackish water-crowfoot*	Marsh sow-thistle
Spiral tasselweed*	Lesser sea-spurrey

* indicates that coastal grazing marshes are the main habitat for the species.

3.3.4 Management requirements of drainage channel plants

Provisional classification of vegetation in drainage channels reveals trends in species richness, with regard to management and mean water depths. Different species and communities exhibit a characteristic range of tolerance of water depth (Table 3.4). A more detailed summary of the water depth tolerances of aquatic plants can be found in Newbold and Mountford (1997). Although aquatic macrophytes occur over a very wide range of water depths, the majority of species can occur in shallow water of 10–100 cm depth. This implies that drainage channel management in wet grassland sites should:

■ maintain a range of water depths

■ conserve shallow water habitat.

Aquatic habitats are highly dynamic, and require maintenance to prevent succession. Appropriate and sympathetic management will enhance biodiversity. The management of drainage channels for conservation is described in Newbold *et al* (1989), and the management techniques available are summarised in Part 4 of this book. Appendix 10 and Table 3.4 suggest that the composition of the drainage channel vegetation and the occurrence of particular aquatic plants is greatly influenced by management.

In determining the need for drainage channel management for plants, the following main factors should be taken into account:

■ Variation in drainage channel depths and profiles provides a range of conditions for aquatic species. Techniques that produce near-vertical drainage channel edges limit this variation in water depth and should therefore be avoided. Fluctuating water levels are important for some of the rare plant species typical of wet mud habitats.

■ Drainage channel sediments contain the seeds, turions and plant fragments that produce the next generation of aquatic macrophytes. Removal of drainage channel sediments should be carried out rotationally to safeguard these propagules and ensure that plants can recolonise (section 4.3.2).

■ Shading by overhanging trees, coarse herbaceous bank vegetation or tall emergent macrophytes can severely limit the light available to floating and particularly submerged species and steps should be taken to keep it to a minimum. Grazing or cutting can be used to control rank growth of bank and/or emergent vegetation and reduce shading, where this is a problem. Care should be taken when managing bankside vegetation as it is often an important habitat in its own right.

■ Removal of sediments on a rotational basis will also remove sediment likely to be rich in plant nutrients and could forestall problems of hypertrophication.

Figure 3.5 Wet grassland micro-habitats and characteristic invertebrates

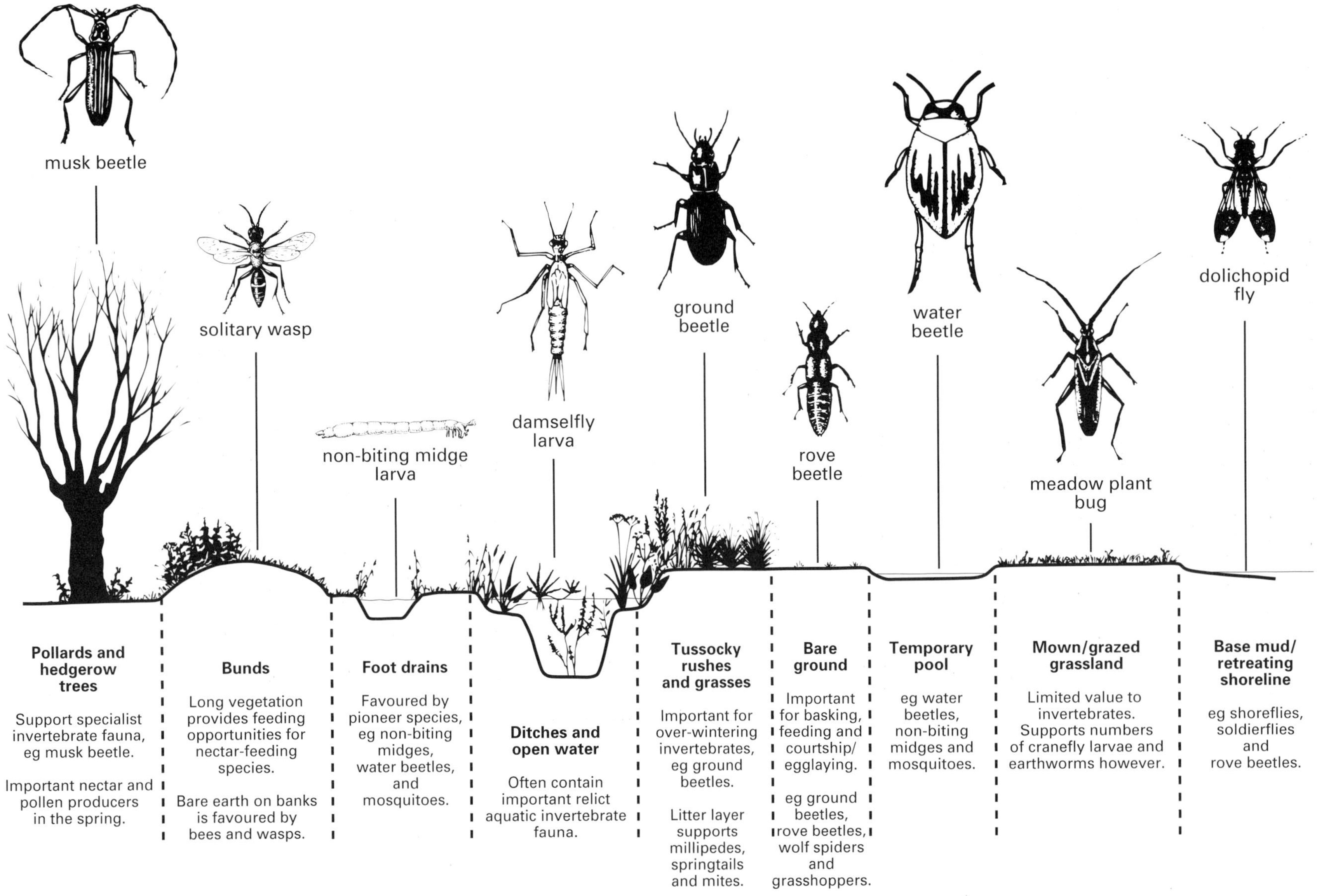

musk beetle

solitary wasp

non-biting midge larva

damselfly larva

ground beetle

rove beetle

water beetle

meadow plant bug

dolichopid fly

Pollards and hedgerow trees

Support specialist invertebrate fauna, eg musk beetle.

Important nectar and pollen producers in the spring.

Bunds

Long vegetation provides feeding opportunities for nectar-feeding species.

Bare earth on banks is favoured by bees and wasps.

Foot drains

Favoured by pioneer species, eg non-biting midges, water beetles, and mosquitoes.

Ditches and open water

Often contain important relict aquatic invertebrate fauna.

Tussocky rushes and grasses

Important for over-wintering invertebrates, eg ground beetles.

Litter layer supports millipedes, springtails and mites.

Bare ground

Important for basking, feeding and courtship/egglaying.

eg ground beetles, rove beetles, wolf spiders and grasshoppers.

Temporary pool

eg water beetles, non-biting midges and mosquitoes.

Mown/grazed grassland

Limited value to invertebrates. Supports numbers of cranefly larvae and earthworms however.

Base mud/retreating shoreline

eg shoreflies, soldierflies and rove beetles.

3.4 Invertebrates

3.4.1 Introduction

Wet grasslands and associated drainage channels provide habitat for a variety of grassland, soil-dwelling and aquatic invertebrates (Figure 3.5). Many invertebrates are highly specialised creatures with precise habitat requirements. They can be very sensitive to quite small changes in their habitat/environment, particularly as a result of management (Table 3.9). Aquatic species found in water-filled drainage channels can also make use of grassland areas when they flood for extended periods. Isolated trees and bushes, droves, lanes and earth walls further diversify invertebrate habitat on wet grassland sites.

This section looks at the habitat requirements of grassland and aquatic invertebrates in turn, then concludes with a brief examination of the requirements of invertebrates of associated habitats.

Table 3.9: Reasons for invertebrate sensitivity to environmental change

- Most have annual life-cycles and lack long-term resting stages. Disruption of the annual cycle can cause a species to disappear from a site.
- Life-cycles are often complex and requirements differ for different stages.
- Many species are highly specialised.
- Many are dependent on apparently insignificant site features which they are able to exploit because of their small size.
- Many species are physically or behaviourally ill-adapted to dispersal.

3.4.2 Grassland invertebrate requirements

Wet grassland supports a wide range of invertebrates including ground beetles, snails and the adult forms of many species which have aquatic larvae, for example dragonflies and caddisflies. Generally, invertebrate interest of wet grasslands is lower than that of associated truly aquatic habitats such as drainage channels.

Vegetation requirements of terrestrial invertebrates

Vegetation structure (ie sward height, tussockiness, etc) and composition (species present) both influence the number and range of invertebrates present at a site. Vegetation structure influences the microclimate at ground level and provides the basic living quarters for animals above ground. There is no ideal structure that will suffice for all species living in grassland.

Many insects require a mixture of sward heights in close proximity to provide the range of conditions needed during different stages of their life-cycle (Table 3.10). Clearly, larger sites with a varied microtopography and range of management offer a greater potential for variation in vegetation structure.

The tussockiness of a sward is a good indication of its value to invertebrates. Tussocks are important because they provide:

- a humid, litter-rich habitat
- refuge from large predators (eg birds)
- protection from extremes of temperature
- overwintering sites (especially in areas subjected to winter floods).

Table 3.10: Vegetation requirements of invertebrates on wet grassland

Habitat feature	Benefit	Invertebrate groups benefiting
Plant species	Provide food.	Correct plant in right condition and position required by herbivores, eg butterflies, root herbivores, seed feeders and some flower visitors.
Tussocks	Provide shelter, refuge from cold, predators and flooding.	Needed year-round, but especially in winter, by ground-dwelling predators such as ground and rove beetles and terrestrial litter feeders, eg cranefly and soldierfly larvae.
Sward height	Varied sward heights and mosaics required. Sward height also controls micro-climate and foodplant condition for herbivores.	Mosaics benefit ground-dwelling predators such as ground beetles. Tall ungrazed or unmown swards are required by seed feeders, eg picture-wing flies and weevils.
Tall emergent plants	Provide shelter, foodplants and emergence sites.	Important as emergence sites and perches for dragonflies and robberflies and water margin predators such as shore bugs and dolichopodid flies. Foodplants for herbivores, eg leaf beetle larvae, seed feeders. Provide good litter layer for water-edge litter feeders.
Flowers	Provide nectar, pollen and seed.	Used as perches and as bait for prey by flying predators. Oviposition sites and larval food for seed feeders. Provide food for flower visitors, eg hoverflies from spring to autumn.
Hedges, bushes, trees, etc	Provide shelter, food (dead and alive), litter source and perches.	Used as hunting stations by flying predators. Foodplants for herbivores, eg brimstone butterfly caterpillars. Litter supply for terrestrial litter feeders.

There is usually a greater density of invertebrates in tussocks than in the surrounding shorter sward, especially in winter, and up to about half of the beetles present in a grassland can be present in its tussocks (Luff 1966). All tussocks have some value, but larger ones (eg of tufted hair-grass) provide better insulation and are therefore more valuable as overwintering sites than, for example, small sparser grasses (eg Yorkshire-fog) (Luff 1965). In pastures, the best time to assess vegetation structure for invertebrates is at the end of the grazing season when stock are removed. At this stage, the grassland should still contain tussocks set in a shorter lawn. A useful rule of thumb is to aim for about a quarter of the area to be tussocky.

Most invertebrates are dependent on vegetation structure and are not associated with single plant species (Sheppard 1994). However, many plant-eating invertebrate species require not only the presence of specific food plants, but also their correct growth-form or stage of development (Kirby 1992). Although it is difficult to be specific about the requirements of wet grassland invertebrates because of their huge variety, certain generalisations can be made. Specific needs are relatively well known for the butterflies. The requirements of this group clearly show how species differ in the foodplants they require, the minimum area needed to conserve them effectively and their management requirements (Table 3.11).

It is important to note that requirements can vary greatly between life-stages as well as between species. In butterflies, adults generally have less exacting requirements than earlier stages (caterpillar and chrysalis). For example, adult butterflies must obtain nectar and may have preferred plant species, but they will use other flowers freely if these are absent. In contrast, females are highly selective in their choice of egg-laying sites as this determines whether caterpillars will have access to their specific foodplant. Most species lay eggs on one or two closely related species of wild flower or grass. An essential first step in managing for butterflies on wet grasslands is to ensure that larval foodplants are established.

Table 3.11: Requirements of some of the butterflies of wet grassland

Species	Habitat	Main foodplant	Growth form of foodplant	Management	Population structure	Min. area for colony	Status
Small skipper	Damp meadows.	Yorkshire-fog	Large tussocks	Very light grazing or leave parts of sward uncut for 2–4 years.	Closed	0.5 ha	Common in southern England and Wales
Essex skipper	Wet meadows, drainage channel edges.	Creeping soft-grass, cock's-foot	Large tussocks	As for small skipper. Can withstand considerable winter flooding.	Closed	0.5 ha	Common in south-east England
Large skipper	Damp, scrubby meadows.	Cock's-foot, purple moor-grass	Medium/large tussocks	Cutting every second year or light winter grazing.	Closed	0.5 ha	Common in south England and Wales
Green-veined white	Damp and wet meadows, drainage channel edges.	Cuckooflower and small crucifers	Young small plants and seedlings in April–August	Considerable disturbance eg heavy poaching by cattle in winter to late spring. Unnecessary on eroding drainage channel sides.	Open	-	Common in all damp habitats throughout UK
Orange-tip	Damp and wet meadows, drainage channel banksides.	Cuckooflower	Large flowering plants in sunny, sheltered locations	Quite heavy grazing or mowing in winter or early spring. Leave undisturbed May–August.	Open	-	Common throughout UK except in north
Marsh fritillary	Damp and wet meadows.	Devil's-bit scabious	Medium-sized, quite prominent plants in warm sheltered sward *c.* 5–15 cm tall	Light winter/early spring grazing, preferably by cattle. Leave spring–autumn. Annual mowing in late June an option but less satisfactory.	Closed	2 ha	Nationally notable

Source: after Treweek et al (1991)

Not only must the right plant species be present, their growth-form is also important. The orange-tip, for example, requires large, established cuckooflower plants because it lays only on the flowers and its caterpillars feed only on the seed pods. The green-veined white butterfly uses the same plant, but lays on younger specimens, including seedlings, because its caterpillars eat only tender young leaves of crucifers. Plant growth-forms are greatly influenced by vegetation management.

Continuity of management is very important, particularly where a site is relatively isolated. Many of these butterflies live in closed populations and are essentially sedentary, existing in close-knit colonies on the same breeding site throughout the year. Even short periods of adverse conditions can be damaging. There have been many instances where a species with exacting requirements has become locally extinct simply because conditions for its foodplant were unsuitable for a season or two. It can take decades for the rarer and more sedentary species to recolonise such an area. Such species may have to be reintroduced to sites where they have become extinct. Methods and practical hints are summarised by Thomas (1989).

Herbivorous insects consume all parts of plants – roots, leaves, stems, seeds, flowers, and nectar and pollen. Probably the most successful species in wet grassland are those feeding on low plants and roots. The former are less likely to be eaten by stock

Table 3.12 Substrate requirements of invertebrates on wet grassland

Habitat feature	Benefit	Invertebrate groups benefiting
Litter	Provides food for litter feeders and humid shelter.	Provides shelter for ground-dwelling predators, water margin predators and root herbivores, eg reed beetle larvae. Unflooded litter layer needed year round by terrestrial litter feeders, eg woodlice. Water-edge litter feeders, eg soldierfly larvae, can withstand prolonged winter flooding.
Bare mud	Provides basking, hunting and courtship areas and food for larvae.	Provides dry ground for hunting and basking for ground-dwelling and flying predators. Wet mud used by water margin predators, eg shore bugs, for hunting and courtship.
Damp soil	High water-table maintains high humidity.	High water-table favoured by most ground-dwelling invertebrates.
Animal by-products	Dung and carrion provide food source.	Dung provides food for dung feeders, eg dung beetles. Carcasses provide food for carrion feeders, eg blowflies.

(together with the vegetation), whereas root-feeders are less susceptible to light trampling. Species such as stem-boring caterpillars and picture-wing flies feeding in seed heads of tall plants are probably the most susceptible to loss as a result of grazing. The intensity and timing of grazing and the type of animal will determine whether species in these groups can survive in grazed grassland.

Pollen and nectar provide a valuable food source for flying insects between March and October. Heavy grazing during this period removes flowers and is damaging to these invertebrates. Some flowers are used more than others, and open-structured flowers are generally more attractive.

Substrate requirements of terrestrial invertebrates

Many grassland and semi-aquatic invertebrates are dependent on bare ground, exposed mud and the litter layer (Table 3.12).

Bare ground is important for a large number of grassland invertebrates. It is used by some species for hunting and courtship. Grasshoppers lay their eggs in drier areas of bare ground or in very short sward. Dry soils on floodbanks, especially those facing the sun, will be used by nesting bees and wasps, which need hot conditions. The extra warmth that reaches exposed wet soil is important in speeding up development of species living at or below ground level.

Exposed mud at water margins is used by some species as a source of organically rich food (Table 3.13). Soft, organic muds at water margins are also important for the larvae of many species of flies, while consolidated mud may hold burrowing species. However, large expanses of wet mud next to water are used by only a small number of mud specialists such as shoreflies. As a general rule, small pockets of bare ground (in the order of centimetres) next to vegetated areas are much more useful than extensive areas (in the order of metres). Management should therefore aim for plenty of bare ground in little patches. Rich invertebrate faunas have often been found at water margins where high levels of poaching have occurred in the previous year. Poaching should be less intensive on damp (not saturated) ground in field centres, because the species most likely to use bare ground are not generally a dominant component of the fauna here.

Table 3.13: Invertebrate species using bare mud at water margins

Role	Species
Organic food	■ shoreflies ■ lesser dung flies ■ soldierflies
Hunting	■ dolichopodid flies ■ muscid flies ■ ground beetles ■ rove beetles ■ shore bugs
Courtship	■ dolichopodid flies ■ shoreflies ■ lesser dung flies

Peat soils are easily damaged by poaching, which can reduce a drainage channel on peat soils to a wide, shallow depression within two or three years. Care is therefore needed in deciding how much access by stock should be allowed to drainage channels on peat soils. Also, it is worth considering whether the drainage channel needs to function as a wet fence or drain, or whether a depression containing swamp vegetation is as valid a habitat as a drainage channel. For many invertebrates, a patch of wet fen is very good habitat.

The litter layer is an important component of grassland for many species and invertebrates play a major role in litter break-down. The main groups involved are earthworms, mites and springtails. In ranker grassland, woodlice, beetles, spiders and millipedes may also use the litter layer. The smaller species are preyed upon by a large contingent of ground and rove beetles (Plate 13). The litter layer is not only important in providing food, but also acts as a buffer against extreme temperatures and as a mulch to retain moisture and maintain humid conditions at ground level.

Water regime requirements of terrestrial invertebrates

It is important to consider the depth, duration, frequency and timing of any flooding and also the position of the soil water-table and the extent to which it fluctuates. Invertebrates of wet grassland are generally adapted to fluctuating water conditions. However, extensive drainage of wet grasslands has resulted in circumstances where species more characteristic of drier habitats can colonise. The invertebrate species composition of embanked floodplain grasslands, for example, may reflect this. The new faunas which colonise such sites are vulnerable to occasional flooding and may also be unable to adapt to increased site wetness where water levels are restored. The time taken for invertebrate faunas characteristic of wet grassland to re-establish is not known, but is potentially faster the nearer the restored site is to a source of colonists.

(Roger Key)

Effects of winter flooding on terrestrial invertebrates

Prolonged winter flooding (November to March) can kill or expel species overwintering in the soil or litter layer, if these are not adapted to continuous submersion. Such species include many moths, but there is little information on the effects of continuous submergence on other groups. Fewer species of flies with terrestrial larvae are found on winter-flooded sites than those which remain merely damp throughout the winter. Shallow flooding is less likely to be damaging than deep flooding because some species may survive in tussocks protruding above the water level.

The timing, duration and rate at which sites are flooded affects the fauna. Some important groups of insects, notably craneflies, are still active in October, and flooding before the end of this month will prevent the autumn-flying species from laying eggs in suitable damp conditions by drainage channel edges. The adults of many beetles are also still active in October and will not have sought winter refuge in tussocks. Managed flooding should therefore be left until at least November when the average temperature is low enough to have reduced activity and stimulated most species to find overwintering sites. During the winter the majority of invertebrates are relatively inactive.

**Plate 13
Carabid beetles, such as *Badister unipustulatus*, are important invertebrate predators in wet grassland.**

Ground beetles appear to be tolerant of prolonged winter flooding. Common and rare species appear rapidly in spring on the Ouse Washes, and Lower Derwent Valley, both of which have a very long history of flooding. The beetle fauna of sites where flooding has been recently introduced or reintroduced seem to respond less favourably. The Nene Washes, which has been only infrequently flooded in recent years and has suffered conversion to arable and subsequent re-conversion to wet grassland, has a poor carabid beetle fauna. The beetle fauna of the site is largely made up of species quick to colonise recently flooded agriculturally improved grassland.

Grasslands that have been regularly flooded over many years, also contain a distinct suite of semi-aquatic earthworm species, that are able to survive prolonged winter flooding. Grasslands where regular winter flooding has been prevented develop an earthworm fauna comprised mainly of terrestrial species, but also invariably including one of the semi-aquatic earthworm species, the green form of the earthworm *Allolobophora chlorotica*. Introducing winter flooding to such sites results in a massive decline in earthworm biomass, with usually only very small numbers of *A. chlorotica* remaining in the flooded areas. It is not known how long it takes a true semi-aquatic earthworm fauna to re-establish.

Temporary pools left after winter flooding are used by aquatic invertebrates, notably water beetles that are normally found in the thickly vegetated edges of drainage channels and in grassy pools. Many of these water beetles are able to complete their larval stage rapidly in spring and the adults fly away when the pool dries out. Some *Limnephilus* caddis, non-biting midges and mosquitoes of pioneer habitats are also abundant in pools in late spring and early summer. The sparsely vegetated retreating shore line is colonised by insects whose larvae live in saturated mud, notably some shoreflies and lesser dung flies.

Effects of summer flooding on terrestrial invertebrates

From mid-March to late September, when soil water temperatures become high enough for the rapid development of anoxic conditions, flooding can damage populations of non-mobile terrestrial invertebrates or those caught out at a vulnerable life stage, such as spiders and the larvae of plant-feeding moths, beetles and bugs. Invertebrates may survive, trapped in air pockets, for a short time, but will eventually die as a result of oxygen depletion and the build-up of toxins from decaying organic matter.

Summer flooding can also have a detrimental impact on larval stages of aquatic insects because some of the population may be stranded when the water recedes. This effect could be particularly damaging to the floating pupae of some soldierflies and snail-killing flies, which could be stranded and dehydrate. Insects in their aerial phases are mobile enough to avoid the effects of summer flooding. Both aquatic and terrestrial invertebrates can be harmed by simple depletion of their habitat when water is pumped on to bunded fields and by flooding in early autumn to encourage birds.

Where water stands for long periods in the summer and becomes stagnant, opportunistic larvae of, for example, non-biting midges and mosquitoes, are likely as the first colonisers, followed closely by water boatmen and water beetles. Such a community may have value in providing food for birds (section 3.5). The potential creation of temporary pools or splashes or more permanent pools should be balanced against the loss of existing botanical and invertebrate communities.

3.4.3 Aquatic invertebrate requirements

The drainage channels of wet grasslands support a range of aquatic invertebrates. These include insects, snails and crustacea. Invertebrate interest is generally higher in drainage channels and water-bodies than on nearby grassland. Some drainage channels may contain nationally rare or scarce aquatic species, such as the great silver water beetle (Plate 14) or the Norfolk hawker dragonfly.

Plate 14 Drainage channels often support diverse invertebrate communities and are important for a range of rare species, including the great silver water beetle.

(Roger Key)

Dragonflies are effective indicators of the condition of aquatic habitats and their immediate environs. In the last 50 years the dragonflies and damselflies of Britain have declined as a result of habitat loss, pollution and abstraction (Chelmick *et al* 1980). Under this pressure, two species have become extinct and a third of the remaining have become rare or local in their distribution.

Plate 15 The hairy dragonfly is an uncommon species, which occurs in still or slow-flowing channels with dense fringing vegetation.

(Malcolm Ausden)

Of the 39 dragonflies and damselflies which breed regularly in the British Isles, 22 species use wet grassland drainage channels (Plates 15 and 16). Several species, such as variable damselfly, Norfolk hawker and hairy dragonfly, show strong associations with wet grassland drainage channels (Table 3.14). Their requirements are given in Table 3.15.

Table 3.14: Uncommon dragonflies strongly associated with wet grassland drainage channels in southern England and Wales

Plate 16 The scarce emerald damselfly occurs in shallow, temporary, freshwater and brackish pools and drainage channels choked with luxuriant growth of emergent and marginal vegetation.

(Malcolm Ausden)

Scarce emerald damselfly (Red Data Book)	Found in shallow habitats, temporary freshwater and brackish pools and drainage channels choked with luxuriant growth of marginal and emergent vegetation. Often associated with emerald damselfly and ruddy darter. The greatest threats to this species are lowering of water-tables at sites where they breed in temporary pools and heavy fertiliser application and the subsequent eutrophication of water-bodies on arable land (Askew 1988, Merritt *et al* 1996).
Norfolk hawker (Red Data Book)	Very rare, restricted to weedy grazing marsh and fen drainage channel systems in Norfolk and Suffolk. Appears to be increasing. Found in drainage channels with good water quality and appears to be associated with water-soldier. Females have been observed laying eggs into this plant, which then sinks to the bottom of the drainage channel during winter (Corbet *et al* 1960).
Variable damselfly (nationally scarce)	Formerly widespread now has a rather restricted distribution. Most numerous in drainage channels on grazing marshes, which have a regular cleaning rotation. Females lay eggs into the underside of floating vegetation, eg pondweeds.
Hairy dragonfly (nationally scarce)	Found in still or feebly flowing waters, tolerates brackish and eutrophic conditions in coastal areas. Dense fringing vegetation such as common reed is characteristic of suitable habitat. Males fly low through such tall emergent vegetation and the females lay eggs into decomposing rushes and sedges floating in the water.

Table 3.15: Dragonflies often recorded on wet grasslands (others can also occur in this habitat)

Habitat and management	Species	Special requirements	Notes
Larger drainage channels managed on short cleaning cycles of 5 years or less; open ponds; sluggish streams.	Emperor dragonfly, common blue damselfly, broad-bodied chaser	Open water for patrolling, tall emergent plants for emergence.	Common blue damselfly tolerates brackish water.
Drainage channels managed on 2–10 year cleaning cycles; ponds; sluggish streams.	Earlier seral stages; blue-tailed damselfly, migrant hawker, southern hawker, hairy dragonfly, four-spotted chaser, common darter Later seral stages; azure damselfly, variable damselfly, large red damselfly	Well vegetated margins for emergence and often for egg-laying; floating vegetation for egg-laying by variable damselfly; clean water for variable damselfly and hairy dragonfly.	Blue-tailed damselfly frequent in brackish conditions, hairy dragonfly tolerates brackish water. Larvae of darters and chasers live in silt. Large red damselfly is more frequent in drainage channels on peat than on clay.
Drainage channels managed for good growth of water-soldier; only a small proportion of plants cleared at any one time.	Norfolk hawker	Very clean water, strong association with water-soldier, high water-table.	Restricted to a few grazing marshes and fen drainage channel sites in Norfolk and Suffolk.
Shallow, densely vegetated drainage channels, in a late seral stage, choked with emergent plants and managed on long cycles of well over 5 years; shallow ponds; seasonal pools.	Emerald damselfly, scarce emerald damselfly, ruddy darter	Dense, tall emergent, soft-stemmed plants (eg sea club-rush and bulrush) for egg-laying by scarce emerald. Their shallow sites are susceptible to lowering of the water-table.	Ruddy darter larvae live in silt. All three species tolerate brackish water, and scarce emerald damselfly can be frequent in brackish drainage channels.

The first column describes where the species will most likely be found but most species have a wide tolerance. General requirements of nearly all species listed are a well vegetated water-body containing a varied structure of submerged plants and a fringe of tall emergent plants used for emergence and often for egg-laying.

Drainage channels offer a range of environmental conditions and micro-habitats for invertebrates (Figure 3.6). Many species have exacting habitat requirements, a range of factors influence their distribution/presence in drainage channels including:

- water depth
- water quality
- sediment
- vegetation type/composition
- shading.

Water requirements, vegetation and other factors are considered in turn.

Water requirements of aquatic invertebrates

Shallow water (<30 cm) generally provides better habitat for aquatic invertebrates than deep water because:

- Water depth influences light penetration which decreases with increasing depth.

- Temperatures are also lower at depth and, for many invertebrates, relatively high water temperatures are essential in spring and summer for rapid development.

- Oxygen concentrations are higher, creating a less stressful environment, especially at night

The edges of drainage channels, where the water is relatively shallow, are particularly valuable. Numbers of species will begin to fall off as the maximum water depth (in early summer) decreases below about

Open water stage

Peltodytes caesus
a crawling water beetle

Open water communities include:
- *Hydroglyphus pusillus* (a diving beetle)
- *Peltodytes caesus* and *Haliplus wehnkei* (crawling water beetles)

Mid-successional stage

Odontomyia ornata
a water soldierfly

Species present include:
- *Limnoxenus niger* (a scavenger water beetle)
- Great silver water beetle
- Dragonflies and damselflies

Late successional stage

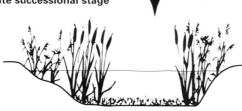

Hydaticus transversalis
a diving beetle

Species present include:
- *Odontomyia tigrina* (a soldierfly)
- *Rhantus grapii* (a diving beetle)
- *Anisus vorticulus* (a ramshorn snail)
- Scarce emerald damselfly

Choked, litter-rich stage

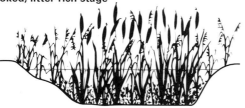

Pisidium pseudosphaerium
a pea mussel

Species present include:
- *Odacantha melaneura* (a ground beetle)
- *Dromius longiceps* (a ground beetle)
- *Aplexa hypnorum* (a bladder snail)

Figure 3.6
The main stages of drainage channel seral succession and their associated invertebrate fauna

30 cm in fresh water and about 15 cm in brackish water (all other factors being equal). As a result, the aquatic fauna is unlikely to benefit from digging or reprofiling of drainage channels deeper than about 60 cm below the normal summer water level.

Transient or temporary water-bodies are an important invertebrate habitat. Remnant creeks (on coastal marshes), pools, depressions and derelict grips, which hold water for short periods are used by a number of insects that grow rapidly as larvae in spring and fly away when adult (eg non-biting midges – see Case Study 8). They are also important where a more or less permanent wetland flora persists and therefore extend the area of habitat for wetland species that require only saturated ground.

There is a marked sequential change in the species composition of invertebrates living in drainage channels as they undergo succession from open, frequently cleaned sites to those which have long ceased to function as wet fences or drains (Plate 17). There is no loss of rare species, merely a shift from rare aquatic species to rare terrestrial species (Figure 3.6).

Plate 17 Ditches choked with vegetation may have low botanical diversity, but can be important for a suite of specialist invertebrate species.

(*Owen Mountford*)

Water quality requirements of aquatic invertebrates

The invertebrate faunas of drainage channels are influenced by water quality parameters such as nutrient status and salinity.

Studies have shown a decline in species richness and a loss of many nationally rare and scarce species from drainage channels where nutrient enrichment has occurred following conversion from permanent pasture to arable or sown grassland. For example, the rare shiny ramshorn water snail and the large-mouthed valve snail disappeared from drainage channels in newly converted arable areas in the Pevensey Levels (Palmer 1986). Many other species of snail also disappear from drainage channels subject to nutrient enrichment, leaving only common, tolerant species such as the wandering snail and Jenkin's spire snail.

The communities of freshwater marshes are very different from those of brackish marshes. A gradient of salinities often exists across coastal marshes (eg Halvergate Marshes, Norfolk, Case Study 8) and important transition communities can be found where fresh and saline influences merge (Table 3.16). When the salinity rises to give conductivity readings in excess of about 4,000 μS, these transitional faunas disappear but may be replaced by lagoon and true saltmarsh species. It is likely that many coastal species can tolerate freshwater conditions for one season but the original gradient should be restored if possible. Whereas brackish marshes support a valuable fauna, irregular inundation by brackish water, for example from tidal rivers that over-top their banks, can eliminate intolerant freshwater species without permitting the faunas typical of brackish marshes to become established.

Water chemistry (and invertebrate diversity) is influenced by the soil type. Drainage channels on peat soils support a slightly richer fauna than those on clay (Drake in press b). A few species, including the lesser silver water beetle, are more common on acidic peat than on fen peat. There appears to be no difference in the richness or composition of the faunas of clay or alluvium drainage channels.

Table 3.16: Examples of invertebrate species tolerant and intolerant of brackish conditions

Species	Intolerant of brackish conditions	Tolerant of brackish conditions but rare	Tolerant of brackish conditions or preferred habitat (*)
Flatworms	all species		
Leeches	all species		
Worms	*Lumbricus variegatus*		
Molluscs	*Anisus vortex, A. leucostoma, Aplexa hypnorum, Bathyomphalus contortus, Bithynia leachii, B. tentaculata, Physa fontinalis, Planorbarius corneus, Sphaerium corneum, Segmentina complanta, Valvata piscinalis*	*Lymnaea palustris, Planorbis planorbis, Sphaerium lacustre*	*Hydrobia ulvae*, H. ventrosa*, Leucophytia bidendata*, Phytia myosotis*, Lymnaea peregra, Potamopyrgus antipodarum*
Crustaceans	*Gammarus pulex*	*Asellus aquaticus, Crangonyx pseudogracilis*	*Corophium* spp.*, *Gammarus duebeni*, G. zaddachi*, Neomysis intiger*, Palaemonetes varians*, Sphaeroma* spp.*
Mayflies	*Caenis robusta*	*Cleon dipterum*	
Dragonflies	most species	Azure damselfly	Scarce emerald damselfly, Blue-tailed damselfly
Water bugs	*Gerris lacustris*	*Iliocoris cimicoides, Microvelia pygmaea*	*Corixa affinis, Notonecta marmorea viridis, Sigara concinna, S. lateralis, S. selecta*, S. stagnalis**
Caddis	*Limnephilus lunatus*	*Athripsodes aterrimus, Limnephilus flavicornis, L. marmoratus*	*Limnephilus affinis*
Moths	China-mark		
Water beetles	*Agabus sturmii, Anacaena globulus, Graptodytes pictus*		*Agabus conspersus*, Berosus affinis, Coelambus parallelogrammus, Dytiscus circumflexus, Enochrus bicolor*, E. halophilus*, Graptodytes bilineatus, Gyrinus caspius, Haliplus apicalis*, Helophorus alternans*, H. fulgidicollis*, Limnoxenus niger, Ochthebius marinus*, O. punctatus*, O. viridis**

Source: Drake (1988c)

Vegetation structure and composition requirements of aquatic invertebrates

Relatively few aquatic invertebrates eat living plants. Predators, parasites, and detritivores together far outnumber herbivores. Many aquatic herbivores, such as mayflies and snails, eat algae rather than macrophytes. Aquatic macrophytes provide living space for invertebrates and in general, the more complex the structure of vegetation, the more species of invertebrates that are present. Management which enhances the variety of the vegetation will benefit the invertebrate fauna as a whole. The small size of invertebrates means that apparently small-scale variations in vegetation structure can have a considerable impact on the availability of habitat.

Although generally, increased structural diversity leads to a more diverse fauna, there are some plant monocultures that support rich invertebrate communities. Drainage channels and depressions dominated almost exclusively by sea club-rush in brackish sites often have a diverse fauna, containing several uncommon or rare coastal insects. Shallow, grassy drainage channels or foot drains with creeping bent and marsh foxtail usually support abundant populations of water beetles. Common reed also has its own large assemblage of herbivores (eg wainscot moths) and their parasites (Fojt and Foster 1992). Even stands of reed sweet-grass and bulrush may contain a diverse fauna within their litter, as well as supporting a few herbivores.

Effects of shading on aquatic invertebrates

Shading reduces the temperature of drainage channel water, as well as the amount of light available to plants. In general, heavily shaded drainage channels (of whatever depth) support a relatively limited aquatic fauna. This may include species that are infrequent in unshaded sites, but these species are usually common and unlikely to need special consideration in terms of management. Continuous hedges are an obvious source of shade. The banks of deep drainage channels also cast shade, especially in drainage channels running in an east–west direction, and are likely to be less valuable for aquatic invertebrates.

3.4.4 Other invertebrate habitats

Additional habitat for invertebrates, is provided by:

- bankside vegetation

- the trees and shrubs occasionally found on wet grassland sites

- droves, lanes and bunds.

Bankside vegetation

Banks of drainage channels are often as important as the aquatic habitat. The soils are often saturated so the flora is more diverse than that of pasture and thus can support a wider range of herbivorous insects. Where banks are ungrazed, they provide a habitat more akin to fen than grassland, with areas of tall vegetation. Species, such as several of the picture-wing flies, that feed within the seed heads of tall composites and other plants find a refuge here. Often, ungrazed or uncut banks have more flowers than elsewhere, and these are an important nectar and pollen source for insects. Umbellifers are especially favoured by species such as hoverflies and soldierflies. Taller vegetation by drainage channels and on their banks provides shelter for flying insects. Emergent plants are used by aquatic insects, such as dragonflies and mayflies, when they emerge as adults.

Trees and shrubs

Trees and shrubs commonly found on wet grassland sites, include willows, poplars, oak, alders, hawthorn and blackthorn. These have the potential to support a large invertebrate fauna, consisting of herbivores and associations of predators, parasites and litter-feeders. These trees and shrubs support many more species than do wild flowers, such as thistles and bird's-foot-trefoil (Sheppard 1994, Southwood 1961). Therefore, trees lining drainage channels and lanes can do a great deal to increase the invertebrate diversity of wet grassland sites, and often support more scarce species than relatively large areas of semi-improved pasture. Some species are found most frequently in isolated trees, for example the larvae of the longhorn musk beetle feed within the small branches of pollarded willows. Willows also support scarce moths, such as the cream-bordered green pea and lunar hornet moth. Another longhorn beetle, *Anaglyptus mysticus*, bores into the dead branches of hawthorns. Isolated trees and bushes also provide shelter, roots and overwintering sites. Spring-flowering trees, with pollen and nectar-producing flowers (eg sallow, hawthorn, blackthorn), are especially valuable for early insects when other flowers are still scarce. Isolated flowering bushes and trees often have many more insects visiting them than those in large clumps and provide important courtship sites for many insects.

Droves, lanes and bunds

Droves and lanes can provide valuable habitat for invertebrates, partly because they are often bordered by trees and bushes and partly because they tend to have more long grass than more heavily managed areas. Some tall flowers that are important nectar and pollen sources, such as hogweed, are also found only along droves. If hedges develop on both sides of a drove, they should not be allowed to shade the drove completely because the valuable sheltered hotspot will be lost.

Bunds built as flood defences can be valuable to terrestrial invertebrates that do not form part of the grassland fauna itself, but can nevertheless contribute to the invertebrate variety of wet grassland sites. Bees and wasps in particular favour sunny banks, especially those with short turf and bare patches of earth (resulting from trampling by sheep, for example). Ungrazed banks, such as sea walls that are inaccessible to stock, may provide the only areas of long grass and associated large flowering herbs on a site. Bunds can also provide an important refuge from flooding for some species.

3.4.5 Management requirements of invertebrates

When managing wet grassland and associated drainage channels for invertebrates, the following general principles should be observed:

- Maintain habitat continuity and variety of vegetation structure on both the grassland and in drainage channels.

- Constant small-scale management such as grazing or trampling is best for keeping vegetation structure varied (Table 3.17).

- Rotational management provides habitat continuity and variety of structure allowing the more mobile species to evade catastrophic management practices, such as drainage channel cleaning and mowing. Care should be taken when assigning management compartments, to ensure that entire plant communities/species are not isolated in one compartment and subjected to management all in one go.

- When creating/reprofiling drainage channels ensure marginal berms/shelves are incorporated into the design (section 4.3.3 and 4.3.4).

- Management should not be undertaken simply to benefit one species.

Table 3.17: Effects of grassland management regimes on invertebrates

ROTATIONAL GRAZING IN SMALL UNITS

Advantages	Disadvantages
Allows growth of longer swards of benefit to species that breed in long grass, eg skippers and brown butterflies, and cone-heads.	Rapid and dramatic change to areas, following periods of no grazing, detrimental to species such as grasshoppers.

CONTINUOUS GRAZING

Advantages	Disadvantages
Maintains mosaic. Carries least drastic change in structure from year to year – of particular benefit to less mobile species, eg molluscs.	None, as long as stocking density is low enough to avoid over-grazing and widespread poaching.

HAY WITH AFTERMATH GRAZING

Advantages	Disadvantages
Few. It is best to consider hay fields as primarily a botanical feature, unless cutting can be delayed until late summer/early autumn.	Loss of short turf and bare, poached areas early in the season. Catastrophic loss of vegetation when many insects are reaching maturity (late cutting from July onwards helps overcome this).

3.5 Wet grassland birds

Over 40 bird species of conservation concern are at least partially dependent on wet grasslands for wintering or breeding (Table 1.4). During the winter months, wet grassland, especially when flooded, can attract large flocks of waterfowl, mainly migrants from northern Europe. Several wet grassland sites in the UK, for example the Ouse Washes, regularly support winter concentrations of waterfowl that are of international importance (>20,000), as well as nationally and internationally important concentrations of individual species. Wintering species of conservation concern include Bewick's swan (Plate 18), bean goose and wigeon (Table 3.18). In spring and summer a number of wader and wildfowl species make use of the wet meadows, water-bodies and drainage channel systems, for breeding. Breeding species of conservation concern include garganey, spotted crake and black-tailed godwit (Table 3.18).

This section focuses on the requirements of wintering and breeding wildfowl and waders using wet grassland.

(Tony Hamblin, RSPB)

Plate 18
Wildfowl of conservation concern that winter in the UK include the Bewick's swan, which occurs in internationally important numbers.

Table 3.18: Waterfowl of conservation concern using wet grassland

Species	Breeding population (<300 pairs or recent decline)	Wintering population (restricted wintering range or >20% of north-west European population wintering in the British Isles)
Bewick's swan		■
Whooper swan		■
Bean goose		■
White-fronted goose		■
Barnacle goose		■
Wigeon		■
Teal		■
Pintail		■
Garganey	■	
Shoveler		■
Pochard		■
Spotted crake	■	
Lapwing		■
Ruff	■	■
Black-tailed godwit	■	
Curlew	■	
Snipe	■	

Source: Avery et al *(1995).*

3.5.1 Requirements of wintering wildfowl and waders

Wintering wildfowl and waders have the following broad requirements:

- suitable feeding conditions
- lack of disturbance
- suitable roost sites.

Flooding in winter is perhaps the most important requirement for wintering waterfowl, providing feeding opportunities and secure roost sites. The presence of shallow surface water on wet grassland sites can attract large numbers of swans, geese and ducks (see Figure 3.7). Large areas of surface water with an average depth of <50 cm are required by the majority of species (Thomas 1982). Deep, permanent flooding is of little use to surface-feeding ducks and geese. Large, shallow winter floods, within a wet grassland complex provide:

- food by releasing seeds trapped in vegetation and flushing terrestrial invertebrates out into the open

- security from ground predators for wildfowl grazing adjacent grassland. Flocks of wigeon, for example, are timid and rarely stray far from the water's edge while grazing during the day

- secure roost sites, close to suitable feeding areas. Many species (eg Bewick's swan), roost on flooded grassland but feed else-where on neighbouring arable farmland.

All wintering waterfowl are sensitive to human disturbance, but wildfowling is thought to be especially significant. Activities such as wildfowling can affect wildfowl distributions up to 400 m from the source of disturbance. Large expanses of open water provide disturbance-free, safe roost sites. Because of the sensitivity of wintering birds to disturbance, access for recreation should be carefully planned and regulated. Creating disturbance-free winter refuges is an important role of nature reserves, allowing the wider countryside to support feeding birds, swans and geese, which use surrounding agricultural land (Case Study 15). It should not be forgotten that attracting grazing wildfowl, such as geese, which may impact on surrounding farmland, can cause conflict with neighbouring landowners/managers.

Wintering wildfowl requirements

The different species of wildfowl are able to utilise the same habitat by having different requirements (Table 3.19). Therefore a mosaic of flooded and unflooded grassland is necessary to attract a diverse wintering waterfowl population (Figure 3.7). Wintering wildfowl can be split into three main groups of species, according to their mode of feeding; grazing wildfowl, dabbling ducks and diving ducks.

Table 3.19: Habitat variables associated with wildfowl species on wet grasslands

Species	Shallow water	Deep water	Short sward	Long sward	Seeds	Arable crops	Cover
Bean goose	0	+	−	+	+	0	−
Greenland white-fronted goose	+	+	+	0	+	+	−
Whooper swan	+	+	+	0	+	+	−
Bewick's swan	+	+	+	0	+	+	−
Wigeon	+	0	+	−	+	+	−
Gadwall	+	−	0	0	+	−	0
Teal	+	0	0	0	+	0	+
Mallard	+	+	0	0	+	+	+
Pintail	+	+	+	0	+	+	−
Garganey	+	−	−	−	+	−	+
Shoveler	+	0	−	−	+	−	−
Pochard	+	+	−	−	+	−	−

+ = positive association, − = negative association, 0 = no association.
Source: Ward et al *(1995) reproduced with kind permission of John Wiley & Sons, Chichester*

**Figure 3.7
Wintering
waterfowl of wet
grassland and their
feeding habitat
preferences**

Dabbling ducks require shallow open water areas. During the winter they feed mainly on plant matter.

Shoveler filter food from the surface of the water, largely seeds during the winter.

Lapwings and **golden plovers** require high soil water tables and secure roosting areas.

Wigeons, unlike the rest of the dabbling duck feed primarily by grazing, favouring short grassy swards.

Teal can feed in water as much as 25 cm deep. Floating seeds of rushes and sedges are an important food source.

Bean geese prefer longer, cattle-grazed grassland which is taller and ranker than the close-cropped sward favoured by many grazing wildfowl species.

Whilst **European white-fronted geese** prefer a short-cropped sward, the sub-species from Greenland favours flooded fields and wetter areas, feeding on the roots and shoots of sedges and rushes.

Bewick's swans, like wigeon and European white-fronted geese, prefer short, sheep-grazed sward. They feed on the softer grasses such as perennial rye-grass.

i) Grazing wildfowl

This group includes swans, geese and the wigeon, which feed on open grassland (Plate 19). Vegetation composition and structure are both important:

Vegetation composition:

- The wigeon and Bewick's swan prefer to feed on a young, grassy sward composed of the softer grass species, eg creeping bent, typical of heavily grazed areas.

- White clover is an important food source for geese and the wigeon, and constitutes up to 60% of the food intake of the barnacle goose at some locations (Owen 1973).

- Coarse grass species such as reed canary-grass, common couch and tufted hair-grass are almost completely ignored (Owen and Thomas 1979).

Vegetation structure:

- Most grazers prefer a short (5–15 cm), even sward.

- Bean geese wintering in the Yare Valley in Norfolk show a preference for pasture grazed by cattle or horses, feeding on taller grass swards than other geese (Allport 1989).

- Shorter, sheep-grazed swards are preferred by the European sub-species of the white-fronted goose but its relative, the Greenland white-fronted goose, favours flooded fields and wetter areas, where they feed on the succulent shoots and roots of grasses, sedges and rushes (Case Study 13).

ii) Dabbling (or surface-feeding) ducks

This group is closely tied to shallow, open water. Dabbling ducks feed on plant matter, especially seeds, and invertebrates, which they sieve from the water. They feed in and around aquatic and marginal vegetation, and can also reach food at the bottom of shallow water by upending. Flooding releases seeds and invertebrates from the vegetation and is an important requirement for this group. The following general considerations apply:

(P J Newman, RSPB)

Plate 19 Barnacle geese graze wet grasslands during the winter (Case Study 13), when the presence of individual food plant species, such as white clover, is important.

- Water depth preferences vary with the size of the bird. Larger, long-necked species such as pintail can feed in water to a depth of 45 cm, whereas the diminutive teal prefers water less than 25 cm deep (Thomas 1982).

- Seed-eating species, such as the teal and shoveler, require the proximity of large seed sources, such as patches of rushes, sedges and docks (Burgess *et al* 1990). Emergent vegetation traps floating seeds and concentrates it. Dabbling ducks therefore benefit from a large edge/surface area ratio on flooded areas.

- Grasslands where flooding creates a succession of surface water areas, or where water levels fluctuate, ensure a steady supply of food throughout the winter.

iii) Diving ducks

The two main species in this group are the tufted duck and pochard. They feed by diving underwater for plant matter and invertebrates. Deep water (>2 m) with high densities of invertebrates in the sediment are required. Larger grassland complexes (eg the Ouse Washes) with big, deep, drainage channels also provide suitable conditions for diving ducks such as the smew and goldeneye.

Wintering wader requirements

Species wintering in large numbers include the lapwing and golden plover. Passage and wintering waders feed on soil-dwelling invertebrates, such as earthworms and cranefly larvae, and require similar feeding conditions to breeding birds (see 3.5.2):

- soft, damp soil

- high soil water-tables

- winter flooding to create islands of grassland and shallow open water suitable for roosting.

Areas of damp pasture, close to suitable woodland, may also be used at night by feeding woodcocks.

3.5.2 Requirements of breeding waders

Wet grassland provides breeding habitat for seven wader species; lapwing, snipe, curlew, ruff, redshank, oystercatcher and black-tailed godwit (Figure 3.8). Two of the UK's rarest breeding waders, the ruff and black-tailed godwit, are almost totally dependent on this habitat during the breeding season. The remaining five species have large breeding populations in other habitats (Table 3.20). Waders nest on the ground and raise a single brood per year. However, most species, for example snipe and lapwing, will lay a replacement clutch if the first fails and conditions remain suitable. Breeding wader distribution and success is linked to a number of factors including:

- water-table depth and soil type

- amount of flooding/surface water in early spring

- food availability

- vegetation structure and composition

- predation

- loss of nests or young from trampling by livestock and destruction by agricultural operations.

Table 3.20: Estimated population of breeding waders on wet grassland in England and Wales and in all habitats in England, Wales and Scotland

Species	Estimated population (pairs) breeding on lowland wet grassland in England and Wales	Estimated population (pairs) in all habitats in England, Scotland and Wales (unless otherwise stated)
Black-tailed godwit	33–36[1]	33–36[1]
Curlew	743[2]	33,000–38,000[3]
Lapwing	4,400–7,539[2]	110,000–138,000 in England and Wales[4] 75,000–100,000 in Scotland[5]
Oystercatcher	845[2]	33,000–43,000[6]
Redshank	2,173–5,095[2]	30,600–33,600[3]
Ruff	<5[1]	<5[1]
Snipe	1,270–2,655[2]	30,000[6]

[1] Gibbons *et al* (1993), [2] O'Brien and Smith (1992), [3] Reed (1985), [4] Shrubb and Lack (1991), [5] Thom (1986) and [6] Piersma (1986).
Source: (Ausden 1996).

Effect of water-table depth and soil type on breeding waders

A high soil water-table during the breeding season (mid-March to end of June) is probably the single most important factor for breeding waders. High soil water-tables ensure that invertebrate prey, for example worms and cranefly larvae, remain close to the surface and increases the biomass accessible to waders. Declines in breeding waders have been noted on sites where drainage channel water levels, and hence soil water-tables, have been lowered (Green and Robins 1993).

Figure 3.8
Breeding birds of wet grassland and their breeding habitat preferences

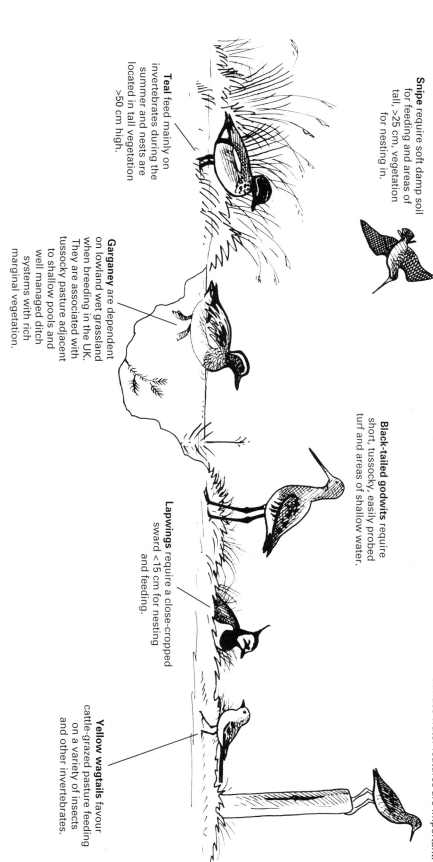

Snipe require soft damp soil for feeding and areas of tall, >25 cm, vegetation for nesting in.

Teal feed mainly on invertebrates during the summer and nests are located in tall vegetation >50 cm high.

Garganey are dependent on lowland wet grassland when breeding in the UK. They are associated with tussocky pasture adjacent to shallow pools and well managed ditch systems with rich marginal vegetation.

Black-tailed godwits require short, tussocky, easily probed turf and areas of shallow water.

Lapwings require a close-cropped sward <15 cm for nesting and feeding.

Redshanks require short swards for feeding, adjacent to tussocky areas in which to conceal their nests. Surface water features are important.

Yellow wagtails favour cattle-grazed pasture feeding on a variety of insects and other invertebrates.

(Malcolm Ausden)

**Plate 20
Surface water
features and large
areas of shallow
edge habitat are
especially
important for
breeding waders
particularly on
clay sites.**

Ideal water-table depth for waders varies according to soil type:

■ On peat soils the water-table should be approximately 20–30 cm below the surface during spring and early summer, depending on exact soil type (Green 1986, Spoor and Chapman 1992). The snipe and black-tailed godwit require soft substrates, and peat soils are ideal, being more penetrable than clays or silts, because of their physical characteristics.

■ On clay and silt soils surface flooding is more important, providing valuable feeding areas for waders such as redshank and lapwing (Plate 20).

Physical characteristics also affect the rate at which the surface moisture can be replenished from the water-table and drainage channels. Clay soils often dry out as a result unless topped up regularly.

Effect of flooding/surface water on breeding waders

Surface water and pool margins are important feeding areas for both adult and young waders:

■ Shallow margins of temporary and permanent pools provide feeding areas for wader species such as lapwing, redshank, ruff and black-tailed godwit.

■ The flooding regime at a site clearly affects invertebrate biomass and its availability to birds. Engineering works (eg floodbanks) on floodplains have, however, led to the drying out of many

sites and probably changed the nature of invertebrate communities. As a result, many sites now have rather erratic flood regimes. Sudden flooding on such sites can create an abundance of drowned terrestrial invertebrates but will lead ultimately to reduced densities of soil invertebrates. Reflooding such sites, for example Pulborough Brooks RSPB Reserve (Case Study 10), initially creates ideal conditions for some species (eg snipe) for the first two years but then numbers can drop, presumably owing to a reduction in prey density. A regime ensuring regular flooding will eventually allow flood-tolerant species to colonise.

■ Ephemeral water-bodies provide suitable conditions for colonisation by invertebrate communities of high biomass, dominated by the larvae of the non-biting midges. These small invertebrates are an important food source for wader chicks (and ducklings). Shallow foot drains or grips, particularly on clay/silt soils, often create suitable conditions for such invertebrate communities.

■ Muddy drainage channel margins accessible to birds create additional feeding areas for waders and provide a refuge for chicks during agricultural operations.

Vegetation structure and composition requirements of breeding waders

Vegetation structure and composition is important for breeding birds. Sward height and structure influences the species potentially using wet grassland. Preferred vegetation structure varies between species from long vegetation, which attracts snipe, to short, intensively grazed swards suitable for the lapwing (Table 3.21).

The presence of mature trees in areas used by ground-nesting birds can greatly reduce breeding productivity in their immediate vicinity, as they provide lookouts and nest sites for predators such as carrion crows (Bell and Chown 1985).

Effect of disturbance on breeding waders

Agricultural operations, such as harrowing and rolling, and grazing in the early part of the breeding season (ie before mid-June) can greatly reduce wader productivity.

Specific requirements of breeding waders

The habitat requirements of the commoner species, lapwing, snipe and redshank, are well known and summarised below and in Table 3.22. Those of the rarer species, such as black-tailed godwit (Plate 21) and ruff are less well understood but generalisations can be made. Most wader chicks are precocial, leaving the nest soon after hatching. In most cases they are capable of feeding themselves immediately,

Table 3.21: The hydro-ecological requirements continuum for three wader species

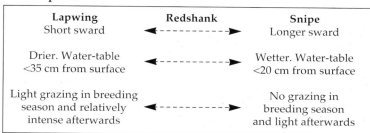

Lapwing Short sward	◄----------►	Redshank		Snipe Longer sward
Drier. Water-table <35 cm from surface	◄----------►			Wetter. Water-table <20 cm from surface
Light grazing in breeding season and relatively intense afterwards	◄----------►			No grazing in breeding season and light afterwards

gleaning invertebrates from plants and the soil surface. The oystercatcher and snipe (Plate 22) are the exceptions to this rule in that the parent birds feed the newly hatched chicks. Species such as lapwing and redshank can, if necessary, move their young considerable distances (up to 2 km) to the nearest suitable feeding habitat.

Table 3.22: Micro-habitat preferences of waders breeding on wet grassland

Habitat	Lapwing	Snipe	Redshank	Black-tailed godwit
Soil/water				
High drainage channel water level	+	+	+	+
Soft soil	0	+	+	+
Early season flooding	+	0	+	0
Surface water	+	0	+	+
Vegetation/land use				
Tall vegetation	–	+	0	–
Species-rich vegetation	–	+	–	0
Tussocks	+	+	+	0
Rushes	0	+	0	0
Grazing/mowing	+	–	–	0
Large field	+	+	+	+
Trees/hedges	–	–	0	–

Where + = positive association, – = negative association and 0 = no association (usually through lack of information). *Source: Self et al (1994).*

Table 3.23: Conditions required by the lapwing at formerly dry grassland sites

March to early May	Early May to mid/late June
1. Very high water-table without surface flooding the previous winter and a short sward preferably maintained without heavy grazing (both usually difficult to achieve). Under such conditions birds feed mainly on abundant earthworms.	1. Permanent pools or grassland left submerged from winter flooding, both of which will now have been colonised by high densities of non-biting midge larvae (providing food for chicks), and with bare and sparsely vegetated ground around their margins (for adults to feed on).
2. Grassland surface flooded during the previous winter. Even if the flooding results in extremely low biomasses of earthworms (as it usually does), these areas are still used in preference to unflooded grassland. Lapwings probably feed mainly on terrestrial invertebrates and cranefly larvae in these areas.	2. Grassland surface flooded during the previous winter, which has since dried out during the spring.
3. Unflooded grassland with a low water-table.	3. Unflooded grassland with a low water-table.

1 = best option, 2 = best alternative if option 1 not achievable, 3 = worst option

(R Williams, RSPB)

(E A Janes, RSPB)

Plate 21 (left) Black-tailed godwits are among the rarer breeding birds that use wet grassland in the UK. They require short, tussocky grass, easily probed soils and nearby surface water features.

Plate 22 (right) Breeding snipe have suffered population declines in many areas of the UK. They require soft, damp penetrable soil for feeding and tall vegetation to conceal their nest in.

Table 3.24: Conditions required by the redshank at formerly dry grassland sites

March to early May	Early May to mid/late June
1. Very high water-table without surface flooding the previous winter (usually difficult to achieve) and a moderately short sward, preferably maintained without heavy grazing. Under such conditions birds feed mainly on abundant earthworms.	1. Permanent pools or grassland left submerged from winter flooding, both of which will now have been colonised by high densities of non-biting midge larvae.
2. Permanent pools. At this time of year these will contain low biomasses of non-biting midge larvae and aquatic oligochaetes, whereas apparently suitable submerged grassland left from winter flooding will contain virtually no aquatic invertebrates (or earthworms).	2. Grassland surface flooded during the previous winter, which has since dried out during the spring.
3. Unflooded grassland with a low water-table.	3. Unflooded grassland with a low water-table.

1 = best option, 2 = best alternative if option 1 not achievable, 3 = worst option.

Lapwing (Table 3.23)

- Is the least dependent on wet or damp conditions, breeding on a range of agricultural habitats. As a result it is the most widespread wet grassland breeding wader.

- Often nests on arable land and moves young to grassland to feed.

- Feeds visually, picking invertebrates from, or close to, the soil surface. Earthworms form an important part of the adults' diet.

- Requires a close-cropped sward of less than 15 cm for nesting and feeding (Green 1986).

- Rears chicks on muddy margins of pools.

Redshank (Table 3.24)

- The majority of wet grassland nesting birds are found in coastal grazing marshes.

- Prefers short swards (<15 cm), but must have tussocky/taller areas (*c.* 20 cm) in which to conceal its nest.

- Requires grasslands with shallow surface water, where invertebrate prey is located visually and picked from the surface of the water, substrate or from vegetation.

- Adults move up to 1.5 km or so to feed at suitable pools and along the edges of fleets and creeks at coastal sites. Newly hatched broods are often escorted some distance to the nearest suitable feeding area.

Snipe (Table 3.25, Plate 22)

- Probes the soil for invertebrates with its long bill.

- Requires soft, damp soil.

- Requires tall vegetation (>25 cm) for concealment.

- Young are fed by adults for first few days.

- Feeding adults and adults with young broods move only short distances and therefore depend on ideal field conditions. The edges of pools and drainage channel edges tend to be used only when field conditions are unsuitable (Green 1986).

Black-tailed godwit (Table 3.25)

- Currently breeds regularly at only five wet grassland sites in England.

- Breeds in areas with short, tussocky, easily probed turf.

- Breeds within 300 m of shallow surface water (Plate 23).

- Chicks actively glean vegetation for invertebrate prey, which includes many flying species, and have a preference for taller vegetation (Beintema *et al* 1991).

Plate 23 Shallow, mid-field drainage channels are an important component of black-tailed godwit breeding habitat at the Nene Washes RSPB Nature Reserve.

(Carl Hawke)

Table 3.25: Conditions required by the snipe and black-tailed godwit at formerly dry grassland sites

March to early May	Early May to mid/late June
1. Very high water-table without surface flooding the previous winter (usually difficult to achieve).	1. Very high water-table without surface flooding the previous winter (usually impossible to achieve).
2. Grassland surface flooded during the previous winter.	2. Grassland surface flooded during the previous winter.
3. Unflooded grassland with a low water-table.	3. Unflooded grassland with a low water-table.

1 = best option, 2 = best alternative if option 1 not achievable, 3 = worst option

Ruff

- Requires raised areas with short turf for the 'lek', an area where groups of males display to, and compete for, females (Beintema 1982).

- Leks are situated on raised areas or on other sites, often close to water, where birds have an unobstructed view in several or all directions (Rhijn 1991).

- Probably requires shallow surface water nearby (Cramp and Simmons 1983).

- Experience in the Netherlands indicates that the ruff is the most demanding wader species and the first to decline if management is not suitable (Beintema 1986).

Curlew

- Is a scarce breeder on wet grassland in England and Wales, found on only 15% of the sites surveyed by Smith (1983), and is largely concentrated in sites in the north and west. In Scotland and Northern Ireland, the curlew is common, even abundant, in some loch-side wet grassland areas.

- Favours damp, extensively managed grassland.

- Requires disturbance-free areas during the breeding season.

3.5.3 Requirements of breeding wildfowl

Breeding wildfowl of wet grassland, most of which are dabbling duck, tend to be associated with drainage channels and spring flooded areas (Figure 3.8). All nest on the ground, usually close to water.

Mute swan

The most conspicuous bird of wet grassland, the mute swan feeds mostly in the water taking submerged vegetation (leaves, stems and roots). It feeds down to

45 cm by dipping its head and neck underwater, by upending it can feed in water depths of as much as 1 m. If undisturbed it will leave the water and graze grassland. Young are fed by the adults on plant fragments, and invertebrates may also be important at this stage.

Dabbling ducks

All species are dependent on invertebrates for the bulk of their food requirements during the summer (Thomas 1980). Nests are located in areas of tall vegetation >50 cm high. Ducklings feed themselves from hatching and rely on abundant supplies of

invertebrates on the water surface, for example hatching midges. The shoveler is adapted to filter zooplankton from the water and its ducklings exploit this abundant spring food source after hatching (Plate 24). Good water quality and vigorous macrophyte growth are important. The garganey is the only wildfowl species to occur solely on wet grasslands when breeding, and is associated with tussocky pasture adjacent to shallow pools and well managed drainage channel systems with rich marginal vegetation (Self *et al* 1994).

Diving ducks

The pochard and tufted duck are usually scarce breeders on wet grassland, except where there are deep soke dykes or fleets. As a result, they tend to occur mainly on coastal grazing marsh sites, for example Elmley Marshes Reserve (Kent). They require deep water (but less than 5 m in depth) with abundant submerged and emergent vegetation. Both species are dependent on high densities of aquatic invertebrates in the breeding season.

Plate 24
The shoveler is a dabbling duck; its large bill contains a fine-sieving fringe that filters zooplankton from the water.

(P R Perfect, RSPB)

3.5.4 Other bird species using wet grassland

Many other birds use wet grassland habitat:

- The corncrake was originally widespread throughout agricultural areas in the UK, but has suffered a serious historical decline and is now considered to be

globally threatened (Collar *et al* 1994). It is now restricted to grassland habitats (many of them wet) largely on islands of the west coast of Scotland (Case Study 13). Corncrakes are summer migrants and require undisturbed, tall (>20 cm) grassland during the breeding season (late April to August) (Plate 25). Early in the season rank cover, such as nettle beds, are also used. Occasionally, corncrakes still breed on wet grassland sites in England and Wales. Managers who detect the presence of calling male birds should ensure that all forms of grassland management cease in the fields used by the bird for the duration of the breeding season. If a hay crop has to be taken then this should be done in a 'corncrake-friendly' manner (Andrews and Rebane 1994).

Plate 25
The corncrake is a rare breeder in wet grassland communities mainly on the islands off the west coast of Scotland (Case Study 13).

(R T Smith, RSPB)

- The spotted crake is a rare and sporadic breeding bird in lowland swamps and fens (usually fewer than 12 pairs per year in the UK – see Case Studies 1 and 2) and little is known of its precise ecological requirements. It appears to favour open swampy wetlands, with some low trees or scrub. Areas where it occurs should be maintained and extended where possible.

- A number of birds of prey use wet grassland, especially during the winter. Barn owls use sites that have areas of rough grassland, with good populations of small mammals, and suitable nest-sites nearby. Ungrazed sea-walls, riverbanks and neglected fields are favoured hunting grounds. Wintering short-eared owls and hen harriers use similar wet grassland areas. Peregrines and merlins are attracted to the high densities of prey during the winter months.

- The yellow wagtail is a summer migrant, primarily breeding on wet grassland. The historical decline and range contraction of this species is linked to the drainage of wet grassland and other intensive agricultural practices. Yellow wagtails are insectivorous. They show great behavioural flexibility when feeding, tailoring their feeding method to whatever prey item is available at the time (Tyler 1993). Tussocky, cattle-grazed pasture seems to be favoured during the breeding season. Nests are concealed in areas of tussocky, long vegetation.

3.5.5 Management requirements of wet grassland birds

It is possible to present generalised seasonal management schedules which benefit breeding and wintering waterfowl. Birds dependent on wet grassland benefit from a water management regime that provides damp grassland, surface water and full drainage channels at appropriate times of the year. Low-intensity sward management is essential for breeding and wintering birds. Management should aim for minimal trampling during the breeding season and maximum structural diversity. The following is a typical scenario incorporating hydrological and vegetation management guidelines:

Spring
Drainage channel water dropped to field surface level, retaining scattered shallow pools in lower parts of fields. A flooded area may be retained. Damp, soft ground and the margins of shallow pools have high densities of invertebrates and are easier to probe. The margins of floods and gently shelving drainage channel edges are especially important on clay sites, which dry rapidly when surface water is removed.

Summer
Drainage channel water levels and any shallow pools (ideally in areas with least biological interest) allowed to drop progressively on part of the site, the remainder kept damp as long as practicable. Livestock grazed on drier parts, or a first hay/silage cut taken no earlier than late June. Wet areas allowed to dry progressively into July and then grazed at low intensity or cut as late as possible. Drop drainage channel water levels to 50 cm below field surface by end of July. Some areas kept partly flooded for breeding wildfowl.

All waders benefit from reduced intensity farming operations during the breeding season, although sward management is necessary for some species. The need to retain areas with a tall sward into July depends on the presence of snipe. All species, on clay sites in particular, benefit from scattered pools and the wet margins of full drainage channels. Breeding wildfowl benefit from areas kept flooded into autumn.

Autumn

Any remaining inundated areas allowed to dry partly. Later in the autumn, drainage channel water levels reinstated to field surface level – rainfall begins to exceed evaporation by this time of year to assist the process. Livestock removed. The muddy remains of previously flooded areas are attractive to passage waders.

Winter

Drainage channels allowed to over-top and flood lowest-lying fields, or only those in selected compartments on very flat sites. A mosaic of floods and grass is ideal. Water at a range of depths to 30 cm. Winter floods providing feeding and roosting areas, and safety for grazing wildfowl. Seeds are floated out of longer vegetation and made available.

Key references

Batten, L A, Bibby, C J, Clement, P, Elliott, G D and Porter, R F (1990) *Red Data Birds in Britain.* T and A D Poyser, London.

Ellenberg, H (1988) *Vegetation Ecology of Central Europe: 4th Edition.* Cambridge University Press, Cambridge.

Evans, C (1991) The conservation importance and management of the ditch floras on RSPB reserves. *RSPB Conserv. Rev.* 5: 65-71.

Fry, R and Lonsdale, D (1991) *Habitat conservation for insects – a neglected green issue.* Amateur Entomologists Society, Colchester.

Green, R E (1986) The management of wet grassland for breeding waders. *Chief Scientists Directorate No. 626.* Nature Conservancy Council, Peterborough.

Kirby, P (1992) *Habitat management for invertebrates: a practical handbook.* RSPB, Sandy.

Part 4
MANAGEMENT TECHNIQUES

Contents

4.1 Introduction

The continued existence of many wet grasslands depends on interventive management of vegetation to arrest succession. The principles of vegetation management, the main techniques and their implications for the different wildlife groups are outlined in this section. The nature of hydrological management which is needed at a site depends upon the degree to which the site has been drained or altered by flood defence measures. On less modified wet grasslands, eg the Derwent Ings (Case Study 12), hydrological management is less intensive than on the highly modified drained peat sites of the Somerset Level and Moors (Case Study 5). These factors are outlined in this chapter, together with the main techniques for water management.

Where characteristic faunas and floras have evolved under long traditions of consistent hydrological and vegetation management, every effort should be made to continue these appropriate regimes.

4.2 Water management

4.2.1 Introduction

The conservation interest of wet grasslands and the ability to manage them effectively are influenced by the physical and chemical characteristics of the water and soil. Two aspects of water management are of particular importance: water regime and water quality; sections 4.2.2 and 4.2.3 examine these in turn. The first section looks at the problems of water availability on sites and how to control and manipulate water levels. The second examines the effects of water quality and measures that can be taken to improve it when problems occur. Table 4.1 outlines the factors which should be considered before undertaking any water management.

Ideally, hydrological management should meet the water requirements of target species and communities as described in Part 3. Where species' requirements are not fully known, it may be possible to mimic the hydrological regimes of other, similar sites which support high-quality wet grassland, or to reinstate historical regimes which supported it in the past. It cannot be stressed enough, however, that where reinstatement is required, wholesale and rapid change of hydrological and grazing regimes is not advisable.

Table 4.1: Considerations for water management

Water-table and water level requirements (ie regime)	■ different community/species needs
Water supply	■ quantity available ■ availability at key periods ■ surety of supply (balance with needs of other users)
Water quality	■ soil type and sediments ■ salinity ■ plant nutrients (eutrophication) ■ chemical pollutants
Water management infrastructure	■ distribution network ■ condition of existing infrastructure ■ need for new structures (drainage channels, bunds, grips, etc) ■ maintenance needs (sluices, pumps, drainage channels, grips, drains)
Legal considerations	■ access to external supplies ■ modification of drainage infrastructure ■ modifications to existing hydrological regime

4.2.2 Water regime

Water regime describes the combination of water-table depth, the length of time that depth is maintained and at what time of year. The water regime of a wet grassland may be influenced by environmental factors and by management. These include:

■ environmental factors such as:
  • catchment area
  • rainfall
  • evapotranspiration
  • surface flows
  • soil type
  • topography
  • groundwater flows.

■ management factors such as:
  • other water demands in catchment
  • drainage infrastructure on site.

The extent to which regimes should and can be managed varies between sites as a result of seasonal and geographical variation, existing drainage infrastructure on the site and adjacent land use (eg spray-irrigated agricultural land). Activities outside a site's boundaries may also affect proposed management and should be evaluated. For example, at Pulborough Brooks in Sussex, when the RSPB sought to restore a major area of wet grassland in the River Arun floodplain it did not look for wholesale removal of floodbanks to reinstate a more natural regime. As a consequence of embankment of much of the Arun floodplain, removal of floodbanks would have resulted in storage of excessive volumes of floodwater from other areas of the catchment for extended periods. In addition it was recognised that the existing drainage infrastructure could be used for managing water levels for the benefit of wildlife.

This section examines factors influencing water supply and distribution on wet grasslands in turn. Methods for water control are then examined.

Water supply

Adequate water supply is essential to enable enhanced management and restoration of wet grassland habitats. Water supply for a site is influenced by climatic conditions (ie rainfall and evapotranspiration), which vary throughout the UK. Sites may be dependent on surface water (eg river flows) or groundwater supplies; however, in many areas these have become increasingly limited, especially where rainfall is low or where there are other competing demands (eg abstraction for spray-irrigation or public water supply). Modification of rivers for flood defence has altered natural flooding regimes and has in many areas resulted in a general lowering of water-tables. Abstraction from rivers and groundwater for domestic, agricultural and industrial use has exacerbated water supply problems in many areas.

The extent to which supply can be managed will vary between sites, and the following factors should be considered:

- seasonal variations

- water source (inputs eg river, groundwater and rainfall)

- access to supply (competing demands)

- losses from site (eg seepage and abstraction).

Natural seasonal variations of water supply should be taken into account when determining proposals for enhanced management and restoration. Evapotranspiration will typically be highest in June, July and August when water levels will naturally be at their lowest. Water availability for sites can be calculated (Appendix 4) and should be examined in conjunction with other water demands to see whether the site is capable of sustaining wet grassland where creation or restoration options are being considered.

In some areas agriculture is now a major user. Shortages are particularly common in the summer months, when evapotranspiration rates are high and supplies are limited. Shortages as a result of abstraction from main rivers could potentially be alleviated by providing on-site storage of winter water – see below (MAFF 1996). Winter water is often available in excess, particularly on washlands or on areas which are natural sinks for water and could be retained to maintain water-tables in summer.

The easiest way to store this water may appear to be on the grassland itself during the spring, using bunds. It must be borne in mind, however, that this can have a negative impact on the species diversity of both the grassland flora and the invertebrate community where water is stored. Holding water at high levels on grassland during spring creates very stressful conditions for grass swards and extensive grass kills may result due to a lack of oxygen in the soil. Where wet grassland conservation is the objective, water should be stored in reservoirs or on areas of swamp vegetation or reedbed.

The many pressures on limited water supplies can make it difficult to meet conservation needs. Water Level Management Plans (WLMPs) are one way of attempting to ensure that environmental requirements are met. WLMPs are discussed in detail in Part 2 and can help to resolve potentially conflicting interests. There is, however, some concern as to how far WLMPs can deal with water supply problems owing to water abstraction. It is essential that action should be taken to integrate water abstraction issues into WLMPs where appropriate. Addressing shortages arising as a result of abstraction is a common problem. The Environment Agency has powers to revoke or vary abstraction licences, where they consider the licence is in conflict with its nature conservation duty. The Agency should be approached to resolve this conflict where there is a concern.

Water distribution

Water distribution or movement at a site is influenced by:

- topography

- surface flows (eg in drainage channels)

- regional and local groundwater flows

- soil type.

i) Topography
Natural variations in topography can provide a variety of wetness regimes in an area. Topography affects plant community composition because of its influence on water-table levels. Localised depressions often provide wetter 'islands' which typically contain inundation grassland (eg MG13) but which may also support swamp or sedge-bed communities. Higher areas may support communities characteristic of drier soils (eg MG6 and MG7). Small-scale variations in micro-topography or soil structure may produce very different water regimes in directly adjacent points, as in ridge and furrow grassland.

ii) Surface flows
Controlled distribution of water and the regulation of water levels is much easier on sites with a well developed water distribution network. Paradoxically, this is more likely on sites which have been intensively managed in the past. Systems of

water-filled drainage channels can be used to both drain or irrigate land, depending on the position of the soil water-table relative to drainage channel water levels.

In areas like the Norfolk Broads and the Somerset Levels and Moors, where the land is essentially flat, hydraulic gradients within the system are almost zero. Where there is gravity-feed from surrounding higher ground, drainage channel water levels can be controlled simply by setting levels at the outlet, for example by using sluices. It is advantageous to create a terraced irrigation system where water flows from one hydrological unit to another (see Case Study 5). Where there is no natural supply from surrounding high ground or from groundwater recharge, it will be necessary to import water to meet evaporative demand, particularly in the summer. This may require the manipulation of inlet sluices, for example to let water onto the site from adjacent carrier channels, or even pumping (Armstrong *et al* 1995).

iii) Groundwater
Knowledge of groundwater levels and gradients (direction of flow is usually down a valley or towards a river) can be very valuable when creating new wet grassland. However, it can be very difficult to make accurate predictions and the advice of a hydrologist or hydrogeologist should be sought.

iv) Soil types and their effect on in-field water levels
Soil type and structure influence the ability to manage water levels on a site. It is generally assumed that clay/silt soils depend on surface flooding to maintain wetness and wildlife interest, whereas water-table levels in peat soils can be influenced by the lateral (sideways) movement of water (eg to and from ditches – Figure 4.1). However, this is a generalisation and should be treated with extreme caution. Soil structure can be the overriding factor controlling water movement in soils. Soil type and structure influence the ability of the soil to hold water (and hence influence plant growth and soil penetrability) and also the degree of water movement through the soil.

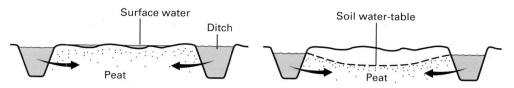

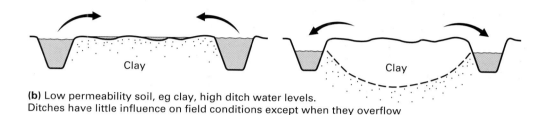

(a) Moderately permeable soil, high ditch water levels all year. Soil water-table maintained at or near field surface level by lateral movement through the soil.

(b) Low permeability soil, eg clay, high ditch water levels. Ditches have little influence on field conditions except when they overflow

Figure 4.1 Examples of management of field water-tables on wet grassland on two substrates – peat and clay (Self *et al* 1994)

Water flow or permeability (which can be measured in terms of hydraulic conductivity in metres per day) is affected by particle size and structure. The flow rate through a sandy soil (with large pore spaces) is greater than in an unstructured clay soil (Figure 4.2). A clay soil with a large block (cube-like) or columnar structure is less permeable than a clay soil with a small granular or crumb-like structure. Peat soils generally have higher hydraulic conductivity enabling faster lateral water movement. These properties have major implications for how a manager can control or manipulate water levels on a site.

On peat soils (which have high hydraulic conductivity), in the Somerset Levels and Moors high drainage channel water levels can be used to keep field water levels high. Conversely low drainage channel levels result in drainage. Figure 4.3 shows how drainage channel level on a typical peat soil in this area influences field water levels throughout the year. It should be noted that there is little influence beyond 40/50 m from the drainage channel edge. The use of drainage channels for sub-surface irrigation (raising water levels) of field centres is considered later in this section.

Peat soils which have been maintained wet and uncompacted have a conductivity of about 0.7–2.0 m/d. However, desiccation or compaction by heavy machinery or

overburdens of other soils can reduce this. Dry peat can actually repel water and, in the 17th century, was used to line and provide the essential seal for some of the fen drainage channels. Re-wetting dry peat is extremely difficult. The point at which drained peat repels water is not known, nor are these physical processes completely understood. An occasional summer draw-down or drought may not damage the ability of peat to absorb water again, whereas prolonged draw-down may have irreversible effects. It is advisable to seek specialist hydrological/soils advice for sites with desiccated peat soils. Actual losses of soil through mineralisation at the surface are also likely with desiccated peats.

In contrast to sites with peat soils, water levels in drainage channels on sites with poorly structured clay and alluvial soils, have little influence over soil water-tables in field centres. This is because of their low hydraulic conductivity (Figure 4.2). Surface inundation is therefore often the only method of maintaining soil wetness (as has been undertaken at sites on clay in North Kent, eg Elmley). These poorly structured clay soils also have a low drainable porosity (a measure of the volume of water which will drain from a saturated soil under gravity). It is measured as a percentage and ranges from 0.5–5.0% for clays and from 15–35% for peats (Smedema and Rycroft 1983). It can be used, when fields are saturated, to estimate the amount

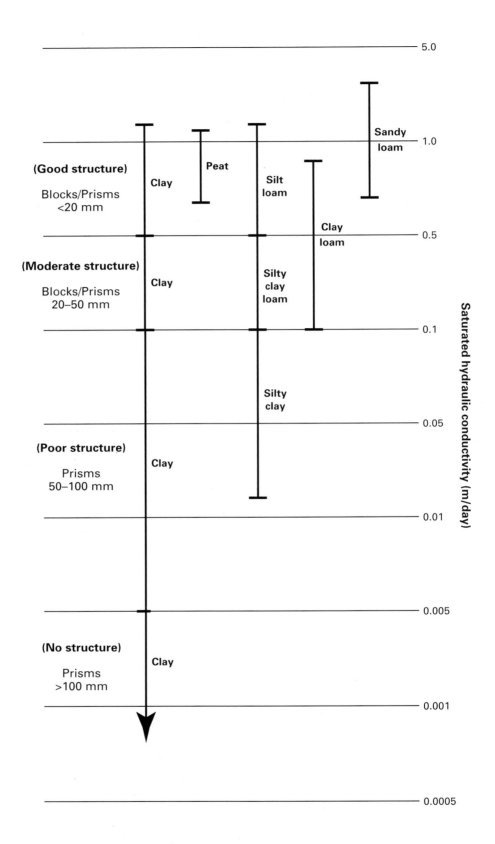

**Figure 4.2
Hydraulic
conductivity of
different soil
types**

of water required to saturate the soil before flooding occurs. Clays absorb less water before they become saturated than do peats.

Compacted clay soils can also form hard surface pans which prevent movement of water to the lower soil profile. Such pans are common on clay soils in the Norfolk Broads, for example, on sites which have been heavily winter-grazed. On such sites, it may be necessary to develop different approaches to soil management, which can be used to assist in re-wetting. Site managers often resort to winter flooding, using natural topographic variation to maintain wet hollows during the summer. It is worth noting that the deposition of dredged soil on drainage channel banks can elevate the areas adjacent to drainage channels and make them surprisingly dry.

Water level control

Water levels on a wet grassland site are controlled by the rate at which water enters and leaves. Although influenced by natural factors, levels can be managed using:

- bunds
- dams
- sluices
- winter water storage
- pumps
- surface irrigation
- sub-surface irrigation.

It should be remembered that all work in or adjacent to watercourses designated as main rivers in England and Wales will require consent from the Environment Agency or, in some cases the relevant IDB.

i) Bunds

Where water is available only during the winter, it may be possible to retain it by constructing levees or bunds (low earth banks keyed into the substrate) – see Case Study 13. These permit water to be stored during the winter to counter summer deficits, create permanent lagoons and also protect areas from the effects of flooding (Armstrong *et al* 1995).

Bund construction follows the same general principles as dam construction (see below),

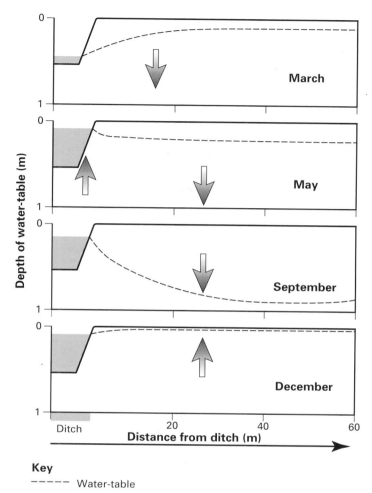

Key
----- Water-table

**Figure 4.3
The effect of drainage channel water levels on in-field water-tables**

but is less complicated and relatively cheap (Plate 1). At Berney Marshes, low bunds with a top width of 75 cm were created at a rate of 25 m per day using a tractor-mounted McConnel PA8 digger-arm. Using a Hymac increased the rate to 80 m per day, at a cost of about £1.50/m.

Bunds should be set well back from the edges of drainage channels to prevent slumping and reduce seepage. Mower-friendly profiles are advisable as bunds are often invaded by rank vegetation such as thistles.

Under the Reservoirs Safety Provisions Act 1975, if bunds or dams are required to impound a volume of water exceeding 25,000 m³ above natural ground level, they must be designed and constructed under the control of a DoE qualified Panel Engineer. They must also be inspected annually by a Supervising Engineer and at least every 10 years by a Panel Engineer (MAFF 1996).

Plate 1
The construction of bunds allows winter water to be retained into spring and can solve summer water supply problems.

Plate 2
Dam construction and the blocking off of drainage channels is a key part of hydrological isolation and subsequent raised water level management.

ii) Dams

Dams can be constructed in drainage channels to retain water in, and isolate, hydrological units (Plate 2). Dividing areas of wet grassland into smaller hydrological units using dams enables independent control of water levels, for example allowing rotational flooding in winter. However, flows of water and consequently the movement of fauna around a site may be inhibited. Movement of water through and around such systems is therefore important to prevent stagnation, build up of nutrients and to allow species access to all parts of the system.

Dam construction is easier in areas with loamy or clay soils. Clay and silt dams can effectively be used across drainage channels up to about 5 m wide. Peat will only make satisfactory dams if well compacted and even then the effective width is less. In general, the basal width of a dam should be five times its height. The top of the dam should be level and at least 50 cm above the normal water level. Table 4.2 outlines the principles which should be adopted when constructing dams.

Dam construction is likely to take up to half a day with a tractor-mounted hydraulic digger-arm and cost from £40 to £200 per unit, depending on size. Diggers or Hymacs accomplish the task more efficiently and cost-effectively but are rarely available in-house and have to be contracted. Additional costs will be incurred in areas grazed by livestock, as it will be necessary to fence the dam against trampling and subsequent erosion.

Table 4.2: Principles to be adopted when building dams

- Construct during the late summer when water levels are lower and rainfall less likely.

- Use temporary dams to block drainage channels on both sides and pump dry before constructing the dam itself. Temporary coffer dams can be constructed from double rows of sandbags or wooden boards with a clay infill.

- Remove topsoil and scarify the sub-soil where the dam is to be built, to enhance keying and minimise seepage.

- Build the dam up slowly, eg in 15 cm layers and then compact. Allow extra material for settling: 10% for mechanical compaction and 20% for compaction by foot. Peat may settle up to twice as much as silt.

- Topsoil can be replaced above the normal water level and sown with a proprietary grass mix. This stabilises the surface and discourages deeper rooting plants. Creeping bent and rough meadow-grass are ideal (ensure seeds are of known provenance).

Table 4.3: Relative advantages of four different sluice designs

Attribute	Flexi-pipe	Dropboard	Lifting-gate	Tilting-weir
SLUICE TYPE				
Flow capacity	■	■■■	■■■■	■■■■
Water level control	■■■■	■■■	■	■■■■
Durability	■■	■■■	■■	■■■
Ease of adjustment	■■■	■■	■■■■	■■■■
Resistance to blockage	■	■■■	■■■	■■■
Resistance to vandalism/tampering	■	■■	■■■	■■■
Construction cost	■■■■	■■■	■	■
Design complexity	■■■	■■	■	■■
Ease of installation	■■■■	■■	■	■■■
Availability of materials	■■■	■■■	■	■■■

Some of these features may vary depending on the design specification, eg concrete or wooded surrounds, the age of the sluice and position/accessibility. Relative benefits: ■ = poor, ■■ = moderate, ■■■ = good, ■■■■ = very good. (Adapted from Merritt 1994)

iii) Sluices

Sluices can perform the same function as dams, but are designed to permit controlled through-flow so that water levels in drainage channels can be regulated. There are four main types: flexi-pipe, dropboard, lifting-gate and tilting-weir. The main factors which should be taken into account when selecting sluices are summarised in Table 4.3 and the different types are described below:

- Flexi-pipe sluices consist of flexible ribbed plastic pipe about 25 cm in diameter (pipes greater than 35 cm in diameter are difficult to adjust). They are usually incorporated into an earth bund or dam (see Figure 4.4). Choose dark-coloured pipe (eg black) as lengths of brightly coloured pipe can be visually intrusive in open landscapes.

■ Dropboard sluices are relatively simple structures, comprising a series of boards which drop into a grooved spillway (Plate 3). To counteract seepage, two parallel sets of boards may be used. Water levels are adjusted by inserting or removing boards as appropriate. At West Moor in Somerset, dropboard sluices consist of dams constructed of trench sheets with a welded steel frame set into it containing the wooden dropboards. Construction details are given in Brooks (1981), see also Case Studies 5 and 7.

■ Lifting-gate sluices are characteristic of old water meadow systems (Plate 4). Traditional style, oak sluices at Sherborne Water Meadows cost only £250 each to construct (Case Study 3). Water level control is, however, difficult using this type of sluice.

■ Tilting-weir or drawbridge sluices are very effective, but relatively uncommon. They are based on a hinged weir that can be adjusted to give very precise water level control. However, they are more expensive (see Case Study 5).

In areas where flooding of adjacent land must be prevented and sluices are not large enough to take predicted storm flows, a spillway must be incorporated into all sluice designs.

iv) Winter water storage

Where summer water supplies are unpredictable, construction of a water reservoir may be the only option (Case Study 9). Water storage systems, such as that found at Elmley RSPB nature reserve, greatly facilitate water management during spring and summer. At Elmley RSPB nature reserve wet grassland is kept wet throughout the spring and summer by using an existing fleet as a water storage reservoir. Previously this fleet took drainage water from the marshes to a sea wall borrow dyke, from where it

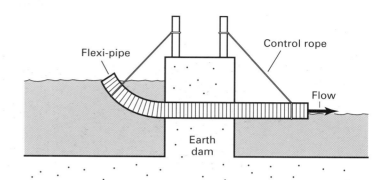

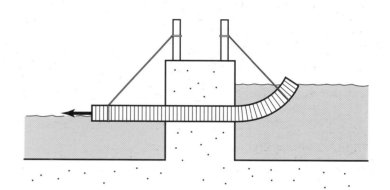

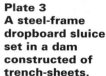

**Figure 4.4
A flexi-pipe sluice**

(Paul José)

**Plate 3
A steel-frame dropboard sluice set in a dam constructed of trench-sheets.**

(Owen Mountford)

**Plate 4
Lifting-gate sluices are unpopular on nature reserves as precise water level control is difficult to achieve.**

(John Leece)

**Plate 5
Diesel pumps can
be used to move
water against a
hydraulic gradient.
Because of
pollution problems
they are slowly
being replaced by
windmills on some
nature reserves
(Case Study 8).**

passed into the intertidal Swale, through a
tidal flap. Impoundment and extraction
licences were obtained from the Southern
Water Authority in 1981 and the Elmley
fleet was enclosed by the construction of
clay dams to isolate it from the remainder
of the system and further increase its
storage capacity. The local IDB agreed to
the diversion of the flow and undertook
work to facilitate this. When flow
commences, usually in late autumn, water
is pumped into the fleet, which acts as a
water storage reservoir and this water is
used in the spring and summer to maintain
shallow pools across the marsh.

Anyone contemplating reservoir
construction should be aware of the
requirements of the Reservoirs Safety
Provisions Act 1975 – see above. Care
should be taken when siting the reservoir
to ensure valuable habitats are not
destroyed. Wherever possible steps should
be taken to ensure a wildlife-friendly
design (see Orford 1996 for details). The
following options greatly enhance the value
of reservoirs to aquatic plants and animals:

- Creating a deep area in the reservoir bed
  provides water for fish and invertebrates
  even when the reservoir is low during the
  summer.

- Creating a shelf for marginal plants and
  maintaining a water flow to the shelf
  during summer draw-down is an
  expensive option but very worthwhile.
  Water can be provided to these areas by
  bleeding off some of the water during
  abstraction from the reservoir.

- Providing floating islands, planted with
  vegetation, which will be used by nesting
  birds and other wildlife.

v) Pumps

Pumps are required to move water against
prevailing hydraulic gradients (Plate 5).
Pumping is often used where more water is
required than can be supplied by inflowing
streams, groundwater or precipitation, for
example to move water from a low-level
drainage channel to supply a raised water
level area. Pumping may also be used to
alleviate the effects of stagnation where
flows have been arrested owing to
construction of dams, bunds or sluices.
Wherever possible wind-pumps should be
considered (Case Study 8).

Pump specifications must match site water
requirements and conditions. The following
considerations should be taken into account
when considering a pumping operation
and what type of pump to use:

- volume of water and rate of delivery
  required

- the height of head (vertical difference
  between input and output levels)

- distance between intake and discharge
  points

- proximity to electricity supply

- whether an abstraction licence is required
  (eg from the Environment Agency in
  England and Wales).

The attributes of the main types of pump
available are provided in Table 4.4.

vi) Surface irrigation
(grips or foot drains)

Grips or foot drains are small spade-sized
channels, connected to the main water
system. Typically a grip is 30–60 cm wide
and no more than 50 cm deep. On sites with
old surface grips or foot drains flooding
them in winter can be an effective way to
keep soils locally wet (surface irrigation).
Grips were often spaced just far enough
apart for natural and efficient sub-surface
feed between them. During the summer,
grips should be kept wet until the need for
the desired high water level has passed.

Table 4.4: Attributes of different types of pumps

Type of pump	Capital cost	Running cost	Capacity	Noise	Pollution	Vandalism risk	Notes
Diesel	High (about £7,000 for a 6" pump).	Low, a 6" pump delivers water @ £5.50 per 1,000 m³.	High (up to 700 m³/h).	High	High, both noise and possible risk of spillages of fuel into drainage channels.	High risk of theft (pump and/or fuel).	Drain when not in use during cold weather (ice can damage pump mechanism).
Tractor-mounted PTO driven	Low (an Alcon 3" pump costs about £1,400).	High	Low	High	High	Low (can be locked away).	Useful on small sites and for small volumes of water, but ties up tractor when in use.
Electric	Cheap, but installation costs can be high.	Low	Moderate	Low	Low	High	Nearby electricity supply essential. Low maintenance costs.
Wind	From £2,500	Very low	Low	Low	Negligible	High	Wind-dependent (Case Study 8). Vulnerable to storm damage.

Water may have to be pumped into the main feeder drainage channel or from the drainage channel to the field to ensure supply. Often the grips can have their own wildlife interest, for example, they are often dominated by yellow iris. Management options for grips are similar to those for drainage channels (Case Study 8). Advantages and disadvantages are discussed in Table 4.5.

vii) Sub-surface irrigation

Sub-surface irrigation (where the infrastructure exists) can be used to raise soil water-tables on sites where the distribution of water channels is too sparse to guarantee the delivery of water to field centres. It is not recommended that sub-surface irrigation systems are installed to achieve this aim, as they act as an efficient and uncontrolled drainage system when drainage channel levels are low (Case Study 16). Sub-surface irrigation can use natural water-soil transfers or water can be helped to reach the centres of fields by the use of sub-surface pipes, either plastic pipes or compression mole drains (sub-surface channels forced through the soil), dug from feeder channels or drainage channels maintained at a higher level. Figure 4.5 shows the principle of sub-surface irrigation. Installation of a new piped

Table 4.5: Advantages and disadvantages of foot drains

Advantages
- Good for creating linear pools in summer.

- Particularly useful on clay and silt where use of sub-surface pipes may be impractical, soil permeability is poor and movement of water through the soil is non-existent.

- A rapid way of creating shallow floods, particularly when drainage channel levels are high, for wintering wildfowl.

- Excellent where the field profile is naturally concave and water can be run on merely by raising drainage channel levels.

- If blocked off at the drainage channel end in early spring, can be used to create valuable feeding areas for breeding lapwings and redshanks.

Disadvantages
- Impractical for transporting water in summer as it is rapidly lost into the soil and through evaporation.

- The channels create extra hazards for machinery, particularly during mowing operations.

- In many cases water must be pumped from the drainage channel into the grip.

**Figure 4.5
Principle of
sub-surface
irrigation**

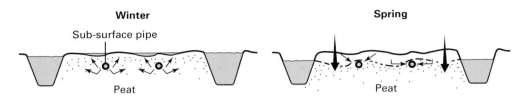

Permeable soil with sub-surface pipes. Field water-table is more uniform in spring.
Ditch water levels must however be high to prevent drainage effect

system or moling should not be considered in areas of archaeological interest, as it can be damaging to remains below the surface.

The pipe systems transport water to the centre of a field using simple gravity feed from a feeder channel. However, there are several important principles and requirements that must be adhered to for success:

- Any smearing or compaction around the plastic pipe must be kept to a minimum to enable the water to move easily in and out.

- Avoid using plastic pipes in soils rich in free iron to avoid blockage with iron ochre. Mole channels could be satisfactory in these situations, being easy and cheap to renew if blockage occurs.

- Milled mole channels (ie where the soil is removed mechanically to create a sub-surface channel) are much more

satisfactory in peat soils than compression moles and can have a life of 3–20 years depending upon the type and density of the peat.

- Milled moles must be installed under saturated conditions with an adequate supply of water in the feeder drainage channel to lubricate the machine. This technique avoids the need to lower water-tables and drainage channel levels before installation as is required with pipe drains.

Subsoiling is another recognised agricultural technique frequently used in cultivated fields. Its potential value in improving soil structure on wet grassland sites is not clear. Anyone wishing to undertake such an operation should seek expert advice and ensure that there is no damage to archaeological interest on their site.

4.2.3 Water quality

Water quality is particularly important for drainage channel plants and invertebrates. The main water quality problems likely to be encountered relate to eutrophication, levels of salinity, the presence of toxic iron and sulphur compounds and the presence of agro-chemicals. Heavy sediment loads are also a problem for some species. To establish the nature of water quality problems at a site it may be possible to use information from the relevant government agency water quality monitoring programmes, or water-testing may be required. Chemical analyses, invertebrate or plant monitoring (section 5.2) may also be used.

Eutrophication
Lowland water courses are frequently polluted by elevated levels of nitrate and phosphate. This may be a result of fertiliser leaching from farmland or from point sources of treated sewage effluent. For all natural trophic states the ratio between nitrogen and phosphorus lies in the range of 10–20 parts of nitrogen to 1 of phosphorus (Part 3, Table 3.6). Changes beyond these ratios may indicate a potential pollution problem. Algal blooms and the presence/absence of different indicator species can indicate pollution problems (Part 5).

Many sites are affected by flood defence works upstream which alter the timing of flows and floods. Uncontrolled winter flooding nowadays can spread silt containing high levels of phosphate over a site and potentially reduce botanical and invertebrate interest. Historically this practice was carried out deliberately by farmers to enhance fertility and probably benefited some grassland plant communities (eg at Southlake on the Somerset Levels and Moors).

Where there is concern about high river nutrient levels:

- abstraction of river water should not be undertaken during the first flood after a long dry period, as the water will contain high nutrient levels flushed from the catchment

- abstraction should be undertaken just after flood peaks, to avoid high sediment concentrations to which phosphate may be bound.

Salinity

Most plant and invertebrate species have a restricted range of tolerance to salinity. Salt is a very efficient herbicide for all freshwater plants and at salinities in excess of 200 mg/l of sodium, freshwater communities may become stressed.

Clay and peat soils lose their structure on exposure to sea water. Clays lattices break down and the soil becomes fluid and de-oxygenated. Sodium replaces calcium in the soil structure and plants and invertebrates which are not adapted to saline conditions die. Even if such extreme conditions are absent, freshwater plants will die when their roots hit a saline water-table. Maintaining conditions of salinity to which the flora and fauna are adapted is very important. For invertebrates, gradients of salinity can be vital in maintaining some species and communities of high conservation value (Case Study 8).

Under stable salinities the tolerance of freshwater plant communities is higher. Fluctuating salinity can reduce tolerance by a factor of 4. Plants found at a stable salinity of 1,000 mg/l sodium will become stressed if the salinity fluctuates between, for example 1,000 mg/l and 250 mg/l and if fluctuations persist, the community will tend to become confined to areas where the water has an average sodium concentration of 250 mg/l or less (Remane and Schleiper 1971). This has major implications for the maintenance of aquatic communities dependent on brackish water.

Toxic effects of iron and sulphur

There can be problems with iron toxicity (ochre) in some peat soils. Under certain conditions peats form a toxic iron pan which plant roots cannot penetrate. Drainage channels dug in such peats can release a toxic tide of iron-rich water.

Pools can be created in iron-rich peats if water levels are kept stable. However, if levels are allowed to fluctuate, ferric sulphates and sulphides can form on exposure to the air as levels fall. These are reduced to the ferrous state as levels rise again and combine with water to form sulphuric acid which, depending on its concentration can be very damaging to the ecosystem.

Solutions to water quality problems

Dealing with water quality problems may require drastic measures including:

- isolating areas of conservation value from a eutrophic water supply

- phosphate stripping.

Isolation of a site from a eutrophic water supply may involve major land-forming works, for example the construction of bunds, though in some circumstances, it may be possible to construct simple dams to isolate drainage channels from eutrophic rivers. However, measures should be taken in the first instance to address the cause of the problem where possible before considering such an option. Phosphate stripping has been carried out by the water companies to remove up to 90% of the phosphate contained in sewage effluent before it is released into rivers. It has been shown to provide benefits over 5–10-year

5-metre wide option

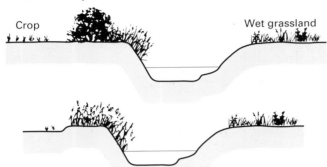

Crop   Wet grassland

- Reed will naturally
  colonise some banks
  in fen areas –
  allow to grow down the slope.

- In light soils some of
  the more attractive and rare
  annual flowers may survive in the seed bank.
- Rotovate after harvesting.
- Cut spring and autumn for two years.
  Remove the cuttings.
- Rotovate thereafter once every two years.

- In heavy soils sow with
  low productivity grasses.
- Cut in spring and autumn for two years
  to keep pernicious arable weeds down.
- Thereafter cut as necessary, perhaps
  every two years. Always remove cuttings.

15-metre wide option

Sterile
strip

Crop

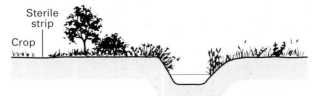

- Plant trees natural for the area.
  Hedgerow/scrub species – hawthorn,
  blackthorn or buckthorn.

periods, reducing algal levels and allowing some plant recovery. The lag-time before recovery takes place is very dependent on the nature of the sediments. It is a relatively expensive technique which should only be considered for large-scale treatment of phosphate-rich water. However, a small experimental system at Slimbridge in Gloucestershire has proved very effective. This uses crushed limestone to absorb phosphorus from nutrient-rich water (Hawke and José 1995). Potential solutions to water quality problems are listed in Table 4.6.

Buffer zones (Figure 4.6) may be used to treat more diffuse sources of nutrients, including agricultural run-off (Large and Petts 1992) – Case Study 3. These are considered in detail in Haycock *et al* (1997), which should be consulted for further details.

Table 4.6: Possible solutions to some water quality problems where the source cannot be tackled

Sediment loading
Construct sediment traps at inflow points to remove sediment.

Phosphorus enrichment
Strip phosphates using limestone, eg in specially constructed channels.

Nitrogen enrichment
Consider use of reedbeds or other wetland plants to breakdown nitrate. Use water-table management to encourage denitrification.

Acidification
Buffer using limestone.

Salinity
Dilute with fresh water. Gypsum can sometimes be effective in reducing salinity in pools.

Iron ochre
Seal drainage channel sides. A precautionary approach should be taken when digging new drainage channels or ponds, to avoid iron ochre deposits.

Figure 4.6
Buffer strips can provide some protection to drainage channels arresting nitrates and suspended solids before they enter water courses

4.3 Drainage channel management

4.3.1 Introduction

Assuming there is appropriate water quality and water level, the most diverse drainage channel floras and faunas are found on sites with:

- extensive networks of drainage channels

- a wide range of drainage channel types

- a range of seral stages, representing habitats from open water to drainage channels choked with well established emergent vegetation

- sympathetic drainage channel maintenance regimes.

Channel maintenance is critically important for both wildlife and drainage. It is clearly important to identify who has responsibility for the maintenance of drainage channels on any site, prior to commencing any work (Table 4.7). Cleaning drainage channels (slubbing) prevents the choking of channels and involves the removal of plant material and accumulated silt (Plate 6). In the past this would have been done manually on a 'little and often' basis, using scythes, peat spades, or sharp chains dragged along the bottom of the drainage channel by two people. These techniques resulted in a great variety in the depth, width, profile and vegetation composition of drainage channels, providing suitable habitat for a diverse range of species. Nowadays, by employing a rotational programme and a 'little and often' philosophy, mechanical management can maintain a similar variety of successional stages.

Before undertaking channel management, it is advisable to undertake a rapid survey, to identify stretches supporting rare plants, such as sharp-leaved pondweed, which may have special requirements. Similarly, some invertebrates like the variable damselfly may be restricted to short lengths of drainage channels.

Table 4.7: Drainage channel responsibility in England and Wales

> **The responsibility for the maintenance of water courses varies:**
>
> - The Environment Agency (previously the NRA) has permissive powers to maintain 'main rivers' which are covered in the Water Resources Act 1991.
>
> - The Internal Drainage Boards have similar permissive powers on designated 'main drains'.
>
> - For 'ordinary watercourses', including smaller streams, drainage channels, drains and dykes, the relevant legislation is the Land Drainage Act 1991 (LDA), and the responsibility for management lies with the landowner fronting the watercourse.

Source: Beardall (1996)

Plate 6 Regular maintenance of drainage channels prevents them choking up with emergent vegetation. Sympathetic management greatly enhances their value to wildlife.

(Owen Mountford)

4.3.2 Drainage channel maintenance

Frequency of management

To maintain a diverse community of plants and associated invertebrates, a range of drainage channel management rotations should be adopted. Infrequent management, or its restriction to a limited part of the drainage channel system at any one time:

- allows a full range of successional stages to develop

- permits less mobile species to escape catastrophic effects

- may require specific intervention to control weeds.

Length of rotation depends on factors such as whether the drainage channels have an important water transport or livestock control function, or the type of grazing animal present. Possible options for drainage channel cleaning cycles are:

- light maintenance every year

- a two-year cycle, cutting half of the channel width each year

- less frequent routine maintenance with targeted control of emergents more often as necessary

- radical cleaning of 10–20% of the drainage channels every year (Plates 7 and 8).

Highest species diversity of floating, emergent and submerged aquatic plants is most often associated with freshwater drainage channels managed every three to five years (Thomas *et al* 1981, Wolsey *et al* 1984, Case Studies 10 and 15). Drainage channels on peat may have to be cleaned more frequently if they are subject to subsidence and are essential as wet fences. Brackish drainage channels require less maintenance and can be managed on a 10-year rotation.

Distribution of management

In drainage channels where the prime function is one of drainage, sympathetic management is still possible. Options for dredging and cutting aquatic and marginal vegetation annually, to cater for the needs of wildlife and drainage are:

- leave a continuous strip of emergent and aquatic plants untouched on one margin (Figure 4.7a)

- leave a fringe of emergents on both sides of the channel

- dredge a sinuous route, leaving plants in patches on alternate sides (scalloping) (Figure 4.7b)

- dredge 30 m for full width of channel then leave 10 m dredged to half the width and so on (Figure 4.7c).

Level-dependent drainage channels, ie those where water flow is less than 20 m/hr and where drainage is of secondary importance, can be managed to include a range of vegetation stages from clear, open water with submerged, floating and emergent plants to developed reedswamp:

- Ideally 10–30% of the ditches in one marsh should be slubbed out annually in late summer and early autumn.

- Care should be taken to work from one side only or to clean only part of each ditch in any one year.

Plate 7
Drainage channel management rotations vary in length (from 2–30 years) depending on a number of factors, including the presence of grazing animals and their importance as water carriers.

(*Tim Callaway*)

Plate 8
Open water habitats, created immediately after cleaning can be important for a number of invertebrate species. Recolonisation by aquatic macrophytes is rapid after sensitive management.

(*Tim Callaway*)

(a)
Clear the ditch from only one side (if it is wide) or for only half its length in any particular year.

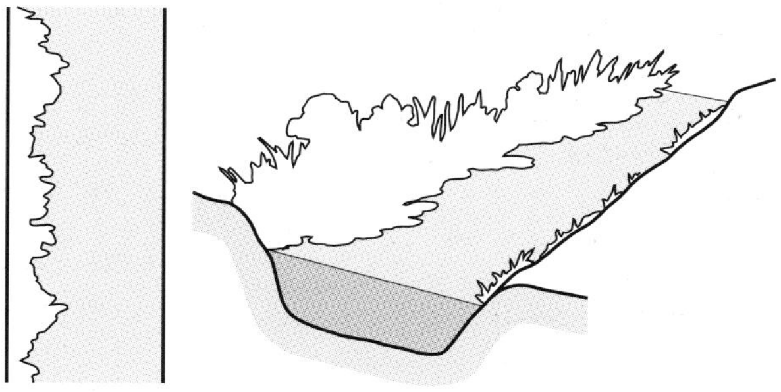

(b)
Use a sinuous dredging route or scallop the vegetation to create meanders.

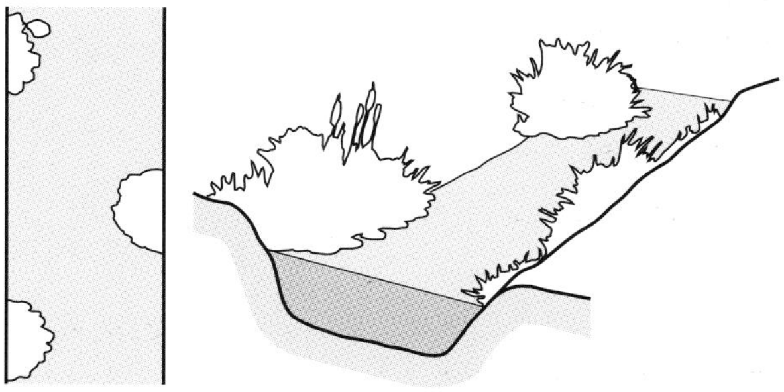

(c)
Leave 10 m blocks of vegetation every 30 m or so.

**Figure 4.7
Sympathetic options for drainage channel management (after Newbold *et al* 1989)**

■ Water levels should preferably be maintained at marsh height during spring and early summer with a water depth of 0.7–1 m.

Maintenance of flow-dependent drainage channels, ie those ditches where water flow exceeds 20 m/h, should be carried out to retain a variety of channel features and flow velocities:

■ always try to leave at least 10% of the channel vegetation uncut

■ create a sinuous, de-silted channel within wider drainage channels to mimic natural meanders, with a wider margin on the inside of bends for wetland plants to establish

■ maintain any natural meanders in the channel

■ where gravel beds and riffles have established try to leave alone as these are important habitats

■ leave channel features that result in variety in flow velocity and substrate. For example, where banks have slumped this often constricts the channel without significantly reducing overall flood capacity (but increases the velocity of water, creating silt-free and valuable habitat)

■ do not over-widen the channel as this will promote siltation, smothering valuable habitats and increasing maintenance frequencies

- maintain or create wet marginal shelves for marginal plants

- work in an upstream direction to keep work area clear of silt

- where rare plants are evident avoid them

- debris in the channel (eg small branches) can modify flow patterns and create useful habitats, so if it is not a drainage or pollution problem leave it

- excavate deeper ponds in the drainage channel bottom to hold water during low flow conditions

- create silt traps, where access and management is easy, to prevent silt from degrading habitats downstream

- avoid chemical control of vegetation wherever possible

- leave headwaters alone.

Costs of drainage channel maintenance vary; Table 4.8 provides a range of costs for different options.

Table 4.8: Drainage channel maintenance options and costs (based on RSPB experience)

Operation	Equipment	Cost/m or m/day (1994)	Timing
Mechanical clearance on a dry site	Hymac or similar	£0.20	Late summer
Mechanical clearance on a wet site	Hymac or similar	£1.00	Late summer
Mud pumping	Mud pump	£1.00	Autumn/winter
Clearing accumulated vegetation by hand using volunteers	Rakes or cromes	10 m/ man-day	Winter
Clearing accumulated vegetation by hand using staff	Rakes or cromes	20–40 m/ man-day	Winter
Mowing edges	Iseki mower (or similar reciprocating mower)	500–800 m/ man-day	Mid-summer
	Scrub cutter	250 m/ man-day	Mid-summer

Timing

Drainage channel management should be undertaken in the late summer or early autumn:

- after plants have seeded

- after the bird breeding season but before wintering birds arrive

- when water levels are low.

Tools and techniques for channel maintenance

The tools and techniques used for drainage channel management can have a significant effect on the outcome of management.

Ideally drainage channels on nature reserves should be managed by hand. Although it is rarely a practical option because it is so labour intensive, it has many benefits. A hand rake or crome may be used to pull plants up, and scythes may be used for hand-cutting. Raking is most effective for the selective removal of nuisance species. Hand removal of emergent vegetation, such as bur-reed and bulrush, maintains drainage channels at their most diverse botanical stage; open water dominated by submerged macrophytes.

At Strumpshaw Fen, hand removal is used to manage hay meadow drainage channels that require mechanical cleaning only every 30 to 50 years. The absence of cattle and other livestock reduces bank erosion and subsequent siltation and so reduces the need for frequent drainage channel management. Such management maintains suitable habitat for the rare Norfolk hawker dragonfly and a rich aquatic flora. Management by hand makes it easier to retain specific rare plants like water-soldier and to identify opportunities for the reintroduction/redistribution of plants prior to and after drainage channel cleaning. The reintroduction of macrophytes can help to prevent algal domination and can speed recolonisation in cases where few plant fragments remain after cleaning.

In large drainage channels a weed-cutting boat may be used for channel maintenance. Otherwise, a tractor and bucket or a Hymac can be used to slub out material or reprofile drainage channels. Tractor-mounted diggers are the best tool to use, as they are relatively inefficient, leaving patches of vegetation undisturbed and creating an irregular profile (Doarks 1994). Cutting should always be carried out above the sediment layer. Spoil is usually disposed of on-site by incorporating into adjacent land. To avoid problems with the disposal of spoil:

■ deposit spoil away from the bank and in areas of low wildlife interest. Avoid smothering important bankside and field habitats (Case Study 10)

■ leave spoil on the bankside for several hours to allow invertebrates and amphibians to return to the water

■ place spoil where eutrophic run-off from plant decomposition does not feed directly into a watercourse

■ do not in-fill wet hollows with spoil as these may provide important habitat for waders and wildfowl

■ ensure that livestock do not have access to spoil that may contain toxic aquatic/bankside plant matter (eg hemlock, iris and water-dropworts)

Where spoil is to be disposed of off-site, and used or sold for bund construction etc, the mineral planning or local planning authority should be consulted.

4.3.3 Drainage channel reprofiling

Profile and depth significantly influence the wildlife value of drainage channels. Some species are dependent on specific water depths. It is important to maintain a variety of depths in the channel, grading to a shallow, wet marginal fringe. Winter levels are not so critical, but some water must be maintained year round. Drainage channel reprofiling offers opportunities to enhance the interest of existing networks, and also removes accumulated sediment full of nutrients (Case Study 10). If drainage channels become regularly choked with algae consider removing the sediment layer on an annual basis, and try to identify the nutrient source and consult the relevant Government agency over its treatment.

For major reprofiling of drainage channels, work should be carried out on one side of the drainage channel only and in alternate 100 m stretches. Remaining sections should be reprofiled only when the originally worked sections have recovered (Figure 4.8).

As a general rule cutting into the substrate should be avoided where problems with ochre are suspected. When disturbed, some peat soils leach iron hydroxide which is toxic to plants and invertebrates. However, susceptible areas of peat with iron-rich deposits are marked on soil survey maps, so this problem can be avoided. Over-deepening of drainage channels should also be avoided.

4.3.4 Drainage channel creation

It may be desirable to create new drainage channels to:

■ improve water transport capacity

■ provide additional aquatic habitat.

Drainage channel creation costs around £1.00/m on dry, accessible sites. New drainage channels should be 70–100 cm deep and have a shallow profile (30–45°).

It should be remembered that physical disturbance of soil when creating new drainage channels may release nutrients and cause eutrophication in the new drainage channel. New drainage channels should not therefore be connected up to pristine drainage channel networks until their nutrient status has stabilised. At Ludham Marshes (Norfolk) this process took three years and involved the annual removal of invasive species such as reed sweet-grass and other eutrophic indicators.

Riparian habitats can be restored or created using grants available within schemes such as Countryside Stewardship or ESAs (Appendix 2).

**Figure 4.8
Options for
drainage channel
enhancement by
reprofiling**

Original ditch
Steep sides, depth 0.7–1 m

- Allows growth of submerged plants
- Maintains water flow

Greatest water flow, minimal conservation value

Option 1
Deepening of the channel bed to more than 1 m and creation of submerged berms

- Allows growth of emergents
- Deepened bed prevents spread of emergents across ditch

Good water flow, increased conservation value, requires no land-take

Option 2
One side steep and the other sloped to about 45°

- Allows growth of emergents
- Cattle can drink without falling in
- Wading birds can feed on shallow edge

Best conservation/farming compromise – minimal land-take

Option 3
Both sides sloped to about 45°

- Gently sloping banks allow greatest light penetration into ditch for plants
- Cattle can drink without falling in
- Wading birds can feed on shallow edge

Best for wildlife conservation – maximum land-take

4.3.5 Bankside management

The design and management of drainage channel banks can contribute greatly to the overall wildlife value of the drainage channel habitat (RSPB *et al* 1994). A steep, deep bank, commonly found in the hydraulically efficient trapezoidal channel, is of relatively little value for wildlife. The most diverse drainage channel margins are invariably of a shallow gradient and lightly grazed by cattle. This creates a damp marginal habitat for numerous invertebrate and plant species.

An edge trampled by stock will cause slumping of the banksides, but there are many ecological advantages to such a trampled zone. Trampling creates a berm which provides a niche for shallow water and bare mud-adapted plants and animals. Many annual plants, some of which are nationally scarce, thrive in such habitats. Bare mud is also a critically important niche for many invertebrate species. The best option is to ensure a diversity of treatments, ranging from trampled, muddy edges to long bankside vegetation (Plate 9).

The most diverse banksides can contain relict fen communities of ancient wetlands and are important refuges. Where drainage channels with an important water-carrying function also support such communities or other scarce or rare species, it may be advisable to dig separate feeder drainage channels, rather than risk losing species through regular maintenance. However, cutting of botanically diverse banksides can sustain communities if the timing and frequency is adjusted to annual reproductive cycles of constituent species.

Recommendations:

- As a general rule, floristic, invertebrate and bird diversity can be maintained by cutting one side of the bank only, in alternate years (ie a two-year rotation). Cutting should take place as late as possible, preferably after the first frost or around October. If it is necessary to cut earlier, cutting in mid-August allows most plants to set seed and gives time for any second broods of birds, such as reed warblers, to fledge. Even so, cutting at

(*Owen Mountford*)

Plate 9 Marginal vegetation has been effectively limited by grazing on the right-hand bank of this drainage channel. Managers should ensure that some bankside areas are ungrazed or only lightly grazed, to provide a mosaic of bankside vegetation heights.

this time will affect the survival of some late-flowering plants and some invertebrates.

- Cutting vegetation on longer than a 1-year rotation encourages coarser species and provides cover for nesting birds.

- It is best to remove cut material to prevent it falling into the drainage channel, as it may impede drainage and cause pollution when it rots. Cutting vegetation on more than a 1-year rotation encourages coarser species and provides cover for nesting birds.

- Where possible grazing of bankside vegetation is preferable to cutting as it introduces greater structural variety (from bare, poached muddy margins to long, rank vegetation) and is less destructive.

Pesticides also have an impact on aquatic flora and fauna (Beardall 1996). A recent report (NRA 1995) concluded that, although surprisingly little ecological fieldwork had actually been completed, 'significant effects were found at disturbingly low water column concentrations for some pesticides ... concentrations likely to arise from normal usage'. This has led the Environment Agency to recommend a minimum 6-m 'no spray zone' for all pesticides adjacent to all watercourses. The Pesticide Safety Directorate (PSD) have already restricted the use of over 150 pesticides from a 6-m buffer zone adjacent to all watercourses, and more will no doubt be restricted as the PSD reviews other products on the market.

4.3.6 Use of aquatic herbicides

Table 4.9: The choice of herbicide formulations and their spectra of weed control. (Where a choice of chemical exists select the one affecting the least number of non-target groups.)

'Weed groups'	Terbutryn	Dichlobenil	Dichlobenil plus dalapon	Diquat	Dalapon*	Glyphosate	Maleic hydrazide	2,4-D	Fosamine ammonium
Algae	K		MR						
Submerged plants	K	K	K	K					
Free-floating plants (small leaf area)	K			K					
Floating-leaved plants (large leaf area)		K	K			K		MR	
Reeds			K		K	MR			
Sedges			MR		MR	K			
Grasses and rushes						K	K		
Broad-leaved weeds						K	K	K	
Docks						K			
Trees and shrubs									K

K = Kill MR = Moderately resistant, * only available from German stockists

Occasionally it may be necessary to use aquatic herbicides, especially for controlling introduced weed species with the ability to regrow from fragments. Mechanical or manual management can promote such plants. For example, aggressive growths of Canadian or Nuttall's waterweed are best controlled using aquatic herbicides. Reference should be made to Table 4.9 to avoid effects on non-target species. Appendix 11 lists those products which have been approved for use as herbicides in or near watercourses and lakes.

All users / operators working with herbicides must have a BASIS certificate gained by attending an appropriate training course.

When using herbicides for drainage channel management the following management principles should be applied:

- always treat small areas only

- use selective herbicides wherever possible

- use broad-spectrum herbicides with great caution. Seek advice as there may be undesirable ecological effects

- always follow the manufacturers' recommendations.

It should also not be forgotten that the use of herbicides on SSSIs / ASSIs will require the consent or approval of the statutory conservation body. Further information on the management of drainage channels can be found in Newbold *et al* (1989), although for up-to-date information on approved products, information should be sought from MAFF.

4.4 Grassland management

4.4.1 Introduction

Wet grasslands in the UK are the products of interventive agricultural management, usually by grazing or mowing. Such management halts the natural succession to coarser vegetation types such as scrub and woodland.

Management may involve:

■ mowing

■ grazing

■ haying, followed by aftermath grazing

■ burning (now rarely used).

The timing of management, its frequency and intensity all influence the outcome which can be expected.

4.4.2 Mowing

Mowing is a non-selective form of management, in that all vegetation is cut to a uniform height (Plate 10). This can lead to uniformity of vegetation cover and an overall reduction in the diversity of plants and invertebrates. However, meadows which have been cut annually at about the same time for many years often have valuable species-rich swards, notably the communities of flood meadows, and old grazed hay meadows.

Equally, many diverse grasslands are the result of very irregular regimes, with mowing at different times each year or in some years not at all. Regular cutting is therefore not the only option. Years without cutting may be particularly important for plants to set seed. Some selectivity can be achieved in effect by altering the time, frequency and height of mowing.

(*Andrew Mayled*)

Plate 10 Mowing for hay removes nutrients from the wet grassland system and encourages a diverse, species-rich sward.

Timing of cutting

It is best to cut fodder crops between 1 July and 31 August. Cutting should be timed to:

■ Allow important species to complete critical phases of their life-cycle (eg flowering and setting seed). In general, late cutting (eg topping in September) favours tall-growing plant species, while lower-growing plants tend to be promoted by earlier mowing (eg in June).

The time of cutting can also affect botanical diversity, but this depends on the fertility of a site and its community composition. Bakker (1989) found that September cuts enhanced species richness on less productive sites, but an earlier cut (eg in July) was more effective on more productive sites, because of the need to control competition from aggressive grasses.

■ Control rank growth or competitive and aggressive species which would otherwise dominate the vegetation. For that purpose it should be timed to coincide with their peak in growth, usually in spring and early summer (although care should be taken not to harm other groups such as birds or invertebrates).

One of the effects of mechanisation has been the ability to complete harvests more rapidly. Where management plans or ESA management prescriptions set restrictions on mowing dates, there is a tendency to try to harvest as rapidly as possible after the official start-date. This is particularly likely if contractors are used. To reduce the tendency to uniformity of management, different parts of a site should be mown at different times. In occasional years, delaying the first cut in some fields until September will benefit late-flowering plants such as devil's-bit scabious and meadowsweet.

Removal of cuttings

Cuttings should never be left *in situ* as this leads to nutrient enrichment and contributes to the development of a mat of litter. This prevents seeds from reaching the soil and reduces light levels at the soil surface, thereby suppressing small flowering plants and mosses. Removing cuttings is also important where aftermath grazing is practised as there is a possibility that mowings may include toxic plants (eg ragwort). Where removal of cuttings is not practical, and toxic plants are present, aftermath grazing should not take place for at least six weeks. Raking (manual or mechanical) to remove cuttings can help to open up the sward for seed germination.

When cuttings are removed, repeated harvests result in gradual nutrient depletion, in marked contrast to their localised return in the dung and urine of grazing animals. In time, the removal of cuttings favours the agriculturally less productive grasses, such as sweet vernal grass, common bent and red fescue, and also wild flowers.

Mowing for fodder production

Mowing is usually carried out for hay or silage production. On sites where grazing is also carried out, mowing can be important to conserve fodder for winter-feeding. There is considerable benefit in using home-grown fodder, because hay bought in from outside may:

■ have been produced from fertilised sites, thus importing added nutrients

■ contain weeds and the seeds of alien species, which may be shed during feeding and establish in the sward.

One of the main consequences of drainage is the earlier onset of vegetative growth in the spring and an increase in the load-bearing capacity of the soil, both of which tend to result in earlier mowing. The nutritional value of hay or silage is also better the earlier the cut is taken. However, early mowing can be extremely damaging to ground-nesting birds (section 3.5) and also tends to reduce flowering and seed-set in plants, leading to a reduction in botanical diversity.

Silage making is generally less beneficial for wildlife conservation. It usually takes place earlier in the year than haying and is therefore particularly damaging to ground-nesting birds. Rapid harvesting early in the growing season means that seeds do not have time to ripen and drop to the ground as they do in hay making. It is also common for more than one silage cut to be taken per season and this increases disturbance. Silage making is also not advisable on sites with high entomological interest, the eggs or larvae of some invertebrate species being adversely affected by the more intensive and rapid cutting and baling process. Whereas during hay cutting and turning there may be more time for eggs and larvae to drop safely to the ground, with silage making they are more likely to be removed from the site with the crop.

Topping

Topping is used to remove coarse or excess vegetation, often to tidy up fields which have been grazed or to control weeds like thistles (Plate 11, Case Studies 1, 13 and 16).

On the Nene Washes for instance the majority of fields are topped to control thistle growth (Case Study 11). Topping can benefit grazing birds. Owen (1983) reported a 32% increase in goose usage on sites which had been topped compared with those left uncut. However, in other circumstances and where there are no weed problems, topping is generally to be discouraged as it reduces sward and invertebrate diversity.

Mowing equipment

Mowers, forage harvesters and toppers may be used. Mowers are designed to cut at ground level and lay mown vegetation in dense, even swathes for later harvesting. For hay making, these swathes are turned and dried until the moisture content has dropped enough for baling and dry storage. Hay making therefore depends strongly on the weather. Silage making is more likely to be done using a forage harvester. Single or double-chop harvesters are available, the latter producing very finely cut material. Forage harvesters can be adjusted to cut at a variety of heights. For silage the vegetation is usually cut relatively close to ground level and then passed through the machine and blown into an accompanying trailer for transport to purpose-built silos or silage pits. The baling of silage is also becoming increasingly common, and can produce high quality fodder.

Toppers generally have a violent cutting action. Integral skids allow blades to be set at anything up to 20 cm above the ground surface. Relatively small volumes of finely cut material are produced which can usually be left to rot down naturally. Typical work rates for topping vary between 0.75–2.5 ha/h, depending on the density of vegetation, the flatness and size of the field and type of topper used.

Practicalities of mowing versus grazing

Mowing is often more practical than grazing on smaller sites. It may also be the only option for sites which are isolated or less accessible, as livestock need to be checked regularly. However, wherever possible, land should be grazed after mowing to create height diversity in the sward.

(Keith Blomerley)

In some areas availability of livestock can be a problem. Livestock management is also labour-intensive and requires special skills.

If skilled labour is unavailable, mowing is more straightforward. Whereas livestock management requires daily labour input for a whole season, mowing can be carried out as a one-off operation and it is much easier to contract out.

Mowing also has drawbacks, however:

- It may cease to be cost-effective on larger sites, for example on sites larger than 3 ha (McLaren 1987), especially if the crop cannot be sold or let.

- Both hay and silage making are very labour-intensive, albeit for a more limited period. On the Nene Washes, for example, harvesting hay from a 4-ha area took 9 days from cutting to carting off. On average, making hay or one cut of silage a year requires about 12 tractor hours/ha. A second silage cut takes about 9 tractor hours/ha.

Plate 11 Topping is often used to remove coarse vegetation (eg thistles or rushes) and to remove excess vegetation before winter flooding.

4.4.3 Mowing with aftermath grazing

Mowing for hay, followed by grazing of the aftermath, is the traditional management practice for some wet grasslands (Case Studies 11, 12 and 14). Fields are usually shut up for hay from April to June or early July. Cutting for hay (or silage) is followed by light cattle or sheep-grazing (50–80 LSU/ha/yr). This regime can promote species-rich plant communities, regeneration niches being created for grassland plants by the trampling of the livestock. As a general rule, sward heights should be between 3 and 10 cm at the end of the grazing period.

4.4.4 Grazing

Grazing predominates in the nature conservation management of wet grasslands in the UK. Many diverse plant communities have evolved under grazing management and these are distinct from those which develop under mowing or mowing with aftermath grazing.

Livestock graze selectively, depending on their preferences and the relative palatability of different plants in the sward. In contrast to mowing, grazing therefore tends to produce a relatively uneven sward. It has different effects depending on the type of grazing animal used, the season of grazing and its intensity and frequency.

Cattle and sheep are most commonly used, but also ponies and occasionally goats. It is possible that some of the hardier and more traditional breeds of livestock may be more effective in managing wet grasslands, particularly where it is necessary to control ranker vegetation.

Plate 12
Heavy poaching by grazing animals is a problem on wet grassland sites, especially in the winter, and should be avoided to prevent damage to the sward and the invasion of ruderal species. Poaching in moderation is beneficial to some invertebrates and provides regeneration niches for plants.

Stock type

i) Cattle

In many wet grasslands, cattle are the preferred grazing animal, because they are:

- more tolerant of wet conditions than sheep and generally easier to manage with wet fences (ie boundary drainage channels)

- relatively unselective in their grazing behaviour compared with sheep and are therefore ideal for removing long or rank vegetation, or for controlling invading scrub

- particularly suited to the management of productive sites which require summer grazing, as they do not graze flowers preferentially. For example, the Culm grasslands were traditionally used as rough summer grazing for suckler or store cattle (Wolton 1992)

- well suited to the control of taller grasses such as reed sweet-grass and reed canary-grass, which can otherwise dominate washlands. Extensive stands of reed sweet-grass are of little use to wintering wildfowl and provide poor nesting habitat for most wetland birds – the exception being spotted crake (Owen and Thomas 1979, Fuller 1982, Thomas *et al* 1981, Burgess *et al* 1990). Reed sweet-grass stands in washlands are also used by rare invertebrates, such as the leaf beetle *Donacia semicuprea*.

Being much heavier animals than sheep, cattle trample the vegetation more and cause more poaching (Plate 12). Poaching can help to create regeneration niches for

(Owen Mountford)

wild flowers (and bare ground useful for insects), but also for troublesome weeds like ragwort and thistles. It is very important to have lie-back areas so that livestock can be taken off the pasture if it is poaching badly. Cattle tend to produce a relatively tussocky sward, which is preferred by nesting waders and invertebrates. In addition, fewer cattle than sheep can be used to achieve the same grazing pressure and the risk of trampling to wader nests and young is therefore lower (Green 1986).

In unfenced areas, as well as creating valuable bare mud habitat along the margins of drainage channels, cattle can browse tall emergents in the channels, encouraging a richer macrophyte flora by enabling more light to reach the water surface (Thomas *et al* 1981). Cattle will also reduce the development of tall, rank vegetation along drainage channel banks and prevent the encroachment of species-poor stands of tall plants like common reed, reed sweet-grass and reed canary-grass into the open water of drainage channels.

The behaviour of cattle varies to some extent between breeds and age groups (Ausden and Treweek 1995). Younger cattle (youngstock) can be very boisterous and are probably a greater trampling threat to ground-nesting birds than older animals. This risk can be reduced by keeping animals in smaller groups. On most nature reserves, dairying is impractical, because it requires too much traffic to and from the site, twice daily disturbance and also special housing and feeding facilities. Also dairy cattle have high nutritional demands that are rarely met by unimproved herbage. Store cattle, youngstock or suckler cows are likely to be the most realistic option (see Appendix 12).

The hardier beef breeds such as Aberdeen Angus, Devon, Hereford and Highland are more likely to thrive on most wet grasslands than breeds adapted to intensive systems, like the continental beef breeds and most dairy breeds.

(Keith Blomerley)

ii) Sheep

Sheep are less often grazed in wet grassland situations owing to their relative intolerance of wet conditions underfoot and associated health problems. However, some breeds are more able to thrive in wet conditions, notably the Romney Marsh breed which was traditionally associated with the Kent/Sussex marshes (Plate 13, Case Study 16).

Intensive shepherding is required for good sheep husbandry, especially for a breeding flock. Wet grasslands are not suitable for lambing or for young lambs (which get cold when wet), so alternative sites will be needed during lambing or when the ground is very wet. Provision for shearing and perhaps dipping (though this is no longer compulsory) will be necessary.

Sheep graze more closely and evenly than cattle, producing a relatively uniform sward structure which is less suitable for breeding waders and invertebrates. However, they do produce a sward well suited to grazing by wintering wildfowl. They are unable to graze effectively on tall, rank pasture and are therefore less useful for early management of neglected or overgrown sites. They graze most effectively on swards maintained between 3 and 6 cm tall.

**Plate 13
Sheep are less commonly used on wet grassland than cattle, although the Romney Marsh breed is traditionally used in North Kent.**

Part 4 Management Techniques

As with cattle, when sheep are used on wet grassland sites the system will usually be extensive and comprise:

- store lambs (females or castrated males), which might need to be finished or fattened on higher quality grassland

- cull or barren ewes

- mature wethers (castrated males) used solely as grazing machines.

iii) Horses

Perhaps unfairly, horse grazing is widely considered to be damaging to species-rich grassland. There are several problems associated with horse grazing:

- It creates a mosaic of tightly grazed turf interspersed with latrine areas that are often dominated by rank growth as horses avoid grazing them.

- Horses are very active and can cause poaching problems (Case Study 14).

- Land is often continuously stocked and over-grazed.

- Supplementary feed causes eutrophication.

However, where over-grazing can be

avoided and stocking densities are low, these problems can be overcome (Gibson 1996). Horses are particularly good at opening up rank vegetation and have been used with success at the Ouse Washes to control dense vegetation and open it up for grazing by cattle. They are useful in areas where:

- horse-grazing is traditional, eg on meadows associated with inns

- other livestock is unavailable or prohibitively expensive

- the grazing is too poor to support profitable/commercial livestock production

- vegetation is particularly coarse and overgrown

- the resultant patchy mosaic is a valuable habitat, favouring a number of key invertebrates

- the target vegetation is a very short turf with low-growing wild flowers, such as marsh pennywort.

Stocking density

As well as diversity in grazing behaviour and selectivity, there is obvious variation in the size of the different species and hence their grazing capacity, production of dung and physical impact through trampling. To make direct comparisons between different types of animals, stock densities are often expressed in terms of livestock units (LSU). This system is based on the average amount of vegetation removed by different ages and types of livestock and uses the dairy cow as the base unit (Table 4.10).

LSU coefficients can be calculated based on the equivalent allowances for other types of livestock, such that one beef cow is considered equivalent to approximately eight sheep (Table 4.10). LSU coefficients are useful for calculating and comparing stocking densities. They can also be used to calculate the extent to which available grassland will meet the annual fodder requirements of livestock and work out when additional or supplementary feed might need to be provided or bought in. Guidance notes produced by ADAS or the

Table 4.10: Livestock unit coefficients

Stock type	Livestock unit coefficient
Cattle	
Dairy cow	1.00
Dairy bull	0.65
Beef cow	0.75
Cattle (0-1 year)	0.30
Cattle (1-2 years)	0.54
Cattle (>2 years)	0.80
Horse	1.00
Sheep	
Ewes (Light, 40 kg)	0.07
Ewes (Medium, 60 kg)	0.09
Ewes (Heavy, 80 kg)	0.11
Rams	0.08
Lambs	0.04-0.08

Source: SAC (1990)

Scottish Agricultural College provide useful background information (ADAS 1983, SAC 1990).

Recommended stocking densities are more rules of thumb than absolute prescriptions (Case Studies 1, 7 and 11). However, inappropriate stocking densities are a common factor in reducing the conservation value of wet grassland. It is important to recognise that identical stocking densities can produce different sward responses in different fields, (or in the same field in different years), depending on other factors, such as water regime, soil type, botanical composition and weather patterns.

In situations where control of rank vegetation is an objective, relatively high stocking densities for shorter periods are often the most effective. However, it is important to bear in mind the potentially adverse effects of severe trampling and disturbance on invertebrates and birds. Furthermore, livestock stocked at high density to graze down rough/rank vegetation may well need supplementary feeding. Feeding areas are likely to get heavily trampled and poached, and there is a risk of nutrient enrichment. Ideally, any additional feeding should take place on lie-back areas where nature conservation interest can be sacrificed. Considerable care should be taken when feeding hay produced on other sites, as this can act as a source of seed and result in the ingress of alien species. Ideally, home- or locally-grown hay should be fed to livestock grazing sites of nature conservation importance.

Planning and managing stocking densities involves the initial evaluation of a long list of factors. Frequent review and adjustment may be necessary as sward production fluctuates relative to the needs of stock. Exceptionally wet or dry years, for example, can necessitate considerable variations in stocking density. Crofts and Jefferson (1994) summarised the factors which should be taken into account when planning and reviewing stocking densities (Table 4.11).

Table 4.11: Factors which should be taken into account when determining stocking densities

Factor	Questions to ask
Soil	■ What is the soil type? ■ Is the site naturally fertile and able to support higher densities?
Climatic variation	■ What is the average climatic regime? ■ Is it relatively warm and wet, supporting high densities? ■ Is temperature/lack of water limiting sward productivity?
Hydrology	■ When does drought occur? ■ When does flooding occur?
Accessibility	■ Are all parts of the site equally accessible? ■ If not, is the prescribed density based on *available* grass? ■ Can stock be guided to use the whole or part of the site?
Vegetation	■ Is the sward quality sufficient to supply the needs of the stock? ■ Should other stock types now be considered, or a mixture? ■ Do certain communities need protection or grazing focused on them?
Productivity	■ Are the grasses present agriculturally productive or not?
Other grazers	■ Has an estimate been made of the impacts of rabbits or deer? ■ Are current populations of wild grazers stable?
Farm system	■ Has the conservation site to be integrated with a commercial farm? ■ What are the current grazing needs of other wet grasslands?

Table 4.12: Suggested medium level stocking rates for wet grasslands

Grazing period	Livestock unit days/ha/year
From mid-May to November, to create a mosaic of short swards and tussocks for breeding snipe, redshank and wildfowl.	100–250
Between mid-July and October on winter-flooded areas, to create a 5–7 cm high sward for breeding lapwing, black-tailed godwit and wintering wigeon, Bewick's swan and other wildfowl.	120–370
Aftermath grazing following a hay cut	50–80

Source: based on Lane (1992), and Tickner and Evans (1991).

Suggested stocking rates for wet grassland are given in Table 4.12, but these should be regarded as a rough guide only. In a botanically rich, old wet grassland in the Somerset Moors, stocking rates were adjusted regularly to maintain a sward height of about 5.5–6.5 cm (Mountford *et al* 1994b). For unfertilised plots on this site, two store cattle per hectare were allocated for aftermath grazing, but others were added and removed according to the availability of grass. Adjusted set-stocking is labour intensive, but ensures that the focus is on the condition of the sward, rather than on adherence to a rigidly defined stocking density.

Sward height measurements can be very useful as a tool in regulating stocking densities, but appropriate heights for nature conservation purposes are less well researched than they are for commercial agricultural production. On swards with very varied structure, a large number of sward height measurements may be needed to estimate the mean sward height and its

variability (see Green 1986 for methodology).

There is a fairly consistent relationship between the type of livestock (cattle or sheep), their stocking density and the numbers of nests likely to be trampled for different breeding birds. Figure 4.9 shows how the percentage of nests likely to be trampled can be estimated. Some managers choose to locate and protect nests with nest protectors, which can be successful in areas where grazing cannot be delayed (Case Study 7).

Timing and duration of grazing

The start of the grazing season depends on a number of factors and is usually a result of a compromise between graziers and conservation managers. Graziers prefer to turn animals out as early as possible (eg in April), depending on their stocks of conserved winter forage, to take advantage of higher feeding value herbage. The main agronomic considerations are the

Figure 4.9 A chart for calculating the risk of nest trampling by cattle and sheep for the whole incubation period of redshank, snipe and black-tailed godwit (Green, 1986)

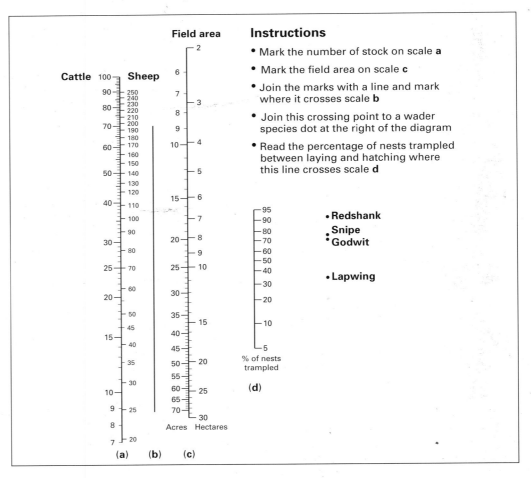

availability of forage, the intended management for the land in that year and the wetness of the site. Fields which are very wet will be prone to poaching and sward damage. Flexibility is important, so that grazing can be delayed if conditions are unusually dry or wet. In such cases it can be helpful not to own stock and be forced to find grazing for them.

The start of grazing in the spring will also depend on the conservation interest of the site. A delay will be required to avoid disturbance of any nesting birds. To some extent, this conflict can be resolved by putting livestock out first onto areas where fewer or no birds nest (Case Study 11). Some species, like snipe, will continue to nest well into July or early August, however, so it can be impossible to avoid damage altogether. Delaying turn-out for too long can result in considerable wastage as mature plant growth forms are often unpalatable and animals trample vegetation down rather than eating it.

The timing and duration of any period of grazing, the type of livestock used and the grazing pressure all contribute to the grazing regime. Duration of grazing will depend on:

- how much defoliation is required

- how long individual field productivity is able to sustain production

- sensitivity of different communities/ species

- window of opportunity for combining species needs.

Grazing regimes may be continuous, rotational or seasonal:

- Continuous year-round grazing at low stocking densities can produce diverse swards with a varied structure, but carries the risk of trampling damage both for invertebrates and nesting birds. Stocking densities must be low enough to ensure that a proportion of flowering plants can flower and set seed despite the constant presence of livestock. Continuous grazing systems are more common in upland environments and are effective only on relatively large sites.

They carry a higher risk of chronic disease for livestock.

- Rotational grazing can be used to produce a variety of sward structures throughout a site and to ensure that sensitive life-stages are avoided on specific areas. It has proved particularly valuable in managing pastures for butterflies. Regular rotations may be preferable to spasmodic, irregular grazing, which species cannot adapt to very easily. When operating a rotational grazing system, care should be taken not to overstock for limited periods, thereby causing catastrophic damage to invertebrates or plants which are sensitive to trampling (orchids for example). However, rapid defoliation can be appropriate to open up foraging areas for species such as lapwing, black-tailed godwit and redshank and their broods.

- Seasonal grazing predominates on wet grasslands. Some general principles can be identified. Grazing in the autumn is most likely to result in botanically diverse swards, as grazing and trampling helps to create regeneration niches for plants. At high stocking rates, however, the establishment of seedlings can become suppressed. Some of the seasonal effects of grazing on plants, invertebrates and birds are summarised in Table 4.13.

Control of livestock

To treat and handle livestock efficiently and with minimal stress, it is necessary to be able to confine animals in a safe, secure working area. Livestock, especially sheep, require regular attention and jobs like foot-trimming and drenching for worms are made a lot easier for everyone concerned if there are good handling facilities. Temporary handling facilities can be constructed using hurdles for sheep, but for cattle more substantial facilities are required (Case Study 11).

Wet or conventional fencing will be required to keep different owners' animals apart, protect sensitive areas, separate livestock from visitors, and also to regulate grazing pressure on different areas.

Table 4.13: Effects of different seasonal grazing systems on wet grassland flora and fauna

Grazing season:	Plants/vegetation	Invertebrates	Breeding waders and wildfowl	Wintering wildfowl
Spring	Creates regeneration niches, but young seedlings may fail to establish. Should not be contemplated in areas with rich hay meadow associations.	Compatible with invertebrate interest if carefully managed. Avoid heavy grazing during drought periods.	Detrimental to seed-eating birds because it inhibits flowering. Risk of trampling nests.	
Summer	Suppresses flowering and seed-set. Can control growth of competitive species.	Heavy summer grazing damages species dependent on flowers, fruits and seeds. Reduces range of egg-laying sites available. Compatible with invertebrate interest if carefully managed. Avoid heavy grazing during drought periods.	Benefits lapwing and black-tailed godwit by providing a mosaic of brood-rearing habitats and short swards the following spring. eg Ouse Washes: minimum of 250–300 LSU days/ha/yr in previous summer gives appropriate structure the following spring.	Produces short swards for winter-grazing and promotes softer grasses favoured by grazing species such as Bewick's swan.
Autumn	Grazing later in the year permits late-flowering species to flower and set seed. Risk of domination by competitive species. Important for creating regeneration niches for autumn-germinators.			@ 120–370 LSU days/ha/yr between July and October can be used to create a short sward (5–7 cm) on areas to be winter-flooded.
Winter (may not be possible on wetter sites)	Controls rank vegetation. Can create bare ground, break up litter layer and create regeneration niches for plants in spring. Grazing densities may have to be lower than 0.25 LSU/ha to prevent damage by poaching.	Many invertebrates hibernating and less vulnerable to trampling damage. May damage species hibernating in litter layer if grazing is heavy. On drier sites, winter grazing is preferable to spring-early summer grazing.	Can help to provide suitable conditions for nesting the following spring (see above).	Grazing animals may compete for biomass with grazing birds, especially if areas are heavily grazed just before arrival of wintering geese. Daily stock-check will cause disturbance. Usually best areas are too wet to graze in winter.

Permanent fencing (consisting of post and rail, post and wire or mains-operated electric wire) is advisable on drier sites where fields are grazed on a regular basis or where it is necessary to keep livestock away from neighbouring land or main roads. Initial investment may be high, but maintenance requirements are relatively low. Poaching is likely along fencelines, so these should be situated away from areas of botanical importance. However, on wetter sites, permanent fences are less stable and on washlands can be damaged by flood-borne debris.

Temporary fencing usually consists of movable electric fencing. The basic electric fence consists of bare wire conductors supported by insulated posts and connected to a fence energiser unit. The energiser unit is earthed and supplies brief pulses of high voltage electricity through the fence conductor so that any animal touching the wire (and in contact with the ground) completes the circuit and receives a small electric shock. Fences may be powered by wet or dry batteries or mains electricity, depending on supply. It can be used to exclude livestock from particular areas for specific periods or to sub-divide large grazing areas into more manageable units. The need to replace batteries regularly can be a problem on remote sites. Battery units are also stolen frequently on less remote sites. Power failures are common owing to shorting out on tall vegetation. It is therefore advisable to mow or herbicide a narrow strip beneath the fence.

On many wet grasslands, wet fences are provided by drainage channels. As well as fencing animals onto discrete areas, these also provide drinking water and are generally more aesthetically pleasing than other types of fencing. However, wet fences are not 100% effective and drainage channels need to be checked regularly to ensure animals have not become stuck in them and are at risk of drowning. In many areas these problems are circumvented by erecting temporary electric fencing along drainage channels in fields grazed by stock.

Ownership and management of livestock

Ownership of livestock should be given careful consideration because of the management input required. Labour requirements are particularly high. For a breeding ewe flock, an average of 4 hours may be needed per ewe per year (very slightly less if shearing is carried out by contractors). A generally accepted rule of thumb is that a full-time shepherd can look after 400 ewes with lambs, given a few weeks help during lambing and shearing. Shepherding stores is less labour-intensive. However, where large numbers of stores are held, grazing management can become quite complicated and sheep bought-in may have health problems that need treating, notably for worms and foot-rot. Treating an outbreak of foot-rot can be particularly time-consuming. For store cattle, out-wintered or summer grazed, average labour hours per head per month will be about 0.9 and 0.2 respectively. Suckler herds of cows need from about 0.9–2.9 hours/head/month depending on how many calves are suckled per cow.

Often it is possible to find graziers who will rent wet grassland for their livestock. It is important to establish the quality and productivity of 'nature conservation' grassland relative to commercial pasture. Grass may have to be let at slightly less than the going rate, though in many cases, lowland wet pastures are regarded as of premium quality because:

- grasses require a lot of moisture for peak production

- forage intake rates are often higher because cattle appear to enjoy the variety of tastes in species-rich swards, provided there are not too many coarse species.

Many wet grassland sites are therefore very popular with graziers, particularly if a reliable shepherding service is provided (Case Study 11). This is a particular asset for non-local graziers. Wet grasslands in some areas have traditionally been used for cattle from other areas. On the RSPB reserve on the Nene Washes, for example, cattle grazing the site in 1990 came from five local graziers (269 head) but also from

Yorkshire, Shropshire, Leicestershire and Hertfordshire (239 head).

If a shepherding service is provided or if livestock are owned by reserve managers, there will be a number of resourcing considerations. For example, livestock enterprises use a certain number of tractor hours each year and there may be a need for capital investment in handling areas or buildings. Useful information on the economics of establishing livestock enterprises can be found in Nix (1996).

The advantages/disadvantages of owning animals are summarised below:

Advantages:
- conservation can be given priority (provided animals remain healthy)
- livestock can be used to graze less productive areas
- can be profitable
- rare/interesting breeds can provide interest for visitors.

Disadvantages:
- ties up large amounts of capital
- high running costs (eg veterinary bills)
- no guarantee of return on investment
- management requires time and expertise.

Plate 14 Cattle grazing requires skilled labour and expensive infrastructure to ensure good livestock care. Site managers often offer a stockcare/ shepherding service in order to attract graziers and their animals (Case Study 11).

(C H Gomersall, RSPB)

Livestock health

Livestock will not graze effectively, or grow satisfactorily if they are unhealthy. Animals should be checked frequently. A head-count should be made at least once a day for cattle and more often for sheep. As well as routine observations of individual appearance and behaviour, regular weighing can be used to estimate growth rates and detect individuals which are obviously under-performing. This is only possible where there are good handling facilities, including a crush and weighing machine (Plate 14, Case Study 11).

On wet grassland sites, some animal health problems are more likely to occur than on drier sites. These include:

- drowning in drainage channels (cattle and sheep)
- blow-fly infestation in sheep (fly-strike)
- liver fluke in sheep and cattle
- foot-rot in sheep
- slow wear of cattle and sheep's feet on soft, damp ground resulting in overgrowth and lameness
- sheep can get stuck on their backs on tussocky ground and will die if left like that for long periods. Rumen gasses cannot escape; this causes the rumen to expand, putting pressure on the lungs and suffocating the animal.

Sheep are prone to fly-strike when blowflies lay their eggs in damp or soiled fleece. Trimming or dagging of dirty wool around the crutch and tail can help to reduce the incidence of strike. Blowfly eggs hatch in about 12 hours and invade the skin and flesh of their host. Further soiling of the fleece occurs over raw areas, often resulting in secondary strikes. If left untreated, sheep are literally eaten alive and may die from toxaemia in three to four days. Sheep grazing damp or waterlogged sites are particularly vulnerable. The blowfly season may extend from May to October, when close vigilance is essential. Spring dipping was often used by farmers to protect sheep from fly-strike up to shearing time, but there are considerable problems with the use and safe disposal of organo-phosphate sheep dips, especially on nature reserves.

Various internal parasites, generally referred to as worms, affect livestock (Figure 4.10). As a general rule, adult animals are worm carriers, but youngstock are most susceptible to injury and disease. Young animals should therefore never follow adults onto a pasture. They should always precede them.

The liver fluke of sheep and cattle (*Fasciola hepatica*) is a parasitic flat worm that can kill livestock if not treated (Figure 4.10). Fluke can be controlled by regular dosing with specific chemicals (like diamphenethide) or by destroying the intermediate hosts, which are various species of *Lymnaea* snail. However, this involves chemical spraying which may also damage non-target organisms. Most of the chemicals used are damaging to fish and most other invertebrates.

Other possible parasites of sheep include keds, lice and sheep scab mites. Compulsory dipping to control sheep scab is no longer required, but it remains a notifiable disease. Ticks are unlikely to be a problem on lowland sites. Cattle are vulnerable to warble fly, the subject of a government eradication scheme in recent years.

Some health problems can be avoided or ameliorated by adopting *clean* grazing systems. Foot-rot, for example, is a contagious disease, but the infective organisms decline after two or three weeks in the absence of sheep. Rested pastures can therefore be regarded as relatively clean and safe. Foot-rot should be treated on a flock-basis. Regular foot-trimming is necessary for sheep, especially when grazing on soft, wet and relatively non-abrasive substrates. If feet are trimmed and checked regularly, foot-rot is more likely to be spotted before it has taken hold in the flock. Otherwise the first notable symptom is lameness in affected animals, which should be isolated from the rest of the flock and treated immediately with a 10% solution of zinc sulphate or formalin, or a 5% solution of copper sulphate.

Sheep and cattle are susceptible to different parasites and can therefore follow one another safely, the exception being liver fluke (see below). Pastures can be regarded as completely clean only if they have not been grazed by sheep or cattle for several years or if they are newly sown. However, a rest of 4–6 weeks during dry weather can help to reduce worm burdens. Dosing for worms does not control larval migrating forms, nor does it prevent dosed animals from becoming infected in future. There are also increasing problems with parasite resistance and many of the products used (notably Ivermectin) may have damaging effects on many non-target invertebrates (Madsen *et al* 1990).

On many sites, flexibility in grazing management for the specific purpose of benefiting or safeguarding animal health is limited. There may be insufficient sacrificial areas where wildlife value can be treated as secondary.

Some weeds, notably ragwort, are poisonous to livestock and may need to be controlled. Cattle and horses are unable to recognise the plant when it is desiccated, eg after cutting and may eat it inadvertently. It should therefore be removed prior to cutting hay or after topping/chemical treatment.

Summary of general principles of grazing management:

- Maintain traditional grazing systems if associated with wildlife conservation.
- Cattle are generally best suited to wet conditions.
- Stocking densities are only rough guides, and should be adjusted to avoid under or overgrazing.
- Grazing regimes must be tailored to the requirements of the priority species present on the site.
- Installing a grazing management system may involve a large capital expense in providing infrastructure and will also require skilled labour.
- If possible, feed concentrates and hay produced off-site away from botanically rich areas.
- Use lie-back areas when the weather is very wet and there is a high risk of poaching.

**Figure 4.10
Life cycle of two
common endo-
parasites of sheep
and cattle**

Life cycle of liver fluke

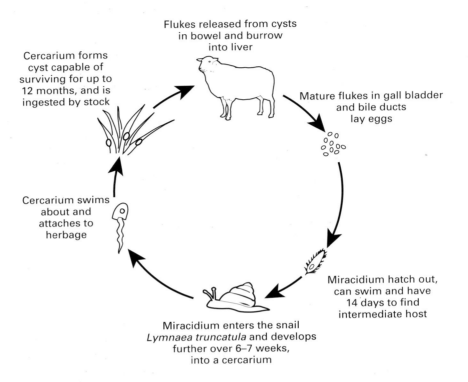

Flukes released from cysts
in bowel and burrow
into liver

Cercarium forms
cyst capable of
surviving for up to
12 months, and is
ingested by stock

Mature flukes in gall bladder
and bile ducts
lay eggs

Cercarium swims
about and
attaches to
herbage

Miracidium hatch out,
can swim and have
14 days to find
intermediate host

Miracidium enters the snail
Lymnaea truncatula and develops
further over 6–7 weeks,
into a cercarium

Life cycle of parasitic roundworm in sheep

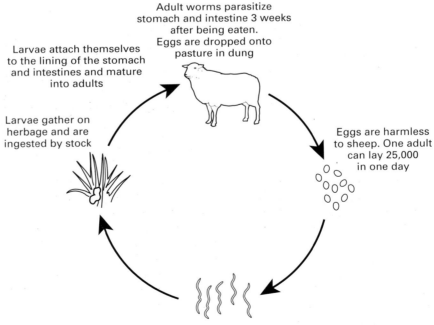

Adult worms parasitize
stomach and intestine 3 weeks
after being eaten.
Eggs are dropped onto
pasture in dung

Larvae attach themselves
to the lining of the stomach
and intestines and mature
into adults

Larvae gather on
herbage and are
ingested by stock

Eggs are harmless
to sheep. One adult
can lay 25,000
in one day

Under warm, moist conditions
the eggs develop into larvae
in 3–4 days

4.4.5 Burning

The only wet grassland plant communities associated with any tradition of burning are those on the Culm measures of Devon, which tend to become dominated by purple moor-grass. On these grasslands, burning is justified to prevent the accumulation of thick litter. When the conservation of the ecosystem is considered as a whole, burning is unacceptable. It damages many animal groups, especially less mobile invertebrates. The only conceivable case where burning might be justified is in extreme situations, to clear large volumes of coarse vegetation from neglected sites prior to the re-establishment of a more sympathetic mowing or grazing regime.

Even if a site manager is convinced that fire is the only feasible option for clearing a site, it should be borne in mind that burning is extremely unpopular. Within the winter period (1 November to 31 March) no licence is required but all burning should be carried out under the guidance of the Heather and Grass Burning Regulations. Outside this period licences from MAFF are now required and are issued only in exceptional circumstances. Burning is a skilled task and should not be tackled by the inexperienced. Burning during January and February is least damaging to conservation interest, but should only be considered as a last resort.

4.4.6 Pesticides

Herbicides

As one would expect, the blanket application of herbicides to botanically rich wet grasslands should always be avoided. It may occasionally be justifiable to use knapsack sprayers or weed-wipers to spot-treat undesirable species (especially scheduled weeds). However, it should not be forgotten that several of the species notifiable under the Weeds Act (1959), eg docks and thistles, are valuable as food-plants for invertebrate larvae, and seed-eating birds. Where spray drift or contamination from adjacent farmland is a problem buffer strips may provide a solution (Figure 4.6).

Infestation of invasive species, such as rushes, ragwort or thistles, is often brought about by inadequate management or the use of inappropriate techniques. When this occurs some form of chemical control may be the only answer, but must be accompanied by a return to sound management practices that will prevent recurrence of the problem. Wherever possible weeds should be physically controlled by topping, pulling or by grazing, eg using sheep to graze off ragwort at the rosette stage in April and May. However, there are many cases where chemical control methods are required.

Managers of nature reserves should read Simpson (1993) for further information. Care should be taken when controlling ragwort to ensure that dead and palatable plants are not available to stock, which could be poisoned.

(E. Allman & Co.)

**Plate 15
The 'Ecowipe' weed-wiper is a recently developed, environmentally friendly method of delivering herbicides to pest species, such as rushes and thistles.**

Use of narrow-spectrum herbicides will ensure accurate targeting of the weed species and minimal impact on the surrounding vegetation. The best method of delivery is to use a weed-wiper (Plate 15, Case Studies 7, 15). Conservation-friendly weed-wipers, such as English Nature's 'Ecowipe' and the 'Rotawipe' have the following advantages:

■ targeted application without ground contamination

■ no spray drift, because there are no spray droplets (very useful when operating near water-bodies or sensitive plant communities)

■ a large proportion of the herbicide is applied to the undersides of the plant, protecting it from being washed off by rain

■ treating weeds as they occur ensures that less herbicide is used (which also saves money)

■ lower volumes of water are needed which is helpful on remote sites.

There are also disadvantages and problems:

■ the technique requires a height differential between target weeds and other vegetation

■ producing this height differential may require a temporary change in grazing regime

■ application windows may be narrower than for spraying because of the above point, because application when there is a height differential may be outside the recommended period, leading to reduced efficacy

■ reduced choice of herbicides with label recommendations for wiper application

■ tractor wheels can flatten target vegetation and prevent contact with the wiper

■ herbicides are mixed at higher concentrations for wipers than for sprayers

■ development of this technique could lead to the tendency to continue to treat the symptoms rather than tackle a remedy

■ at temperatures over 20 °C herbicides containing triclopyr may volatise and be carried as fine particles to non-target vegetation.

Under the Control of Pesticides Regulations (1986) there are two herbicides that have label approval for use with weed-wipers – 'Broadshot' and 'Roundup' – and another two which have off-label approval – 'Dow Shield' (0662/92) and 'Grazon 90' (0692/95). 'Broadshot', 'Dow Shield' and

'Grazon 90' control pernicious grassland weeds, while 'Roundup' is a broader spectrum foliage-acting herbicide. Details of these products can be found in two annually published guides: the *UK Pesticide Guide* and *Pesticides 1997* (see Appendix 11 for further details).

Other herbicides can be used with weed-wipers, providing they are not expressly prohibited from use in wipers on the label. Subject to this, reduced volume application via a weed-wiper is acceptable up to 10x the recommended maximum concentration on the label. This is subject to carrying out a comprehensive COSHH assessment and compliance with paragraph 88 of the Approved Code of Practice for use of Pesticides in Agriculture and Horticulture. Paragraph 88 states that pesticides should not be applied with lower volumes of water than the label recommends for that dose if the label: prohibits reduced or low volume application; requires the use of PPE for protection against the pesticide diluted to the minimum volume rate recommended on the label for that dose; or has one of the following hazard warnings 'corrosive', 'very toxic', or 'toxic', or carries the phrase 'risk of serious damage to the eyes'.

It should be noted that the above text is only a general introduction and no liability is accepted. Operators should always read the label and comply with any off label requirements including those of FEPA, COPR and COSHH and approved Codes of Practice (Appendix 13).

It should also not be forgotten that the use of herbicides and weed-wipers on SSSIs/ASSIs and NNRs will require the consent or approval of the statutory conservation agency.

Insecticides and animal health products

Selection of insecticides and animal health products should be done with great care, since most compounds affect non-target organisms (including invertebrates, fish and livestock) as well as the target pest. A particular problem is Ivermectin, one of the main drugs used to combat internal parasites in livestock. The active ingredient is excreted in the dung, where it can limit dung-living invertebrates. It may also kill the Crustacea of drainage channels and ponds. Alternatives should be sought and are discussed in the leaflet *Chemical alternatives to treatment of cattle with Ivermectin* available from the JNCC, Peterborough (Appendix 3 for address).

If possible livestock should be treated against internal parasites such as worms on areas that can be sacrificed. If it is necessary to dip sheep and a mobile dipping unit is used, it is important to make sure the dip is disposed of safely and well away from valuable areas.

4.4.7 Soil disturbance

Methods leading to the large-scale disturbance of soil (eg rotovating or ploughing) are generally incompatible with the needs of grassland plants and animals. Digging of shallow water-bodies can benefit wetland birds, however, and is a common feature on many reserves where management for birds is a priority, but has landscape implications and should not be considered on botanically rich grassland.

Less drastic procedures, notably rolling and chain-harrowing, are used in farmed wet grasslands and may have a limited role in conservation management.

Rolling
Rolling is generally used to stimulate the tillering of grasses, flatten mole-hills and poached ground and make sites more amenable to other machinery, especially mowers. It is clearly out of the question during the bird nesting season because of damage to ground-nesting species. Rolling should also be avoided when tender plants like orchids are flowering.

Chain-harrowing
In wet grassland, the scattering of localised dung and the dispersal of dense, tangled litter can help to provide regeneration niches for grassland plants and prevents the build-up of localised areas of rank vegetation. Harrowing is less beneficial for invertebrates and should be avoided at sensitive times, eg flowering and bird nesting periods of spring and summer.

4.4.8 The zero management option

Most of the wet grassland habitats valued for their wildlife have evolved under active management, usually for farming. Neglect results in the loss of pastures and meadows and the development of vegetation dominated by taller, coarse species. Eventually succession to scrub or woodland occurs. In the absence of regular defoliation, thick litter layers build up, which prevents short-lived species from regenerating.

However, coarse, litter-rich plant communities sustain distinctive invertebrate faunas. Enhanced cover for small mammals also encourages raptors, such as hen harriers and owls. In the particular case of wet grasslands, several species of duck, as well as snipe, may be encouraged to nest in small areas of unmanaged grassland. It may therefore be desirable to leave some small areas unmanaged or to preserve long-established fragments of coarser habitat as part of an overall integrated site management programme. Botanically poor areas in existing grassland should be chosen if this option is to be used.

4.5 Grassland establishment

4.5.1 Introduction

It is sometimes desirable to diversify existing grasslands, or create new ones, for example on land taken out of arable production. There are a number of possible ways to establish wet grassland, and the choice of method will depend on geographic location, site factors and also economic considerations (Case Study 17).

Reversion of arable to wet grassland is problematic because ex-arable sites may have:

- high nutrient availability, which gives ruderal and agricultural species a competitive advantage over slower-growing perennials

- impoverished seed banks

- altered hydrological regimes.

Restoration is more likely to succeed on sites:

- which have been under cultivation for only a short time

- that are adjacent to existing semi-natural grassland which can act as a seed source, via seed rain or floodwater transport

- where appropriate hydrological conditions can be re-established.

The options are to rely on regeneration from soil seed banks and natural dispersal from other established vegetation communities or to transplant the desired species onto the site. Species may be transplanted as seeds or pot-grown plants. It will also be necessary to decide whether to alter site conditions to enhance establishment or to leave the site as it is.

4.5.2 Restoration techniques

Natural regeneration

It may not always be necessary to reintroduce species to a site artificially (Case Studies 12, 16 and 17). The soil may contain seeds derived from plants still growing on the site, but also seed from plants which previously existed there and seeds that have rained in from further afield. Although the seed of some plants remains viable for many years, viability generally declines with time. Many species characteristic of semi-natural grasslands do not form persistent seed banks. Seeds may germinate but fail to establish under cultivation and others may rot or be eaten by soil fauna. Seed reserves of diverse grassland species therefore tend to decline with time under cultivation, and soil seed banks become dominated by seeds of annual arable weeds.

Because of the increasing isolation of many sites from other areas where native species persist, natural dispersal can be slow and unreliable (Johnson and Bradshaw 1979). As a general rule, the longer a site has been cultivated or improved and the further it is from existing stands of species-rich vegetation, the more likely it is that desired species will have to be introduced deliberately.

Species reintroduction

The first problem is deciding which plant species should be introduced. In general, suitable species are:

- ecologically suited to the site's soil / hydrological conditions

- perennial

- not highly competitive or invasive

- able to germinate readily

- available from native sources.

Sowing and transplanting are expensive. Although commercial sources are available, supplies of native species are often limited. Some species may be very difficult to obtain in some years. Use of non-native seed should be avoided if possible, to prevent genetic alteration of local populations. Addresses of seed suppliers are included in Appendix 3.

Further information on all methods of plant reintroduction can be found in works by Wells *et al* (1981, 1986, 1989) and Wells (1983).

Container-grown plants, plant plugs, and turfing and habitat transplant

These techniques may be used either for the establishment of new grassland or for diversification of existing grasslands. They represent useful methods for rapid establishment or where establishment from seed may be unsuccessful, for example on more productive sites. The provenance of container-grown plants should be checked to ensure that garden varieties or foreign strains are not used.

If used for the diversification of existing swards, gaps in the vegetation should be created to allow the plant to establish without competition from other plants. The plants should not be allowed to dry out, either in the pot or after planting.

Plants for transplanting may also be purchased as plugs, usually supplied in plastic trays of up to 200. The plugs tend to be small and dry out quickly. Plants will need to be kept moist until established, so the spring and autumn are the most appropriate planting times. Holes for planting should match the size and shape of the plug. If planting into established swards, competition from established plants should be reduced by gap creation as for container-grown plants.

Turves may be transplanted to inoculate areas with established species. Turf area is perhaps not so important as depth, but will

affect the number of species transplanted. Turves should be cut to a depth of between 20 and 50 cm, depending on the rooting depth of the plants. Turf must be replaced level, and gaps between turves should be packed with subsoil. Large-scale use of turfing is constrained by the high costs involved with stripping, storage and replacement, not to mention the problems of finding a suitable donor site.

Research indicates that changes in the community composition, and abundances of individual species, can be expected owing to factors such as damage to plants during the transplant process, severing of roots by shallow turf-stripping, or differences between the donor and receptor sites in terms of environmental conditions or management (Bullock *et al* 1995). In general, communities typical of wetter sites do not transplant as successfully as those characteristic of drier sites.

Seeding
i) Site preparation

A seedbed will need to be prepared before species are introduced. Ideally, seedbeds should have a fine tilth, good drainage and aeration, and be free of plant litter and weeds. For sites with excessive weed problems, spraying with a compound such as 'Roundup' may be desirable before ploughing or rotovating and then harrowing to produce a fine seedbed (Case Study 3). Seeds should be lightly raked into the soil after sowing, and light rolling is recommended to firm the soil surface and increase contact between seeds and soil.

ii) Seed from hay bales

Hay baled from species-rich grasslands contains seeds of many grassland species. Use of seed from hay negates the need for hand collection of seed or commercial purchase, and the provenance of the seed can be guaranteed. Seed can be extracted from the hay before conventional sowing, or the hay can be shaken and spread on the ground, either being left or removed after the seed has been shed. If the hay is left on the ground, care should be taken to ensure that it does not form a thick mat since this will inhibit seed germination and seedling establishment (Case Study 17).

The species composition of hay is difficult to determine, and may vary between bales, being influenced by the species with ripe seed at the time of the hay cut.

iii) Seed mixtures

Seed mixtures are often recommended for re-establishment of grassland, and can be particularly useful in isolated situations where naturally occurring seed sources may be absent or too distant for seeds to disperse to the site. In addition, the use of seed mixtures enables the reintroduction of a far wider range of species than would be possible by other methods or natural dispersal alone (Case Studies 3, 16 and 17).

Grasses should always form the major part of seed mixtures since all semi-natural grasslands tend to have a grass cover of at least 60%. Grasses remain winter-green and protect the soil surface. In addition, grass seed is not as expensive as wild flower seed.

Seed mixtures are usually approximately 80% grasses to 20% wild flowers by weight. Indigenous strains of native species should be chosen, and in areas adjacent to habitats of conservation value, seed of local provenance should be used. All species should be regionally appropriate, ie species should not be introduced to areas where they would not normally grow.

It is not always possible to acquire seed of local provenance commercially, although many seed houses now offer seed mixtures derived from specific counties/meadows/NVC communities. Seed of British provenance may not always be available for all species and, if available, may cost more than foreign strains of the same species.

iv) Sowing rates

Sowing rates of 3–5 g/m^2 (30–50 kg/ha) are generally recommended for grassland/meadow re-establishment. Higher sowing rates will increase the ground cover of desirable species, but not the species richness. In addition, increased sowing rates tend to reduce weed cover and diversity (Stevenson *et al* 1995). However, care must be taken that high sowing rates do not produce a dense sward that would hinder establishment of other species. Higher sowing rates, thus larger quantities of seed, generally necessitate the use of commercial seed, while lower sowing rates may allow seeds of local provenance to be used.

v) Sowing times

Sowing in spring (April–May) or autumn (late August–September) is recommended. The best results are often obtained from autumn sowings as the climatic conditions are more favourable, and plants can be established over winter for rapid growth the following spring. In addition, some species will not germinate without vernalisation or scarification. Vernalisation is the requirement of repeated chilling of moist seeds before they can successfully germinate and is characteristic of species such as yellow-rattle. Seed may be artificially vernalised by mixing with wet sand and subjecting to freeze/thaw conditions for approximately a month. Scarification is a requirement of many hard coated seeds, eg species of pea and vetch, and may be achieved artificially by abrading with sandpaper. Both these processes occur naturally when seed is sown onto soil, but for spring sowings, species with these requirements may not germinate until after the first winter.

vi) Nurse or cover crops

Nurse crops may be beneficial on some sites to establish ground cover, protect soil from erosion and provide a sheltered environment for the germination and establishment of sown wild flowers. Suitable nurse crops are short-lived and not persistent. Westerwolds rye-grass is often recommended. Alternative nurse crops are cereals such as oats or barley or cornfield annuals. A sowing rate of about 1–2 g/m^2 (10–20 kg/ha) is appropriate. Follow-up management is very important to control the growth of the cover crop so it does not out-compete desirable and generally slower-growing grassland species. Cover crops are not always easy to eliminate even under repeated mowing. They may even suppress establishment of other species (Case Study 17).

vii) Seed collection

Seed harvesting guarantees seed provenance and can provide extra income for owners of donor sites (Case Study 14). It is also a cheaper way to procure seed than purchasing it from commercial suppliers.

Hand-harvesting is laborious. The variable size and scattered distribution of source populations and the variation between years and areas in the seeding times of species can make hand-harvesting prohibitively time-consuming. Information on seeding times for most British wild plants is limited, but documents such as that by Wells *et al* (1981) provide a guide to the months suitable for the seed collection of many grassland plant species.

The harvesting of seed from species-rich grasslands is potentially damaging to them (Porter 1994). Timing of hay cuts influences the rate and timing of seed deposition by sward component species. Seed-harvesters therefore usually maximise their yield and the ripeness of harvested seed by delaying hay cuts. This practice results in more seed of later-flowering species being shed than would normally be the case. Repeated later hay cuts and extra movement of machinery on the meadow will eventually alter the floral composition and may adversely affect the fauna present. Harvesting is generally only about 20% efficient, so the process can result in rapid changes in species composition. Harvesting is particularly likely to influence the persistence of species like yellow-rattle, which rely on annual

recharge of the seed bank to produce flowers in the following year.

It is important to regulate seed harvests on important wet grassland sites. Playing it safe by harvesting a quarter to a fifth of the site in any one year and rotating the section harvested is advisable. Strip harvesting is the preferred approach, one strip in five being left for seed-harvesting and the remainder being cut for hay at the normal time. The type of harvester used is also important. Suction machines harvest invertebrates as well and can damage the invertebrate fauna or alter its species composition (Kirby 1992). Recently developed brush harvesters may be a partial solution, but tests have shown that they too can be damaging to certain groups of invertebrates, for example they collect more burnet moths than do suction harvesters (Porter 1994).

viii) Slot seeding

This is a method suitable for the diversification of existing grasslands, whereby seed of desirable species is introduced into a sward. The sward should be closely mown prior to seeding, and strips of existing vegetation killed by spraying narrow bands of herbicide. Seeds are then drilled into slits within the sprayed areas (Plate 16). The theory is that seedlings arising from the introduced seed can establish before the existing grass reinvades. Spring or autumn are the most suitable times for slot seeding since the ground needs to be workable.

**Plate 16
Slot-seeding creates rows of successfully established wild flowers, which can then spread throughout the wet grassland.**

(Terry Wells)

4.5.3 Aftercare management of restored swards

More complex seed mixtures have a wide range of responses to factors such as germination, competitive ability, time taken to mature and flowering time. Some species will be short-lived and need to replace themselves by seed in order to persist in the sward. Management must take account of this, for example by not cutting during flowering and seeding periods.

During the first year, the aim of management is to establish plant cover quickly to protect the site from soil erosion, to control weed competition and to provide conditions favourable for the survival of sown wild flowers. For autumn-sown sites, species may well flower the following summer, but if sown in late autumn, winter or spring, many species will not flower until the second summer after sowing. The sward should be cut to about 8 cm when the vegetation height exceeds 20 cm to reduce competition from annual weeds, encourage tillering of grasses and prevent dense shading of establishing wild flowers (Case Study 16). All cut material should be removed. Cutting should cease as the first flowering period approaches. If annual species have been included, the sward should not be cut from April or mid-May until flowering has finished. During autumn and winter, the sward may be cut occasionally if necessary or grazed if conditions are suitable (ie not too wet).

In the case of existing grassland diversification, where container-grown plants, plant plugs or direct transplants have been used, the site will probably have been mown prior to planting. After planting, the over-topping sward should be cut at a height that avoids damage to the inserted plants. During subsequent years the sward will require cutting at least once a year, and may be grazed after cutting.

4.6 Managing associated habitats

4.6.1 Introduction

Peripheral habitats associated with wet grassland include:

- drove roads
- springs and seepages
- bushes and trees.

These boost diversity of a number of species groups and are especially important for invertebrates. Care should be taken when managing these features to ensure against damage to specialised animal communities.

4.6.2 Associated habitats

Drove roads

Droves or earth tracks are used for access to many wet grasslands. The most practical management is by cutting, with removal of mowings where possible (Newbold *et al* 1989). The timing of the cut and the number of cuts per year can be manipulated to modify effects on invertebrates and plants (see earlier section on the effects of mowing). A good compromise is probably to cut once in late summer or autumn. Leaving a strip a metre or so away from the road to revert to rough grassland (eg by not cutting for two to four years) diversifies the range of habitats provided and can benefit different birds, invertebrates (especially butterflies) and mammals such as field mice and bats.

Bare soil, cracked soil and water-filled ruts are used by a variety of invertebrates. Repairing tracks may eliminate such small features which may be scarce on a site. Unless access is becoming difficult tracks are best left alone.

Springs and seepages

Springs and seepages can occasionally be found on wet grasslands, even if only as seepages through a river wall. These are often botanically interesting but are also especially valuable for a specialised insect fauna. They need to be kept open by light grazing and trampling. Shading, for instance by tall rushes, will reduce their value.

Bushes and trees

Trees and shrubs are often found on the banks of drainage channels and bordering drove roads. In some wetlands, pollarded willows are an important landscape feature (Plate 17). On the Fens, they were traditionally used as markers for drove roads during floods. Although relatively unusual, drainage channels associated with hedge systems, such as on the Gwent Levels, support diverse invertebrate communities. Scrub is to be encouraged in discrete patches on drainage channel banks. Small thickets of bramble and blackthorn provide valuable habitat for frogs, toads and newts. Larger mammals such as foxes and badgers, as well as otters and stoats, may benefit from dense cover on slightly drier grasslands. Scrub and bramble thickets also provide suitable breeding habitat for many songbird species, including whitethroat, blackbird, song thrush and robin. Their presence may, in turn, encourage predators such as sparrowhawks. Encouraging mammalian predators is obviously not appropriate in areas important for ground-nesting birds.

Management of bushes and trees involves the use of brush-cutters and other power-tools, such as chainsaws, all of which are

(Alison Lea)

Plate 17 Pollarded willows are an important landscape feature on many wet grassland sites and require regular management.

potentially dangerous. Health and Safety precautions and regulations should be adhered to at all times (Appendix 13).

i) Tree-planting

Advice on native trees and shrubs appropriate for planting in different regions can be found in Soutar and Peterken (1989). Moisture tolerant tree species include willow and alder, but a number of other species are also suitable. Species like oak and ash have extensive root systems which bind drainage channel banks and can provide habitat for otters. Downy birch, blackthorn, dogwood, field maple, hawthorn, hazel, holly and rowan are all found on drainage channel and/or river banks. Mature trees of whatever species provide bat roosts and bird nesting sites. The English black poplar is one species that has become particularly scarce. Black poplars require closely adjacent male and female plants to reproduce and will only germinate successfully in fresh bare mud where there is no competition from other seedlings. They therefore have very exacting requirements, but reintroduction schemes have met with some success and trees can be propagated vegetatively (Purseglove 1988).

Tree-planting in field corners, where sizeable patches of habitat can develop, is preferable to the planting of trees in narrow strips. Fencing helps a shrubby layer to develop and enhances the wildlife value of woodland. Blackthorn will sucker to form a dense stand if protected from grazing and can provide habitat for blackcaps and nightingales. In many areas, fencing alone will allow regeneration from existing woodland remnants.

Where trees are to be planted along drainage channel banks, it is better to choose the northern bank as this minimises light restriction to the water in drainage channels. Planting of trees and shrubs to overhang the confluence of drainage channels, or feeder streams with a river, is also particularly valuable, enabling birds and other animals to travel undisturbed (Purseglove 1988).

Care should be taken when tree-planting to avoid areas used by breeding waders, as trees are used as vantage points by nest predators, such as carrion crows.

ii) Coppicing

Coppicing was traditionally used to control the size of trees growing on the banks of drainage channels. Outgrown coppice in the form of spreading, multi-stemmed trees, can restrict access and may cause excessive shading of drainage channels. Rotational coppicing allows sufficient cover to be retained for invertebrates and birds like moorhens (which use low branches and dense shrubs for cover and protection from predators), while also leaving some stretches relatively unshaded. Trunks should be cut on the slant so that the cut area sheds rainwater. Regeneration occurs from the base or stool. Where access is important, singling the stems may be advisable to allow a mature standard to develop. The resulting tree can be pollarded or re-coppiced at a later date (Newbold *et al* 1989).

iii) Pollarding

Pollarding of crack and white willows was traditionally carried out to control the size of trees and rejuvenate them. At the same time the process provides stakes or poles for hammering into river or drainage channel banks as a fast-growing and cheap source of new trees (Purseglove 1988). Pollarding is an excellent way of retaining local genetic strains and preserving regional biodiversity. It is best carried out in winter and the young poles should be protected from damage by livestock until they are well established. Poles should be about 20 cm in diameter, 3 m long and cut at an oblique angle to shed rain water and prevent rotting. They should be driven in to a depth of about 1 m. A height of at least 2 m is required if machinery or livestock are to have access to the bank base for management. Shorter pollards may be acceptable elsewhere (Newbold *et al* 1989).

iv) Scrub control

On sites with very low grazing densities, or with histories of neglect, invasion by scrub (especially willow) is an undesirable possibility. Scrub will have to be winched out or cut and the stumps treated to prevent regrowth (Case Study 1).

4.7 Managing for multiple objectives

4.7.1 Introduction

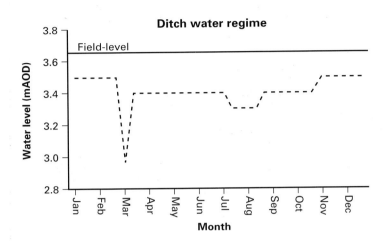

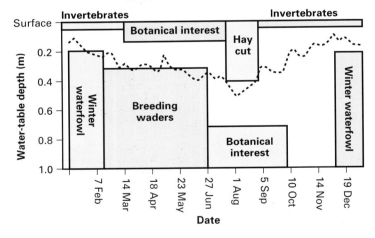

Figure 4.11 Management of water levels to achieve multiple objectives (after Spoor *et al* 1996)

On most sites, there will be a range of management objectives. Careful prioritisation of nature conservation objectives should minimise potential conflicts. Figure 4.11 shows that for a peat site, with a drainage channel spacing of 30 m, it is possible to manage water levels to meet the varying requirements of different species. The white zone in the lower graph represents the range of acceptable water-table levels for different wetland species groups. This approach also shows that farming interests can be effectively integrated into the management scenario. The regime of drainage channel water levels shown in Figure 4.11 necessitates a rapid draw-down of water levels in spring to prevent excess surface water which could damage botanical interest. Raising drainage channel levels soon afterwards enables the soil to be kept moist for breeding wader interest. A decline in water levels during the summer period enables agricultural operations, such as hay cutting, to be carried out. Tables 4.14, 4.15 and 4.16 are intended to give some indication of potential conflicts and to assist in reaching a workable compromise.

Table 4.14: Effects of grazing on wet grassland flora and fauna

Operation	Plants/Vegetation	Invertebrates	Breeding waders and wildfowl	Wintering wildfowl
Grazing	Promotes structural diversity of vegetation and species able to maintain themselves without seeding.	Structurally diverse swards provide more niches for invertebrates.	Many breeding birds prefer to nest in tussocky vegetation, which can result from grazing.	Feeding benefit during shallow floods as tussocks protruding above water level give sanctuary to invertebrates and trap floating seeds.
Trampling	Important for creation of regeneration niches, particularly in the spring and autumn. Too much can damage plants.	Trampling can reduce populations directly. Indirectly it can be beneficial, by creating patches of bare ground important for basking and courtship.	Damages nests. Risk highest for breeding waders. Species most at risk benefit from a delayed start to the grazing season Do not exceed 2 animals per ha until mid-July to minimise risk.	
Dunging	Sporadic dunging enhances species and structural diversity. Latrine areas can become dominated by rank vegetation, eg nettles.	Can boost invertebrate biomass.	Can obliterate nests (particularly cow pats). Dung invertebrates are an important food source for waders such as lapwing.	Can be beneficial by boosting invertebrate biomass.
No grazing (neglect)	Results in domination by less palatable species like canary-grass, common couch and reed sweet-grass. Eventually leads to loss of habitat via scrub encroachment.	Promotes many invertebrates in the short/ medium term. Results in loss of species needing short swards and bare ground.	Creates poor conditions for breeding waders, apart from snipe.	Rank growth and thick litter layer deters grazers, such as wigeon.
Grazing animal: **Sheep**	Produce relatively short, even sward. Encourage low-growing perennial species.	Generally poorer than cattle for invertebrate interest.	Few waders prefer short, even swards, except lapwing.	Produces short sward suitable for grazing by geese and wigeon.
Cattle	Control rank vegetation and prevent domination by competitive species. Produce a more tussocky sward.	Fewer animals required to achieve same grazing pressure, so less trampling. Tussocky swards are better for invertebrates than close-cropped sheep-grazed turf. Bare, poached patches provide valuable niches.	Fewer animals required to achieve same grazing pressure, so trampling risk lower. However, cattle will eat or lick eggs and their dung can obliterate nests.	Useful to bring rank swards down to a level at which they can be grazed by birds.
Grazing regime: **Rotational**	Encourages grazing tolerant species.	Can benefit many invertebrates, particularly butterflies and other more mobile species.	Usually associated with higher stock numbers, resulting in more trampling damage to breeding birds. Frequent disturbance is damaging.	Can produce suitable swards for winter grazing birds.
Year-round (low density)	Maintains a varied structure and a diverse sward, so long as stocking densities are low.	Compatible with invertebrate conservation so long as densities are very low.	Trampling damage will occur during the breeding season.	Swards suitable for grazing are maintained, but stock compete for herbage in the winter.

cont'd

Table 4.14: continued

Operation	Plants/Vegetation	Invertebrates	Breeding waders and wildfowl	Wintering wildfowl
Seasonal	See above for seasonal effects. Can be adjusted to allow certain species to flower and set seed.	Seasonal grazing generally the preferred option for invertebrates. Scope for avoidance of key life-stages. See above for seasonal effects.	See above for seasonal effects. Permits avoidance of key periods (nesting).	See above for seasonal effects. Allows avoidance of competition for herbage.
Late hay crop with aftermath grazing	Provides an opportunity for flowering/fruiting. Creates bare soil for regeneration. Variable defoliation creates heterogeneous sward.	Tall swards in spring/early summer benefit some species. Dung for dung-eaters but loss of bare soil and short sward areas in early part of season is detrimental. Catastrophic loss of vegetation in peak growing season as larvae reach maturity.	Ground-nesting birds can breed without disturbance and risk of trampling.	Can produce suitable swards for winter grazing birds.

4.7.2 Management for breeding waders and wintering wildfowl – an example

The following suggested optimum management prescription for breeding waders and wintering waterfowl is an example of the integration of management for a target species group, without affecting other interests – in this case herb-rich grassland (Ausden 1996):

Agricultural operations

■ No mechanical operations to be carried out between 31 March and 1 July.
Rationale: prevents wader and other ground-nesting birds' eggs and nests being destroyed.

■ Apply no inorganic fertiliser. Do not increase current application levels of organic manure, which should not exceed 25 t/ha/year. Do not apply slurry.
Rationale: application of fertiliser will tend to increase grass growth, thereby decreasing suitability for waders that prefer short swards. More grass will also allow, or require, a higher grazing density, increasing the risk of trampling.

Grazing

■ Do not graze between 1 April and 31 May. Between 1 June and 30 June grazing density should not exceed one bovine animal per 0.75 ha. Avoid grazing with sheep.
Rationale: prevents trampling of young and nests. Low-intensity grazing in the latter part of the breeding season is required to prevent the sward from becoming too tall. Cattle are preferred as they produce structural variety and trample fewer nests per quantity of vegetation eaten.

Surface water

On agriculturally improved grassland and grasslands of low botanical conservation interest (MG6, MG7, MG9, MG10, MG11 and MG13) little damage occurs when such areas are reflooded, the following prescriptions apply:

■ 1 December to 31 March. Maintain shallow (<20 cm) surface water over 30–60% of the site (Plate 18).
Rationale: surface water will attract

Table 4.15: Effects of fertiliser addition and mowing on wet grassland flora and fauna

Operation	Plants/Vegetation	Invertebrates	Breeding waders and wildfowl	Wintering wildfowl
Addition of fertiliser	Damages botanical interest. Reduces diversity. Results in domination by few, competitive species. Light dressings of FYM (single dressing <20 t/ha every 3–5 years) acceptable where nutrient losses are high.	Reductions in botanical diversity result in fewer niches for invertebrates. Invertebrate biomass of a few species may go up.	Fertilised areas are more productive earlier in the growing season. Earlier cutting and/or heavier grazing are required, which is damaging to nesting birds.	Wildfowl species such as geese and wigeon may benefit from increased biomass. Use of fertilised areas by geese 42% higher than unfertilised areas (Owen 1983).
Mowing (cuttings must be removed)	Favours tall, palatable wild flowers, grasses with poor tillering capacity and species that set seed early in the year (before sufficient grass to harvest).	Sudden/catastrophic changes in sward structure can cause invertebrate populations to plummet. Cutting generally reduces invertebrate diversity.	Time of mowing is critical for nesting birds, ie no cutting before 15 July.	Mowing in late summer/autumn can be useful to create a sward suitable for grazing wildfowl.
Early mowing	Prevents flowering and seed setting for earlier-flowering species.	Relatively un-disruptive management regime may benefit some invertebrates. However, stem and seed-head feeders will be unable to complete their life-cycles.	Damaging for nesting birds and for chicks still in vegetation when mowing commences. Delay mowing to avoid damage. Delay longer on wetter sites, where species like snipe may re-lay and have eggs/chicks on nests as late as July/August.	Grazing likely to be necessary to reduce the aftermath (eg 50–80 LSU days/ha/yr).
Late mowing	Promotes taller-growing species (meadow specialists). Forage quality declines, particularly if the first cut is delayed beyond the end of June.	Allows seed-head and stem feeders to complete their life-cycles.	May still damage late-nesting birds or birds which have re-laid.	Tends to result in shorter swards in the autumn/winter which are suitable for grazing by geese.
Frequent mowing	Maintains grasses in a vegetative state and inhibits flowering. Reduces diversity.	Disruptive and damaging for invertebrates.	Very damaging for nesting birds and chicks.	May reduce invertebrate and seed availability, but can create suitable swards for grazing birds.
Topping (eg for control of invasive plants in July–September or for sward height reduction where grazing is insufficient)	Controls ingress of thistles, ragwort and rushes and can help to maintain a species-rich sward. However, frequent topping tends to reduce diversity.	Frequent/regular topping produces a more uniform sward structure, reducing the niches available for invertebrates. Beetle diversity has been shown to decline with mowing.	Removal of stalky material helps to give a clear vista for species such as lapwing and black-tailed godwit. Shorter swards are preferred by lapwing, black-tailed godwit and redshank.	Helps to promote more palatable feed grasses. Very short swards are preferred by the wigeon.

cont'd

Table 4.16: Seasonal effects of flooding on wet grassland flora and fauna

Operation	Plants/Vegetation	Invertebrates	Breeding waders and wildfowl	Wintering wildfowl
Early spring (March)	Before temperatures rise and the growing season commences, most species can tolerate early spring flooding. Maintains botanical diversity and suppresses grass growth.	Beneficial for many aquatic species and those that require seasonal pools that dry later in the spring.	Provides damp soil and high water-table through April and May.	Flooded areas provide roosting and feeding sites.
Late spring (April/May)	Flooding/waterlogging not tolerated for extended periods by many grasses (ie > 4–5 days).	Later flooding becomes increasingly damaging to active stages of terrestrial species that have survived winter flooding.	Provides brood-rearing habitat.	
Summer	Prolonged flooding during this period will be tolerated by only swamp communities. Grasslands subjected to flooding at this time will revert to swamp vegetation. Prevents grassland management.	Summer flooding is particularly damaging to terrestrial species and can cause stranding of aquatic species, when waters subside.	Widespread summer flooding is unusual and prevents waders from nesting. This often occurs at the Ouse Washes (Case Study 2).	
Autumn		Flooding in late autumn (October) may prevent autumn flying species from egg-laying on damp ditch margins. Adult beetles which are still active will not have found winter refuges and may drown.		
Winter	Flooding/waterlogging tolerated by many grasses, sedges, and wild flowers.	Most invertebrates inactive. Prolonged winter flooding can kill invertebrates in soil/litter layer, that are not adapted to continuous submersion, eg some worm species. Can be a problem on newly restored sites if large areas of previously dry grassland are flooded for lengthy periods.		Shallow winter flooding provides feeding and roosting conditions. Flooding provides food by releasing seeds trapped in vegetation and pushing invertebrates from their winter refuges.

(G Downey, RSPB)

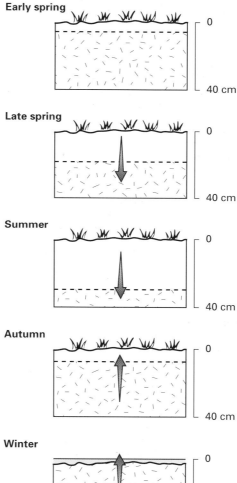

(C H Gomersall, RSPB)

Plate 18 (far left) During the winter, wildfowl and waders, such as lapwing, require shallow water over 30–60% of the site.

Plate 19 (left) During the spring, gradually decreasing the area of shallow water until 20% cover is attained at the end of April, provides ideal conditions for breeding waders, such as redshank.

wintering wildfowl and roosting waders and will usually result in the development of MG13 grassland favoured by feeding wigeons and Bewick's swans. MG13 also produces a short open sward favoured by breeding lapwings. Unflooded areas provide areas for waders to feed on soil invertebrates and reduce the risk of the total loss of any existing wildlife to flooding.

■ 1 April to 30 April. Allow the area of shallow water on fields to decrease to 20% of the site by the end of this period (Plate 19).
Rationale: concentrates aquatic invertebrates into small pools that are suitable feeding areas for broods of waders and ducks.

■ 1 May to 30 June. Maintain areas of shallow flooding on fields so that they still cover about 10% of the site by the end of June.
Rationale: provides lapwings with muddy margins at a time when sward height is increasingly unsuitable. Surface waters present will contain high biomasses of non-biting midge larvae and other aquatic invertebrates, and are good feeding locations for wader broods.

On agriculturally unimproved grasslands and mires of existing high botanical conservation interest (MG4, MG8, M22, M23 and M24) the following prescription applies:

■ Follow the above winter flooding regime but ensure that surface water does not lie on fields after 1 April (Figure 4.12).
Rationale: whilst it may be advantageous for breeding birds to maintain areas of

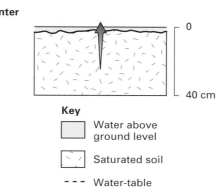

Early spring

0

40 cm

Late spring

0

40 cm

Summer

0

40 cm

Autumn

0

40 cm

Winter

0

40 cm

Key

☐ Water above ground level

☐ Saturated soil

- - - Water-table

Figure 4.12 An annual water management regime, favoured by breeding waders and wildfowl and wintering waterfowl, that does not harm areas of high botanical interest

131

surface water throughout the spring and early summer, this is likely to damage the existing botanical interest of unimproved grassland and mires.

Drainage channel water levels

■ On silt and clay soils these should be maintained within 45 cm of mean field level between 1 April and 15 June.
Rationale: drainage channel water levels on silts and clays have little influence over field water-table height and therefore have little effect on the softness of the upper soil. Drainage channel levels should be kept as high as possible, however, to maintain surface flooding via foot drains and to provide habitat for drainage channel plants and animals (especially wildfowl).

■ On peat soils drainage channel water levels should be maintained within 20 cm of mean field level between 1 April and 15 June.
Rationale: maintaining high drainage channel water levels ensures high field water-table and soft upper soil on peat soils, allowing snipe to feed.

Creation of new drainage channels and foot drains

■ On clay and silt soils the creation of foot drains should be encouraged.
Rationale: foot drains greatly facilitate maintenance of shallow surface flooding on clay sites.

■ On peat sites the distance between drainage channels should be reduced to about 20 m.
Rationale: increases the proportion of the field over which it is possible to maintain high field water levels when maintaining high drainage channel water levels.

Key references

Ausden, M and Treweek, J (1995) 'Grassland' In: W J Sutherland and D A Hill (Eds) (1995) *Managing Habitats for Conservation*, pp 197-229. Cambridge University Press, Cambridge.

Newbold, C, Honnor, J and Buckley, K (1989) *Nature conservation and the management of drainage channels*. The Association of Drainage Authorities and the Nature Conservancy Council, Peterborough.

Nix, J (1996) *Farm Management Pocketbook. Twenty-sixth Edition*. Farm Business Unit, School of Rural Economics, Wye College, London.

Perry, J and Vanderklein, E (1996) *Water Quality Management of a Natural Resource*. Blackwell Science, Oxford.

Simpson, N A (1993) *A summary review of information on the autecology and control of six grassland weed species*. English Nature Research Report No. 44. English Nature, Peterborough.

Wells, T C E, Cox, R and Frost, A (1989) The establishment and management of wildflower meadows. *Focus on Nature Conservation*, No. 21. Nature Conservancy Council, Peterborough.

Part 5
SURVEY AND MONITORING OF FLORA AND FAUNA OF WET GRASSLAND

Contents

5.1 Introduction

Surveying and monitoring form an essential part of conservation management. Without them, the effectiveness of management cannot be assessed. Survey and monitoring can be time-consuming and expensive, so requirements should be built into management planning from the outset (section 2.2.7) and the necessary resources allocated. The importance of monitoring systems is emphasised in the new management plan guidelines adopted for CMS (Alexander 1996, Appendix 5).

Surveys essentially produce a `snapshot' of the conditions which prevailed at the time of the study. A series of surveys can be used to build up an understanding of temporal trends and to establish baselines for key organisms and groups so that subsequent changes can be monitored. Monitoring is an essential part of management assessment. Feedback from monitoring programmes (positive or negative) can be used to adjust management to ensure that objectives are met.

Monitoring is important because it can be used to:

■ assess the effectiveness of site management, schemes, policy and legislation

■ provide an early warning system if things are going wrong, allowing management to be modified where appropriate (Case Study 15).

To design a monitoring system, it will be necessary to answer the following questions (after Hellawell 1991):

■ What are the objectives of the monitoring system?

■ What is to be monitored? The selection of key indicator species or groups and physical parameters to measure is not easy. Few species are known well enough. The NVC system has however provided tried and tested plant groupings that can be used for monitoring purposes (Case Study 15, section 5.2.1).

■ What is the standard or baseline to be? This can only be provided by surveillance (ie a series of surveys).

■ What methodology should be employed? A number of methodologies are discussed below.

5.2 Survey and monitoring of vegetation

Surveying and monitoring may be required for either grassland or drainage channel plant communities within a wet grassland site. Reference to a standard textbook on ecological methods (eg Moore and Chapman 1986), will supply details of the more basic techniques, including those listed in Table 5.1.

Table 5.1: Monitoring methods for vegetation

Information required on:	Technique	Disadvantages	Advantages
Vegetation composition	Line intercept	Time consuming, requires large sample.	Minimal equipment, can monitor size of gaps.
	Point count	Time consuming, requires large sample.	Minimal equipment, can monitor size of gaps.
	Quadrats	Time consuming, requires large sample.	Minimal equipment.
	Cover maps	Only identifies general vegetation types.	Quick, especially if aerial photos or base maps exist.
	Aerial photos	Only identifies general vegetation types.	Accurate for establishing continuous measure of change.
	LANDSAT	Expensive unless imagery borrowed (may require special equipment).	Accurate for establishing continuous measure of change.
	Photo stations	Only identifies gross changes.	Permanent record of major change. Cheap.
Plant density	Quadrat	Time consuming, requires large sample.	Minimal equipment.
(applied to individual species)	By eye	Results vary between individual recorders.	Quick – minimal equipment.

Source: Frederickson and Reid (1988)

5.2.1 Grassland vegetation

Wet grassland vegetation is commonly monitored in relation to water levels and grazing pressure (all aspects which need to be monitored). In this way, if changes are negative, it should be possible to trigger a change in management (Case Study 15).

The standard way to monitor grassland vegetation is by recording plant cover using a quadrat – a square frame inside which the percentage cover or presence of each plant species is recorded:

- Monitoring points are laid out in a regular grid or transect, with each position accurately mapped (allowing them to be relocated). This ensures adequate coverage of hydrological, micro-topographic and floristic variation within the site.

- At each position, all species are recorded. Simple presence/absence information may be sufficient, provided the number of samples is high.

135

- Alternatively, the recorder may use visual assessment of percentage cover (or the DOMIN scale) or, where time allows, the use of a sub-divided quadrat to provide frequency information. Such cover/abundance estimates supplement the distribution data.

Quadrat analysis forms the basis of the NVC survey technique and is a valuable method of recording community change. The NVC is a comprehensive framework for classifying vegetation in the UK. It enables plant quadrat data collected in the field to be matched against a definitive hierarchical classification using a key or computer software package (such as MATCH – see Case Study 15), by fitting samples to a range of phytosociological groups or classes (eg mesotrophic grassland, swamp or mire communities). Field sampling requires the collection of 5 quadrats from a representative area. The frequency of plants (ie the number of

quadrats each occurs in), is recorded as a roman numeral (I–V). The abundance (ie how much of the plant is represented in each quadrat) is calculated on a percentage basis and converted to the DOMIN scale where:

Cover of 91–100% is recorded as DOMIN 10
76–90% ... 9
51–75% ... 8
34–50% ... 7
26–33% ... 6
11–25% ... 5
4–10% ... 4

< 4% { with many individuals 3
with several individuals 2
with few individuals 1

The percentage cover range of each plant (in terms of DOMIN score) is then recorded on a table next to the frequency score (Table 5.2).

Table 5.2: An example of an NVC floristic table – MG13 creeping bent and marsh foxtail inundation grassland (Rodwell 1992). Species occurring with an overall frequency of IV or V are known as community constants. Survey results should be presented in this way to allow keying out of community.

Creeping bent	V	(3–9)	Meadow foxtail	I	(2)
Marsh foxtail	V	(3–9)	Meadow fescue	I	(1)
Creeping buttercup	II	(2–9)	Spear-leaved orache	I	(1)
Yorkshire-fog	II	(2–5)	Cock's-foot	I	(2)
Rough meadow-grass	II	(2–7)	Marsh-marigold	I	(3)
Soft-rush	II	(2–5)	Tufted hair-grass	I	(5)
Floating sweet-grass	II	(1–5)	Oval sedge	I	(5)
Small sweet-grass	I	(3–7)	Autumn hawkbit	I	(1)
Plicate sweet-grass	I	(5–8)	Sharp-flowered rush	I	(3)
Toad rush	I	(2–4)	Carnation sedge	I	(3)
Jointed rush	I	(3–5)	Soft-brome	I	(2)
Red fescue	I	(3–4)	Creeping thistle	I	(2)
Lesser spearwort	I	(2–3)	Bog stitchwort	I	(2)
Curled dock	I	(1–3)	Tubular water-dropwort	I	(4)
Sweet vernal grass	I	(1–3)	Water forget-me-not	I	(3)
Water mint	I	(2)	Marsh valerian	I	(1)
Water-pepper	I	(2–4)	*Ceratodon purpureus*	I	(2)
Marsh arrowgrass	I	(1–5)	Blinks	I	(2)
Sea arrowgrass	I	(2–3)	*Brachythecium rutabulum*	I	(5)
Saltmarsh rush	I	(3)	Greater chickweed	I	(1)
Celery-leaved buttercup	I	(3)	Clustered dock	I	(1)
Silverweed	I	(2–5)	**Number of samples**	**17**	
Annual meadow-grass	I	(2)	**Number of species/sample**	**8**	**(3–15)**

5.2.2 Drainage channel vegetation

A standard technique for monitoring ditch vegetation uses this methodology:

■ Measure out a 20-m length of ditch, and list all species rooted in submerged substrate. Their abundance may be assessed in terms of visual estimates of percentage cover and/or percentage frequency within a regular grid of cells. Species abundance should be separately assessed for the submerged, floating and emergent components of the vegetation – one species may contribute to two or all components.

■ Over the same 20-m length, record the presence of species rooted on the adjacent channel banks, noting which bank they occur on. These data may again be supplemented by either visual estimates of percentage cover, or percentage frequency within a grid cell.

■ Measure channel width, maximum depth, freeboard (both banks), bank width and slope angle. Record evidence of management, supplemented with data from landowner and appropriate water management agency.

■ At each subsequent monitoring date, re-record all data categories above.

5.2.3 Aquatic flora – as indicators of water quality

Because aquatic plant communities and species are sensitive to water quality (section 3.3.3) they can be used to determine the general water chemistry of a water-body, ie availability of phosphate and nitrate and pH – Table 5.3 (Palmer *et al* 1992). Table 5.4 lists some of the more characteristic plants which may be found in slow-flowing wetland systems, each is assigned a number from 1–10 according to their tolerance/preference for enriched or clean water, this is known as the Species Trophic Rank (STR). Depending on the Species Cover Value (SCV) of listed taxa within a 100-m stretch of drainage channel (recorded on a nine-point scale), a Mean Trophic Rank (MTR) can be assigned and used to monitor water quality.

A 100-m length of drainage channel is surveyed once or twice a year between June and September. Using the standard list of species, SCVs are estimated on a nine-point scale: 1 = <0.1%, 2 = 0.1–1.0%, 3 = 1.1–2.5%, 4 = 2.6–5.0%, 5 = 5.1–10.0%, 6 = 10.1–25.0%, 7 = 25.1–50.0%, 8 = 50.1–75.0%, 9 = >75.1%.

Two examples are given below showing how to calculate the scores. The examples have the same species present, but in different proportions. Take the SCVs recorded during the survey and calculate the Cover Value Score (CVS) by multiplying the STR by the SCV. CVSs for the whole sample are summed, and divided by the sum of the SCVs to give a MTR (which is multiplied by 10).

Example 1

Species	STR	SCV	CVS
Enteromorpha	1	1	1
Cladophora	1	1	1
Amblystegium riparium	1	1	1
Common duckweed	4	7	28
Fennel pondweed	1	1	1
Horned pondweed	2	1	2
Yellow water-lily	3	1	3
River water-crowfoot	7	7	49
TOTAL		20	86

MTR = sum of CVSs ÷ sum of SCVs x 10 or (86 ÷ 20) x 10 = 43

Example 2

Species	STR	SCV	CVS
Enteromorpha	1	7	7
Cladophora	1	7	7
Amblystegium riparium	1	1	1
Common duckweed	4	1	4
Fennel pondweed	1	7	7
Horned pondweed	2	7	14
Yellow water-lily	3	7	21
River water-crowfoot	7	1	7
TOTAL		38	68

MTR = sum of CVSs ÷ sum of SCVs x 10 or (68 ÷ 38) x 10 = 17.9

Table 5.3: Plants used as indicators of water quality

Signs of good water quality in drainage channels and open water are:

- a mixture of floating, emergent and submerged plants

- a range of pondweed species, especially fine-leaved species (other than fennel pondweed)

- a lack of algal dominance

- bladderworts, water-violet and white water-lily in lowland drainage channels and ponds

- no single macrophyte species thriving at the expense of other species

- a mixture of low and medium scoring trophic species in lowland habitats, where this is not as a result of acidification (see Table 5.4).

Signs of poor water quality in drainage channels and open water are:

- monocultures or massive dominance of single species

- abundant fennel pondweed or horned pondweed in the absence of other fine-leaved pondweeds or crowfoot

- low species numbers and lack of diversity of plant forms, such as emergents, broad and narrow-leaved submergents, and so on

- abundant filamentous green algae

- poor water clarity due to turbidity caused by phytoplankton.

Signs of salt water intrusion:

- a loss of variety of plants and the presence of brackish water-crowfoot and soft hornwort (Section 3.3.3, Table 3.8). Such communities are intrinsically important in their own right.

Table 5.4: Plants as indicators of water quality

Calcareous	Neutral	Acid	Trophic rank	Species	Calcareous	Neutral	Acid	Trophic rank	Species
				Algae					**Higher plants (macrophytes)**
	■		2	*Vaucheria* sp.		■		8	Lesser water-plantain
■			1	*Enteromorpha* sp.	■			5	Flowering-rush
■			3	*Hydrodictyum reticulatum*	■			5	Whorl-grass
■			1	*Cladophora* agg.		■		6	Common spike-rush
				Bryophytes		■		5	Canadian waterweed
	■		1	*Amblystegium riparium*		■		3	Nuttall's waterweed
		■	10	Sphagnum		■		3	Reed sweet-grass
					■			3	Opposite-leaved pondweed
				Higher plants (macrophytes)		■		6	Frogbit
		■	9	Lesser marshwort			■	10	Bulbous rush
	■		4	Fool's water-cress	■			7	Blunt-flowered rush
■			5	Lesser water-parsnip					
	■		9	Pedunculate water-starwort		■		2	Fat duckweed
■			5	Blunt-fruited water-starwort		■		4	Common duckweed
■			2	Rigid hornwort	■			2	Greater duckweed
■			4	Soft hornwort			■	9	Floating water-plantain
■			4	Mare's-tail					
■			6	Water-violet	■			5	Sharp-leaved pondweed
	■		9	Bogbean		■		7	Red pondweed
						■		4	Small pondweed
		■	8	Alternate water-milfoil	■			7	Fen pondweed
■			3	Spiked water-milfoil	■⁵	■⁴		5 / 4	Grass-wrack pondweed
■			3	Whorled water-milfoil		■		3	Curled pondweed
	■		3	Yellow water-lily		■		3	Flat-stalked pondweed
	■		6	White water-lily		■		7	Various-leaved pondweed
	■		2	Fringed water-lily		■		3	Shining pondweed
■			5	Water-cress					
■			5	Fine-leaved water-dropwort		■		5	Broad-leaved pondweed
■			5	River water-dropwort				2	Loddon pondweed
■			9	Marsh cinquefoil		■		1	Fennel pondweed
						■		4	Perfoliate pondweed
	■		5	Common water-crowfoot			■	10	Bog pondweed
■			5	Stream water-crowfoot (ssp) *pseudofluitans*	■	■		6	Long-stalked pondweed
	■		6	Stream water-crowfoot (ssp) *penicillatus*		■		4	Lesser pondweed
■			4	Fan-leaved water-crowfoot		■		5	Blunt-leaved pondweed
		■	7	Lesser spearwort		■		2	Hairlike pondweed
■			7	River water-crowfoot					
	■		6	Ivy-leaved crowfoot		■		3	Arrowhead
	■		8	Round-leaved crowfoot			■	10	Floating club-rush
	■		4	Pond water-crowfoot				3	Common club-rush
■			6	Thread-leaved water-crowfoot				3	Sea club-rush
	■		2	Celery-leaved buttercup		■		3	Unbranched bur-reed
								3	Branched bur-reed
	■		3	Great yellow-cress		■		3	Water-soldier
■			4	Blue water-speedwell				2	Bulrush
	■		5	Pink water-speedwell				2	Lesser bulrush
		■	7	Marsh speedwell	■			6	Rootless duckweed
	■		2	Sweet-flag	■			2	Horned pondweed
			3	Water-plantain					
			3	Narrow-leaved water-plantain					

5.3 Surveying and monitoring invertebrates

Table 5.5: Monitoring methods for invertebrates

Group	Methods	Reference
Dragonflies	transect walk	Brooks (1993), Moore and Corbet (1990)
Butterflies	transect walk	Pollard and Yates (1993)
Moths	light trapping	Dickson (1985)
Aquatic assemblages	pond netting; ten separate samples from drainage channels in comparable stages of succession; standardise samples as suggested in text; take samples from mid-April to end of May or mid-September to end of October.	Pond Action (1994)
Ground-dwelling assemblages	pitfall trapping; ten traps spaced at *c.* 2 m intervals in a line at each location, and treat each trap as a separate replicate unit; set traps for at least one two-week period during May to mid-June or September to October; use the same period(s) each year.	Sheppard (1991)
Vegetation-dwelling assemblages	water trapping, interception trapping; use at least five, and preferably ten traps at each location, treat each as a separate replicate unit; set traps for at least one two-week period from early June – end July; use the same period(s)	Sheppard (1991)

Invertebrates can be good indicators of environmental conditions because they have short life-cycles and their populations respond rapidly to environmental changes. Many aquatic species are sensitive to water quality. There are, however, problems with monitoring invertebrates. Their populations can fluctuate wildly and, except for butterflies, there is no national framework against which to compare these fluctuations – are they the result of local changes in management or are they national trends caused by climate or other wide-ranging factors? To obtain statistically useful results requires a large number of samples, which can make expensive monitoring.

There are no standard methods for invertebrate survey and monitoring. Table 5.5 lists the main methods used.

5.3.1 Aquatic invertebrates

The most species-rich groups in drainage channels are water beetles, water bugs and snails. Surveys should include these three groups as a minimum requirement. Other groups that are worth including, because they contain uncommon species, are larger crustacea in brackish marshes, and leaches and some flies whose larvae are easily identified (soldierflies and meniscus midges).

Pond netting is the most effective method to sample drainage channel species. It will not give quantitative results but sampling units can be standardised to allow comparison between similar sites. Using a set number of sweeps is not recommended because, firstly, the structure of the vegetation can radically alter the catch quite independently of the numbers of animals present so untargeted sweeping will not take account of local variation in the vegetation and, secondly, not all micro-habitats will be investigated.

The following methods of standardising catches have been used:

- National Pond Survey method (Pond Action 1994) for still water.
  - divide the water-body into micro-habitats which appear distinctively different.
  - apportion a 3-minute sampling period evenly among the micro-habitats; if one micro-habitat covers a large area, subdivide the area into smaller blocks to ensure a wide coverage of the area.
  - sample as much as possible of each micro-habitat with the net actually being used in the water for the time allotted.
  - time the period using a stop watch – guessing the time does not work.
  - supplementary collecting is recommended (see below).
  - lump the sub-samples and preserve for sorting in the laboratory.

- As above but allot the time spent sampling each micro-habitat according to its approximate area. The disadvantage of this approach is that a lot of time can be apportioned to large but species-poor micro-habitats, for example large beds of submerged plants, at the expense of those that are small but species-rich, such as areas of marginal emergents.

- Timed search. Rather than time the period that the net is being used, time the period spent at a site. This method is appropriate if the catch is sorted on the bankside. A period of between 30–45 minutes has been found to be adequate to collect the bulk of species in drainage channels, and in this period, about 6–8 net-hauls can be taken and searched. This number of hauls usually takes about 3 minutes so the results will be similar to those obtained using the National Pond Survey method. Supplementary collecting is recommended (see below).

- Search until no new species are recorded. This method works only for experienced collectors who can identify most species in the field. It fails when the surveyor tires and forgets what has already been recorded. A recording form is essential.

- Supplementary collecting. If the objective of the survey is to record as many species as possible from a site, further collecting is recommended using a tea strainer or kitchen sieve to probe vegetation at the water margins, searching by eye for amphibious species at the wet margins, and, using the pond net, taking very vigorous long sweeps to collect large, fast-swimming beetles that often escape gentle netting.

In still water, the most effective way to catch as wide a range of species as possible is to net vigorously to dislodge animals from the vegetation and banks, using a mixture of short thrusting strokes and occasional long sweeps to cover all micro-habitats. Avoid netting soft sediments and leaf litter which quickly clog the net and prevent the animals being seen and vastly increase the sorting time if the catch is preserved in the field and processed in the laboratory.

The entire catch, including weed and litter, may be preserved in the field, or it may be sorted on the bank-side. Formalin is the most appropriate preservative for bulky, saturated material; alcohol will become too dilute to preserve the animals. It should be noted that COSHH assessment and appropriate training and instruction are required before using formalin. Bank sorting is carried out by tipping the net haul on to a pale-coloured polythene sheet (eg a fertiliser sack), and spreading out the material into a thin layer over the whole sheet so the animals can be seen crawling out of the debris. Before tipping out the catch, arrange the sheet so that a pool can form in a depression in the middle. This will allow swimming species to escape and be more easily spotted. Readily identifiable species and those that become unidentifiable when preserved (leeches, flatworms) are recorded on a form and the others are preserved for identification in the laboratory. An alternative or adjunct to the sheet is a white tray (about 30 x 20 cm) with shallow water which is better than a sheet at enabling weak animals, such as mayflies, to escape from the debris and be seen.

5.3.2 Terrestrial invertebrates

Which method to use to collect terrestrial invertebrates depends upon the target group selected. Where stock are present pitfall traps are recommended because they are least vulnerable to disturbance although they may be trampled.

■ Pitfall traps are small containers, such as disposable plastic cups or polypropylene tubs (which are stronger), sunk into the ground to their rim. The container is one-third filled with a preservative, usually ethylene glycol (this is anti-freeze, so caution is needed, as it is poisonous). This will preserve animals well for up to two weeks.

In areas without grazing animals, water traps and interception traps are good substitutes for sweep netting:

■ Water traps are containers with water, preservative (eg formalin or dilute ethylene glycol), a few drops of detergent to reduce surface tension, and about 3% salt (sodium chloride) to reduce the swelling of soft-bodied animals through osmotic absorption of water. Any shallow, wide container will suffice (small washing-up bowls or ice-cream cartons). White and yellow bowls attract a larger catch than many other colours. It

is more important to keep the same colour for comparable catches. Flies, bees and wasps, and some beetles are collected well by water traps. Catch rates vary with the height of the trap above the vegetation.

■ Interception traps are vertical walls of fine black gauze, perspex or acetate sheet below which a gutter is placed containing preservative (as for water traps). Flying insects collide with the wall and fall into the gutter. The size of the wall is not important, but the size of the catch is almost proportional to its area so the same size of trap must be used for comparable catches. A wall about 1-m square will catch a large number of insects, especially beetles, in mid-summer.

Table 5.6 summarises a useful selection of species to survey and appropriate methods. Details of other traps can be found in Sheppard (1991).

Table 5.6: Terrestrial invertebrates to include in survey and monitoring

Taxonomic groups	Methods	Peak time of year
Flies:		
snail-killing flies	sweep netting or water trapping	June to late July; second peak for craneflies in October
hoverflies		
soldierflies		
Dolichopodid flies		
craneflies		
many other families can usefully be included		
Beetles:		
ground beetles	pitfall trapping	May to late June (July)
rove beetles		
leaf beetles	sweep netting, interception trapping	
weevils		
many other families can usefully be included		

5.3.3 The Butterfly Monitoring Scheme

Butterflies are best monitored using the Butterfly Monitoring Scheme (BMS) methodology (Hall 1981, Pollard and Yates 1993). Butterflies are identified and counted within an imaginary box no more than 5 m wide and 5 m ahead of the observer who walks at a steady pace along a predefined route. The length of the route varies but about 3 km is recommended. The route is divided into a maximum of 15 sections, determined by features of the route and by local changes in vegetation. Separate counts are made in each section during weekly visits from 1 April to 30 September. The following rules apply:

- The temperature must be above 17 °C in the shade irrespective of sunshine, or between 13–17 °C if at least 60% of the route is sunny, or 11 °C in northern upland areas.

- The counts must be made between 1015 and 1545 hrs BST, ie 2 ¾ h either side of noon GMT.

- The wind, in the open, must be less than force 5 on the Beaufort Scale (small trees beginning to sway), although the effect of wind on the flight of butterflies varies with the immediate habitat; wind speed in woods will be less than in exposed habitats, so this rule is flexible.

- Species that are difficult to identify in the field, such as small and Essex skippers, will need to be caught using a black butterfly net. There is no need to kill or keep any British butterfly; there are innumerable identification guides available to take into the field if needed.

5.3.4 Monitoring adult dragonflies

Dragonflies are highly visible, relatively easy to identify and are good indicators of water quality.

The following methodology sets out a standard technique to be used to monitor adult dragonflies; it is especially suited to recording populations of damselflies and Libellulids (Brooks 1993). It allows different observers following a set route – during optimum conditions for dragonfly activity – to produce comparable results. Transects should be mapped, divided into sections and walked every week during the summer period (1 May to 30 September). Alternatively, individual species can be targeted and transects walked only during their flying periods (see Merritt *et al* 1996); for example hairy dragonfly (1 May to 7 July), white-legged damselfly (mid-May to mid-August) and variable damselfly (mid-May to end of July).

The following conditions must be met:

- The survey should not start earlier than 1100 or later than 1300 hrs.

- Air temperature in the shade should be above 17 °C.

- There should be at least 50% sunshine. As each section is entered the surveyor should record whether a shadow is cast. If half the sections are recorded as sunny then the survey is valid.

- Wind conditions should be light. If trees are bending the wind is too strong.

Method

1. Transects should be walked at a continuous slow stroll keeping to the edge of the river or drainage channel.

2. In each section every identifiable specimen is recorded (perched or flying) in front of and to the side of the surveyor, but not behind. For the purposes of the survey it does not matter if the same individual is counted more than once. Hawkers (Aeshnidae) are likely to be counted several times, but this will be a consistent error. The surveyor should not stop and search vegetation but keep walking.

3. Where red-eyed damselfly occur the observer should stop periodically in each section and scan floating vegetation systematically with binoculars counting all individuals.

4. Distinguishing between common blue damselfly, variable damselfly and azure damselfly while walking is not possible; they must be recorded together as blue coenagrionids. If specific identification can be made then this should be noted.

5. Transects should always be walked following the same route.

This method is not suitable for accurately recording populations of the variable damselfly. This species occurs in localised colonies which should be mapped and counted on a weekly basis between mid-May and the end of July. Care should be taken to avoid confusion with other blue coenagrionids.

5.4 Surveying and monitoring birds

During the winter, birds are simply monitored by counting at regular (eg monthly) intervals. Monitoring breeding bird numbers is slightly more problematic and the techniques used vary with each group of birds – see Bibby *et al* (1992) for more details. Techniques used to census breeding wildfowl, rails and crakes are summarised in Table 5.7.

Table 5.7: Bird census techniques for breeding wildfowl, rails and crakes

Type of bird	Count unit	Method
Wildfowl Obvious species, eg mute swan	Territorial bird with nest	Map and count when nests are conspicuous in April–May.
Secretive species, eg shoveler	1. Off-duty males	Count groups of males (<5 birds) just after females start incubating and become elusive. Different species lay at different times, which should be taken into account.
	2. Females with young	Count either by direct observation or by flushing broods into open water by walking the banks with dogs.
	3. Nesting females	Rigorous searching for nests is labour-intensive and can cause desertion. Rarely used and not recommended.
Rails and crakes Obvious species, eg moorhen	Breeding territory	Map territories during several visits early in the season (late March–early April)
Secretive species, eg spotted crake	Breeding territory	Calling birds are mapped during several night visits (2300–0200) in late May to mid-June. Territory is occupied if bird is heard calling for more than 5 days.

Source: adapted from Bibby et al *(1992).*

5.4.1 Surveying and monitoring breeding waders

The field-by-field method is the best method for counting breeding waders on wet grassland (O'Brien and Smith 1992). Wader distributions are marked on large-scale maps during three visits:

■ visit 1 between 15 April and 30 April

■ visit 2 between 1 May and 21 May

■ visit 3 between 22 May and 18 June.

Each field is walked through on a route that takes the observer within 100 m of all points. Cold, wet and windy weather is avoided. Ideally, all compartments should be surveyed within three hours of dawn or dusk. Numbers, behaviour and position of all wader species are recorded on a map. Data from the maps are summarised onto recording forms:

- For lapwing and redshank, record the total number of birds per compartment.

- For snipe, record the number of chipping/drumming birds.

- For curlew and oystercatcher, record the number of pairs.

To calculate the number of pairs of breeding birds, from the mapped information, consult Table 5.8.

Table 5.8: Interpreting mapped wader distribution and behaviour

Species	Count unit	Method for calculating number of pairs/nests
Snipe	Displaying male	Number of nests is equal to the maximum number of displaying males in any one visit in April/May multiplied by 1.74.
Redshank	Flying bird showing alarm	Average number recorded between 15 April and 20 May is equal to the number of pairs.
Lapwing	Individual bird	The maximum number of birds observed on site during any one visit in April/May, divided by two gives a good estimate of the number of breeding pairs.
Curlew/ oystercatcher	Pairs or single birds with young	The maximum number of pairs recorded alarm-calling or with nests or young on any single visit gives the number of pairs present.

Source: O'Brien and Smith (1992).

5.4.2 Surveying and monitoring breeding passerines

Breeding populations of passerines (eg yellow wagtail) are counted using mapping methods, point counts or transects. The 'Common Bird Census' technique which involves mapping the distribution and behaviour of birds over a series of visits is more than adequate – see Bibby *et al* (1992) for further details.

5.5 Monitoring water levels

Water levels can be monitored visually, by checking whether water is present in drainage channels and pools. Level indicator boards in channels, or levels marked on the side of a sluice or bridge and related to Ordnance Datum make rapid, comparable observations possible (Coles 1995).

Measuring in-field water levels can be very useful for predicting the effects of management on target wildlife and requires more sophisticated methods. Transects or networks of dipwells (which measure water-table height) or piezometers (which measure actual water pressure and can therefore be used to determine the direction of groundwater flow) may be used (Case Study 6). Dipwells need to be placed firmly in the ground, preferably down into the mineral horizon on peat soils, so they don't move up and down. The top must be protected from any grazing livestock (Plate 1). Dipwells should be capped to stop them collecting rain. Once tubes are in place, they should be levelled to ordnance datum. Levelling should be periodically repeated to check for movement.

Dipwell spacing should be determined by the level of monitoring required and the soil type (section 4.2). Closer spacings will be needed on soils with low hydraulic conductivity. Spacings should also be closer near field boundaries than in field centres because of the greater variation in water-tables adjacent to drainage channels. Dipwells will not always give valid results on slowly permeable soils, such as clays, especially where perched water-tables occur. Advice should be sought in interpreting data.

Measuring of levels in dipwells can be undertaken with a spring tape, a light weight on a string or an electronic dip-meter. Measurements should be taken weekly in the first year of monitoring. Subsequent monthly monitoring may

suffice during wet periods. However weekly or fortnightly monitoring should be maintained during the spring/early summer period when levels are most critical to flora and fauna.

(Peter Roworth)

Plate 1
Dipwells allow water-table levels to be monitored throughout the year, building up a picture of site water regime.

Key references

Armitage, P D, Furse, M T and Wright, J F (1979) *A bibliography of works for the identification of freshwater invertebrates in the British Isles.* Freshwater Biological Association Occasional Publication No. 5.

Bibby, C J, Burgess, N D and Hill, D A (1992). *Bird Census Techniques.* Academic Press, London.

Croft, P S (1986) *A key to the major groups of British freshwater invertebrates.* AIDGAP, Field Studies Council.

Hammond, C O (1983) *The dragonflies of Great Britain and Ireland.* Harley Books, Colchester.

Moore, P D and Chapman, S B (1986) *Methods in plant ecology.* Second edition. Blackwell, Oxford.

Pollard, E and Yates, T J (1993) *Monitoring butterflies for ecology and conservation.* Chapman and Hall, London.

Sheppard, D A (1991) Site survey methods. In R Fry and D Lonsdale (Eds) Habitat conservation for insects: a neglected green issue. *The Amateur Entomologist,* 21, 205-208.

Stace, C (1991) *New Flora of the British Isles.* Cambridge University Press, Cambridge.

Sutherland, W J (Ed) (1996) *Ecological census techniques: a handbook.* Cambridge University Press, Cambridge.

Thomas, J and Lewington, R (1991) *The butterflies of Britain and Ireland.* National Trust/Dorling Kindersley.

Part 6
CASE STUDIES

Contents

Introduction

This part of the Guide contains a series of case studies that provide practical examples of techniques mentioned in the preceding text. Projects and sites chosen are scattered around the UK (see Figure 6.1) and have all had demonstrable benefits to conservation/wildlife.

Case studies follow a standard format:

- General Information – such as site name, managing body, location, area, designations, soil type, National Vegetation Classification communities occurring on site and techniques illustrated in the case study.

- Main Management Objectives – provides details of main conservation objectives for the site.

- Background – provides background information about the site/project.

- Techniques – describes in detail the implementation of the chosen technique(s) highlighted in the case study. Techniques are cross-referenced against the appropriate text in Chapters 1–5.

- Benefits – describes the benefits of the management undertaken in both wildlife terms but also in socio-economic terms where appropriate.

**Figure 6.1
Location of sites
presented as
case studies**

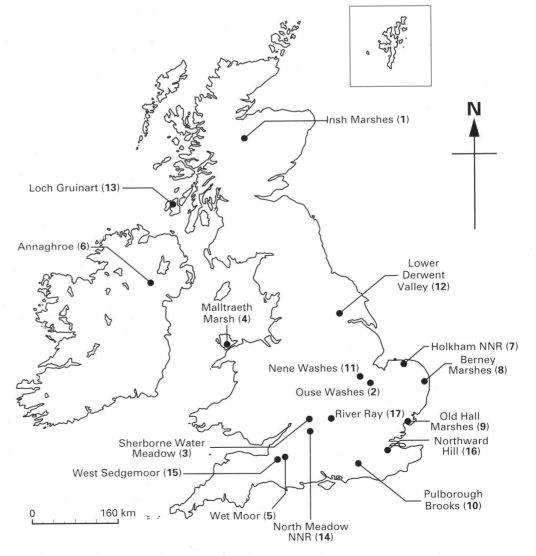

Insh Marshes (**1**)

N

Loch Gruinart (**13**)

Annaghroe (**6**)

Lower
Derwent
Valley (**12**)

Malltraeth
Marsh (**4**)

Holkham NNR (**7**)

Berney
Marshes (**8**)

Nene Washes (**11**)

Ouse Washes (**2**)

River Ray (**17**)

Old Hall
Marshes (**9**)

Sherborne Water
Meadow (**3**)

Northward
Hill (**16**)

West Sedgemoor (**15**)

0   160 km

Wet Moor (**5**)

North Meadow
NNR (**14**)

Pulborough
Brooks (**10**)

Insh Marshes

Case Study 1

(RSPB)

Location:	Between Kingussie and Kincraig, Inverness-shire OS 1:50,000 sheet no 35 GR NH800020
Area:	936 ha total 589 wet grassland/swamp
Designations:	SSSI, IBA, ESA, NSA, proposed Ramsar and SPA

Soil Type(s):	Peat, alluvium and sands/gravels
NVC Type(s):	M23, M25, S22
Technique(s):	

NATURAL FLOODING (section 1.1)
LOW-INTENSITY GRAZING (section 4.4.4)
Scrub control (section 4.6.4)

MAIN MANAGEMENT OBJECTIVES

To maintain the nature conservation value of this nationally important floodplain mire and its associated river system.

To manage and protect the site for the benefit of breeding and wintering birds, plants and invertebrates.

BACKGROUND

The Insh Marshes are situated along the middle River Spey, Scotland at an altitude of *c.* 220 m (Figure 1) and represent the least damaged large floodplain remaining in the UK. Past attempts to restrict flooding by embankment proved ineffective and all banks are now breached in one or more places. The whole area was formerly grazed or cut for hay and small areas were ploughed and re-seeded or converted to arable. The presence of a network of open and occluded drainage channels is a vestige of past, largely unsuccessful, efforts to drain the area. Since the RSPB began ownership in 1973 the only farming activity has been light grazing and the land is subject to a more or less natural flooding regime. In 1995, work began on controlling scrub invasion on some of the ungrazed wet areas.

WATER REGIME (NATURAL FLOODING)

- The River Spey is one of the least modified rivers in Europe. It has a large catchment area of 819 km^2, comparable to half the size of Norfolk. The Insh Marshes are considered to be the most important floodplain wetland in the UK.

- Despite being at a relatively high elevation (>200 m) the floodplain grades gently, falling only 15 m over 18 km, causing the river to meander across the floor of the valley. Loch Insh, a deep basin downstream of the Marshes, effectively slows the flow of the Spey and causes ponding of water upstream under high flows.

- Flood events, usually in winter, result in massive volumes of water inundating the marsh. High rainfall at any time causes localised flooding on the reserve. The reserve also receives water from groundwater upwellings on-site and from adjacent slopes, but the situation is rather complex and inadequately understood.

- A range of natural river features such as backwaters and ox-bow lakes occurs on the reserve. These provide permanent open water.

- The semi-natural water regime creates a very wet site, the ground generally being free of surface water only in mid-summer. The mire is flat with a relief of about 50 cm and water levels vary over the year by 3 m. Even the higher areas, in the centre of the marsh, are flooded for 150 days per year on average. Some parts remain wet all year round. Marsh water levels remain higher than river levels for most of the year following flooding.

- In spring, water levels fall naturally leaving large areas suitable for breeding waders and other birds.

LOW-INTENSITY GRAZING

- Wet grassland on the reserve is subjected to variable levels of low-intensity grazing. Some areas are ungrazed. Grazing is let to four local farmers who use sheep and/or cattle. The intensity and duration of grazing varies annually depending on ground conditions.

- Approximately 126 ha on Insh Fen and Coull Fen (Figure 1) are grazed most intensively whilst a further 66 ha is almost ungrazed. The grazing regime for each main compartment is shown in Figure 1.

- In general, the more intensively grazed areas support most breeding redshank and lapwing whilst snipe and curlew are spread over the less intensively grazed areas. Grazing starts in May on the higher, drier areas which support fewer ground-nesting birds. As the lower land becomes less wet, the stock move on and start to graze.

- Topping is undertaken while the stock are present to prevent invasion by less palatable rank vegetation and rushes. Grazing (plus browsing by roe deer) has kept scrub invasion under control in most of the open areas.

- Some drainage channels have been maintained to function as wet fences, but a network of stock fencing and gates facilitates control of grazing.

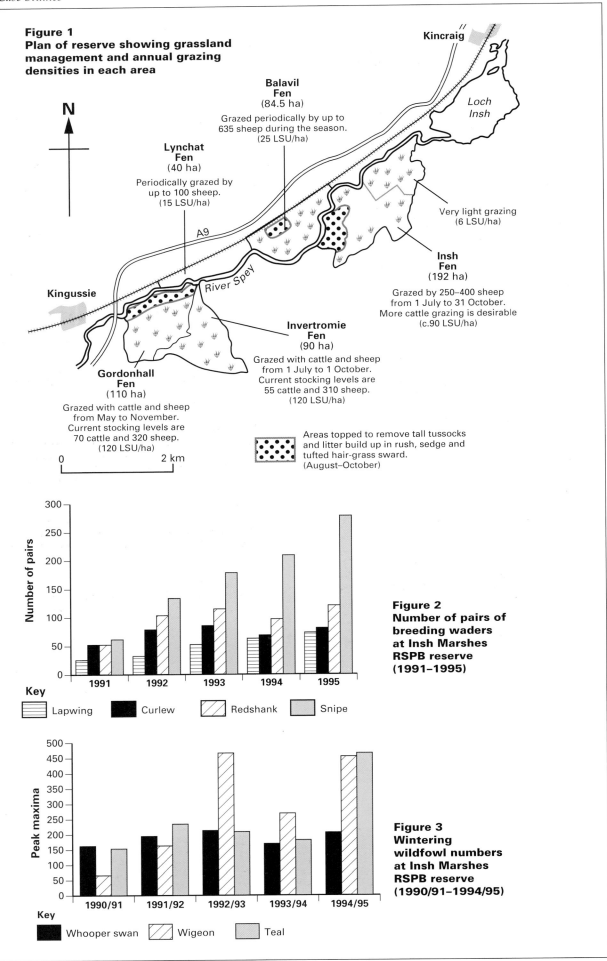

Figure 1
Plan of reserve showing grassland management and annual grazing densities in each area

N

Kincraig

Loch Insh

Balavil Fen
(84.5 ha)
Grazed periodically by up to 635 sheep during the season.
(25 LSU/ha)

Lynchat Fen
(40 ha)
Periodically grazed by up to 100 sheep.
(15 LSU/ha)

A9

Very light grazing
(6 LSU/ha)

Insh Fen
(192 ha)
Grazed by 250–400 sheep from 1 July to 31 October.
More cattle grazing is desirable
(c.90 LSU/ha)

Kingussie

River Spey

Invertromie Fen
(90 ha)
Grazed with cattle and sheep from 1 July to 1 October.
Current stocking levels are 55 cattle and 310 sheep.
(120 LSU/ha)

Gordonhall Fen
(110 ha)
Grazed with cattle and sheep from May to November.
Current stocking levels are 70 cattle and 320 sheep.
(120 LSU/ha)

0   2 km

Areas topped to remove tall tussocks and litter build up in rush, sedge and tufted hair-grass sward.
(August–October)

Figure 2
Number of pairs of breeding waders at Insh Marshes RSPB reserve (1991–1995)

Key

Lapwing   Curlew   Redshank   Snipe

Figure 3
Wintering wildfowl numbers at Insh Marshes RSPB reserve (1990/91–1994/95)

Key

Whooper swan   Wigeon   Teal

SCRUB CONTROL

- Over a ten-year period willow scrub is being thinned in each floodplain block to densities shown on 1965-70 aerial photographs.

- Cutting is by hand and chainsaw, the scrub is burnt *in situ* on corrugated iron. Large pieces of timber are removed from the site. All stumps are treated with glyphosate, within two hours of cutting, to prevent regrowth.

BENEFITS

- The natural flooding regime creates ideal conditions for breeding spotted crake, waders and ducks. Insh Marshes has the highest density of breeding waders in mainland Britain and is one of the top five sites in the UK. The current grassland management regime has ensured that this has remained stable and in some areas, has been improved greatly (Figure 2). Wintering birds also benefit from the periodic inundation, the site regularly supporting 1% of the Icelandic population of whooper swans (Figure 3).

- The varied grazing regime, together with spatial variation in vegetation controls (such as water-table regime and soil water chemistry), produces a mosaic of sward heights and vegetation types across the reserve to maximise the benefits for all wildlife.

- Site conditions favour a rich flora with 26 species of sedge being recorded on the site and a total vascular plant list of 514. Included are species of conservation importance (Table 1).

- Despite incomplete entomological coverage, the site is known to support more nationally rare invertebrates than any other site in Scotland (Table 2). The marshes are particularly rich in flies, with 6 RDB and 13 notable species being present.

- Scrub control will offset the significant increase in scrub coverage that has been noted over the last thirty years, while recognising the intrinsic value of the scrub itself.

- Additionally, there is a large otter population locally on the River Spey, and Loch Insh supports a nationally rare fish, the Arctic char.

Table 1: Wetland vascular plants of conservation importance found at Insh Marshes

String sedge	(RDB)
Pillwort	(NSC)
Smallreed *Calamagrostis purpurea*	(RDB)
Slender-leaved pondweed	(NSC)
Cowbane	(NSC)
Six-stamened waterwort	(NSC)
Bog hair-grass	(NSC)
Least yellow water-lily	(NSC)
Shady horsetail	(NSC)

Table 2: Invertebrate groups of conservation importance at Insh Marshes

- **Beetles**
  Only 113 species recorded to date of which two are nationally rare, 16 nationally notable and 11 of local occurrence.

- **Butterflies and moths**
  19 species of butterflies have been recorded. Only the pearl-bordered fritillary is of conservation significance. 208 species of moth are listed of which 50 are of national importance and 81 are local.

- **Flies**
  At least 20 species of national significance, including two endangered and two vulnerable species. 73 species of hoverfly have been recorded.

- **Spiders**
  249 species of spiders are known from the Cairngorms of which 93 were recorded on the reserve, including the first Scottish record of *Tmeticus affinis*.

Ouse Washes

Case Study 2

(Environment Agency, various nature conservation bodies and private owners)

Location:	Located on the border between Cambridgeshire and Norfolk, 10 km NW of Ely. OS 1:50,000 sheet no 143 GR TL495880
Area:	Total 2,400 ha Wet grassland 1,900 ha
Designations:	Ramsar, SPA, cSAC, SSSI and IBA

Soil Type(s): Alluvial clay and peat

NVC Type(s): MG9, MG13, S5, S22

Technique(s):
FLOOD STORAGE (section 1.1)

MAIN MANAGEMENT OBJECTIVES

The Environment Agency aim to maintain the traditional water management regime, which produces flooding in winter, moist soil conditions in spring and drier soil conditions in the summer. This allows the Washes fully to realise their value as a wildlife habitat, while also fulfilling agricultural and flood defence requirements.

BACKGROUND

The Ouse Washes lie between the Old Bedford and Hundred Foot Rivers and are the largest example of a functioning flood storage washland in the UK (Figure 1, Plate 1). The system was created in the 17th century when the two rivers were excavated and the Middle Level and South Level Barrier Banks were built. The Ouse Washes are still of strategic importance in providing flood defence for the Great Ouse catchment.

Unimproved neutral grassland, which occupies the majority of the site, is regularly flooded during the winter months (Plate 2). The sward provides haying and grazing during the summer. An increasing incidence of summer flooding since the mid-1970s has adversely affected breeding bird populations and encouraged the spread of mire and swamp vegetation communities at the expense of neutral wet grassland. This situation has been exacerbated by an increase in nutrient loading of floodwater in the last four decades.

FLOOD STORAGE

- Between the main drainage channels lie 1,900 ha of grassland fields separated by a network of drainage channels (Figure 1). The main function of these drainage channels is to allow management of summer water levels within the Washes. They also act as wet fences and assist with the evacuation of water off the washes after floods.

- A flood of 1 m in depth across the Washes contains 20,000,000 m³ of water.

- Flooding can occur at any time and its depth, extent and duration is largely dependent on rainfall within the catchment. Winter flooding is the norm, only one winter in the last twenty has been without surface flooding. Recently there has been an increased incidence of summer flooding, with only four flood-free summers since 1975.

- The site slopes along its east–west axis, water being 1 m deeper on the west side than on the east. This creates a diverse range of habitats.

- During the summer, water is obtained from the Hundred Foot River (east side) through a system of tidal slackers. Fresh water is available for only about six days in every fortnight due to the tidal cycle. Water flows into a header ditch and is then transferred through the Washes. Input of water during the summer prevents stagnation (and subsequent eutrophication and deoxygenation) and maintains drainage channel water levels.

- About 80% of the Washes are owned/managed by nature conservation bodies, further optimising the value of the site to wildlife. The RSPB warden acts as Wash Superintendent for the IDB regulating the flow of water onto the site during the summer.

BENEFITS

- During periods of high rainfall and high tides, flood-water contained between the banks of the Ouse Washes provides flood protection for the Cambridgeshire Fens. Complete towns and villages, as well as 29,000 ha of agricultural land are protected.

- Much of the conservation importance of the Ouse Washes is due to its continued use as a functional washland, with extensive flooding in the winter and traditional forms of agriculture during the summer.

- Drainage channels and rivers in the area support a diverse flora, accounting for 44% of the British aquatic flora, including six nationally scarce species (Table 1).

Table 1: Nationally scarce plant species occurring at the Ouse Washes

Greater dodder
Tasteless water-pepper
Whorled water-milfoil
Greater water-parsnip
Fringed water-lily
Hairlike pondweed
Narrow-leaved water-dropwort
Marsh sow-thistle

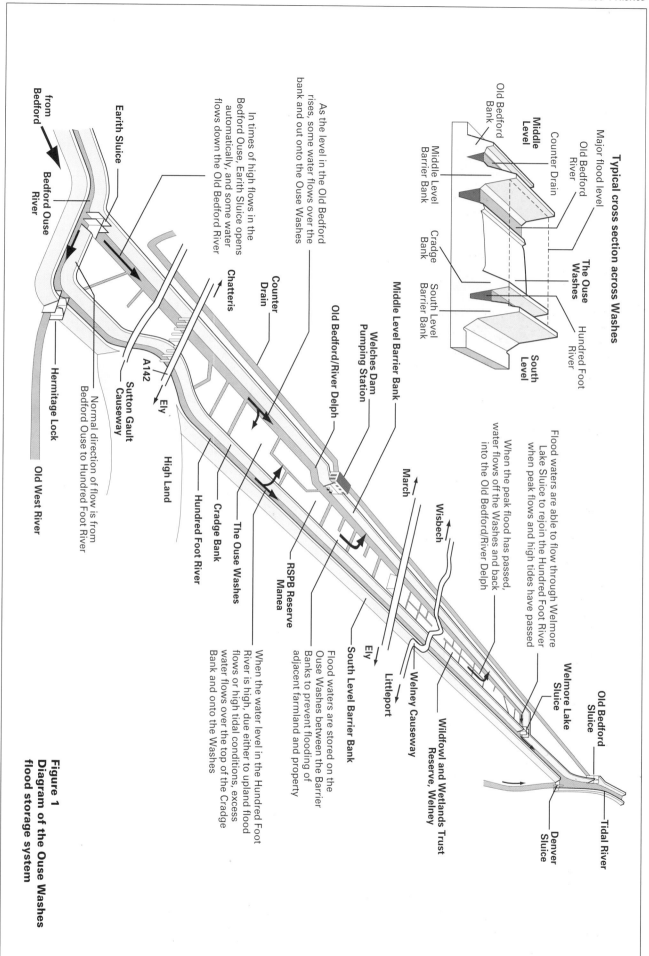

Typical cross section across Washes

Major flood level

Old Bedford Bank

Old Bedford River

Counter Drain

Middle Level

Middle Level Barrier Bank

Cradge Bank

The Ouse Washes

South Level Barrier Bank

Hundred Foot River

South Level

Middle Level Barrier Bank

Welches Dam Pumping Station

Old Bedford/River Delph

Flood waters are able to flow through Welmore Lake Sluice to rejoin the Hundred Foot River when peak flows and high tides have passed

When the peak flood has passed, water flows off the Washes and back into the Old Bedford/River Delph

March

Wisbech

Ely

Littleport

Welney Causeway

Wildfowl and Wetlands Trust Reserve, Welney

Welmore Lake Sluice

Old Bedford Sluice

Denver Sluice

Tidal River

from Bedford

Earith Sluice

Bedford Ouse River

Hermitage Lock

Old West River

In times of high flows in the Old Bedford Bedford Ouse, Earith Sluice opens automatically, and some water flows down the Old Bedford River

As the level in the Old Bedford rises, some water flows over the bank and out onto the Ouse Washes

Normal direction of flow is from Bedford Ouse to Hundred Foot River

Chatteris

Counter Drain

A142

Sutton Gault Causeway

Ely

High Land

The Ouse Washes

Cradge Bank

Hundred Foot River

RSPB Reserve Manea

South Level Barrier Bank

Ely

Flood waters are stored on the Ouse Washes between the Barrier Banks to prevent flooding of adjacent farmland and property

When the water level in the Hundred Foot River is high, due either to upland flood flows or high tidal conditions, excess water flows over the top of the Cradge Bank and onto the Washes

Figure 1
Diagram of the Ouse Washes flood storage system

155

■ Invertebrate fauna includes, at least, 53 nationally scarce species, as well as 12 nationally rare species, including the scarce chaser dragonfly and the compressed river mussel.

■ During the winter the Ouse Washes host internationally important concentrations of seven wildfowl species: Bewick's swan, whooper swan, wigeon, teal, gadwall, pintail and shoveler. Additionally cormorant, mute swan, mallard, pochard, tufted duck, coot and ruff winter in nationally important numbers. Numbers of wildfowl using the site have regularly exceeded 20,000 in winter, the criterion used to judge wetlands of international importance. In the five-winter period 1990/91 to 1994/95 the average peak total count for all waterfowl was in excess of 55,000 birds (Table 2).

■ 94 species of bird have been recorded breeding including species of conservation concern, such as garganey, spotted crake, ruff and black-tailed godwit (Table 3).

Plate 1 The sluice at Earith (upstream of the Washes) opens automatically in times of high flow, letting water into the washland system.

Plate 2 Bank to bank flooding on the Washes during the winter creates a sheet of water 20 miles long and half a mile wide.

Table 2: Wintering wildfowl and wader maxima at the Ouse Washes 1990/91 to 1994/95

Species	90/91	91/92	92/93	93/94	94/95
Mute swan	414	365	615	1,025	726
Bewick's swan	5,100	5,542	5,169	4,172	4,234
Whooper swan	578	778	856	986	1,142
Wigeon	24,715	37,064	28,879	23,791	33,326
Gadwall	352	683	417	455	378
Teal	5,225	5,157	2,688	2,349	4,663
Mallard	3,530	3,203	4,342	5,693	4,511
Pintail	1,332	1,969	1,745	1,082	1,601
Shoveler	625	567	1,019	1,066	993
Pochard	1,135	1,596	3,279	3,087	3,786
Tufted duck	365	273	1,507	1,737	761
Coot	1,248	1,904	2,289	3,182	2,225
Ruff	160	128	136	228	195
Black-tailed godwit	800	1,469	800	1,407	2,068
Peak count of all wildfowl	60,954	59,809	57,404	49,779	52,927

Table 3: Birds of conservation concern breeding on the Ouse Washes, average number of pairs and percentage of British population, 1991–1995

Species	Average 1991–95	Percentage of UK breeding population
Pintail	2	5
Garganey	12	24
Pochard	7	2
Quail	1	–
Spotted crake	2	29
Snipe	222	–
Ruff	1	9
Black-tailed godwit	5	9
Barn owl	1	–

Sherborne Water Meadows

(National Trust and NRA/Environment Agency)

Case Study 3

Location:	8 km west of Burford, Oxfordshire OS 1:50,000 sheet no 163 GR SP154187
Area:	57 ha total
Designations:	ESA

Soil Type(s):	Alluvial soils
NVC Type(s):	Not applicable
Technique(s):	

WATER MEADOW RESTORATION
(section 1.1)

MAIN MANAGEMENT OBJECTIVES

To reinstate, as accurately as possible, a traditional water meadow management infrastructure and regime.

BACKGROUND

Water meadows were developed between the 16th and 19th centuries and represented one of the most intensive forms of land management of the period. Water meadows were intentionally flooded using a flowing water system, to boost soil fertility (through the capture of water-borne silt) and stimulate early grass growth. Water meadows declined early this century with the advent of new husbandry techniques, improved fodder crops and strains of grass and artificial fertiliser.

At Sherborne, a water meadow system was constructed alongside the River Windrush in the 1840s. The meadows fell into disuse 90 years later and were ploughed for arable in 1965. In 1991 the National Trust (as new owners of the estate) decided to reinstate a water meadow system. The Countryside Commission accepted the project for grant aid under the Waterside Landscape category of the Countryside Stewardship Scheme and the NRA also became involved. It was this partnership that tackled the ambitious project of faithfully restoring the water meadow system.

WATER MEADOW RESTORATION

- The NRA and National Trust located old features (drainage channels, carriers and sluices) using aerial photographs and old OS maps (Plate 1).

- A detailed topographic survey was undertaken by the NRA, using total stations (electronic theodolites combined with infra-red ranging devices). This produced a computer model of the landscape.

- A new drainage channel system was excavated using a caterpillar-tracked hydraulic excavator, and the spoil was levelled using a bulldozer (Plate 2). The topographic survey was used to guide spreading and land-forming. Approximately 10,000 m of drainage channel were re-excavated or de-silted between 1992 and 1994.

- The old sluice system was replaced, 15 lifting-gate sluices were installed at an average cost of £250 per unit (Plate 3).

- Twelve footbridges and nine vehicular bridges were installed to allow land managers and stock to move around the site. Footbridges cost £140 per unit and vehicular bridges £300.

- Fencing was erected around the perimeter of every field to give greater stock control and prevent trampling of drainage channel edges. Cost: £22,688 (including stiles and gates).

(Andrew Mayled)

**Plate 1
Aerial photographs were used to identify old water control structures.**

- When all the water control features had been installed the area was re-seeded. The former arable fields were sprayed with glyphosate, ploughed, power-harrowed and re-seeded at 15 kg/ha with a mixture of grasses specified in the Countryside Stewardship agreement. The seed mix comprised the following species: meadow fescue, smooth meadow-grass, red fescue, tall fescue, crested dog's-tail and cock's-foot. The cultivation and re-seeding cost £200/ha.

- Since 1996, water management has been that between November and February/March water flows across the water meadows. In early spring the water levels in the carriers are lowered and sheep graze, the numbers and timing varying according to grass growth and ground conditions.

- Stock is removed by early summer and a hay or silage crop is taken and then aftermath grazed. A late hay cut is taken every third year to allow plants to seed, in accordance with the terms laid down by the Countryside Stewardship Scheme. Under these terms stock must graze for a minimum of ten weeks in the year, cattle are occasionally used in some fields.

- The valley-side fields adjacent to the floodplain are in arable and have been isolated from the water meadow system by a 20–30 m grass buffer strip to prevent nutrient run-off into the wetland. This buffer strip qualifies for long-term set-aside.

BENEFITS

- Work to date has reinstated a managed water meadow, a system of considerable historical and landscape value.

- Even before the completion of the project, wet areas created were attracting breeding waders. Two pairs of redshanks bred in 1994.

- In the 1995 season one pair of redshanks and at least 10 pairs of lapwings bred on the site. Additionally, 12 pairs of mute swans held territory. Barn owls and grey herons regularly feed in the area. There has also been an increase in winter duck and passage wader use of the site.

- The removal of 57 ha of arable land from the Windrush floodplain, with its associated silt, nutrient and pesticide impacts on the river system, is likely to improve river water quality.

Plate 2
Drainage channels, vital for the control of managed flooding and subsequent draw-down, were cleaned and reprofiled.

Plate 3
Lifting-gate sluices are the traditional type of water control structure associated with water meadows.

Malltraeth Marsh

Case Study 4

(RSPB)

Location:	10 km west of Menai Bridge, Anglesey, Gwynedd OS 1:50,000 sheet no 114 GR SH452718
Area:	154 ha total 100 ha proposed reedbed 50 ha proposed wet grassland
Designations:	cSAC, ESA, SSSI

Soil Type(s):	Sandy to loamy marine alluvial deposits
NVC Type(s):	MG6, MG10, M23
Technique(s):	
MANAGEMENT PLANNING (section 2.2.7)	

MAIN MANAGEMENT OBJECTIVES

To manage the nature reserve as a wetland complex comprising maximum area of wet grassland and reedswamp in order to increase the quality of the local landscape and its conservation value.

BACKGROUND

Malltraeth Marsh was reclaimed for agricultural use in the 19th century by the embankment of the Afon Cefni and construction of a sea wall at the mouth of the estuary. At the same time an extensive network of drainage channels was established linking the marsh to the Afon Cefni via tidal gates. Malltraeth Marsh now forms an extensive area of grazing marsh, much of which is semi-improved grassland, dominated by rushes. Additionally there are some improved fields grazed by cattle, sheep and ponies.

RESERVE PLANNING

■ Site potential originally identified by the Anglesey Wetland Strategy – a joint CCW/Environment Agency/RSPB project, in association with WOAD and the North Wales Wildlife Trust – which aimed to identify regionally important wetlands.

■ CCW funded a hydrological feasibility study, which concluded that it would be possible to create a wetland reserve at Malltraeth (Gilman 1993). This calculated the amount of water needed to counter leakage and increased evapotranspiration from the site and to allow for some surface water losses.

■ The feasibility study recommended that the following should be undertaken:

• a topographic survey. This was funded by the Environment Agency and included all the area within the potential acquisition zone. This survey enabled reserve managers to identify areas suitable for reed and the slightly higher areas which would be managed as wet grassland (Figure 1).

• water quality analysis of the Main Drain to assess source of water, possible saline influence and degree of eutrophication if any.

• a soil survey, to identify underlying pockets of sand that would affect the site's hydrological integrity and influence the position of water control structures in some areas of the reserve.

■ Information provided by these studies was used to write a Management Plan for the site. The management plans includes an audit of the site and states management policies and objectives. It also contains detailed management prescriptions to enhance the wildlife interest of the site (Table 1), and lays out a five-year work programme. Mechanisms by which the effectiveness of the work programme can be assessed, such as species targets, are also included (Table 2).

Table 1: Grassland prescriptions in the Malltraeth Marsh Management Plan

Prescription	Description
Seasonal grazing	Grazing from end of June to end of October with cattle only, at a density of 2.5 LSU/ha. No fertiliser to be used.
Topping	Fields topped following grazing to control rush infestation. Start in late July, two cuts before autumn flooding.
Silage cutting	Single field under silage management not to be cut before end of June.
Rush control	Chemical control with weed-wiper to be used, on an experimental basis, if mechanical means fail.

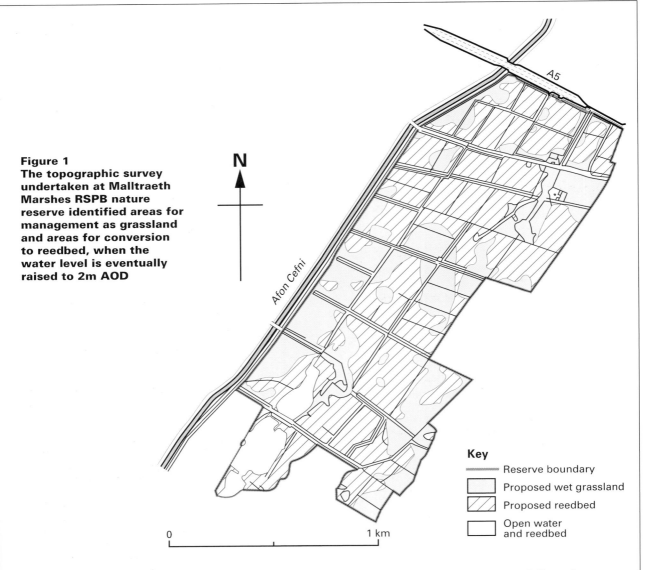

Figure 1
The topographic survey undertaken at Malltraeth Marshes RSPB nature reserve identified areas for management as grassland and areas for conversion to reedbed, when the water level is eventually raised to 2m AOD

N

Afon Cefni

A5

0   1 km

Key

═══════ Reserve boundary

▭ Proposed wet grassland

▨ Proposed reedbed

▭ Open water and reedbed

BENEFITS

- The Management Plan identified target species and gives an indication of target numbers for bird species in wet grassland and reedbed in the future (Table 2). This will allow assessment of project success when the Plan is reviewed after five years.

- Current wildlife interest is limited although the reserve does support breeding curlews, lapwings and snipe. Reed warblers breed in the reedbed. Numbers of wintering wildfowl, notably teal, may reach nationally important numbers in some winters. There are some records of wintering bitterns using the reserve.

- Planned management will also benefit the species-rich aquatic flora of the drainage channels which host a number of species that are scarce in Wales, such as the starwort *Callitriche hermaphroditica*. The associated invertebrate fauna includes three nationally scarce dragonflies; hairy dragonfly, variable damselfly and scarce blue-tailed damselfly.

Table 2: Management targets at Malltraeth Marsh contained within the Management Plan

Species	Number of breeding pairs (1993)	Target number of breeding pairs
Curlew	4–6 prs	10–20
Shoveler	2–3 prs	10–15 (1% UK)
Water rail	2 prs	
Lapwing	10 prs	30
Grasshopper warbler	6–8 prs	
Reed warbler	5–10 prs	
Garganey	1 pr (?)	5 (5% UK)
Bittern		4–5 (30% UK)
Marsh harrier		2–3 (2–3% UK)
Spotted crake		2–3 (10% UK)
Redshank		10–12
Snipe		4–5

Other potential colonists: black-tailed godwit, bearded tit, ruff and corncrake

Wet Moor

(Private landowners and Environment Agency)

Location:	Langport, Somerset OS 1:50,000 sheet no 193 GR ST450240
Area:	265 ha
Designations:	SSSI, ESA, IBA and proposed Ramsar and SPA

Soil Type(s):	Thin clay layer overlying peat
NVC Type(s):	MG6, MG7, MG9 and MG13
Technique(s):	WATER MANAGEMENT: RAISED WATER LEVEL AREAS - TERRACED IRRIGATION (section 4.2.2) CONTROL STRUCTURES (section 4.2.2)

MAIN MANAGEMENT OBJECTIVES

To install water level control structures and associated works to allow independent water level management to be undertaken.

BACKGROUND

Wet Moor is part of the Somerset Levels and Moors, an area heavily affected by drainage for agriculture in the past. Steps to reverse this have been taken by the introduction of an ESA scheme and an NRA (now the Environment Agency) Strategy on Water Level Management.

Wet Moor floods in most winters. The land is up to 2 m lower than the spring high tide levels at Bridgwater and is mostly at a lower level than the water levels in the River Yeo. The Moor is pump-drained and in early winter water levels are dropped by about 20 cm to increase the floodwater storage capacity. In summer, water levels are penned relatively high in field drainage channels to provide irrigation, cattle watering and wet fencing.

By 1980, conservation organisations had successfully lobbied for the notification of SSSIs in the area. The Wessex Water Authority undertook to ensure that there would be no further lowering of water levels. However, greater changes were required to benefit breeding birds. It was nearly 10 years before the Somerset Levels and Moors ESA scheme was introduced and strengthened to Tier 3 level, which included raised water level prescriptions and incentives in 1992. This coincided with the development of the NRA's Somerset Levels and Moors Water Level Management and Nature Conservation Strategy which would be a mechanism to facilitate Tier 3. It also undertook to review flood defence procedures and adopt a presumption in favour of positive water level management for nature conservation benefits.

RAISED WATER LEVEL AREAS (RWLAs) – TERRACED IRRIGATION

- The aim of the plan was to produce a terraced system of discrete hydrological units, where water levels were held high and water flowed from one unit to another (Figure 1).

- In general, the water regime retains winter water above maximum drainage channel level so that

patchy, splash-flooding occurs on the fields into spring. Levels gradually recede such that by late spring/early summer drainage channel water will have reached and will be held at summer penning levels (no greater than 30 cm below average field level).

- For the scheme to be effective, discrete blocks of land holdings are sought wherever possible. This enables water level controls to be integrated across an area.

- Where an individual landowner wishes to be excluded from the scheme it is usually possible to engineer-out the holding (Figure 1). It may be possible for the owner to engineer the land back into the scheme at a later date. At nearby West Moor, a siphon pipe was installed under the main drain to connect previously engineered-out land to raised water level land on the other side. This has enabled the newly engineered-in land to achieve the same raised water levels as the rest of the area without affecting the drainage function of the main drain.

- The NRA is not resourced to manage the water levels and maintenance of structures beyond the initial establishment phase (2–3 years). After one year of satisfactory operation these functions, where structures not on the Main River are concerned, are handed over to the local Internal Drainage Board.

- Entry into ESA Tier 3 is entirely voluntary. The NRA's strategy is an added incentive as it covers the capital costs of the necessary works to be undertaken. In addition, the landowner can receive a £415/ha/annum ESA payment from MAFF.

- Additionally, farmers within ESA areas may enter into a raised water level agreement on their own and apply for an 80% grant from MAFF towards capital costs. They also receive the annual Tier 3 payment provided the criteria are met (Table 1).

CONTROL STRUCTURES

- Determining overall plan feasibility and control structure siting involved detailed topographic and hydrological surveys which were undertaken at the start of the project.

Figure 1
Plan of the Wet
Moor RWLA

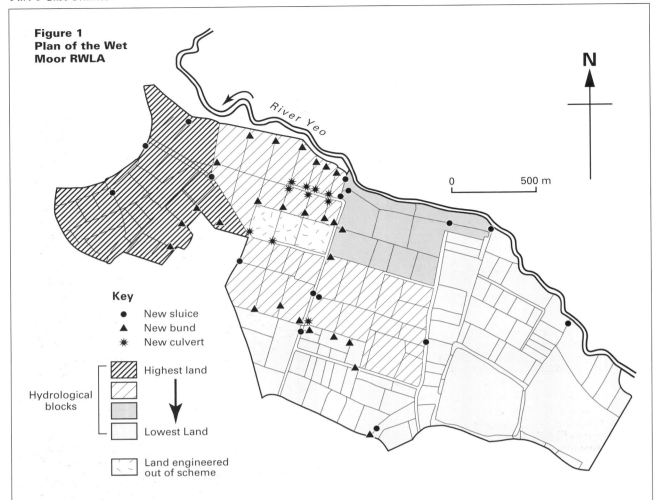

Key

● New sluice
▲ New bund
✳ New culvert

Hydrological blocks

[▨] Highest land

[▧]

[▥]

[▫] Lowest Land

[▱] Land engineered out of scheme

Table 1: Criteria for receiving payments under the three tiers of the Somerset Levels and Moors ESA Scheme.

Prescription	TIER		
	1	2	3
No new under-drainage, sub-soiling or moling	■	■	■
Maintain existing ditches and other drainage structures	■	■	■
No spraying of ditches or field drains	■	■	■
Ditch water levels at or above IDB penning level	■	■	■
Ditch water level within 30 cm of field surface from May–Nov	□	□	■
Ditch water level at mean field surface level from Dec–Apr	□	□	■
Maintain grassland, no ploughing, re-seeding, etc	■	■	■
Graze with cattle or sheep	■	■	
If mown, the area should be aftermath grazed	■	■	■
Do not exceed stated levels of inorganic fertiliser	■	■	
Do not use insecticides or fungicides	■	■	■
Use of herbicides controlled	■	■	■
Do not add lime or other material to reduce soil acidity	■	■	■
No chain-harrowing or rolling between 31 Mar and 1 July	■	■	■
Mow at least one year in three		■	■
No cutting or topping after 31 Aug		■	■
No sheep grazing from 1 Sept to 1 Mar		■	
No mechanical operations between 31 Mar and 1 July			■
No inorganic fertiliser			■
Cattle grazing only and not before 20 May			■
No silage making			■

■ = mandatory, □ = optional, for additional payment

- Water level control was achieved by constructing a series of dams, culverts, bunds and sluices at appropriate points in the system (Plate 1).

- To ensure that unwanted flooding does not occur, a large diameter penstock sluice was installed in the system, enabling the site to be evacuated if necessary.

- Figure 1 shows the discrete hydrological blocks which have been established, and the necessary water control structures. The Wet Moor scheme is one of the biggest Raised Water Level Areas in Britain and cost £63,000 (@ £238/ha) to implement (see Table 2 for costs of water control structures). Smaller schemes generally cost more per hectare, eg the 77 ha West Moor Raised Water Level Area cost £506/ha.

BENEFITS

- The overall result is the recreation of traditional extensive farming, while maintaining landowners' income and improving the habitat for breeding and wintering wet grassland birds.

- The flooding regime that results in most years from the RWLA scheme benefits nesting birds, particularly waders and yellow wagtails, by providing suitable nesting and feeding habitat and shortening the grazing season (Plate 2). Prior to implementation of the scheme, Wet Moor supported only 2–3 pairs of breeding waders. After one year this had increased to more than 30 pairs. Throughout the Somerset Levels and Moors ESA there are on average ten times more breeding birds per hectare on RWLAs than on areas outside the scheme.

- In winter, shallow floods interspersed with grazed sward provide valuable feeding and roosting areas for many wintering bird species, especially snipe, lapwing, wigeon and teal.

- As water retreats to the drainage channels in spring and is retained at summer penning levels, they continue to function as wet fences and for stock watering. In addition, the wildlife value of the drainage channels is retained or even enhanced owing to smaller fluctuations in summer and winter levels.

- The principles and practices at Wet Moor have been adopted at RWLAs at 12 other sites in the Somerset Levels and Moors, which now have a combined area of 1,217 ha.

(Carl Hawke)

(Carl Hawke)

Plate 1 (top)
The water management infrastructure at Wet Moor includes this tilting weir sluice, which allows very fine adjustments of water level to be made.

Plate 2 (bottom)
Raised water levels have created suitable conditions for breeding waders, such as lapwing.

Table 2: Approximate cost of materials for water control structures

Structure type	Cost (£)	Note
Dropboard sluice	1,500	Cost varies with size. Framework usually of trench-sheets with wooden dropboards supported in a welded, steel frame.
Tilting-weir sluice	4,500	Comes as a pre-made flat-pack. Enables very fine water level control. Easy to operate and low maintenance (Plate 1). Can require a substantial support structure.
Earth dams	200	Including cost of post and rail fence to prevent cattle access.

Annaghroe Meadows

Case Study 6

(Caledon Estate and Department of Agriculture Northern Ireland)

Location:	4 miles south-west of Caledon, County Tyrone, Northern Ireland OS 1:50,000 sheet no 19 GR H 737440
Area:	Total 50 ha Wet grassland 50 ha
Designations:	IBA, proposed Ramsar and SPA

Soil Type(s):	Alluvial
NVC Type(s):	MG10
Technique(s):	WATER MANAGEMENT (section 4.2) HYDROLOGICAL MONITORING (section 5.5)

MAIN MANAGEMENT OBJECTIVES

To manage the site for the benefit of regionally important populations of wintering wildfowl.

BACKGROUND

The Annaghroe Meadows are situated adjacent to the Upper River Blackwater. Between 1984 and 1990 an arterial drainage scheme in the Blackwater valley had the potential to seriously reduce the wildlife interest of the area. To prevent this happening at Annaghroe, the Department of Agriculture (DANI) undertook measures designed to maintain the site's high water level regime.

During the summer the site is leased for grazing and fertiliser is applied every year. Soil drainage is dependent on a series of inter-linked open channels throughout the site. These discharge into the Annaghroe minor watercourse, which in turn discharges into the Blackwater. The site is managed jointly by DANI and the landowner, with an advisory input from the RSPB.

WATER MANAGEMENT

- In 1991 three sluice gates were installed by DANI, isolating the site from the drainage scheme. The sluice gates are closed from 15 October to 15 March to hold back water to create suitable conditions for over wintering wildfowl (Figure 1, Plate 1).

HYDROLOGICAL MONITORING

- In 1992, to determine the success of the mitigation measures, DANI undertook a topographic survey and installed a total of 170 dipwells on the site to monitor the water-table across the managed area (Figure 1).

- These dipwells comprise 100 cm lengths of perforated pipe, installed vertically to a depth of 90 cm (Figure 2).

- Levels were recorded every two weeks until the area flooded in winter. This was repeated for another two years.

Plate 1 Installation of sluices has allowed raised water level management; winter flooding still occurs in most years and attracts wintering wildfowl in regionally important numbers.

(*Godfrey McRoberts*)

BENEFITS

- Mitigation measures have resulted in the wintering bird interest being maintained. As a result of the raised water level management, the site continues to support 70–150 Greenland white-fronted geese (about 30% of birds wintering in Northern Ireland), as well as up to 30 whooper swans and ducks such as wigeon, mallard and teal during flood conditions.

- The water regime provides very good conditions for wintering wildfowl in wet winters. Benefits could potentially be enhanced for breeding waders by maintaining higher water levels into spring and early summer (Figure 3). Currently the site supports a small lapwing population.

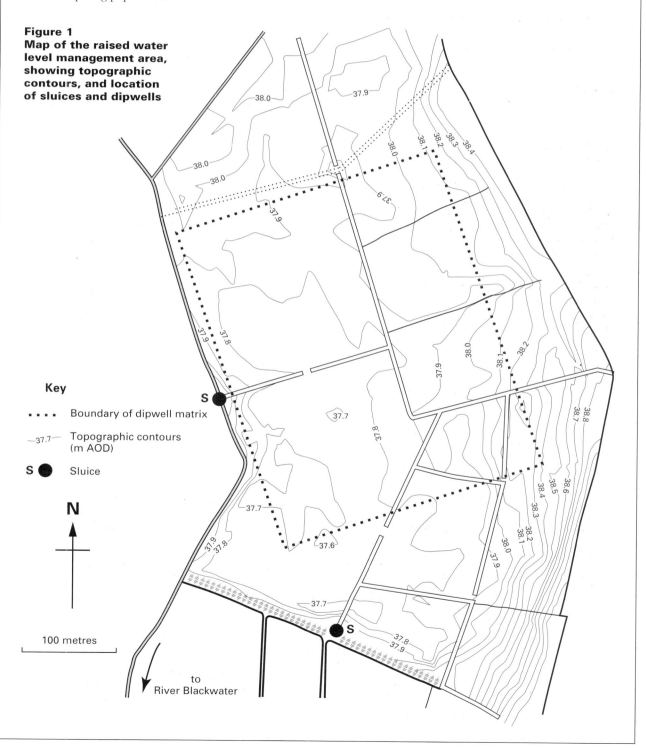

Figure 1
Map of the raised water level management area, showing topographic contours, and location of sluices and dipwells

Key

- • • • Boundary of dipwell matrix
- —37.7— Topographic contours (m AOD)
- **S** ● Sluice

N

100 metres

to River Blackwater

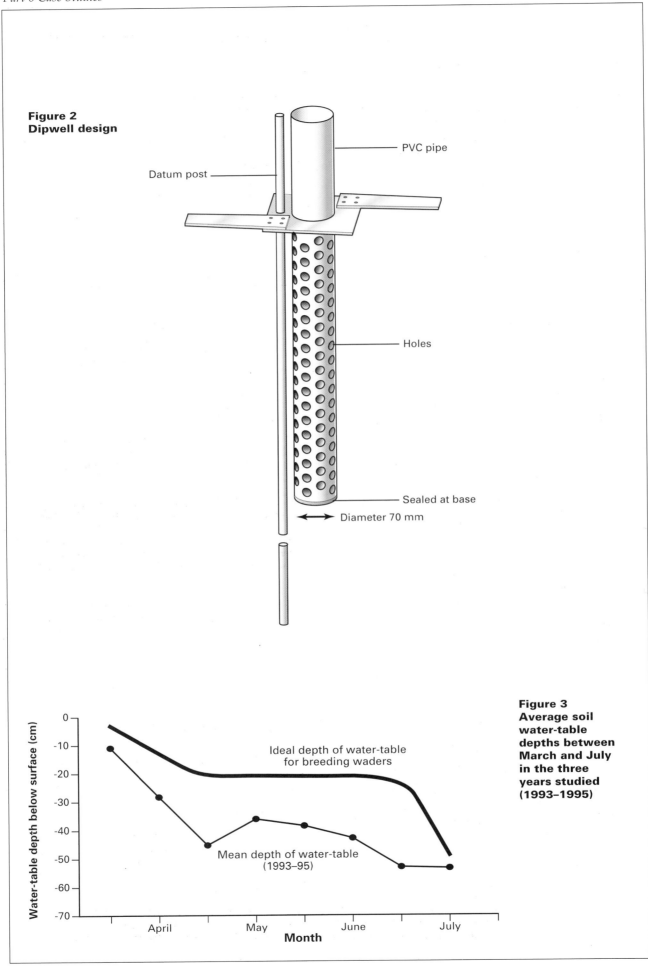

**Figure 2
Dipwell design**

PVC pipe

Datum post

Holes

Sealed at base

Diameter 70 mm

**Figure 3
Average soil
water-table
depths between
March and July
in the three
years studied
(1993–1995)**

Ideal depth of water-table
for breeding waders

Mean depth of water-table
(1993–95)

Water-table depth below surface (cm)

Month

April   May   June   July

Holkham National Nature Reserve

Case Study 7

(English Nature and Holkham Estate)

Location:	Between Burnham Norton and Blakeney, North Norfolk OS 1:50,000 sheet no 132 GR TF875445 Holkham Marshes TF855445 Overy Marshes TF830445 Norton Marshes
Area:	4,000 ha total 401 ha grazing marshes
Designations:	Ramsar, SPA, NNR, SSSI and IBA

Soil Type(s):	Silts
NVC Type(s):	Not surveyed.
Technique(s):	
REHABILITATION: WATER MANAGEMENT (section 4.2) GRASSLAND MANAGEMENT (section 4.4)	

MAIN MANAGEMENT OBJECTIVES

To enhance the conservation interest over the 401 ha of permanent grassland by improved water level control, grazing and mowing regimes.

BACKGROUND

The Holkham grazing marshes were formerly saltmarsh. Reclamation began in the 16th century with the construction of sea wall embankments around Overy Marshes. This was extended around Holkham Marshes in the following years and was completed in 1859 with the Wells sea wall.

The reclaimed saltmarsh was used as grazing for cattle and sheep up to the Second World War, when some areas were converted to arable. By 1985, nearly half of the grassland area was under arable cultivation. The wildlife interest of the marshes was extremely limited, largely confined to drainage channel flora and fauna. The National Nature Reserve was established in 1967 and is managed by English Nature (EN) under an agreement with the Holkham Estate.

The grassland consists of three separate units, each with independent hydrology (Figure 1). Each hydrological unit is spring-fed, a supply providing sufficient water even in dry summers. In 1986 improved water level and grassland management was introduced to increase the wildlife interest of the area.

WATER MANAGEMENT

- A hydrological study was undertaken in 1986, to determine the correct siting of water control structures.

- A series of clay dams and piped water controls were then installed on Holkham Marsh.

- In 1987/88 work was undertaken by contractors which involved strengthening clay dams and constructing a new pile-driven timber sluice at the main outfall at Norton Marsh.

- At Overy Marsh two piped water control points were constructed to isolate the northern half of the marsh to accommodate high water-table management. This was necessary to avoid flooding neighbouring arable land which continues to drain via the south marsh, to the Burnham Overy sea wall outfall.

- In 1990 a series of timber dams were installed on Holkham Marsh, some complete with water control structures (Figure 2).

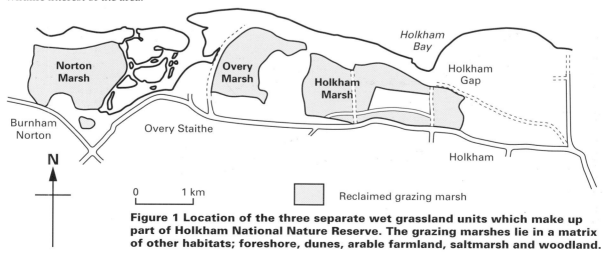

Figure 1 Location of the three separate wet grassland units which make up part of Holkham National Nature Reserve. The grazing marshes lie in a matrix of other habitats; foreshore, dunes, arable farmland, saltmarsh and woodland.

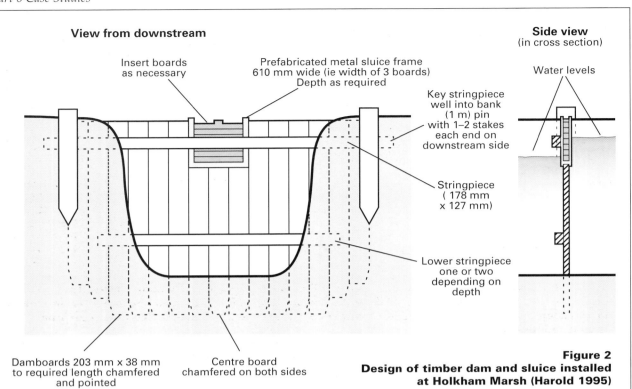

View from downstream

Insert boards as necessary

Prefabricated metal sluice frame 610 mm wide (ie width of 3 boards) Depth as required

Side view
(in cross section)

Water levels

Key stringpiece well into bank (1 m) pin with 1–2 stakes each end on downstream side

Stringpiece (178 mm x 127 mm)

Lower stringpiece one or two depending on depth

Damboards 203 mm x 38 mm to required length chamfered and pointed

Centre board chamfered on both sides

**Figure 2
Design of timber dam and sluice installed at Holkham Marsh (Harold 1995)**

- Using these control structures, partial flood conditions are created in winter on at least 10% of the areas and spring floodwater is retained for breeding waders and wildfowl, with at least 5% of the area permanently flooded.

- To facilitate water level management a seven-year rotation of ditch slubbing has been implemented over 40 km of drainage channel length.

GRASSLAND MANAGEMENT

- Grazing agreements have been established with tenants and licensees, the grazing period running from 20 May to 15 October. Early in the season stock graze higher, drier fields of lower conservation interest. The local farmers tend to the stock with some assistance from EN staff.

- Stocking densities are within the range 1.25–3.75 LSU/ha, with the average at 2.5 LSU/ha. This achieves an end of season sward length of 5–8 cm. Cattle (mostly small suckler herds) are the preferred grazer, sheep are used only when cattle are unavailable.

- Nest protectors (simple cages) are used to cover wader nests at risk from trampling by stock (Plate 1).

- On higher, dry fields with no value for breeding birds, hay is cut from 1 July and grazed thereafter. Most of Overy Marsh is managed in this way and includes some silage making on fertilised fields in spring. Silage cutting is due to stop after 1996.

- Use of fertilisers and herbicides is now limited by agreement with licensees.

- Thistles are controlled by topping using a tractor and 'Votex' topper or by applying herbicide with an 'Ecowipe' weed-wiper.

BENEFITS

- A mosaic of grassy fields, reedbeds, scrapes, flashes, drainage channels and open water has been created. Situated as they are in a prime coastal location, they have succeeded in attracting large numbers of birds and the results have exceeded planned targets.

- A high water-table has been maintained with water levels at or within 10 cm of the surface from October–June in most years. Water-table depths are not uniform across fields however, and field centres can become very dry in mid-summer. Breeding populations of wader species, such as snipe and lapwing, have become nationally important (Table 1).

- Stable, high water levels have been maintained in the drainage channels which function as wet fences thus facilitating stock management. In addition, this has benefited breeding waterfowl species, such as garganey, as well as aquatic plants and invertebrates.

- Since the introduction of the new regime, breeding waders have achieved a higher breeding success rate owing to reduced nest trampling and improved feeding conditions in terms of water-table depth and sward height (Table 2).

- Winter wildfowl numbers have increased, and the site is now internationally important for the number of duck and geese that it supports in winter (Table 3).

- Breeding yellow wagtails have increased in numbers because of improved nesting and feeding conditions (Table 1). Declines in 1994 and 1995 are thought to be associated with problems on the wintering grounds.

Table 1: Breeding birds at Holkham NNR 1986–95

Species	Prior to management		After introduction of management							
	1986	1987	1988	1989	1990	1991	1992	1993	1994	1995
Little grebe	0	5	8	20	38	40	39	43	39	46
Gadwall	0	1	3	8	9	12	15	12	15	15
Mallard	12	19	23	36	48	61	68	82	62	56
Garganey	0	0	0	0	1	2	1	1	2	0
Shoveler	0	2	5	13	16	17	15	16	12	12
Pochard	0	0	2	3	8	11	9	14	19	21
Tufted duck	0	2	6	12	8	11	9	13	16	16
Coot	5	31	36	50	89	109	111	175	155	176
Oystercatcher	0	2	6	5	10	17	20	22	27	25
Lapwing	81	73	84	112	148	178	201	240	226	221
Snipe	5	8	18	25	27	28	27	26	17	11
Redshank	8	8	18	26	39	51	50	56	79	85
Yellow wagtail	5	9	10	13	22	23	21	21	8	11

Table 2: Improved breeding success of lapwing, following management at Holkham NNR. The improved breeding success may be attributed to improved habitat management, but other factors should be considered, eg the effects of predator control or weather. Potential and expected figures are from Cramp and Simmons (1983).

Breeding success	1990	1991	improved management			
			1992	1993	1994	1995
No of pairs	148	178	201	240	226	221
Potential young hatched (@ 2.6/pair)	385	463	523	624	588	575
Expected fledged young (@ 0.43/pair)	64	76	86	103	97	95
Actual young fledged	15	90–110	130	150	140	100–120
% actually fledged of total expected	23	118–145	151	146	144	105–126

Table 3: Average peak counts of selected wintering wildfowl species prior to, and after management at Holkham NNR

Species	Pre-management 1983/84 to 1987/88	Post-management 1989/90 to 1994/95
Pink-footed goose	1,651	9,521
White-fronted goose	275	342
Wigeon	<1,000	8,245
Teal	128	1,460

(Ron Harold)

Plate 1
Nest protectors protect bird nests from trampling by stock and can increase breeding productivity.

Berney Marshes

(RSPB)

Location:	Just west of confluence of Rivers Yare and Waveney and Breydon Water, Norfolk OS 1:50,000 sheet no 134 GR TG 466055
Area:	Total 405 ha Wet grassland 393 ha Reserve forms part of the 6,000 ha Halvergate Marshes system
Designations:	SSSI, ESA and IBA

Soil Type(s): Estuarine silty clay

NVC Type(s): MG6, MG11, MG13

Technique(s):
WATER MANAGEMENT STRUCTURES:
FOOT DRAINS (section 4.2.2)
WIND-POWERED PUMPS (section 4.2.2)

MAIN MANAGEMENT OBJECTIVES

To maintain and enhance the traditional Broadland landscape and ecosystems.

To maintain the nature reserve as a disturbance-free roosting and feeding area for internationally important numbers of wintering wildfowl.

BACKGROUND

Berney Marshes forms part of the 6,000 ha Halvergate Marshes complex. The site is predominantly coastal grazing marsh with small areas of saltmarsh, reed, scrub and artificial ponds. Management aims to reinstate traditional systems of agriculture, which created a typical Broadland landscape dominated by wet grassland and drained by wind-pumps through a series of drainage channels connected to a network of shallow foot drains.

Botanically the grassland is species-poor but the reserve supports six nationally scarce plant species. Little is known of the invertebrates of the reserve but at least one nationally rare dragonfly occurs, the Norfolk hawker. Saline influences owing to the proximity of the sea create brackish water conditions which can support interesting invertebrate communities. The soil consists of silty estuarine clay, which presents a challenge to managers trying to create ideal conditions for breeding and wintering birds. Poorly structured clay lacks the porosity and penetrability of peat.

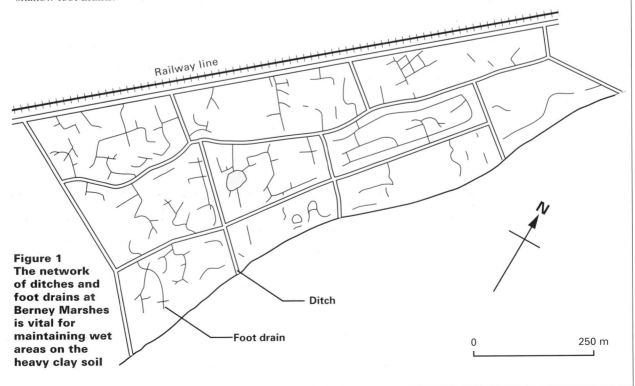

Railway line

Ditch

Foot drain

0   250 m

Figure 1 The network of ditches and foot drains at Berney Marshes is vital for maintaining wet areas on the heavy clay soil

FOOT DRAINS

- The poorly structured clay soils have very low hydraulic conductivity and low drainable porosity. As a result drainage channels have far less influence on field water levels than on peat sites. To facilitate the flooding (and drainage) of such areas at Berney the existing network of foot drains has been restored (Figure 1).

- Foot drains are cut and cleaned with a tractor-mounted PTO-driven (Melleti) cutter (cost £2,000). About 500 m can be cut in an hour at a cost of £0.20/m. This operation is restricted to the summer months as the cutter requires dry soil conditions (Plate 1).

- Foot drains are cut to a maximum depth of 50 cm and a width of 1 m. Profiles are initially steep but are gradually modified by cattle poaching (Figure 2).

- Most foot drains have a piped section into the main drainage channel to allow tractor and cattle access around the perimeter of the field.

- Foot drains are re-cut (cleaned) on a five-year rotation.

- At Berney, saline seepage creates brackish water conditions. Fresh water is less dense than salt water; foot drains are therefore often fresher than their feeder drainage channels as they are supplied from the top of the water column. Wind action and position of pumps can affect these haloclines. Sometimes hypersaline conditions (up to 8,000 μS) are created when water is drawn down, trapped in foot drains and evapotranspiration occurs.

BENEFITS

- Foot drains greatly facilitate the flooding and draw-down of water on clay sites such as Berney.

- Water level management has created suitable conditions for internationally important numbers of Bewick's swans to use the site in winter. Additionally other species, such as white-fronted goose, shoveler and ruff, reach nationally important levels during the winter (Table 1).

- Studies of invertebrate density at Berney show the importance of foot drains for non-biting midge larvae. Pioneer invertebrate communities are typically low diversity–high biomass systems providing a valuable food source. Spring draw-down concentrates these invertebrate resources into foot drains making them accessible to waterfowl and their young. Drying out

Figure 2
The different stages of foot drain development at Berney Marshes

Soon after management (0–4 months)

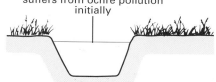

Water is turbid and often suffers from ochre pollution initially

A period of drying out after cutting may facilitate vegetation establishment

Intermediate phase (4 months – 5 years)

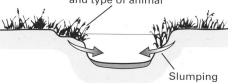

Poaching process begins - dependent on grazing pressure and type of animal

Slumping

Vegetation composition and establishment is dependent on water regime and quality

Established foot-drain (5–15 years)

Abundant dead organic matter (good for non-biting midge larvae)

Water usually static

Vegetation established with the following being present, brackish water-crowfoot, celery-leaved buttercup, sea club-rush, saltmarsh rush and mare's-tail

Table 1: Increases in waterfowl species wintering at Berney Marshes; those occurring in internationally (in bold) and nationally important (italic) numbers are particularly important

Species	Pre-management winter 1986/87	Post-management winter 1994/95	Mean maxima 1988/89 – 1992/93
Bewick's swan	38	186	**495**
European white-fronted goose	37	100	*108*
Wigeon	480	2,700	1,918
Gadwall	2	47	61
Teal	20	925	331
Pintail	12	89	70
Shoveler	-	213	*126*
Ruff	4	124	*42*

also allows oxidation of substrata detritus and subsequent release of nutrients, boosting productivity.

■ Creating a network of foot drains increases structural diversity allowing a range of salinity conditions to occur. Brackish water communities are less diverse, but are scarcer in a UK context, than freshwater ones. Hypersaline foot drains can be detrimental to stock, but can also harbour interesting vegetation and invertebrate communities.

■ Foot drains allow water features to remain on the fields in the late spring and early summer without causing the fields to be excessively poached by cattle.

WIND-POWERED PUMPS

■ Windmills are used in place of diesel and electric pumps.

■ Windmills are built on site and consist of a centrifugal pump, driven by a 4-m wind tower with a four-sail 3-m diameter rotor (Plate 2). The effective output of such a windmill is only 1.2 hp or 900 W; as a result the water intake must be protected to prevent jamming of the impeller by debris or even water voles. The design includes a stall protection device which turns the windmill out of the wind in the event of gusts or very strong winds. Total cost of materials for each unit, excluding VAT, was £4,000.

■ Capacity – lifts 16 litres/s over a 40-cm head, at a constant wind speed of 11–16 knots (force 4). Capacity is reduced with increasing head (the vertical height difference between input and output levels). Taller towers result in increased power as a result of a smoother, less interrupted airflow.

■ Careful consideration must be given to siting windmills. Flow capacity will change depending on input/output levels. In spring input levels may drop drastically owing to evapotranspiration, increasing effective head of pump and lowering capacity. It is also necessary to make sure that the hydrological system supplying the windmill and delivering water to the target area is as efficient as possible.

BENEFITS

■ Environmentally friendly method of maintaining water levels in managed areas, cutting out the need for diesel or electric pumps. Additionally there is no noise pollution as windmills are almost silent.

■ Very low running costs.

■ Artificial flow characteristics of wetland systems can be enhanced. Water can be circulated around and through the site without having to consider financial or environmental costs. It is important to replace water in small managed units such as Berney as often as feasibly possible. At Berney inputs are high but outputs occur only through evapotranspiration and flow rates are low. Maintaining flow and exchanging water when possible is therefore important to prevent build up of nutrients and salinity.

(Dave Barrett)

Plate 1 Foot drain cutting and cleaning using this machine requires dry soil conditions and is therefore restricted to the summer months.

(Dave Barrett)

Plate 2 The windmill design used at Berney incorporates a centrifugal pump, driven by 4 metre wind tower with a four-sail 3 metre diameter rotor.

Old Hall Marshes

(RSPB)

Location:	15 km south of Colchester, Essex OS 1:50,000 sheet no 168 GR TL975125
Area:	Total 459 ha Wet grassland 361 ha
Designations:	Ramsar, SPA, NNR, ESA, IBA

Soil Type(s):	Clay
NVC Type(s):	Not known
Technique(s):	
WINTER WATER STORAGE (section 4.2.2)	

MAIN MANAGEMENT OBJECTIVES

To manage the site for the benefit of nationally important assemblages of wintering and breeding waterfowl, plants and invertebrates.

To enhance the wildlife value by manipulation of water levels and grazing.

BACKGROUND

Old Hall Marshes was reclaimed from saltmarsh during the 15th century, with a large proportion of the site lying below mean sea level. The majority of the site comprises unimproved coastal grazing marsh, with smaller areas of improved grassland, reedbed, saltmarsh and brackish water-bodies. There has been a long tradition of cattle and sheep grazing.

The Essex coast is one of the driest places in the country. Old Hall Marshes has a very low mean annual rainfall (526 mm) coupled with a high annual evapotranspiration rate (550 mm). Because of this it is essential to retain as much water as possible during the period from October to April, to enable effective water management during the spring and early summer.

WINTER WATER STORAGE

- Low rainfall and high evapotranspiration, coupled with the absence of significant surface and groundwater sources, means that it is essential to store winter water to meet the summer water deficit.

- Old Hall Marshes has an extensive network of creeks formed into eight major water control units (Plate 1). These systems are topped to capacity using a combination of internal rainwater run-off and water taken under licence from the nearby Salcotstone Brook, the only flowing source of freshwater. Water is abstracted using a 6" Sykes Univac pump with a level-dictated automatic on/off switch.

- Any excess water is pumped through the water control units, to create circulation in the otherwise closed system.

- During the period May to September five of the eight water control units are allowed to draw-down naturally through evapotranspiration (410 mm). In the remaining three systems the rate of draw-down is slowed by pumping water, using the largest system as a reservoir.

(Bob Glover)

Plate 1 One of the water control units at Old Hall Marshes. Such units are filled to capacity during the winter using internal rainwater and water taken from a nearby brook.

(Chris Tuas)

Plate 2 High winter water levels, followed by a controlled spring draw-down, create ideal conditions for wintering wildfowl and breeding waders.

BENEFITS

- The current water management regime, instigated in 1992/93 winter, fixes reasonable and constant winter and summer water levels throughout the system (Plate 2).

- Holding extra freshwater and controlling summer draw-down has reduced salinity fluctuations, reducing the mean summer conductivity peak from 25,000 μS to 14,000 μS and reducing the difference between maxima and minima from 10,000 μS to 5,000 μS.

- The controlled spring/summer draw-down produces wet edge feeding for waders throughout, but still leaves sufficient open water for wildfowl at the summer minimum.

- The control regime, combined with effective cattle and sheep grazing, has increased the numbers of key breeding waterfowl from 58 pairs in 1991 to 197 pairs in 1994 (Table 1).

- This management also increased the peak maxima of key wintering species, from 6,600 birds in 1991/92 to 13,852 in 1993/94 (Table 2). The number of passage waders using the site has also increased.

Table 1: Numbers of breeding waterfowl at Old Hall Marshes RSPB Nature Reserve, before and after installation of winter water storage regime. Nationally important numbers are in bold

Species	Number of breeding pairs in 1991 (pre-management)	Number of breeding pairs in 1994 (post-management)	Five-year mean (1991–95)
Garganey	0	3	1.5
Gadwall	3	8	7
Shoveler	3	16	12
Pochard	12	24	19
Avocet	0	14	5
Lapwing	19	44	33
Redshank	21	88	48

Table 2: Numbers of wintering waterfowl at Old Hall Marshes RSPB Nature Reserve, before and after installation of winter water storage regime. Nationally important numbers are in bold

Species	Winter peak maxima pre-management 1991/92	Winter peak maxima post-management 1993/94	Five-year mean 1990/91–1994/95
Brent goose	**3,450**	4,528	**4,522**
Wigeon	608	**3,685**	2,005
Teal	**1,778**	2,839	**1,829**
Shoveler	51	**110**	92
Golden plover	630	**2,500**	**2,858**
Ruff	40	**80**	**54**
Black-tailed godwit	43	**110**	60

Pulborough Brooks

(RSPB)

Location:	2 km south of Pulborough, West Sussex. OS 1:50,000 sheet no 197 GR TQ 054170
Area:	Total 207 ha (171 ha freehold) Wet grassland 147 ha (121 ha freehold)
Designations:	SSSI and IBA

Soil Type(s):	Mainly silts and clays
NVC Type(s):	MG9, MG13
Technique(s):	DRAINAGE CHANNEL REHABILITATION (section 4.3.2) DRAINAGE CHANNEL MANAGEMENT (section 4.3.2)

MAIN MANAGEMENT OBJECTIVES

To manage the site for the benefit of nationally important assemblages of wintering and breeding waterfowl.

To enhance the wildlife value by manipulation of water levels and grazing and mowing regimes.

BACKGROUND

The Pulborough Brooks are part (8%) of the River Arun floodplain, which were managed for centuries as water meadows (Figure 1). Drainage improvements, including canalisation of the River Arun, and intensive farming practices, have had a significantly detrimental effect on the wildlife of the whole valley. In addition, this area of the Brooks fell into dereliction during the mid to late 1980s when farming ceased altogether. The water supply is from the River Stor, backed up by the tidal influence of the River Arun and a number of springs along the eastern boundary of the north Brooks. Water levels on the Brooks are, for most of the year,

dependent on water levels in the rivers. The grassland is fairly species-poor, aquatic plants in the drainage channels continue to hold the main botanical interest.

The RSPB purchased the site in 1989 and set about restoring the wet grassland and its associated drainage system.

DRAINAGE CHANNEL REHABILITATION

Owing to several years of neglect, the majority of the drainage channels required slubbing and reprofiling to enhance their value for wildlife. The starting condition of the drainage channels varied depending on previous use/management and individual characteristics (see Table 1 for costs).

■ Drainage channel rehabilitation is ongoing and is followed by a three to seven-year rotational management programme (Figure 1). By 1994, 67% of the drainage channels had been treated (10 km of the 15 km length).

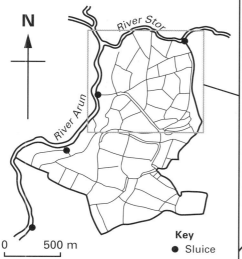

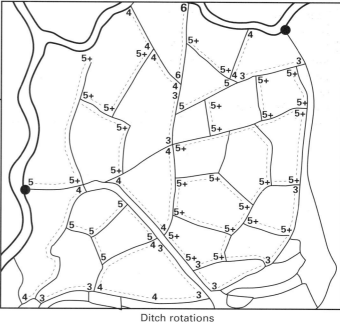

Ditch rotations (years)

Figure 1 Water control structures and ditch management rotation at Pulborough Brooks. Spring water and run-off is used in preference to river water whenever feasible because of the poor quality of the latter. Ditch management takes place on roughly a four-year rotation

Key
● Sluice

0   500 m

- Plant and invertebrate surveys were undertaken prior to commencement of work.

- Work was carried out in July–October period when water levels were lowest.

- All work was undertaken using a tracked, long-reach hydraulic digger with a 1-m ditching bucket. Drainage channels with little silt to clear were cleared/partially cleared of accumulated vegetation using a 1.5-m weeding bucket.

- Drainage channels were also reprofiled so that one or both edges have *c*. 45° gradient profile (Figure 2). Most drainage channels were also widened along some or all of their length.

- Drainage channels with spoil banks from successive clearing over the years were reprofiled such that the raised bank was removed (Figure 2).

- Spoil was placed at least 5 m from the drainage channel edge and was subsequently rotovated and spread when dry.

- At appropriate points, spoil was used to construct low bunds designed to produce temporary or permanent pools on adjacent grassland. Spoil was also used to repair earth gateways with culverted flexipipes to facilitate control of water levels across the site.

- At sharp intersections of drainage channels, the corners were removed to produce small, deep pools or small islands (Figure 3).

DRAINAGE CHANNEL MANAGEMENT

In order to ensure maintenance of the wildlife value of the rehabilitated drainage channel system, a programme of rotational management was begun in 1993/94.

- Drainage channels are cleared of accumulated silt and the aquatic and marginal vegetation reduced by variable degrees. This occurs on a three- to seven-year rotation depending on the requirements of individual drainage channels.

- Short sections (<500 m) are cleaned along only one side of the drainage channel, to reduce the impact of the operation.

- Selected drainage channels are managed as above but on a rigid programme and monitored closely for the effect this may have on wildlife.

- Along the edges of selected drainage channels, electric stock fencing is used to prevent grazing and allow common reed to grow.

Table 1: Cost of drainage channel management in 1995

Technique	Cost (£/m)
Ditching:	
Clearing with vegetation bucket	0.50
De-silting	0.75
Widening	1.75
Reprofiling:	
Spoil used locally	1.00
Spoil removed	1.75
Rotovating spoil	0.05–0.10*
Rotovating and spreading spoil	0.25**

* Varies with quantity of spoil and soil type ** maximum
The figures are based on minimum drainage channel lengths of 200 m and do not include transport costs. Costs increase with shorter lengths.

BENEFITS

- Pulborough Brooks supports nearly 50 species of aquatic plant, which represents a third of the drainage channel flora of Great Britain. Additionally, 24 species of nationally important invertebrate have been recorded, including the scarce chaser dragonfly.

- The clearing and reprofiling of the drainage channels have increased the area of open water benefiting aquatic plants and breeding wildfowl (Table 2 and Figure 4).

- The reprofiled drainage channel edges have provided ideal feeding margins for many birds in particular breeding wader species, such as lapwing, redshank and snipe (Figure 4).

- The drainage channels now function as effective stock barriers. The reprofiled edges allow access to cattle for drinking and make it easier for cattle to climb out should they fall in.

- The use of spoil to provide permanent and temporary pools has benefited breeding and wintering birds, plus aquatic invertebrates such as dragonflies.

- The removal of old spoil banks along drainage channels enables water to spill out, producing muddy margins suitable for feeding waders, and is of potential benefit to emergent vegetation.

- The use of spoil to construct flexi-pipe sluices enables water levels to be controlled independently in the drainage channels. This produces stable water levels (65–100% full) throughout the summer, principally for the benefit of breeding waterfowl and aquatic plants.

- The use of electric stock fencing along selected drainage channel edges has permitted linear reedbeds to develop, benefiting reed warbler, sedge warbler and water rail.

- Well maintained drainage channels enable efficient water level control. In winter, more than 24,000 waterfowl can occur, typically 55–75% of the Arun Valley wintering population may be present on the reserve. Wet grassland birds which breed include garganey, shoveler, lapwing, snipe, redshank and yellow wagtail.

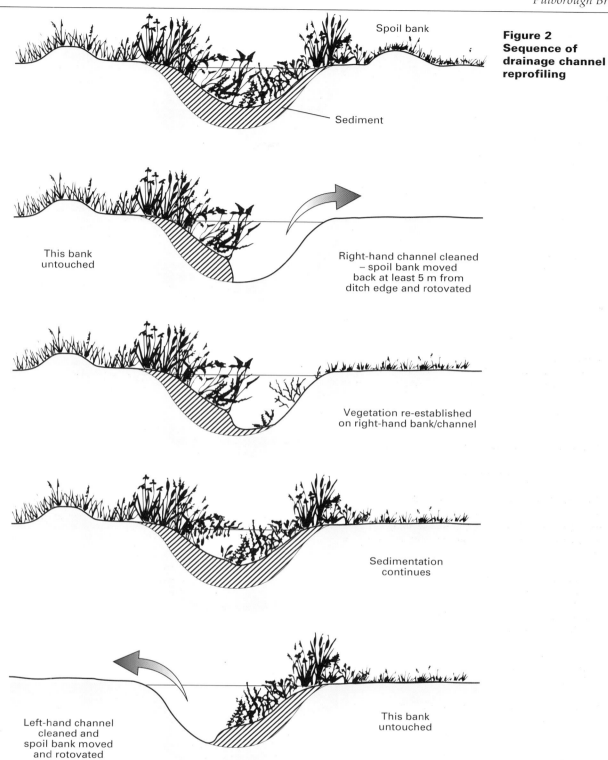

Figure 2
Sequence of drainage channel reprofiling

Spoil bank

Sediment

This bank untouched

Right-hand channel cleaned – spoil bank moved back at least 5 m from ditch edge and rotovated

Vegetation re-established on right-hand bank/channel

Sedimentation continues

Left-hand channel cleaned and spoil bank moved and rotovated

This bank untouched

Table 2: Increases of rare and nationally scarce plant species at Pulborough Brooks.

Species	1990	1994
Sharp-leaved pondweed (Red Data Book)	Recorded from 11 ditches.	Recorded from 30 ditches.
Hairlike pondweed (Nationally scarce)	Recorded from 5 sites.	Recorded from 6 sites.
Greater water-parsnip (Nationally scarce)	Recorded from 2 sites.	Decline at 1 site but found in 4 new sites.
Narrow-leaved water-dropwort (Nationally scarce)	Recorded from 1 site (hayfield).	Recorded from 3 new sites (hayfields).

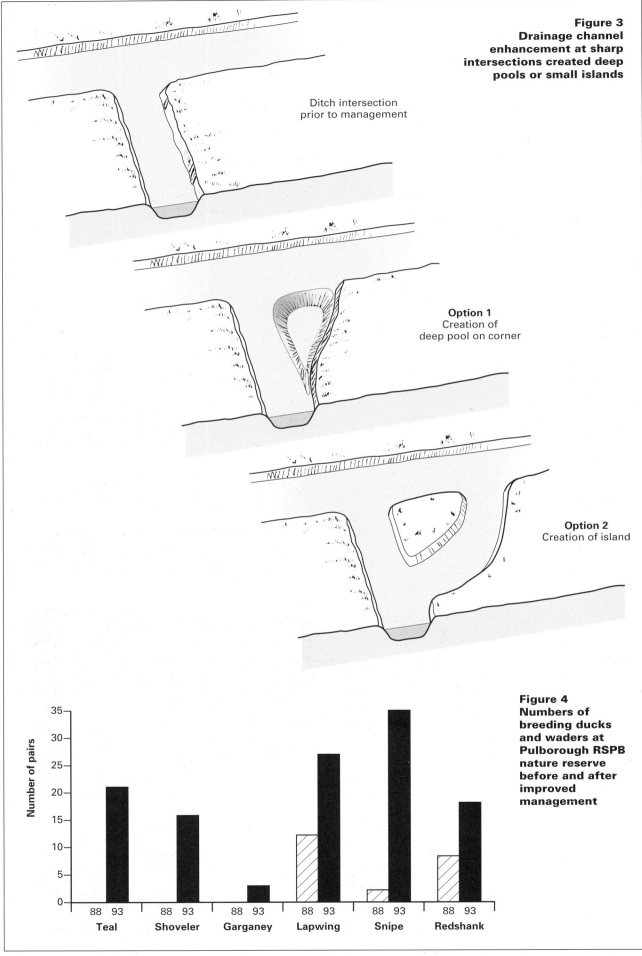

Figure 3
Drainage channel enhancement at sharp intersections created deep pools or small islands

Ditch intersection prior to management

Option 1
Creation of deep pool on corner

Option 2
Creation of island

Figure 4
Numbers of breeding ducks and waders at Pulborough RSPB nature reserve before and after improved management

Nene Washes

(RSPB)

Location:	Whittlesey, Cambridgeshire OS 1:50,000 sheet no 143 GR TL294995
Area:	Nene Washes 1,300 ha Total reserve area 319 ha Wet grassland 283 ha
Designations:	Ramsar, SPA, cSAC, SSSI and IBA

Soil Type(s):	Peat
NVC Type(s):	MG7, MG9, MG13, S5

Technique(s):
GRAZING (section 4.4.4)
SHEPHERDING (section 4.4.4)
Water Management (section 4.2)

MAIN MANAGEMENT OBJECTIVES

To continue traditional grazing and mowing regimes on reserve wet grassland and swamp habitats to benefit the wintering and breeding waterfowl.

BACKGROUND

The Nene Washes in the Cambridgeshire Fens were created in the 17th century to store floodwater from the River Nene. The RSPB Nature Reserve covers about a quarter of this area. It is bounded by the River Nene to the north and Moreton's Leam to the south. The fields are divided by numerous drainage channels (Figure 1). Most of the reserve has been arable in the recent past but has been restored to wet grassland by natural regeneration and re-seeding, particularly since acquisition began by the RSPB in 1982. There are only 8 ha of unimproved pasture which have never been ploughed. About 100 ha of the reserve is very low-lying and readily floods in winter. The remainder is affected by natural flooding which does not occur every year. The water levels in Moreton's Leam and the adjacent drainage channels are lowered in winter to increase the

flood storage capacity of the washland. The levels are raised in spring to provide wet fencing.

GRAZING

Summer grazing with cattle is undertaken from mid-May to the end of October (Figure 1). Flooding may delay the start of the grazing season or require an early evacuation of livestock. Grazing regimes vary between 50 and 300 LSU days/ha/year depending on stock availability and the effects of weather and flooding on grass growth. Generally about two-thirds of the cattle used are suckler herds (cows and calves) and one-third are stores.

- The Cradge Bank is grazed heavily from mid-May to the end of October using cattle at a stocking density of 150–300 LSU days/ha/year.

- Early season grazing is concentrated on the higher ground to avoid nest trampling on wetter fields and areas of high wildlife interest. Grazing is followed by topping to provide short swards (less than 10 cm) in the autumn.

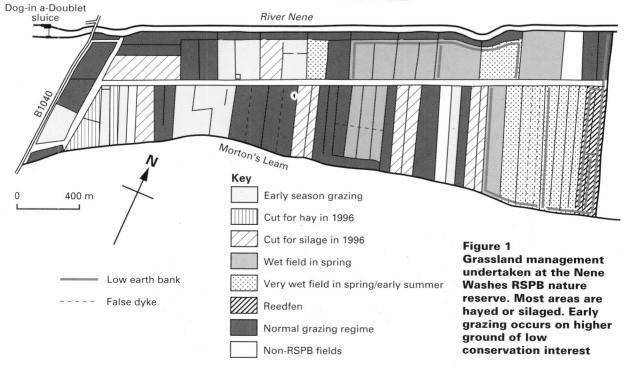

Dog-in a-Doublet sluice

River Nene

B1040

Morton's Leam

N

0   400 m

Key

- Early season grazing
- Cut for hay in 1996
- Cut for silage in 1996
- Wet field in spring
- Very wet field in spring/early summer
- Reedfen
- Normal grazing regime
- Non-RSPB fields

······· Low earth bank

- - - - - False dyke

Figure 1
Grassland management undertaken at the Nene Washes RSPB nature reserve. Most areas are hayed or silaged. Early grazing occurs on higher ground of low conservation interest

- 161 ha are grazed moderately heavily by cattle and sheep from mid-May to the end of October to promote a varied vegetation structure (sward height 5–15 cm). Stock density: 100–250 LSU days/ha/year.

- 49 ha of the wettest grassland are grazed moderately heavily by cattle from mid-July to October to maintain swards (10-30 cm). Stock density: 50–150 LSU days/ha/year.

- Fields which are cut for hay or silage (approximately 50 ha in 1994 and 1995) are afterwards grazed lightly to achieve short swards (5–15 cm). Availability of stock determines the extent of the aftermath grazing. Aftermath grazing by sheep is used to control ragwort.

SHEPHERDING

All the grazing on the reserve is let on a headage basis. The region is largely arable so finding stock can be difficult. The provision of a shepherding service allows greater control of grazing and is essential for attracting graziers from as far afield as Shropshire (Table 1).

Table 1: Shepherding services in 1995

- 604 cattle was the highest total number on the reserve (average 543/month, June–October)

- Charges were on a headage basis of £53 for a cow and calf and £37.50 for a store, for the 24-week season.

- This yielded approximately £20,000 income.

- The charge included grazing, haylets and shepherding.

- The cost of medications and veterinary bills were separately recovered from graziers.

- Shepherding services occupied 162 person days.

- Shepherding is carried out from May to October by the warden plus two contract assistants, one of whom is employed as a stockman. Assistants are trained in basic stock-handling skills.

- All stock is counted and checked each morning. Daily checks are made for animals which have crossed wet fences or fallen into drainage channels.

- Regular worming and basic veterinary care is undertaken and, in agreement with the owner, sick animals are treated by a local vet. There are two large pens for the handling, treating and worming of cattle (Table 2).

Table 2: Costs of building cattle pens at the Nene Washes

Typical field cattle pen (30 m x 15 m)	■ Gates	£ 640
	■ Timber	£ 990
	■ Surfacing	£ 3,230
	■ Total	£ 4,860
Large loading pen (55 m x 18 m), capable of holding 400+ cattle in seven compartments, including lorry-turning area	■ Total cost	£ 8,500
	■ Man hours to construct 390	

- Cattle are moved by reserve staff when the required sward height has been achieved or when ground conditions become too wet. Most of the suckler herds are set-stocked in July to reduce the risk of fog fever.

WATER MANAGEMENT

- Many of the 43 km of drainage channels on the reserve area had silted up or become choked with vegetation. These have gradually been opened up again so they form effective wet fences between fields and valuable wildlife habitat. The drainage channels are now slubbed on a five- to seven-year rotation.

- In 1985 the RSPB and Nene Washland Commissioners (the local IDB) agreed to raise the summer water level in the drainage channels by 30 cm, which in turn raised the soil water-table in the fields. The RSPB warden also became the Wash Superintendent responsible for maintaining water levels in the summer.

- Since 1991 the Environment Agency (formerly the NRA) has operated the levels in Moreton's Leam which determines the level in the drainage channels. The flexible approach of raising summer levels early in the spring and maintaining them late into the autumn, when practical to do so, has continued.

Table 3: Peak wintering wildfowl counts at the Nene Washes RSPB Nature Reserve, 1988–95. Totals in bold are internationally important

Species	1988/89	1989/90	1990/91	1991/92	1992/93	1993/94	1994/95
Bewick's swan	**489**	**740**	**741**	**1,139**	203	567	**1,538**
Whooper swan	9	16	47	48	57	32	19
Wigeon	3,204	2,500	1,912	1,300	2,441	3,440	6,650
Gadwall	54	300	104	80	239	296	140
Teal	514	164	942	900	785	1,800	1,400
Pintail	**843**	200	122	140	**768**	577	**1,794**
Shoveler	152	278	134	48	309	330	390
Pochard	33	25	120	7	353	200	270

■ From 1985 control pipes have improved the water management of the lowest lying bunded land, allowing up to 100 ha of guaranteed flooding in winter and the retention of some floods into the spring.

BENEFITS

■ Figure 2 shows the benefits of improved management, including the traditional grazing regime, on breeding ducks and waders at the Nene Washes 1983–95. The breeding colony of black-tailed godwits on site is of special importance, being the largest in the UK.

■ The reserve holds internationally important numbers of Bewick's swan and nationally important numbers of other species during the winter (Table 3).

■ The drainage channels support important plant and invertebrate communities.

■ Moderate grazing and aftermath grazing to produce a sward height of 5–15 cm has increased the numbers of breeding waterfowl species, especially snipe, redshank, black-tailed godwit and shoveler.

■ Early and heavy grazing of higher, drier areas and areas of low wildlife value to produce a short sward (maximum 10 cm) has provided feeding for wintering wildfowl, although numbers tend to fluctuate annually in relation to extent and depth of flooding (eg the maximum count of wildfowl over the whole washland in 1969 was 19,900 and in 1970, 1,277).

■ The relatively late start to the grazing season (mid-May) and RSPB control of livestock allows the driest fields, those with the fewest ground-nesting birds, to be grazed first. This reduces trampling of eggs and young birds and improves wader breeding success. Similarly there is no mowing for hay or silage until mid-June.

■ The maintenance of 5–15 cm swards on artificially flooded areas has benefited grazing winter wildfowl species, especially wigeon and Bewick's swan.

■ The headage system and RSPB shepherding allows fields to be grazed at the required stocking density and cattle to be removed when the required sward height has been achieved.

■ Between 1989 and 1993, the management regime has maintained stable populations of important breeding birds, such as garganey (2–5 prs), shoveler (10–39 prs), ruff (0–2 reeves) and gadwall (8–27 prs).

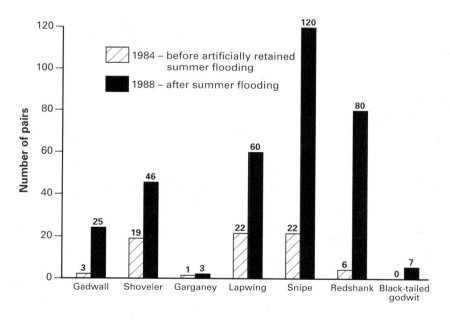

Figure 2
Numbers of breeding ducks and waders at the Nene Washes RSPB Nature Reserve, before and after sympathetic grazing regimes and artificial retained floods were introduced

Lower Derwent Valley

Case Study 12

(English Nature)

Location:	Between Newton-on-Derwent and Wressle. 12 km SE of York, North Yorkshire OS 1:50,000 sheet no 106 GR SE690380
Area:	Total 1,089 ha Wet grassland 1,000 ha
Designations:	Ramsar, SPA, NNR, SSSI and IBA

Soil Type(s):	Clay predominantly, small areas of peat soils
NVC Type(s):	MG4, MG5, MG7, MG8, MG9, MG10, MG11, MG13, S5, M22 and M23
Technique(s):	

GRASSLAND MANAGEMENT (section 4.4)

MAIN MANAGEMENT OBJECTIVES

To maintain and enhance the nature conservation value of the Lower Derwent Valley, with particular emphasis on the conservation of the internationally important flood meadow (MG4) grassland community.

BACKGROUND

The Lower Derwent Valley (Figure 1) consists of a series of flood meadows, fens, swamps, alder woodland and open water features. Within the site are areas that combine to provide an excellent and diverse range of floodplain grassland. The hydrological regime has been altered by embankments, which have reduced the frequency of flooding from the river. Land use and flooding intensity vary across the site, largely controlled by topography. Duration of flooding varies from three weeks (for the majority of the site) to 11 months of the year. Areas flooded for long periods of time are dominated by reed sweet-grass, reed canary-grass, bladder-sedge and slender-tufted sedge.

In addition to the River Derwent SSSI, the 1,000-ha area contains four other grassland SSSIs. Since the 1970s half the site has been purchased by nature conservation bodies (Yorkshire Wildlife Trust, English Nature and the Carstairs Countryside Trust). This area forms the NNR, which is managed and wardened by English Nature. The majority of the landowners of the other half of the site are party to positive management agreements with English Nature (now being converted to Wildlife Enhancement Scheme agreements – see Box 1). Prior to this there was no control over farming activities, water levels or public access in the area. Currently management involves maintaining traditional practices of hay cutting and grazing.

GRASSLAND MANAGEMENT

- About 70% of the grassland of the valley is cut for hay, the remainder is grazed. All MG4 grassland is hayed.

- Summer grazed areas are often those too wet for hay cropping, (eg MG13 sweet-grass stands).

- The management regime is controlled by English Nature through licences and management agreements with local farmers. The following conditions are laid down:

- no cutting before 1 July
- no fertiliser input
- weed species to be controlled by spot-spraying or weed-wiping only – no boom spraying
- stock densities generally follow the regime set in the WES agreement (Box 1).

- After the hay crop is taken the aftermath is grazed by sheep until the area gets too wet, usually about October. MG4 areas are grazed hard at a stocking density of 25 ewes/ha during this period.

Box 1 The Wildlife Enhancement Scheme (WES)

The WES is a pilot project operating on SSSIs in selected areas, one of which is the Vales of Yorkshire. This scheme is essentially an upgraded version of the existing management agreement system.

Its objectives on the wet grassland sites of the Yorkshire Vales are to:
- improve the grassland for specialist components of the flora and fauna.
- show that farming skills can be used to benefit wildlife.

Agreements follow a prescriptive Agreed Management Practice:
- Meadows are cut from 1 July onwards and hay should be removed by 31 August. Hay fields should be aftermath grazed with cattle or sheep, when grass is available, but normally only until the end of October.

- Pasture grazed from 1 May to 31 October, to avoid both disturbing nesting birds in early spring and damaging turf in the winter. Poaching of the ground is to be avoided at all times.

- Stocking rates vary according to the time of year; in May 4 sheep or 1 cow/ha, in June 6 sheep or 1.5 cows/ha, and from 1 July to 31 October there is no limit with the proviso that poaching will be avoided.

- Managers of all areas are required to control ragwort and thistles. Topping is not allowed before 1 July. Artificial fertiliser and farmyard manure application is not allowed. All fences and water and drainage infrastructure has to be maintained.

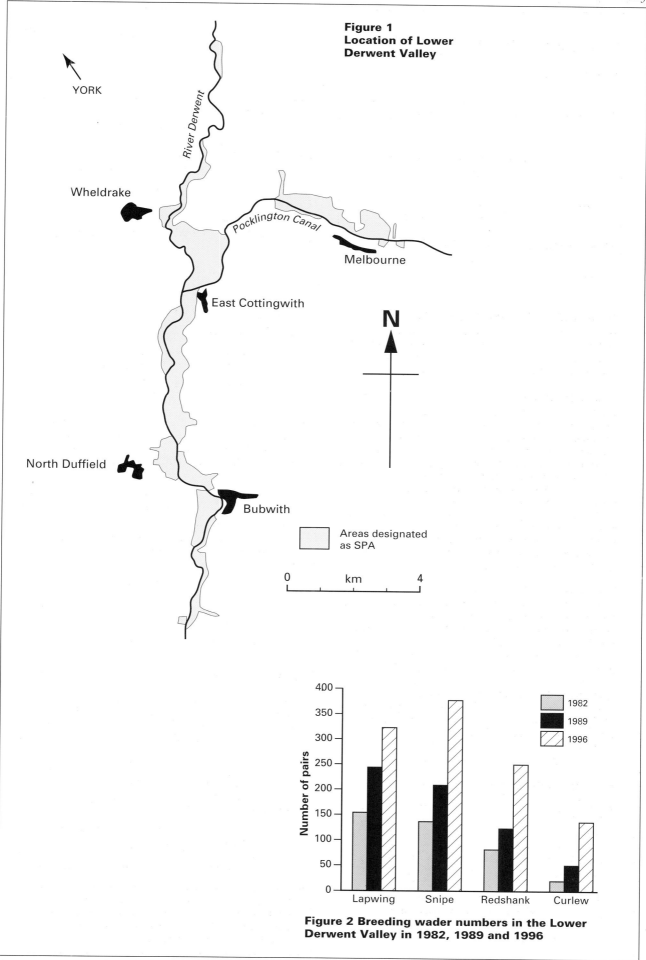

**Figure 1
Location of Lower
Derwent Valley**

YORK

River Derwent

Wheldrake

Pocklington Canal

Melbourne

East Cottingwith

N

North Duffield

Bubwith

Areas designated
as SPA

0   km   4

**Figure 2 Breeding wader numbers in the Lower
Derwent Valley in 1982, 1989 and 1996**

Number of pairs

1982
1989
1996

Lapwing   Snipe   Redshank   Curlew

- Some arable fields, included within the SSSI because of regular flooding, have been converted back to grassland by natural regeneration. In the first year *Persicaria* took hold; it was topped in July and then lightly grazed by sheep through the autumn to encourage grass to tiller. Light grazing by sheep in the following season effectively removed weed species and created a decent grass crop. The following season the grassland was ready for hay cropping.

- In conjunction with improved grassland management water levels have been raised in hydrologically isolated blocks and the drainage channel network has been rehabilitated.

BENEFITS

- Breeding waders have increased following improved management; recently, black-tailed godwits bred for the first time in many years and the site regularly supports breeding ruff (Figure 2). Fields converted from arable may have species-poor swards but are being utilised by breeding waders.

- Breeding ducks have also benefited with increases in key species such as garganey, pintail and shoveler.

- Wintering waterfowl species, especially wigeon, are favoured by the combination of flooded areas and adjacent short turf created by sheep grazing (Table 1). The site has become internationally important for wintering waterfowl.

- Invertebrates flourish under the current management regime:
  - a quarter of the UK beetle fauna (1,000+ species) has been recorded.
  - Moths present on the site include the marsh carpet (an RDB species) and the nationally scarce purple-bordered gold (Plate 1).

- The Lower Derwent Valley also supports the nationally scarce variable damselfly and is the most northerly station in the UK for the red-eyed damselfly.

- Low-intensity grassland management maintains the largest expanse of meadow foxtail–great burnet grassland (MG4) in the UK (see also Case Study 13). Additionally, the site supports a quarter of the UK flora including nationally scarce plant species such as marsh pea and greater water-parsnip.

(Roger Key)

Plate 1 The purple-bordered gold moth is one of many nationally scarce invertebrates found in the Lower Derwent Valley.

Table 1: Wintering waterfowl numbers for the Lower Derwent Valley from 1968/69 to 1995/96. Internationally important totals are in bold

Counts	Winter periods			
	68/69 – 75/76	76/77 – 82/83	83/84 – 89/90	90/91 – 95/96
Average peak count – all wildfowl	2,793	12,877	15,523	24,199
Average peak count – all waders	1,635	5,135	8,690	17,225
Average peak count total – waterfowl	4,428	18,012	**24,213**	**41,424**
Average peak counts for individual species				
Wigeon	1,562	4,570	6,902	**10,308**
Lapwing	1,031	2,683	4,612	7,674
Golden plover	331	1,931	3,277	5,358
Dunlin	264	405	513	1,045
Curlew	2	62	137	280
Redshank	6	42	82	170
Ruff	2	8	37	131

Loch Gruinart

(RSPB)

Location:	Isle of Islay, Argyll, Scotland OS 1:50,000 sheet no 60 GR NR 285665
Area:	Total freehold 1,667 ha Wet grassland 331 ha
Designations:	Ramsar, SPA, SSSI, ESA and IBA

Soil Type(s):	Alluvial soils, peat
NVC Type(s):	MG5, MG7, MG9, MG10, MG13, S22, M23, M25
Technique(s):	
GRASSLAND MANAGEMENT (section 4.4)	

MAIN MANAGEMENT OBJECTIVES

To maintain and enhance on the reserve prime examples of a suite of typical Hebridean habitats and species, particularly corncrake, hen harrier, chough, wintering geese, and wintering and breeding waders and wildfowl. An essential requirement to achieve this will be an efficient, environmentally sound, farming operation.

BACKGROUND

The Loch Gruinart reserve includes areas of re-seeded and semi-improved grassland (Figure 1). During the 19th century reclamation of an extensive floodplain

marsh and saltmarsh complex created grassland now used for hay/silage making and grazing. The RSPB acquired the reserve in 1984 and embarked on creating an agricultural operation that would ensure optimum management of the wet grassland for geese. The need for grazing made it necessary for the RSPB to run its own beef suckler herd and small sheep flock. Since then the main focus has shifted to management for corncrake, chough and breeding waders.

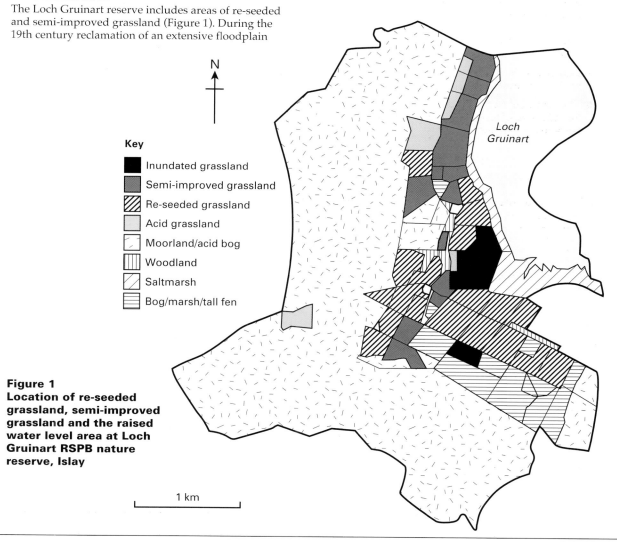

Key

- ⬛ Inundated grassland
- ▨ Semi-improved grassland
- ▨ Re-seeded grassland
- ▨ Acid grassland
- Moorland/acid bog
- ▥ Woodland
- ▨ Saltmarsh
- ▤ Bog/marsh/tall fen

Figure 1
Location of re-seeded grassland, semi-improved grassland and the raised water level area at Loch Gruinart RSPB nature reserve, Islay

1 km

GRASSLAND MANAGEMENT FOR BIRDS

Grassland management for birds at Loch Gruinart follows a system that embraces the needs of a variety of key species. Past management was targeted primarily at wintering geese. Barnacle geese prefer to feed on high-quality swards. In the 1980s, in order to attract geese away from neighbouring farmland, grassland production was intensified, but the associated drainage of low-lying wet grassland had adverse effects on the number of breeding waders using the site.

Recently an improved and more integrated management regime has been introduced, aiming to meet the needs of the globally threatened corncrake, as well as those of wintering geese and breeding waders. Corncrake management revolves around the provision of tall vegetation in April/May and undisturbed hay/silage fields which are cut after mid-August in a manner that ensures young and adults are not killed (for more details see Andrews and Rebane 1994).

- During grass-growing periods, ie early autumn and early spring, geese are likely to be in conflict with local farmers' interests. During these periods the reserve aims to attract as many of the geese on the island as possible.

- The low-lying wet grassland is all roughly at sea level. Each field has a managed drainage channel at each end to drain water into the main drain and out to the sea through a flap valve. Sub-surface drainage systems have been allowed to fall into disrepair. As a result the area is very wet for most of the year.

- **Raised water level management.** Since 1990 three of the lowest lying fields (totalling some 30 ha - see Figure 1) have been managed as a raised water level area. Bunds have been placed around the field margins and dropboard sluices installed in each to control water levels. Drainage channels are kept full during summer and shallow flooding is maintained throughout the winter. Roughly half to two-thirds of the field area is flooded (maximum depth 30–40 cm) during the winter, with 80% of this area under shallow flooding and the remainder splash flooded. Water levels are dropped from mid-May, allowing the grass to grow. No fertiliser is added. Cattle graze from mid-August until the sward has been sufficiently grazed (usually mid-September). Remaining tall vegetation (rushes, ragwort and docks) is topped before flooding. Topping followed by flooding effectively controls rush invasion.

- **Silage.** Up to 90 ha of grassland is cut for silage annually. There is little disturbance in these areas during spring apart from the application of organic-based fertiliser in mid-May. Fertiliser application rates change yearly according to the results of soil sampling. Cutting dates have got later in recent years to cater for the needs of the corncrake; fields are now cut in mid-August. The mowing pattern has also been altered to favour corncrakes. Fields are now cut from the centre outwards using a 'Hydroflex' mower, leaving a strip in the centre unmown. This uncut area is manured and early-growing species are introduced, eg nettles, which provide excellent early cover for corncrakes. This involves sacrificing areas of silage and lowers the quality of goose and cattle grazing, but greatly enhances corncrake survival. Aftermath grazing with cattle takes place until the geese arrive or ground conditions get too wet (mid to late September), when areas are topped if necessary to achieve the desired sward length of 10–15 cm for the wintering geese.

- **Re-seeding.** Low-lying silage fields are re-seeded on a five-year rotation. This is necessary as barnacle geese require a high-quality grass sward. This, however, affects breeding waders and corncrakes, so a move to autumn (late August) re-seeding has been undertaken recently. Grassland is re-seeded using commercial varieties (Table 1) at a rate of 42 kg/ha, and then grazed by sheep before the geese arrive in the following winter. Sheep grazing helps to consolidate the sward and removes broad-leaved weed species.

Table 1: Seed mix used to re-seed silage fields at Loch Gruinart

Seed	kg/ha
Rye-grass	28.5
Timothy	7.0
Fescues	2.0
Clovers	5.0
TOTAL	42.5

Table 2: Wintering populations of key species at Loch Gruinart 1989/90–1994/95

Species	1990/91	1991/92	1992/93	1993/94	1994/95	1995/96
Barnacle goose	13,079	18,354	15,224	18,164	14,926	18,726
% of barnacle geese on Islay using reserve	43%	70%	57%	71%	53%	64%
Greenland white-fronted goose	821	894	980	755	1,009	1,314
Wigeon	281	324	431	311	502	488
Teal	211	322	597	858	991	858
Pintail	6	5	5	4	20	36

- The reserve runs 250 suckler cows (plus followers), 30 heifers and 50 sheep. Permanent pasture exists for these animals on higher and drier parts of the reserve, but they also play a key part in the management of wet grassland areas. Cattle play an important role in aftermath grazing on areas cut for silage and breaking up dense areas of rushes. Sheep have been used effectively to control ragwort in permanent pasture.

BENEFITS

- Initial grassland management created ideal wintering habitat for both barnacle and Greenland white-fronted geese, which occurred in internationally important numbers. Peak numbers of barnacle geese of the Greenland population represent over half the wintering population of the UK. Since 1990 more integrated management has benefited a wider range of species, without reducing the number of geese using the reserve (Table 2).

- The reserve is successful in providing a core area for feeding geese, reducing pressure on neighbouring farmland. During the autumn period two-thirds of the geese using the island are present on site. As grazing becomes exhausted, birds travel farther afield to feed, but by early spring numbers increase again as the geese muster prior to migration.

- Silage cutting and subsequent grazing, as well as regular re-seeding have provided high-quality swards and open feeding areas specifically required by barnacle geese. Goose numbers on the reserve have steadily increased as a result.

- On fields flooded since 1990 white-fronted goose usage has increased dramatically, reflected by the steady increase from under 400 in 1989/90 to the 1995/96 maximum of 1,300. Greenland white-fronted geese favour the flooded fields and wetter areas, where they feed on the succulent shoots and roots of grasses, sedges and rushes. These plants were formerly confined to the drainage channels of silage fields. A corresponding decline in usage of the flooded fields by barnacle geese has not detracted from the continued steady increase on the reserve as a whole.

- The recently flooded areas also provide a wintering habitat for duck species, especially teal and wigeon, but also regionally important numbers of pintail, shoveler, gadwall and mallard. The topping process and the large extent of rushes provide a huge seed source for wintering wildfowl which is made available by flooding.

- Breeding ducks are now a feature of the reserve with the shoveler recently colonising (increasing from 0 to 13 pairs in three years) and the garganey nesting occasionally.

- Within the wetter areas, as well as in the silage fields, wader numbers have increased in response to the more benign regime implemented in 1990 (Figure 2). Breeding wader densities are high compared with sites in lowland England; for example lapwing (4 pairs/ha) and redshank (2 pairs/ha).

- Autumn re-seeding allows the field to be used for silage production before the re-seeding starts thereby increasing the annual yield for winter fodder. It also provides new growth for geese and maintains cover for breeding corncrakes.

- Corncrakes have responded to management, increasing from 0 to 7 calling males in 5 years.

- The area also provides excellent hunting for barn owls (which have increased from 0 to 5 pairs in the last 5 years), hen harriers and golden eagles. In addition, otters use the area.

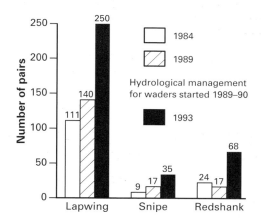

Figure 2 Numbers of breeding waders at the Loch Gruinart RSPB Nature Reserve before and after hydrological management for waders which began in 1989/90

North Meadow National Nature Reserve

(English Nature)

Case Study 14

Location:	13 km north-west of Swindon, Wiltshire. OS 1:50,000 sheet no 163 GR SU092947
Area:	Total 44.7 ha Wet grassland 44.7 ha
Designations:	NNR, SSSI

Soil Type(s):	Alluvial silt and clays
NVC Type(s):	Predominantly MG4, plus MG5 and MG13
Technique(s):	
GRASSLAND MANAGEMENT (section 4.4)	

MAIN MANAGEMENT OBJECTIVES

To maintain the rich and diverse neutral hay meadow flora, especially the population of snake's-head fritillary. This is to be achieved by continuing, largely unmodified, the traditional management regime.

BACKGROUND

North Meadow is actually a low-lying island, with the Rivers Churn and Thames and two of their tributaries providing the site's boundaries. These rivers are connected by an underground gravel layer that ensures a high water-table year round across the site. The close proximity of both rivers also ensures periodic flooding especially during the winter (Figure 1).

A traditional Lammas haying and grazing regime has continued unchanged for several centuries. The grazing rights are held in perpetuity by the people of the Manor of the Hundred and Borough of Cricklade and can be exercised between 12 August and 12 February. After mid-February a hay crop is allowed to grow. The majority is harvested under licence from English Nature, who now own most of the meadow, though some areas remain in private hands. This regime provides suitable conditions for a large tract of herb-rich wet grassland, which hosts the UK's largest colony of snake's-head fritillaries.

GRASSLAND MANAGEMENT FOR PLANTS

- Floodwater entry/exit points are maintained through active management to ensure that periodic flooding of the site continues.

- Cattle graze the area from mid-August until Christmas. Horses are present on the site throughout the grazing period. Preferably the site would be grazed only by cattle but if horses have to be accommodated English Nature prefer to see a 5:1 ratio of cattle to horses.

- Horse numbers are kept below 30. Larger numbers result in poaching of the ground when herds gallop about.

- The following conditions are laid down in the haying licences:
  - no cutting prior to 1 July
  - sward to be cut no lower than 5 cm
  - all grass within allotment must be cut and cleared
  - all hay to be baled using a small baler and removed by 12 August.

- Silage cutting is not allowed.

- No manuring, fertilising, liming or application of pesticides/herbicides is allowed.

- Since 1982 English Nature have also licensed the harvesting of wild flower seed to Emorsgate Seeds, the resulting harvest being marketed as 'Cricklade Mixture' (Box 1). In the past seed has been gathered using a tractor-mounted vacuum, but in 1995 7.5 ha were harvested by using a 'Brush Harvester'. Areas allocated for harvesting are rotated, and only three swathes out of four are harvested in any one area.

(Julian Jones)

Plate 1 Haying benefits a range of plant species, such as snake's-head fritillary, which flower early before harvesting takes place.

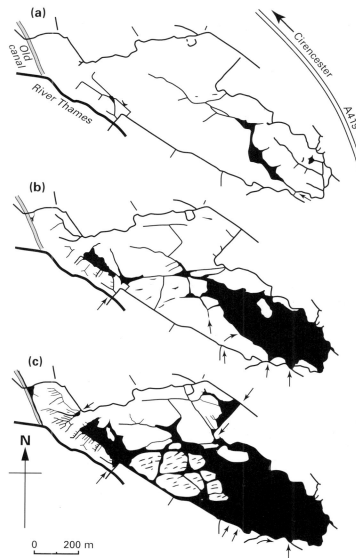

Figure 1 North Meadow is effectively an island bordered by the Rivers Thames and Churn and their tributaries. The site floods regularly when either or both of these rivers tops their banks: (a) regularly attained flood levels during winter and early spring, (b) 2–3 times a year and (c) once every 3 or 4 years. Points of entry are shown with arrows

BENEFITS

- Continuity of the centuries-old management regime has allowed a very old meadow community to survive. The majority of the site comprises MG4, meadow foxtail and great burnet flood meadow, a community scarce enough to be included under Annex 1 of the Habitats Directive (see also Case Study 11). A few scarce plant and invertebrate species occur (Table 1). The sward also contains unimproved strains of species such as perennial rye-grass and creeping bent.

- Open sward early in the season, created by haying and aftermath grazing in the preceding season, favours plants, such as snake's-head fritillary, which mature early in the spring. The situation also benefits annual plants allowing them to set seed in an open sward.

- Haying, as opposed to silage making, promotes sward diversity by allowing seeds to ripen and fall before the crop is removed (Plate 1).

- Harvesting seed using a 'Brush Harvester', as opposed to vacuuming, reduces the impact on invertebrates and results in a higher yield of seeds. Resultant seeds can be used on restoration projects in other areas.

Box 1: Typical composition of 'Cricklade Mixture' produced by Emorsgate Seeds.

Suitable for sowing on most lowland soils and contains a large number of native species including knapweed, meadowsweet, fairy flax, yellow-rattle, oxeye daisy, red clover, great burnet, pepper-saxifrage, sweet vernal grass and quaking-grass.

Table 1: Scarce species recorded at North Meadow

Snake's-head fritillary	North Meadow is the largest natural colony of this plant in the UK. It occurs in damp meadows and pastures, the species range has contracted in response to agricultural improvement. Now frequent only in Suffolk and the Thames Valley.
Club-tailed dragonfly	A rare riverine dragonfly that feeds along hedgerows and over grassland at the site.

West Sedgemoor

(RSPB)

Location:	Between Curry Rivel and Stoke St Gregory, 12 km east of Taunton, Somerset OS 1:50,000 sheet no 193 GR ST361258
Area:	Reserve area 561 ha Wet grassland 491 ha Reserve area under ESA agreement 487 ha Total area of West Sedgemoor SSSI 1,016 ha
Designations:	SSSI, ESA and IBA, proposed Ramsar and SPA

Soil Type(s):	Peat
NVC Type(s):	MG5, MG6, MG7, MG8, MG9, MG10, MG13, M22, M23, S5, S6, S22
Technique(s):	INTEGRATED MANAGEMENT: REFUGE CREATION (section 3.5) WATER MANAGEMENT (section 4.2) DRAINAGE CHANNEL MANAGEMENT (section 4.3) GRASSLAND MANAGEMENT (section 4.4) SPECIES AND HABITAT MONITORING (Part 5)

MAIN MANAGEMENT OBJECTIVES

To continue to rehabilitate and maintain the whole of the West Sedgemoor SSSI by positive management of RSPB land, including hydrological management of selected areas to provide desirable conditions for wintering waterfowl, and breeding wader species especially snipe, redshank and black-tailed godwit.

To influence the land and water management of others, to benefit breeding waders, plant communities and invertebrate populations.

BACKGROUND

West Sedgemoor is a discrete hydrological unit within the Somerset Levels and Moors, comprising a tributary valley of the River Parrett. In 1978 the RSPB recognised the value of the area for birds, and the threats it faced, and started to purchase land. By buying suitable land when it became available the RSPB now owns and manages over half the moor. However, lowering of water levels in the system resulted in a substantial decline in breeding waders, between 1977 and 1987:

- snipe declined by 70%

- lapwing declined by 59%.

Subsequent reserve management has reversed this decline.

During the winter, water is pumped from the site by the Environment Agency into the River Parrett to reduce the risk of flood events. During the summer, water is let in via sluices from the River Parrett, raising drainage channel levels so that they act as wet fences. Traditional grassland management of the site has revolved around grazing, and haying and subsequent aftermath grazing, of the grasslands during the short summer season.

West Sedgemoor is part of the Somerset Levels and Moors ESA and the majority of the reserve is under ESA management agreement (for details of ESA prescriptions see Case Study 5).

REFUGE CREATION

- For wintering wildfowl, it is essential to provide refuge areas where shooting and other forms of disturbance are kept to a minimum.

- The RSPB pursues a policy of purchasing shooting rights wherever cost-effective at West Sedgemoor. Currently 156 ha are leased to the RSPB annually at a cost of £1,346 per year.

- Managed flooding provides a regular, safe winter roost site for wildfowl.

BENEFITS

- Lack of disturbance has been a major contributing factor to the steady increase in wildfowl usage on the site in recent winters (Table 1).

Table 1: Mean yearly peak counts of key wintering wildfowl and wader species at West Sedgemoor prior to raised water level management and after 290 ha had been hydrologically isolated.

Species	Pre-management, 1985/86–1989/90	Post-management, 1990/91–1994/95
Bewick's swan	107	98
Wigeon	726	9,076
Teal	1,520	8,467
Shoveler	35	313
Golden plover	488	3,248
Lapwing	7,500	23,591
Snipe	206	969
Mean peak maxima all waterfowl	10,400	43,347

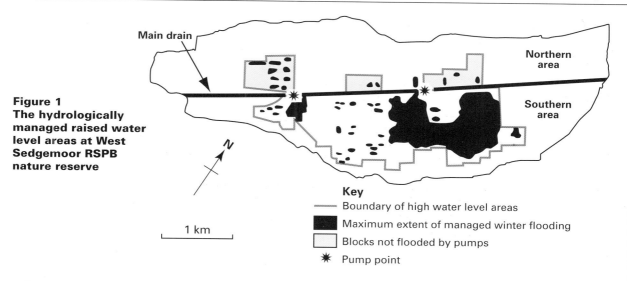

**Figure 1
The hydrologically managed raised water level areas at West Sedgemoor RSPB nature reserve**

Main drain

Northern area

Southern area

1 km

Key
— Boundary of high water level areas
■ Maximum extent of managed winter flooding
☐ Blocks not flooded by pumps
✳ Pump point

■ Provision of disturbance-free open water at the site allowed Bewick's swans to roost on the site for the first time in 1992.

■ Disturbance is also kept to a minimum for breeding waders in the summer by the late start of agricultural operations.

WATER MANAGEMENT

■ Flooding in winter takes two forms:

● natural flooding, caused by storm and flood conditions, which often covers 95% of the entire Moor, but which varies in extent and duration

● managed shallow flooding, on RSPB land, which can cover up to 30% of the Moor, the extent and duration of which can be managed, by a mixture of retention of natural floodwater and pumping if necessary in early winter (Figure 1).

■ Contiguous blocks of land have been bunded off and excluded from the IDB drainage system. Water levels are either pump-maintained or rely on rainfall and flood events (Figure 1). Hydrological isolation enables water levels to be maintained at much higher levels during winter, spring and early summer, than in surrounding areas.

■ Raised water level areas are isolated by blocking off managed ditches, at their junction with IDB managed ditches, with peat/clay dams installed with flexi-pipe sluices. Bunds are constructed along the perimeter of each area to hold back water.

■ As the reserve has grown in size and isolated blocks have become united, the area under hydrological control has increased from 50 ha in 1986 to 290 ha in 1994.

BENEFITS

■ Managed flooding guarantees habitat for wintering wildfowl. Prior to hydrological management, floods were often unreliable and short-lived, resulting in variable numbers of wildfowl (Figure 2).

■ Raised water level management, in spring and early summer, has arrested and, in many species, reversed the decline in breeding waders (Table 2, Figure 3). The current breeding distribution of waders is such

that 80% of all breeding waders on the Moor use the 30% of the land under raised water level management (Figure 4).

DRAINAGE CHANNEL MANAGEMENT

■ A total of 56 km of drainage channels are under RSPB management and are cleaned on a three-to-seven-year rotation.

■ Former drainage channels have been identified using old maps and some have been reinstated.

■ Where possible half-widths are cleaned out or half the length surrounding a field.

■ Some drainage channels are reprofiled to give a shallow slope (or batter) on one side.

BENEFITS

■ Maintained drainage channels are important in providing the infrastructure for hydrological control and act as wet fences for livestock.

■ Rotational drainage channel management ensures the survival of the important ditch flora and fauna of West Sedgemoor.

■ Drainage channels with a shallow profile provide permanent water for stock and birds as well as feeding areas and shelter for wader chicks (especially during agricultural operations).

GRASSLAND MANAGEMENT

■ Usually 45–60% of the grassland on the reserve is cut annually for hay. Mowing generally takes place between 1 July and 31 August and is followed by aftermath grazing.

■ Fields are cut at least one year in three.

■ Grazing alone occurs on only 11–25% of the unimproved grassland area annually. Grazing usually takes place between 1 July and 31 October – but may start earlier on fields of low conservation interest. Both cattle and sheep are used, although sheep are excluded from Tier 3 ESA land. Wet autumns necessitate an early finish to grazing.

Figure 2 Yearly wintering wildfowl maxima and mean winter rainfall 1984/85–1994/95

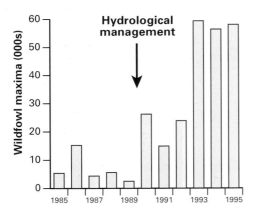

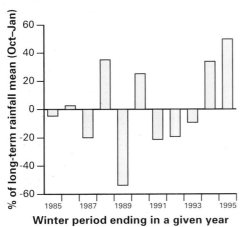

Winter period ending in a given year

■ A limited amount of topping is necessary to control thistles before they flower (June), to control rushes, to reduce sward height in areas inadequately grazed during the season, and where drainage channels have been fenced off from stock. Up to a third of the reserve area has required topping in any one season.

■ Although the use of herbicides is generally undesirable, occasionally the use of glyphosate is sanctioned to treat invasive stands of rushes. Application is by ATV-mounted weed-wiper. Invasion by rushes is common after the rehydration of improved fields, especially those that have been

ploughed. Benefits of the reduction of rush coverage must be balanced against their value as a seed source for the teal. As a result not more than 20% of the total rush coverage is treated in any one year.

BENEFITS

■ Haying is the most important technique for maintaining herb-rich grassland. The practice removes nutrients, maintaining the grasslands' low nutrient status, which allows forbs to compete with grasses, promoting sward diversity.

■ Cutting prevents the invasion of woody plants.

■ Aftermath grazing is important in reducing sward height before winter, creating conditions suitable for wintering wildfowl and breeding waders in the following season.

■ Cattle grazing leads to a structural mosaic of short and tussocky areas, ideal for breeding waders. Grazing intensity varies between ages and breeds of cattle.

■ Sheep produce a short, uniform sward ideal for wintering species, such as Bewick's swan and wigeon, as well as breeding black-tailed godwit and lapwing.

■ The timing of the grazing and mowing season at West Sedgemoor allows waders to breed without the risk of trampling or disturbance.

SPECIES AND HABITAT MONITORING

■ Numbers of both breeding and wintering birds are monitored, with the emphasis being on key species that use the reserve.

■ All water and grassland management at West Sedgemoor is monitored to gauge its efficacy as well as its impact on other groups. In managing wet grassland for birds the RSPB needs to know whether its prescriptions are compatible with the requirements of non-avian taxa of conservation importance.

■ A sward monitoring programme was set up in 1988, and monitoring has continued annually since then. The sward monitoring is integrated with dipwell monitoring, so that the response of the vegetation can be linked to hydrological management, as well as grassland management.

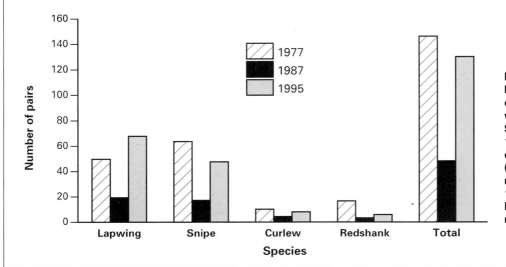

Figure 3 Numbers of pairs of breeding waders at West Sedgemoor in 1977 (pre-decline), 1987 (pre-hydrological management) and 1995 (post-hydrological management)

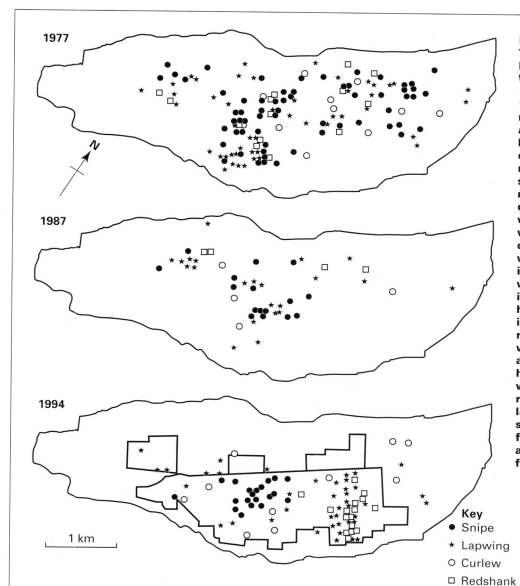

Figure 4
The distribution of breeding waders on West Sedgemoor in 1977, 1987, and 1994 (lines enclose raised water level areas). In 1977, before intensive drainage, wader nests were widely scattered over the moor. After drainage in 1987 wader numbers were low. By contrast, in 1994 waders had increased and nests were concentrated in the hydrologically isolated areas receiving pumped water. Snipe were all in the damp herb-rich meadows, while lapwing and redshank were largely in the area subjected to most flooding (the lower areas which were formerly arable)

Key
● Snipe
★ Lapwing
○ Curlew
□ Redshank

BENEFITS

A complete monitoring programme enables managers at West Sedgemoor to record change, assess achievement of objectives and make informed management decisions.

■ Management aimed at breeding waders and wintering wildfowl has been shown to be effective (Tables 1 and 2).

■ The sward monitoring programme is still ongoing. Results so far indicate that in pump-maintained raised water level areas herb-rich MG8 grassland quickly starts to convert to mire, this occurs within 1–2 years of hydrological management being introduced (Figure 5).

Table 2: Impact of raised water level areas on the number and distribution of breeding waders at West Sedgemoor

Year	Total no of pairs	Percentage nesting in RWLA	Area of RWLA (ha)
1984	106	no RWLA	
1985	76	no RWLA	
1986	56	30	50 (5)
1987	48	33	70 (7)
1988	74	55	70 (7)
1989	54	59	170 (17)
1990	90	43*	170 (17)
1991	66	67	170 (17)
1992	79	84	230 (23)
1993	102	89	230 (23)
1994	96	82	290 (29)
1995	130	70	290 (29)

* the decrease in the 1990 usage of the raised water level area was brought about by inadequate grassland management in the previous farming season and the fact that protracted flooding during the 1989/90 winter provided ideal nesting conditions for lapwings which nested in greater numbers than normal over the entire Moor.

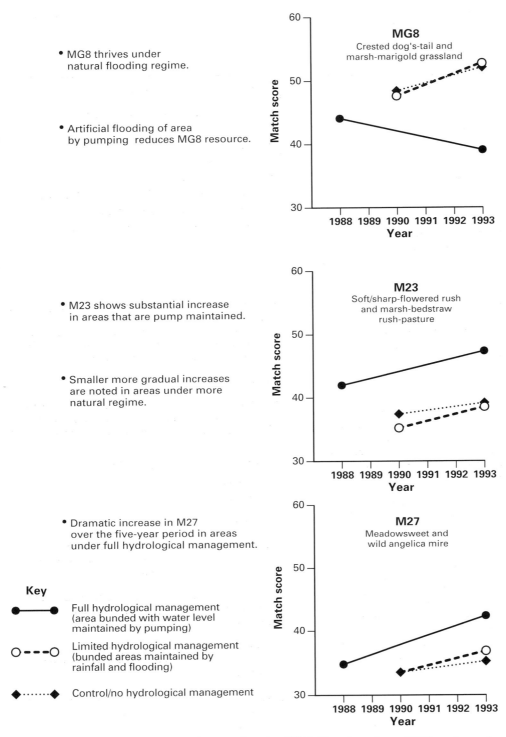

- MG8 thrives under natural flooding regime.

- Artificial flooding of area by pumping reduces MG8 resource.

MG8
Crested dog's-tail and marsh-marigold grassland

- M23 shows substantial increase in areas that are pump maintained.

- Smaller more gradual increases are noted in areas under more natural regime.

M23
Soft/sharp-flowered rush and marsh-bedstraw rush-pasture

- Dramatic increase in M27 over the five-year period in areas under full hydrological management.

M27
Meadowsweet and wild angelica mire

Key

Full hydrological management (area bunded with water level maintained by pumping)

Limited hydrological management (bunded areas maintained by rainfall and flooding)

Control/no hydrological management

Figure 5 Changes in NVC MATCH score for the MG8 flood pasture, M23 rush pasture and M27 mire communities, in response to hydrological and grassland management regimes. MATCH is a software package that compares vegetation data collected in the field with published NVC data (Prosser and Wallace 1995)

Northward Hill

(RSPB)

Location:	Rochester-upon-Medway, Kent OS 1:50,000 sheet no 178 GR TR780775
Area:	248 ha total 141 ha wet grassland 137 ha entered into ESA scheme
Designations:	SSSI, ESA and IBA, proposed Ramsar and SPA

Soil Type(s): Alluvial silt

NVC Type(s): MG6, MG7, MG13

Technique(s):
CREATION:
SEEDING (section 4.5.2)
NATURAL REGENERATION (section 4.5.2)
Water management (section 4.2)
Aftercare management (section 4.5.2)

MAIN MANAGEMENT OBJECTIVES
To create wet grassland on an area of arable land. Subsequently, to manage the habitat for breeding, passage and wintering waders and wildfowl and to enhance the grassland and drainage channel plants and invertebrates.

BACKGROUND
Northward Hill reserve is part of the North Kent Marshes much of which was ploughed up in the 1960s. Drainage channels and hollows were filled in, fields underdrained and pumps installed. Little wet grassland remained. On the nature reserve the RSPB has embarked upon a restoration programme to recreate wet grassland from arable fields. The North Kent Marshes have been designated as an ESA, providing opportunities for further restoration schemes in the area.

The reserve is of limited botanical interest at present, though some nationally notable species occur in the drainage channels. The only unimproved area belongs to the NVC community MG6. This resembles a degraded form of the typical North Kent Marshes pasture (the meadow barley variant of MG6) which retains some value, and provides a template for restoration. Numbers of breeding birds on the reserve prior to restoration were very low (Table 1).

CREATION
Several potential obstacles to restoration have been identified including; low rainfall, limited water availability for summer flooding, the existence of a very

extensive land drain system (often unmapped) and the need to avoid back-flooding neighbours' land. Management is therefore proceeding cautiously and experimentally. Two recreation approaches have been tried, seeding and natural regeneration.

SEEDING

- In April 1991, contractors re-seeded 58 ha of arable fields, which were prepared by ploughing and harrowing and then sown with the following mix at 30 kg/ha:
  - 75% Kent perennial rye-grass
  - 10% red fescue
  - 10% timothy *erecta*
  - 5% Kent white clover.

- Contractors charged £4,916 for preliminary cultivation and sowing, plus the cost of the seed (£2,222), a cost of £123/ha.

- Within two months there was sufficient growth to permit licensed sheep grazing from 15 June to 15 December.

- After grazing, the area was topped to prevent invasive thistles and other rank vegetation from seeding.

- From 1992, the seeded areas were grazed by sheep from April–December (mainly June to October) and were afterwards topped.

- Dry ground conditions encouraged thistles to invade which were sprayed with methyl-chloro-phenoxy acetic acid (MCPA) by contractors in 1992 (@ £18.60/ha). Subsequent signing of an ESA agreement meant that tractor-based herbicide application was no longer permitted.

- During 1993 there was some regrowth of thistles and the fields were topped 2 or 3 times between July and September.

Table 1: Increase in number of pairs of breeding waders at Northward Hill, 1991–95

Breeding population pairs	1991	1992	1993	1994	1995
Lapwing	3	2	16	35	56
Snipe (drummers)	0	0	2	0	0
Redshank	1	1	5	27	35
Avocet	0	0	0	5	33

NATURAL REGENERATION

■ In 1991, 59 ha of arable land was left un-seeded and allowed to regenerate naturally.

■ By October 1991, the area had developed a tall, rank vegetation of self-sown wheat, grass and thistle (Plate 1). The area was topped by contractors (cost £943) and the cut material allowed to decay on the ground.

■ In summer 1992, the area was topped again by reserve staff, and selected fields were grazed by sheep in autumn.

■ Dry ground conditions in 1992 encouraged thistles to invade which were sprayed with MCPA by contractors (@ £18.60/ha).

■ From 1993 fields have been sheep-grazed between April and December and topped two or three times between July and September.

(Alan Parker)

Plate 1 In the early stages of restoration to wet grassland the sward was dominated by rank vegetation.

WATER MANAGEMENT

■ A drainage channel was constructed and dams with flexi-pipe sluices installed to facilitate water level control. This was effective in maintaining high drainage channel water levels but led to back-flooding of neighbouring arable land, during a period of high rainfall.

■ Consequently, low bunds were constructed 10 m in from the field edges with the aim of retaining water after rapid flooding and then dropping drainage channel water levels to avoid flooding of neighbouring land. All bunds were 60–100 cm high with gentle, easily topped slopes.

■ Because of lower drainage channel water levels it became essential to disable the field drainage system thoroughly. Pipes were located by using maps, looking for pipe ends during low water conditions, probing with sticks and even by dowsing. Pipes were then blocked by digging them up close to where they entered the ditches, using a Hymac with a 2-m wide bucket.

■ Topping up flooded areas in spring and early summer is possible using water from an existing 1-ha reservoir, previously used for irrigation. The reservoir is filled from the drainage channel system in the winter in accordance with the abstraction licence.

AFTERCARE MANAGEMENT

■ Most fields are grazed between April and December –grazing is by sheep owned by grazing tenants and deployed to RSPB requirements between February and December. Between 1 April and 31 May grazing density does not exceed 5 sheep/ha.

■ Most fields are topped off after grazing in July to September to improve the sward. Topping takes place from 1 July onward (or earlier if necessary, and approved by the ESA Project Officer), and is particularly used as a means of thistle eradication.

■ Up to 25% of fields are shallow-flooded from October to March.

■ Up to 5% of fields are shallow-flooded from July to September.

■ 5–25% of fields are shallow-flooded from April to June.

BENEFITS

■ Creation of grassland sward and wet flooded areas in summer greatly increased the number of waders breeding at the site (Table 1, Table 2, Plate 2).

■ Control of grazing and low densities of livestock during spring ensure minimal disturbance for ground-nesting birds.

■ Flooded areas and grassland in winter provide suitable habitat for an increasing number of wildfowl, especially dabbling ducks (Table 3).

■ On the sown areas the weedy grasses, barren brome, wild-oat and wall barley are declining and there have been increases in other grasses: rough meadow-grass, timothy, soft-brome, common couch and marsh foxtail. Other grasses have appeared in the sward for the first time: Yorkshire-fog, creeping bent, common bent and meadow barley. Increases in wild flowers are less well marked but there have been increases in bristly oxtongue, scented mayweed and spear thistle. Overall species richness has increased.

■ Sown areas are still MG7 perennial rye-grass leys but are showing diversification and typical species of the Thames Estuary (meadow barley) variant of MG6 have appeared or increased in these fields.

■ On the natural regeneration areas the weedy grasses, barren brome and wild-oat, have declined. Several grass species have increased in abundance; perennial rye-grass, rough meadow-grass, meadow barley, common bent and marsh foxtail (the latter in response to flooding in the winter). Thistles have declined as have a number of other tall herbs, such as prickly sow-thistle, prickly lettuce and orache species. Several mainly smaller wild flowers have increased in abundance; bristly oxtongue, white clover, cut-leaved crane's-bill, hairy buttercup, greater plantain and curled dock. Some of these, such as hairy buttercup and curled dock, have probably been favoured by winter flooding. Additional species have taken advantage of the bare mud areas created by flooding, eg sea barley (a nationally scarce species) and golden dock (locally rare).

- Naturally regenerating areas were not ascribed an NVC code in 1992, being essentially a ruderal community. In 1996 non-flooded parts of these fields more closely resembled grassland consisting of what may be a transitional community destined to become MG6. MG6 is not uncommon but the Thames Estuary (meadow barley) variant is notable.

- Flooded areas of both sown and naturally regenerating areas have developed into MG13 creeping bent–marsh foxtail grassland sward. Although this community is widely distributed, it always occurs in small patches. The amount present at Northward Hill is of considerable importance.

(Keith Blomerley)

Plate 2 The resultant sward after five years may not be herb-rich, but is attractive to breeding waders.

Table 2: Summary and benefits of main management undertaken at Northward Hill, between 1991 and 1993

Management	Area (ha)	Conservation benefit
1991–93, sowing of former arable land with grass mix and grazing by sheep.	58	The establishment of wet grassland sward.
1991–93, grazing and topping of former arable land.	59	The establishment of wet grassland sward.
1992, creation of several dams to raise drainage channel water levels.		Water available for flood pumping, improved wildlife interest in ditches.
1993, creation of experimental flood by pumping.	1	10 broods of wader chicks reared – 6 lapwing / 4 redshank.
1994/95, creation of bunded areas capable of holding floodwater, topped up by pumping.	117	Widespread winter flooding held through breeding season. Nationally important numbers of wintering pintail and shoveler. Over 100 pairs of breeding wader.

Table 3: Peak winter wildfowl numbers at Northward Hill, 1990/91 to 1994/95. Note the increases in the number of dabbling ducks using the reserve, particularly after the introduction of experimental flooding in 1993.

Species	1990/91	1991/92	1992/93	1993/94	1994/95
Shelduck	13	4	0	50	107
Wigeon	2	322	63	10	90
Teal	160	155	125	335	915
Mallard	295	114	56	50	400
Pintail	1	2	0	289	346
Shoveler	6	8	1	8	117

River Ray Catchment

Case Study 17

(Private, ITE, ADAS, Environment Agency)

Location:	Near Marsh Gibbon (8 km east of Bicester), on the Oxfordshire/ Buckinghamshire border. OS 1:50,000 sheet no 165 GR SP651202
Area:	Total 900 ha Wet grassland c.200 ha
Designations:	SSSI and ESA

Soil Type(s): Clay

NVC Type(s): MG4, MG5, MG8

Technique(s):
WET GRASSLAND RESTORATION
(section 4.5)

MAIN MANAGEMENT OBJECTIVES
Restoration of arable land and intensive grassland to herb-rich wet grassland.

BACKGROUND
The Upper Thames Tributaries ESA includes much of the catchment of the River Ray. The floodplain is underlain by impermeable clay soils and the hydrology dominated by surface run-off following rainfall. River water levels respond rapidly to rainfall events, frequently flooding the low-lying land either side of the river. In many respects the floodplain resembles Otmoor, a better known site on the River Ray, which occupies a similar basin downstream. Like Otmoor the area supports some herb-rich grassland.

The combination of periodic flooding and impermeable soil makes drainage and cultivation difficult. Despite this, drainage improvements during the 1970s led to conversion of traditional hay meadows to arable land. Recently the difficulties of farming such wet, low-lying areas have led to a large uptake of agri-environment schemes. Land within the catchment makes up the largest contiguous area under the Countryside Stewardship Scheme in the UK and additional areas are entered into the Upper Thames Tributaries ESA. In total 600 ha of the catchment have been entered into the two schemes.

Since 1993 ITE and ADAS have been using this part of the River Ray catchment for field trials to assess techniques used for the restoration of herb-rich meadows.

WET GRASSLAND RESTORATION
- The first process in any restoration attempt is to precisely identify the desired end-point, in this case the exact species composition of the herb-rich grassland. Nearby herb-rich meadows were examined and found to consist of a mixture of mesotrophic grassland types: MG4 (meadow foxtail and great burnet flood meadow), MG5a (meadow pea sub-community of crested dog's-tail and common knapweed hay meadow) and MG8 (crested dog's-tail and marsh-marigold water meadow). All three communities occur typically under traditional agricultural management and are damaged by intensification. MG4 and MG8 are characteristic of

frequently inundated land and are therefore damaged by drainage. The species composition of this rich and varied sward was adopted as the template for the restoration project. Additional potential constituent species (ie species that preferred wetter, less fertile areas) were identified using their water and nitrogen indicator values. Ruderal or weed species were not included and this gave a total of 36 species.

- Efficient drainage of the site depended in the past on frequent renewal of mole drains. This practice was abandoned. In the absence of maintenance the land reverts to an undrained state in about five years.

- A dropboard sluice was installed on the main drain holding back water, raising the water level.

- The following restoration techniques were experimentally tested to determine which was the most effective on land released from arable agriculture:
  - **natural regeneration** – relying on the seed bank in the soil and seed drift from nearby herb-rich areas. Seed banks in areas that have been cultivated are likely to be degraded and unrepresentative of the original vegetation type. Seeds are buried deeper by cultivation, or germinate and are removed by agricultural operations, meanwhile the number of seeds of arable weeds species within the bank increases.
  - **hay bales** – scattering hay cut from local species-rich grassland. Timing of cutting is important in determining the species composition of the seed harvested in this way. Also the amount of time the crop spends on the ground prior to baling will affect the amount of seed present and its ripeness.
  - **sowing seed mixes** – can greatly accelerate the restoration process and is the recommended technique for restoration projects funded under the agri-environment schemes. Three seed mixes were tested and sown (Table 1):
    - Mix 1 contained four grass species (as recommended by the Countryside Commission in their guide-lines for waterside habitat).
    - Mix 2 was a compromise between Mix 3 and what was commercially and economically viable.

Table 1: Seed mixes used in restoration experiment (species in parentheses were not available)

Seed mix 1 (basic)
Grasses - meadow foxtail, (sweet vernal grass), crested dog's-tail, red fescue and smaller cat's-tail.

Seed mix 2 (intermediate)
Grasses - common bent, meadow foxtail, (sweet vernal grass), crested dog's-tail, red fescue, meadow fescue and Yorkshire-fog.

Wild flowers - (cuckooflower), meadowsweet, oxeye daisy, common bird's-foot-trefoil, meadow buttercup and red clover.

Seed mix 3 (comprehensive)
Grasses, sedges and rushes - common bent, meadow foxtail, (sweet vernal grass), crested dog's-tail, red fescue, Yorkshire-fog, (common sedge), (carnation sedge), quaking-grass, (sharp-flowered rush), meadow barley, (brown sedge) and yellow oat-grass.

Wild flowers - sneezewort, (cuckooflower), common knapweed, (meadow thistle), meadowsweet, meadow vetchling, oxeye daisy, (greater bird's-foot-trefoil), ragged-robin, (creeping-jenny), tubular water-dropwort, (narrow-leaved water-dropwort), meadow buttercup, (lesser spearwort), yellow-rattle, common sorrel, great burnet, (saw-wort), pepper-saxifrage, common meadow-rue, white clover and tufted vetch.

- Mix 3 contained as many of the potential species as possible (26 species).

- **nurse cropping** – a traditional method in the area for establishing grass leys on arable land was to undersow with spring barley or annual rye-grass. The idea being that the shelter provided by a vigorous nurse species will provide an ideal micro-climate for germinating seedlings. The use of a nurse crop with the five treatments above was investigated.

■ While compiling the seed mixes it was discovered that many of the desired species that form vital components of wet grassland communities (eg sweet vernal grass) were commercially unavailable. Gathering seed by hand may be an option at some sites, but clearly this problem could affect restoration costs and results.

BENEFITS
Preliminary results indicate that:

■ On ex-arable sites natural regeneration would take many years to restore a semi-natural vegetation type. Analysis of the available seed bank found that small quantities of desirable species were represented, but not in great enough abundance or reasonable diversity to restore original communities. Seed rain or floodwater seed dispersal from neighbouring herb-rich areas appeared to be limited. However, several species, for example cuckooflower and lesser spearwort, did appear in the sward by natural regeneration.

■ Scattering hay bales has compelling advantages: it ensures that the supply of seeds are of known provenance and is a very cheap method. This technique was, however, unpredictable and less effective than sowing seed.

■ Sowing seed mixtures resulted in significantly greater numbers of species in the resultant sward than either natural regeneration or hay bales. The most comprehensive seed mix produced the sward with the highest species richness and also the highest number of desired/potential species.

■ Sowing seed in this way is far cheaper than transplanting mature plants or turfing areas, neither of which were considered in the experiment.

■ Nurse cropping was ineffective in boosting the establishment of other species.

Appendix 1
Nationally scarce and Red Data Book invertebrate species that occur widely on wet grassland sites (from Drake in press)

Dragonflies	Hairy dragonfly, variable damselfly
Beetles	
Ground beetles	*Bembidion clarki, B. fumigatum, Pterostichus anthracinus, Stenolophus skrimshiranus, Chlaenius nigricornis, Odacantha melanura, Demetrias imperialis*
Crawling water beetles	*Peltodytes caesus, Haliplus apicalis*
Noteridae	*Noterus crassicornis*
Water beetles	*Agabus conspersus, Dytiscus circumflexus, Coelambus parellelogrammus, Rhantus frontalis, R. grapii*
Hydrophilidae	*Hydrochus elongatus, Helophorus alternans, H. nanus, Cercyon convexiusculus, C. sternalis, C. tristis, C. ustulatus, Limnoxenus niger, Anacaena bipustulata, Helochares lividus, Enochrus bicolor, E. melanocephalus, E. ochropterus, E. halophilus, Hydrophilus piceus, Berosus affinis, B. signaticollis*
Hydraenidae	*Ochthebius marinus, O. nanus, O. viridis*
Rove beetles	*Paederus fuscipes, Philonthus punctus, Gabrius bishopi*
Cantharidae	*Silis ruficollis*
Weevils	*Bagous cylindrus, B. subcarinatus, B. tempestivus, Hydronomus alismatis, Notaris bimaculatus, Litodactylus leucogaster, Drupenatus nasturtii, Gymnetron villosulum*
Butterflies and moths	
Cossidae	Goat moth
Sesiidae	Lunar hornet moth
Cochylidae	*Phalonidia alismana*
Pyralidae	*Calamotropha paludella, Schoenobius gigantella, Evergestis extimalis, Synaphe punctalis*
Vanessidae	Marsh fritillary
Geometridae	Rosy wave, shaded pug
Arctiidae	Water ermine
Noctuidae	Obscure wainscot, flame wainscot, reed dagger, crescent striped, twin-spotted wainscot, brown-veined wainscot, Webb's wainscot, silver hook, silky wainscot, cream-bordered green pea, dotted fanfoot
Flies	
Craneflies	*Limonia ventralis, Helius pallirostris, Pilaria scutellata, Erioptera bivittata*
Soldierflies	*Vanoyia tenuicornis, Odontomyia ornata, O. tigrina, Stratiomys singularior*
Hoverflies	*Neoascia geniculata, N. interrupta, Lejogaster splendida, Lejops vittata*
Lauxaniidae	*Sapromyza opaca*
Snail-killing flies	*Colobaea punctata, Pherbellia brunnipes, P. grisescens, P. dorsata, Sciomyza simplex*
Anthomyzidae	*Anagnota collini*
Chloropidae	*Elachiptera pubescens*

Appendix 2
Current schemes offering financial incentives for wet grassland management, rehabilitation and creation

Scheme	Mechanism	Eligibility	Annual payments	Admin. body
Countryside Stewardship Scheme	10-year agreements for management and re-creation of waterside landscapes including wet grasslands. Extra payments available for public access agreements.	All farmers and landowners in England, including voluntary bodies and local authorities, at the discretion of MAFF.	£225/ha for 10 years for grassland restoration, £70/ha for grassland management. Includes a supplementary payment in initial year for major restoration jobs and capital payments grant for creation and management of features, eg pollarding willows and ditch management.	MAFF
Countryside Premium Scheme	5-year agreements. Catch-all scheme combining farm and conservation grants, as well as the Habitat Scheme and Moorland Scheme. Applications assessed after croft/farm audit.	All Scottish crofters and farmers outside ESAs.	Payments discretionary	SOAEFD
Tir Cymen	10-year agreements to encourage management for wildlife and landscape benefit.	All registered farm holdings within three pilot areas of Wales only.	£20–£280/ha, plus similar grants as Countryside Stewardship for 'one-off' capital projects.	CCW
Environmentally Sensitive Areas (ESAs)	10-year agreements to adopt environmentally beneficial practices to protect important landscape and wildlife areas.	All farmers and landowners within designated ESA boundaries, throughout UK.	£8–£415/ha. Capital grants available, plus two-year renewable conservation plans for management and creation of conservation features, which can result in funding for 40–80% of the costs.	DANI, MAFF, SOAEFD, WOAD
Habitat Scheme (called Habitat Improvement Scheme in Northern Ireland)	Mostly 10- and 20-year agreements for creation and management of selected habitats such as water margins. Each country has slightly different arrangements.	All farmers and landowners in England, Wales and Northern Ireland, although may be limited to pilot areas.	£200–£360/ha for 20-year agreement £125–£260/ha for 10-year agreement.	DANI, MAFF, WOAD
Landscape and Nature Conservation Grants	Covers a wide range of small-scale projects to encourage the conservation and creation of landscapes, wildlife and habitats. Includes agreements for management of SSSIs and ASSIs.	Open to all farmers and land managers in the UK.	Grants cover part of management and capital costs, (usually up to 50%). Becoming restricted now.	CoCo, Coed Cymru, CCW, EN, DoENI, SNH, BA, LAs, NPAs
Wildlife Enhancement Scheme	Provides incentives for positive management agreements on SSSIs.	Scheme currently available in 4 wet grassland areas in England.	£75–£200/ha	EN
Nitrate Sensitive Areas	5-year scheme designed to reduce nitrate pollution in designated areas by changing farming practices. Incentives to convert arable and intensive grassland to extensive grassland.	Open to all farmers in England, within NSA boundaries.	Range from £65/ha to £590/ha, according to NSA and option.	MAFF

The information given here is reviewed from time to time by the relevant organisations. For more detailed and up to date information contact the relevant organisation directly (addresses in Appendix 3).

MAFF has produced a leaflet *Conservation Grants for Farmers* (addresses in Appendix 3).

Appendix 3
Addresses of Government Organisations,
Voluntary Organisations, and Seed Suppliers

Government organisations

1. Agriculture Departments
Department of Agriculture Northern Ireland (DANI),
  Dundonald House, Upper Newtownards Road,
  Belfast BT4 3SB. Tel 01232 520000.

Ministry of Agriculture, Fisheries and Food (MAFF),
  3 Whitehall Place, London SW1A 2HH. Tel 0645 335577
  (Helpline – all calls charged at local rate).

Scottish Office Agriculture, Environment and Fisheries
  Department (SOAEFD), Pentland House, 47 Robb's Loan,
  Edinburgh EH14 1TY. Tel 0131 556 8400.

Welsh Office Agriculture Department (WOAD),
  Cathays Park, Crown Buildings, Cardiff CF1 3NQ.
  Tel 01222 825111.

2. Countryside and Conservation Departments/Agencies
Broads Authority (BA), Thomas Harvey House, 18 Colegate,
  Norwich NR3 1BQ. Tel 01603 610734.

Countryside Commission, John Dower House, Crescent
  Place, Cheltenham, Glos GL50 3RA. Tel 01242 521381.

Countryside Council for Wales (CCW), Plas Penrhos, Fford
  Penrhos, Bangor LL57 2LQ. Tel 01248 370444.

Department of the Environment Northern Ireland
  (DoENI), Environment and Heritage Service,
  Commonwealth House, 35 Castle Street, Belfast BT1 1EU.
  Tel 01232 254754.

English Nature (EN), Northminster House, Peterborough
  PE1 1UA. Tel 01733 455000.

Joint Nature Conservation Committee, Monkstone House,
  City Road, Peterborough PE1 1JY. Tel 01733 62626

National Parks Authorities (NPAs). Details in relevant local
  telephone directory.

Scottish Natural Heritage (SNH), 12 Hope Terrace,
  Edinburgh EH9 2AS. Tel 0131 447 4784.

3. Water Management Agencies
Association of Drainage Authorities (ADA), The Mews,
  3 Royal Oak Passage, High Street, Huntingdon PE18 6EA.
  Tel 01480 411123. (For details of local IDBs).

DANI, Rivers Agency, Hydebank, 4 Hospital Road,
  Belfast BT8 8JP. Tel 01232 253380.

Environment Agency (EA), Rio House, Waterside Drive,
  Aztec West, Almondsbury, Bristol BS12 4UD.
  Tel 01454 624400.

Scottish Environment Protection Agency (SEPA),
  Erskine Court, The Castle Business Park, Stirling FK9 4TR.
  Tel 01786 457700.

4. Other Departments
Local Authorities (LAs) including Planning Authorities.
  Details in relevant local telephone directory.

Voluntary Organisations

National Trust (NT), 33 Sheep Street, Cirencester, Glos
  GL7 1RQ. Tel 01285 651818.

The Royal Society for the Protection of Birds (RSPB), The
  Lodge, Sandy, Bedfordshire SG19 2DL. Tel 01767 680551.

The Wildlife Trusts, The Green, Witham Park, Waterside
  South, Lincoln LN5 7JR. Tel 01522 544400.

Wildfowl & Wetlands Trust (WWT), Slimbridge GL2 7BT.
  Tel 01453 890333.

Seed Suppliers

A * indicates a supplier who sells wild flower seeds collected
from sustainable native British sources or harvested from
plants grown from such seed. *Note:* the range of species
offered is often wide but large quantities of seed may not
always be available.

*BTCV Enterprises Ltd – Trees and Wildflowers,
  The Conservation Centre, Balby Road,
  Doncaster DN4 0RH. Tel 01302 859522.

*Chiltern Seeds, Bortree Stile, Ulverston, Cumbria LA12 7PB.
  Tel 01229 581137.

*Emorsgate Seeds, The Pea Mill, Market Lane,
  Terrington St Clement, King's Lynn, Norfolk PE34 4HR.
  Tel 01553 829028, Fax 01553 829803.

*William Evans, 9 Breval Terrace, Charlton Kings,
  Cheltenham, Glos GL53 8JZ. Tel 01242 234355.

*Landlife Wildflowers Ltd, The Old Police Station, Lark
  Lane, Liverpool L17 8UU. Tel 0151 7287011, Fax 0151
  7288413. email info@landlife.v-net.com

*Heritage Seeds, Osmington, Weymouth, Dorset DT3 6EX.
  Tel 01305 834504.

*Johnsons Seeds, London Rd, Boston, Lincolnshire
  PE21 8AD. Tel 01205 365051, Fax 01205 310148.

John K King & Sons Ltd, Coggleshall, Colchester, Essex
  CO6 1TH. Tel 01376 561543, Fax 01376 562218.

*Meadowlands Ltd, The Park Lodge, Park Avenue, Wortley,
  South Yorkshire S30 7DR. Tel 01142 830322.
  email 100664.227@compuserve.com

*Naturescape Wild Flower Farm, Lapwing Meadows, Coach
  Gap Lane, Langar, Notts NG13 9HP. Tel 01949 860592.

Sharpes International Seeds Ltd, Sleaford, Lincs NG34 7HA.
  Tel 01529 304511, Fax 01529 303908.

*Suffolk Herbs, Monks Farm, Pantlings Lane, Kelvedon,
  Essex CO5 9PG. Tel 01376 572456.

*Y.S.J. Seeds, Kingsfield Conservation Nursery,
  Broadenham Lane, Winsham, Chard, Somerset TA20 4JF.
  Tel 01460 30070.

Appendix 4
Calculating water budgets

It is possible to calculate basic water budgets using climatic data alone, as the following example illustrates. However, in practice, a number of other factors influence the range of surface wetness conditions likely to be found. These include the relative hydraulic conductivity of different soil types and topography, which influences the upward movement of water through the unsaturated part of the profile and the drainable porosity of the soil water-table relative to the surface.

Firstly, information is required on average precipitation and on potential losses of water through evapotranspiration. This makes it possible to identify potential periods of water deficit. Data on potential water excesses and deficits for a site over a year can be used to produce an annual water balance. It is useful to find out if there is a meteorological station nearby which can provide locally relevant meteorological data. Small weather stations can be set up (costing from £80). Otherwise, precipitation and transpiration figures can be found in MAFF (1974) or derived from MORECS data from the Meteorological Office. MAFF (1974) splits England and Wales into areas with similar climate and geography and tabulates their average precipitation and transpiration figures. Average rainfall and transpiration figures together with the area of the site can be used to calculate the average water balance and hence the average demand for water per hectare and for the whole site. Using this source of data, it is necessary to assume that the transpiration rate for wet grassland is the same as listed for the land types used in the Bulletin. The figures

obtained can therefore only be used as an approximation, but this will usually suffice. By measuring the flows of potential sources of water in the area (such as streams and rivers) and comparing them to the site's water demands an initial assessment of its viability can be made. Depending on the complexity of local hydrology, investigations into seepage into and off the site, the needs of other water users and water courses running onto and off the site will also have to be considered in the water balance. In the example given in Table 1, rivers and streams in the area must provide a combined flow of at least 1,566 m³/day in June to provide enough water to meet the peak average deficit of the wet grassland. Note that, to raise water levels to achieve a new target regime, additional water may be required.

Figure 1 illustrates graphically the trends in the water availability detailed in Table 1. Such diagrams can help by providing a visual representation of water movement on the site. The water balance in this example is based on average figures and indicates the minimum flows required by contributing streams and rivers to meet the peak average deficits for the proposed area of wet grassland. It was assumed that rainfall was relatively uniform throughout the year, with the fluctuations in water availability caused by increased rates of evapotranspiration during the summer months. Obviously, it is always better to use actual site-specific figures for precipitation and evapotranspiration rather than average figures for a region over time.

Table 1: Wet grassland water balance at a site in Central England

Area of proposed wet grassland 100 ha						
Month	Average Rainfall mm	Wet Grassland Transpiration mm	Water Balance mm	Water Deficit mm	Site Water Demand m³/month	Site Water Demand m³/day
Jan	62	1	61	0	0	0.00
Feb	47	10	37	0	0	0.00
Mar	42	32	10	0	0	0.00
Apr	43	56	−13	13	13,000	433
May	50	81	−31	31	31,000	1,033
June	46	93	−47	47	47,000	1,566
July	58	93	−35	35	35,000	1,166
Aug	64	76	−12	12	12,000	400
Sept	60	47	13	0	0	0.00
Oct	64	22	42	0	0	0.00
Nov	76	5	71	0	0	0.00
Dec	65	0	65	0	0	0.00
Year total	677	516	161	138	138,000	

Figures produced are average figures and reflect the minimum flows required by contributing streams and rivers to meet the peak average deficits for the proposed area of wet grassland.

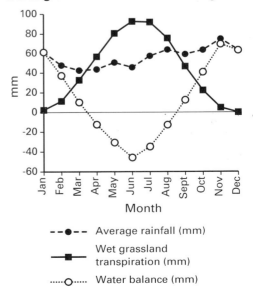

Figure 1 Graph of the water balance for a wet grassland site in Central England

--•-- Average rainfall (mm)

■ Wet grassland transpiration (mm)

·····○····· Water balance (mm)

Appendix 5
Contents for a Full Management Plan
(from Alexander 1996)

PLAN SUMMARY

1. Policy statement

2. Description

2.1 General information
2.1.1 Location
2.1.2 Land tenure
2.1.3 Management infrastructure
2.1.4 Map coverage
2.1.5 Photographic coverage
2.1.6 Compartments or Zones

2.2 Environmental information
2.2.1 Physical
    2.2.1.1 Climate
    2.2.1.2 Hydrology
    2.2.1.3 Geology
    2.2.1.4 Geomorphology / Landform
    2.2.1.5 Soils
2.2.2 Biological
    2.2.2.1 Flora
    2.2.2.2 Fauna
    2.2.2.3 Communities
2.2.3 Cultural
    2.2.3.1 Archaeology / past land use
    2.2.3.2 Present land use
    2.2.3.3 Past management – nature conservation
    2.2.3.4 Past status / interest
    2.2.3.5 Present conservation status
    2.2.3.6 Landscape
    2.2.3.7 Public interest / community relations
    2.2.3.8 Educational use / facilities
    2.2.3.9 Research use / facilities
    2.2.3.10 Interpretation use / facilities
    2.2.3.11 Recreational use / facilities

2.3 Bibliography

3 Confirmation of features

3.1 The site in wider perspective and implications for management

3.2 Provisional list of important features

3.3 Confirmation of features - previously recognised

3.4 Evaluation
3.4.1 Evaluation for nature conservation
    3.4.1.1 Size
    3.4.1.2 Diversity
    3.4.1.3 Naturalness
    3.4.1.4 Rarity
    3.4.1.5 Fragility
    3.4.1.6 Typicalness
    3.4.1.7 Recorded history
    3.4.1.8 Position in ecological unit
    3.4.1.9 Potential for improvement / restoration
3.4.2 Evaluation for Landscape
3.4.3 Evaluation for Public use / access
3.4.4 Evaluation for Education
3.4.5 Evaluation for Interpretation
3.4.6 Evaluation for Research / study

3.5 Confirmed list of important features

4 Factors which influence or may influence the features

4.1 Owner/occupier's objectives

4.2 Internal natural factors

4.3 Internal man-induced factors

4.4 External factors

4.5 Factors arising from legislation or tradition

4.6 Physical considerations/constraints

4.7 Available resources

4.8 Environmental and other relationships which may influence the features

4.9 Summary of factors which influence or may influence the features

5 Objectives, limits and monitoring

5.1 Identification selection of attributes

5.2 Objectives, limits and monitoring

5.3 Current condition and status of features

5.4 Rationale, operational limits and management options
5.4.1 Rationale
5.4.2 Operational limits and monitoring projects
5.4.3 Management options

5.5 Action plan - outline prescription and projects

6 Project register and work programmes

6.1 Project register

6.2 Work programmes

7 Project records and review

7.1 Project records

7.2 Annual review

7.3 Long-term review

Appendices

Appendix 6
Requirements of typical wet grassland plant communities (MG4–MG13)

NVC Vegetation Type (Code)	Dominant (D) and Rare (R) species	Occurrence (habitat)	Soil type
Flood meadows: meadow foxtail and great burnet grassland. (MG4)	D: meadow foxtail, common mouse-ear, crested dog's-tail, red fescue, meadowsweet, Yorkshire-fog, meadow vetchling, autumn hawkbit, perennial rye-grass, meadow buttercup, common sorrel, great burnet, dandelion – agg., red clover and white clover. R: snake's-head fritillary, six dandelion spp and narrow-leaved water-dropwort.	River floodplains in central and southern England.	Alluvial (neutral or calcareous).
Old grazed hay meadows: crested dog's-tail and common knapweed grassland. (MG5)	D: common bent, sweet vernal grass, common knapweed, crested dog's-tail, cock's-foot, red fescue, Yorkshire-fog, common bird's-foot-trefoil, ribwort plantain, red clover and white clover. R: tuberous thistle, corky-fruited water-dropwort, greater yellow-rattle and sulphur clover.	Widespread in lowlands of Britain – especially in the clay farmland of English Midlands. Often on ridges of ridge-and-furrow.	Circumneutral brown soils – but over a wide range (with consequent variation in the make-up of flora).
Dairy and fatting pastures: perennial rye-grass and crested dog's-tail grassland. (MG6)	D: common mouse-ear, crested dog's-tail, red fescue, Yorkshire-fog, perennial rye-grass and white clover. R: corky-fruited water-dropwort.	Very common in pastures of lowland Britain.	Circumneutral brown soils, especially deep loams.
Improved and sown swards: perennial rye-grass leys and related grasslands. (MG7)	D: perennial rye-grass. (Other species locally important).	Very common throughout Britain, especially in highly intensive farmland and amenity areas.	Circumneutral brown soil typically – but agricultural improvement may produce the type on a wide soil range.
Water meadows: crested dog's-tail and marsh-marigold grassland. (MG8)	D: sweet vernal grass, marsh-marigold, common mouse-ear, crested dog's-tail, red fescue, Yorkshire-fog, autumn hawkbit, rough meadow-grass, meadow buttercup, common sorrel and white clover.	Rare (or under-recorded) in traditional water-meadows and elsewhere by rivers in lowland England.	Gleyed brown earths, often silty and calcareous, or locally peaty.

Water-table	Flooding regime	Management
Soils moist to very locally damp. Free-draining above, or sometimes waterlogged (and gleyed) at depth.	Winter flooding – occasionally persisting into the spring.	No fertiliser. Shut up for hay from the flooding onward. Mown in July and the aftermath grazed from August onward.
Soils moist. Where soil particles are finer, drainage may be impeded – with waterlogging in furrows/hollows.	Normally none – standing water in winter is normally associated with other types.	No (or minimal) improvement for farming. Shut up for hay from April–June, when cut and the aftermath grazed through to next spring.
Soils moist but free-draining, eliminated by long waterlogging and encouraged by under-drainage.	No flooding – or only in very exceptional years.	Prefers intensive pasture improvement and often treated with artificial fertilisers. Though often shut up for hay for short periods in spring – usually regularly and intensively grazed.
Soils moist to very locally damp, (like MG6) encouraged by under-drainage and eliminated by long waterlogging.	Where flooded regularly in winter, rye-grass is accompanied by meadow species of foxtail and fescue. Where not flooded, the sward is species-poor.	Heavy use of fertiliser, herbicide and sown cultivars of rye-grass. May be grazed or mown but both intensively.
Soils constantly damp, due to flood regime or seepage and springs.	Deliberately flooded in past for long period in the winter and spring. This tradition is now rare, and the community is found where natural floods occur by rivers.	In addition to the water management, grazed when dry, and occasionally a hay crop taken. Some tradition of hand-weeding, but no use of artificial fertilisers.

NVC Vegetation Type (Code)	Dominant (D) and Rare (R) species	Occurrence (habitat)	Soil type
Tussock wet meadows: Yorkshire-fog and tufted hair-grass grassland. (MG9)	D: tufted hair-grass, Yorkshire-fog.	Very common in lowland Britain, in woodland rides and roadsides, as well as meadows and pastures.	Circumneutral gleyed brown earths, especially where these are infertile.
Ordinary damp meadows: Yorkshire-fog and soft-rush rush-pasture. (MG10)	D: creeping bent, Yorkshire-fog, soft-rush and creeping buttercup.	Common from the lowlands into the upland fringe in pastures and derelict farmland.	Gleyed brown earths and alluvial soils – neutral to slightly acid. In more calcareous sites, hard rush may replace the soft-rush.
Inundation grassland: red fescue, creeping bent and silverweed grassland. (MG11)	D: creeping bent, red fescue and silverweed.	Probably frequent (especially in west) in floodplains, upper salt-marsh and marginal habitats (ie by ditches, ponds and shores).	Brown earths and alluvial soils (sand and shingle possess particular variants). Circumneutral but often brackish.
Upper saltmarsh ungrazed swards: tall fescue grassland. (MG12)	D: creeping bent, tall fescue and red fescue.	Uncommon at the upper edge of saltmarshes and estuaries or on clay coastal cliffs.	Clays and silts.
Inundation grassland: creeping bent and marsh foxtail grassland. (MG13)	D: creeping bent, marsh foxtail.	Widespread by water, especially in the east, on washland, floodplains and in seasonally wet hollows/furrows.	Circumneutral silts.

NOTES: Definition of terms

I.   The usage of the terms 'dry', 'moist', 'damp' and 'wet' follows that defined by the water indicator (F) values of Ellenberg (1988), ie occurrence in the gradient from dry shallow-soil rocky slopes to marshy ground, and thence from shallow to deep water (see Table 3.2).

II.   'Dominant' and 'rare' adapted from usage in the community description in the National Vegetation Classification (Rodwell 1991, 1992, 1995):

Dominant, ie species which occur in the majority of samples, but with ground cover in excess of 5% and which also form a major part of the vegetation cover in at least some examples of that community.

Rare (as used by Rodwell) applies to plants either i) given an A rating in Perring and Walters (1962); ii) included in lists of nationally scarce species, occurring in <100 10-km squares in Great Britain (Stewart *et al* 1994); or iii) bryophytes occurring in <20 vice-counties (Corley and Hill 1981).

Water-table	Flooding regime	Management
Soils permanently moist to damp, and with consequent poor aeration.	Periodically inundated as in the furrows of ridge and furrow – not flooded deliberately.	Stimulated by light to quite heavy grazing, but can be eliminated by an intensive mowing regime.
Soils permanently damp due to ground or surface water.	Not normally flooded, other than in far west, where yellow iris becomes very abundant.	Endures (moderate) grazing, but regular mowing eliminates the rush. Tends to be associated with abandoned or neglected farms.
Soils moist to damp, but free-draining.	Inundated by fresh or brackish water, but also prone to periods of drying out.	Regularly grazed and locally treated with artificial fertilisers, but rarely mown.
Soils damp, but free-draining.	Prone to inundation by brackish water, more rarely tidal water or salt spray.	Usually unmanaged – but rarely grazed, cut or burnt.
Soils damp, and sometimes waterlogged.	Regularly flooded by fresh water – sometimes for long periods.	Flooding regime produces naturally fertile soils, which are exploited for summer grazing (and occasionally hay).

Appendix 7
Requirements of mire plant communities (M22–M25) included within the term wet grassland

NVC Vegetation Type (Code)	Dominant (D) and Rare (R) species	Occurrence (habitat)	Soil type
Rich-fen meadows: blunt-flowered rush and marsh thistle fen-meadow. (M22)	D: marsh thistle, marsh horsetail, meadowsweet, Yorkshire-fog, blunt-flowered rush, greater bird's-foot-trefoil, water mint and the moss *Calliergon cuspidatum*. R: milk-parsley and *Homalothecium nitens*.	Occasional in central and eastern England, where rich fens have undergone some reclamation.	On neutral to rather alkaline soils (pH 6-8) often peaty but also on alluvium and base-rich clays.
Western fen-meadows: Soft/ sharp-flowered rush and marsh-bedstraw rush-pasture. (M23)	D: common marsh-bedstraw, Yorkshire-fog, sharp-flowered rush, soft-rush and greater bird's-foot-trefoil.	In Scotland, Wales and western England from lowlands to moderate altitudes around mires, wet heaths and neglected farmland.	On moderately acid to neutral minerals soils (pH 4-6) with high humus content.
Litter and wet Culm grasslands: purple moor-grass and meadow thistle fen-meadow. (M24)	D: carnation sedge, meadow thistle, greater bird's-foot-trefoil, purple moor-grass and tormentil. R: milk-parsley, wavy St John's-wort and Cambridge milk-parsley.	Local in lowland southern England, where mires (fen or bog) have been affected by cutting/grazing.	On peats and peaty mineral soil, neutral to mildly acidic.
Purple moor-grass grassland: purple moor-grass and tormentil mire. (M25)	D: purple moor-grass. R: bristle bent, cornish heath and heath lobelia.	Throughout western Britain, and common in south-west England, Wales and southern Scotland on heaths and moors.	Acid to neutral (pH 4-6) peats, or peaty mineral soil.

NOTES: Definition of terms

I.   The usage of the terms 'dry', 'moist', 'damp' and 'wet' follows that defined by the water indicator (F) values of Ellenberg (1988), ie occurrence in the gradient from dry shallow-soil rocky slopes to marshy ground, and thence from shallow to deep water (see Table 3.2).

II. 'Dominant' and 'rare' adapted from usage in the community description in the National Vegetation Classification (Rodwell 1991, 1992, 1995):

Dominant, ie species which occur in the majority of samples, but with ground cover in excess of 5% and which also form a major part of the vegetation cover in at least some examples of that community.

Rare (as used by Rodwell) applies to plants either i) given an A rating in Perring and Walters (1962); ii) included in lists of nationally scarce species, occurring in <100 10-km squares in Great Britain (Stewart *et al* 1994); or iii) bryophytes occurring in <20 vice-counties (Corley and Hill 1981).

	Water-table	Flooding regime	Management
	Soils moist to damp for most of year, often due to flushes or springs.	Often flooded in winter, but very variable in duration with resultant variety in the flora.	Derived from fens that have a) had surface drainage partly improved by ditches; b) been cut or grazed (reeds etc eliminated); but c) not fertilised or herbicided.
	Soils moist to wet throughout the year, where the drainage is impeded.	Not usually flooded.	Generally grazed by sheep and/or cattle, but not cut. Some lowland sites have been partly improved – drained, fertilised, re-seeded – but the typical sward occurs where these treatments are discontinued.
	From fairly moist to quite dry (especially in summer) with little fluctuation in water-table or throughput.	Very seldom flooded.	Derived from drier fringes of mires by regular cutting but now often maintained by grazing alone. No fertiliser, herbicide or re-seeding.
	Moist, but well-aerated, often on gentle slopes with lateral water movement.	Not usually flooded.	Affected by burning and grazing in many cases. No fertiliser, herbicide or re-seeding.

Appendix 8
Requirements of swamp communities (S5–S7 and S22) included within the term wet grassland

NVC Vegetation Type (Code)	Dominant (D) species	Occurrence (habitat)	Soil type
Washland: reed sweet-grass swamp. (S5)	D: reed sweet-grass.	Regularly inundated floodplain washland (also common as a fringing swamp to still or sluggish eutrophic water).	Nutrient-rich, circum neutral or basic alluvium, or organic soil with regular inputs of mineral-rich water (pH >6.0).
Tall sedge meadows: great pond-sedge swamp. (S6)	D: great pond-sedge.	Wet hollows within flood-meadows (also common dominant of swamp by still or sluggish, often eutrophic, water).	Mesotrophic to eutrophic, circumneutral mineral soils, more rarely on peat (pH 5.8-7.0).
Tall sedge meadows: lesser pond-sedge swamp. (S7)	D: lesser pond-sedge.	Wet hollows within flood-meadows (also a dominant of swamp by still or sluggish, often calcareous, water).	Moderately eutrophic, circumneutral to basic mineral soils (pH 6.0-6.8).
Floating sweet-grass hollows: floating sweet-grass water-margin vegetation. (S22)	D: floating sweet-grass.	Wet depressions in grassland, and along the margins of pools and drainage channels.	Mesotrophic to moderately eutrophic water on mineral, or more rarely, organic substrates (pH 5.0-7.0).

NOTES: Definition of terms

I.   The usage of the terms 'dry', 'moist', 'damp' and 'wet' follows that defined by the water indicator (F) values of Ellenberg (1988), ie occurrence in the gradient from dry shallow-soil rocky slopes to marshy ground, and thence from shallow to deep water (see Table 3.2).

II.   'Dominant' and 'rare' adapted from usage in the community description in the National Vegetation Classification (Rodwell 1991, 1992, 1995):

Dominant, ie species which occur in the majority of samples, but with ground cover in excess of 5% and which also form a major part of the vegetation cover in at least some examples of that community.

Rare (as used by Rodwell) applies to plants either i) given an A rating in Perring and Walters (1962); ii) included in lists of nationally scarce species, occurring in <100 10-km squares in Great Britain (Stewart *et al* 1994); or iii) bryophytes occurring in <20 vice-counties (Corley and Hill 1981).

	Water-table	Flooding regime	Management
	Usually in waterlogged sites – with water at soil surface for most of the summer (also as an emergent or marginal 'hover' in standing water).	Regular very prolonged winter-flooding.	Tolerant of fertiliser application, as well as summer mowing and grazing by cattle (or wildfowl).
	Continuously waterlogged sites (community also occurs in up to 20 cm of water).	Regular prolonged winter-flooding.	Probably suppressed by high levels of fertiliser application. Intolerant of intense cutting or grazing, especially early in the year.
	Continuously waterlogged sites (community also occurs in up to 20 cm of water).	Regular prolonged winter-flooding.	Probably suppressed by high rates of inorganic application. Favoured intermittent grazing, but usually reduced or checked by mowing.
	In grassland in waterlogged sites (community also occurs in up to 20 cm of water).	Regular prolonged winter-flooding, often through into late spring or even summer.	Probably favoured by low rates of inorganic application. Favoured by annual cutting, and light to moderate grazing.

Appendix 9
Typical plant species of wet grassland and their requirements

Species name (Scientific name)	Soil type	Soil pH	Reaction to salinity
Yarrow (*Achillea millefolium*)	Alluvium (and other coarser mineral soil).	5.5–7.0 (–8)	Intolerant.
Velvet bent (*Agrostis canina*)	Nutrient-poor peats.	3.5–6.0	Intolerant.
Common bent (*Agrostis capillaris*)	Acid mineral soil.	Esp. 4.0–6.0	Intolerant.
Creeping bent (*Agrostis stolonifera*)	Widespread in fertile soil.	Esp. 5.5–>8.0	Moderately tolerant.
Marsh foxtail (*Alopecurus geniculatus*)	Fertile alluvial soil.	5.5–7.0	Occasional in saline sites.
Meadow foxtail (*Alopecurus pratensis*)	Fertile mineral soil.	5.0–7.0	Intolerant.
Sweet vernal grass (*Anthoxanthum odoratum*)	Widespread at lower fertility.	Esp. 4.5–6.0	Intolerant.
False oat-grass (*Arrhenatherum elatius*)	Mineral soils.	Esp. >5.0–8.0	Usually absent.
Daisy (*Bellis perennis*)	Widespread on mineral soils.	(5–) 7.0–8.0	Usually absent.
Soft-brome (*Bromus hordeaceus*)	Mineral soils of moderate fertility.	>5.5	Intolerant.
Smooth brome (*Bromus racemosus*)	Mineral and peat soils.	5.0–7.0	Intolerant.
Marsh-marigold (*Caltha palustris*)	Mineral and peat soils.	Esp. 6.0–7.0	Intolerant.
Cuckooflower (*Cardamine pratensis*)	Mineral and peat soils.	>5.0	Intolerant.
Brown sedge (*Carex disticha*)	Mineral and peat soils.	5.5–8.0	Intolerant.
Glaucous sedge (*Carex flacca*)	Especially on alkaline mineral soil.	(5) 7.0–8.0	Occasional on saline soils.
Hairy sedge (*Carex hirta*)	Mainly on fertile mineral soil.	Esp. 5.0–6.0	Intolerant.
Common sedge (*Carex nigra*)	Infertile, especially organic soil.	Esp. <5.0	Intolerant.

Soil water-table	Reaction to flooding	Reaction to grazing and cutting	Reaction to fertiliser application
Dry to moist – somewhat drought tolerant.	Intolerant.	Favoured by defoliation.	Suppressed.
Wet, waterlogged, poorly aerated.	Tolerant – will colonise still water.	Favoured.	Strongly suppressed.
Widespread, but commoner in well-drained sites.	Normally intolerant.	Strongly favoured by defoliation.	Suppressed.
Moist to damp soils.	Tolerant, will grow floating in still water.	Favoured by mowing, but eaten by stock.	Somewhat favoured.
Intolerant of long drought, typical of wet soils.	Prefers winter-flooded sites – tolerant of poor aeration.	Favoured by late mowing.	Favoured by moderate application of nitrogen.
Damp but well-drained sites, will tolerate short droughts.	Rarer where waterlogging or flooding is prolonged.	Favoured by late mowing, will tolerate some grazing.	Favoured by moderate application of nitrogen.
Widespread, but commoner in moist sites.	Intolerant.	Favoured by late mowing and aftermath grazing.	Favoured by manure, but suppressed by inorganic fertilisers.
Moist, but not waterlogged. Tolerates drought.	Intolerant.	Intolerant of grazing but prefers annual hay-cut.	Favoured by moderate application of nitrogen.
Widespread, preferring moist but well-aerated soil.	Intolerant.	Dependent on regular defoliation.	Suppressed by heavy rates of fertiliser.
Intolerant of waterlogging.	Intolerant.	Favoured by late mowing, but suppressed by heavy grazing.	Strongly favoured by fertiliser use.
Damp to wet sites, able to tolerate quite long droughts.	Very tolerant of flooding in winter but not spring.	Favoured by late mowing, and by light to moderate grazing.	Favoured by fertiliser application.
Damp to wet sites, able to tolerate quite long droughts.	Will grow in shallow water – tolerates aeration stress.	Will tolerate late mowing, but rare with heavy grazing.	Probably suppressed by heavy rates of fertiliser.
Damp sites, but tolerant of change.	Tolerant of winter floods.	Favoured by grazing of tall species.	Suppressed by heavy rates of inorganic fertiliser.
Wet, waterlogged, poorly aerated soil.	Tolerant of winter floods.	Favoured by mowing.	Somewhat suppressed by inorganic fertiliser.
Mainly on moist to damp soils, but with wide tolerance.	Tolerant of prolonged winter flooding.	Favoured by defoliation.	Somewhat suppressed by inorganic fertiliser.
Moist to damp soils, but tolerant of drought.	Intolerant of prolonged waterlogging.	Favoured.	Suppressed by inorganic fertiliser.
Damp to wet sites, and intolerant of prolonged drought.	Tolerant.	Favoured.	Suppressed by inorganic fertiliser.

Species name (Scientific name)	Soil type	Soil pH	Reaction to salinity
False fox-sedge (*Carex otrubae*)	Mainly on mineral soil.	Esp. >5.5	Occasional on saline soils.
Carnation sedge (*Carex panicea*)	Mainly on organic soil.	(4–) 5.0–6.0 (–7.5)	Intolerant.
Greater pond-sedge (*Carex riparia*)	Mineral and organic soil.	>5.5	Intolerant.
Whorled caraway (*Carum verticillatum*)	Nutrient and calcium-poor mineral soils, sometimes with peaty topsoil.	4.0–6.0	Intolerant.
Common knapweed (*Centaurea nigra*)	Mainly on moderately fertile mineral soil.	Esp. >5.0	Intolerant.
Common mouse-ear (*Cerastium fontanum*)	Mainly on moderately fertile mineral soil.	Esp. >5.0	Intolerant.
Creeping thistle (*Cirsium arvense*)	Mainly on fertile mineral soil.	Esp. >5.0	Occasional in saline soils.
Meadow thistle (*Cirsium dissectum*)	Infertile organic soil.	Esp. <7.0	Intolerant.
Marsh thistle (*Cirsium palustre*)	Widespread on moderately fertile soils.	4.5–6.5	Intolerant.
Crested dog's-tail (*Cynosurus cristatus*)	Mainly on moderately fertile mineral soil.	Esp. 5.0–7.5	Intolerant.
Cock's-foot (*Dactylis glomerata*)	Especially on moderately fertile mineral soil.	Esp. 5.0–8.0	Intolerant.
Tufted hair-grass (*Deschampsia cespitosa*)	Widespread, but especially in infertile mineral soil.	Esp 4.5—6.5	Intolerant.
Common spike-rush (*Eleocharis palustris*)	Mineral and peat soils.	5.0–7.5	Intolerant.
Marsh horsetail (*Equisetum palustre*)	Moderately fertile organic and mineral soils	>5.0	Intolerant.
Tall fescue (*Festuca arundinacea*)	Especially on moderately fertile mineral soil.	>5.5	Occasional in saline soils.
Meadow fescue (*Festuca pratensis*)	Especially on fertile clay and alluvium.	>5.0	Intolerant.
Red fescue (*Festuca rubra s.l.*)	Widespread, but most common on mineral soil.	Esp. >5.0	Some sub-spp. common in saline soils.
Meadowsweet (*Filipendula ulmaria*)	Mineral and organic soil.	>4.5	Intolerant.

Soil water-table	Reaction to flooding	Reaction to grazing and cutting	Reaction to fertiliser application
Typical of wet sites.	Tolerant.	Intolerant of intense grazing.	Somewhat suppressed by high levels of inorganic fertiliser.
Typical of damp sites, intolerant of prolonged drought.	Tolerant.	Favoured by defoliation.	Suppressed by high levels of fertiliser.
Typical of wet sites, intolerant of drought.	Tolerant, often emergent in drainage channels.	Intolerant of frequent cutting or grazing.	Probably suppressed by high levels of fertiliser.
Tolerant of water-logged sites prone to some fluctuation.	Intolerant.	Favoured by autumn and winter defoliation, especially cattle grazing.	Probably suppressed by heavy rates of fertilizer.
Typical of moist sites, tolerant of drought.	Intolerant.	Favoured by (late) mowing but suppressed by intense grazing.	Strongly suppressed by moderate to high levels of fertiliser.
Typical of moist sites, tolerant of drought.	Intolerant of prolonged flooding.	Favoured by mowing and grazing.	Favoured by moderate applications of fertiliser.
Widespread, rare where waterlogged.	Intolerant of prolonged flooding.	Can be suppressed by intense mowing, avoided by stock.	Favoured by moderate applications of fertiliser.
Typical of damp to wet, often waterlogged sites.	Tolerant of moderate flooding.	Favoured.	Suppressed by high levels of fertiliser.
Typical of damp to wet sites, but with wide tolerance.	Tolerant of prolonged winter flooding.	Tolerant of annual cut, avoided by stock.	Suppressed by high levels of fertiliser.
On moist sites, tolerant of long drought.	Intolerant of prolonged flooding.	Strongly favoured by grazing.	Strongly suppressed by inorganic fertiliser.
On moist sites, tolerant of drought.	Intolerant of prolonged flooding.	Favoured by occasional defoliation, tolerant of summer grazing.	Favoured by lower applications of nitrogen.
On damp sites, but tolerates moderate droughts.	Intolerant of prolonged flooding.	Reduced by frequent cutting, avoided by stock.	Suppressed by higher levels of application.
Typical of waterlogged, inundated sites, does not tolerate drought.	Prefers regular flooding.	Favoured by mowing of tall grasses, and light grazing.	Probably suppressed by heavy rates of fertiliser.
Mainly in damp sites, but tolerates some drought.	Occasionally found where flooded for short periods.	Suppressed by frequent mowing, often avoided by stock.	Probably suppressed by heavy rates of fertiliser.
On damp soils, tolerates short drought.	Rare where flooding is prolonged.	Commonest under light grazing and/or annual mowing.	Favoured by moderate application of nitrogen.
On moist to damp sites.	Intolerant.	Intolerant of neglect, or intense grazing.	Favoured by moderate application of nitrogen.
Widespread.	Tolerates moderate flooding in winter.	Found over a wide range of management.	Suppressed by even low levels of fertiliser.
Damp to wet sites, not permanently waterlogged; tolerates some drought.	Intolerant of prolonged flooding.	Prefers an annual cut and light grazing.	Suppressed by moderate rates of inorganic fertiliser.

Species name (Scientific name)	Soil type	Soil pH	Reaction to salinity
Snake's-head fritillary (*Fritillaria meleagris*)	Alluvial soil.	6.0–7.5	Intolerant.
Common marsh-bedstraw (*Galium palustre*)	Organic and mineral soil.	Esp. 5.0–7.0	Intolerant.
Fen bedstraw (*Galium uliginosum*)	Infertile organic soil.	5.5–8.0	Intolerant.
Ground-ivy (*Glechoma hederacea*)	Mainly on fertile mineral soil.	5.5–7.5	Intolerant.
Floating sweet-grass (*Glyceria fluitans*)	Fertile, organic and mineral soil.	Esp. 5.0–7.0	Intolerant.
Reed sweet-grass (*Glyceria maxima*)	Fertile, organic and mineral soil.	5.0–7.5	Generally intolerant.
Yorkshire-fog (*Holcus lanatus*)	Widespread, but especially on quite fertile soil.	Esp. 5.0–6.0	Intolerant.
Cat's-ear (*Hypochaeris radicata*)	Mainly on infertile mineral soil.	Esp. 4.5–5.5	Intolerant.
Yellow iris (*Iris pseudacorus*)	Fertile mineral and organic soil.	Very wide-spread.	Intolerant.
Sharp-flowered rush (*Juncus acutiflorus*)	Especially on infertile organic soil.	Esp. <6.0	Intolerant.
Jointed rush (*Juncus articulatus*)	On moderately infertile mineral and organic soil.	Esp. >5.0	Intolerant.
Soft-rush (*Juncus effusus*)	Organic and mineral soils.	Very wide-spread esp. <7.0	Intolerant.
Saltmarsh rush (*Juncus gerardii*)	Mainly on mineral soils.	Very wide-spread.	Generally on saline soils.
Hard rush (*Juncus inflexus*)	Mainly on relatively infertile mineral soils.	Esp. >5.5	Occasional on saline soils.
Blunt-flowered rush (*Juncus subnodulosus*)	Relatively fertile organic soils.	6.5–8.0	Occasional on saline soils.
Meadow vetchling (*Lathyrus pratensis*)	Mainly on relatively fertile mineral soils.	Esp. 5.0–7.0	Intolerant.
Autumn hawkbit (*Leontodon autumnalis*)	Mainly on relatively fertile mineral soils.	>5.0	Occasional on saline soils.

Soil water-table	Reaction to flooding	Reaction to grazing and cutting	Reaction to fertiliser application
Damp to wet sites, but free-draining.	Tolerates winter flooding with moving water.	Late mowing followed by aftermath grazing.	Intolerant of fertiliser application.
Wet, waterlogged sites, intolerant of prolonged drought.	Will grow in shallow water, especially where winter flooded.	Prefers annual cut and light grazing.	Suppressed by higher levels of fertiliser application.
Damp to wet sites, not in drought-prone sites.	Tolerant of winter floods.	Prefers annual cut and light grazing.	Probably suppressed by high levels of fertiliser application.
Widespread, especially in moist to damp sites.	Intolerant.	Shade-tolerant, often absent under intense defoliation.	Possibly tolerant of light applications of fertiliser.
Typical of wet sites, intolerant of drought.	Often aquatic, preferring prolonged flooding.	Prefers annual cut and light grazing.	Probably favoured by low rates of fertiliser.
Waterlogged sites, intolerant of long droughts.	Frequently aquatic, prefers sites that are regularly inundated.	Prefers annual cut and light grazing.	Favoured by fertiliser application.
Moist–damp sites, tolerant of moderate droughts.	Intolerant of very prolonged floods.	Limited by very intense grazing, but otherwise widespread.	Strongly favoured in short term by fertiliser application.
Typical of dry sites, and tolerant of prolonged drought.	Intolerant of prolonged floods.	Favoured by frequent mowing and grazing.	Suppressed by high levels of fertiliser application.
Usually in wet sites, intolerant of drought.	Often aquatic, prefers regular flooding.	Prefers annual cut and light grazing.	Possibly suppressed by heavy rates of fertiliser.
Typical of damp to wet sites, intolerant of long droughts.	Tolerates moderate flooding.	Favoured by defoliation, avoided by stock at light grazing pressures.	Suppressed by high levels of fertiliser application.
Typical of damp to wet sites, intolerant of moderate droughts.	Occasionally behaves as an aquatic, frequent where floods are regular.	Favoured by defoliation, avoided by stock at light grazing pressures.	Suppressed by high levels of fertiliser application.
Damp sites, probably tolerant of short droughts.	Tolerant of winter floods, but usually absent from standing water.	Favoured by grazing (avoided by sheep and cattle), and annual cutting.	Suppressed by heavy rates of inorganic fertiliser.
Damp sites, intolerant of prolonged droughts.	Tolerant of winter and tidal flooding.	Tolerates quite intense grazing (avoided by sheep and cattle), and moderate cutting.	Probably suppressed by heavy rates of inorganic fertiliser.
Damp sites, tolerant of prolonged droughts.	Tolerant of winter flooding.	Tolerates intense grazing (avoided by sheep and cattle), and moderate cutting.	Suppressed by heavy rates of inorganic fertiliser.
Damp to wet sites, intolerant of prolonged droughts.	Tolerant of winter flooding, occasional as an aquatic.	Favoured by defoliation, avoided by stock at light grazing pressures.	Possibly suppressed by heavy rates of inorganic fertiliser.
Moist to damp sites, tolerant of short-duration drought.	Intolerant of moderate flooding.	Prefers lightly grazed and / or annually mown sites.	Probably suppressed by heavy rates of inorganic fertiliser, but favoured by light dressings.
On moist sites, tolerant of some droughting.	Intolerant of regular flooding.	Favoured by mowing or grazing of taller species.	Suppressed by even moderate rates of inorganic fertiliser.

Species name (Scientific name)	Soil type	Soil pH	Reaction to salinity
Rough hawkbit (*Leontodon hispidus*)	Mainly on relatively infertile mineral soils.	Esp. >7.0	Intolerant.
Perennial rye-grass (*Lolium perenne*)	Especially on fertile mineral soils.	5.0–8.0	Intolerant.
Greater bird's-foot-trefoil (*Lotus pedunculatus*)	Organic and mineral soils.	Esp. 4.5–6.5	Moderately tolerant.
Field wood-rush (*Luzula campestris*)	Mainly on relatively infertile mineral soils.	Very wide-spread. Esp. 4.5–6.0	Intolerant.
Ragged-robin (*Lychnis flos-cuculi*)	Organic and mineral soils.	Esp. >5.0	Intolerant.
Creeping-jenny (*Lysimachia nummularia*)	Organic and mineral soils.	Esp. >5.0	Intolerant.
Water mint (*Mentha aquatica*)	Organic and mineral soils.	>5.0, esp. >6.0	Intolerant.
Purple moor-grass (*Molinia caerulea*)	Mainly in infertile organic soils.	Widespread esp. <4.0 and >7.0	Intolerant.
Changing forget-me-not (*Myosotis discolor*)	Mainly in infertile organic and mineral soils.	Esp. <6.5	Intolerant.
Tubular water-dropwort (*Oenanthe fistulosa*)	Organic and mineral soils.	5.5–-7.5	Intolerant.
Parsley water-dropwort (*Oenanthe lachenalii*)	Mineral and organic soils.	Esp. >6.0	Generally on saline soils.
Amphibious bistort (*Persicaria amphibia*)	Relatively fertile mineral and organic soils.	Esp. >5.0	Intolerant.
Timothy (*Phleum pratense*)	Especially on moderately fertile mineral soils.	>5.0	Intolerant.
Ribwort plantain (*Plantago lanceolata*)	Widespread, but especially on mineral soils.	Esp. 5.0–8.0	Intolerant.
Spreading meadow-grass (*Poa humilis*)	Especially in infertile mineral and organic soils.	Esp. <6.5	Possibly occasional in saline soils.
Smooth meadow-grass (*Poa pratensis s.l.*)	Especially on moderately fertile mineral soils.	>4.5	Intolerant.

Soil water-table	Reaction to flooding	Reaction to grazing and cutting	Reaction to fertiliser application
On dry to moist sites, drought-tolerant.	Intolerant of regular flooding.	Favoured by mowing or grazing.	Probably suppressed by heavy rates of inorganic fertiliser.
On moist sites, reduced by extreme drought.	Tolerates regular, but not prolonged floods.	Favoured by (even intense) mowing or grazing.	Favoured by all applications of fertiliser.
Damp to wet sites, but relatively drought-tolerant.	Tolerates regular (though usually not prolonged) flooding. Rare as an emergent in aquatic sites.	Prefers lightly grazed and / or annually mown sites.	Suppressed by heavy, but possibly favoured by light rates of inorganic fertiliser.
On dry to moist sites, drought-tolerant.	Intolerant of prolonged flooding.	Favoured by mowing or lighter grazing.	Probably suppressed by heavy rates of inorganic fertiliser.
On moist to damp sites, intolerant of prolonged droughts.	Most common where flooded regularly.	Prefers lightly grazed and / or annually mown sites.	Suppressed by heavy rates of inorganic fertiliser.
On moist to damp sites, intolerant of very prolonged droughts.	Most common where flooded regularly.	Prefers lightly grazed and / or annually mown sites.	Suppressed by even low rates of inorganic fertiliser.
On wet sites, intolerant of drought.	Flood-tolerant, often found as an emergent.	Suppressed by frequent grazing or cutting.	Probably suppressed by heavy rates of inorganic fertiliser.
Damp sites, typical of fluctuating water-table.	Intolerant of prolonged flooding and waterlogging.	Favoured by annual cutting, but suppressed by intense grazing.	Probably suppressed by heavy rates of inorganic fertiliser.
Dry soils, often occurring on mole- or ant-hills in wet sites. Tolerant of drought.	Tolerates regular (though not prolonged) flooding.	Favoured by grazing (and trampling) and mowing.	Suppressed by higher rates of inorganic fertiliser.
Wet sites, intolerant of drought.	Most common where flooding regular, frequently emergent in shallow water.	Favoured by annual cutting, toxic to stock.	Probably suppressed by heavy rates of inorganic fertiliser.
Damp to wet sites, intolerant of prolonged drought.	Tolerates regular (though not prolonged) flooding.	Favoured by annual cutting, toxic to stock.	Probably suppressed by heavy rates of inorganic fertiliser.
Very wet sites, intolerant of prolonged drought.	Favoured by regular and prolonged flooding – occurs in both terrestrial and floating aquatic forms.	Favoured by annual cutting, and light grazing.	Possibly favoured by light applications of fertiliser.
Moist sites, tolerant of short periods of drought and / or waterlogging.	Frequent in sites liable to regular winter flooding eg water meadows.	Favoured by mowing for hay, and grazing.	Favoured by fertiliser.
Widespread and tolerant of drought.	Occurs in regularly flooded sites, but not those liable to prolonged waterlogging.	Favoured by cutting, and (even intense) grazing.	Suppressed by moderate levels of inorganic fertiliser.
Damp sites, intolerant of prolonged drought.	Frequent in sites liable to regular winter flooding.	Favoured by mowing for hay, and grazing.	Possibly favoured by light applications of fertiliser.
Moist sites, tolerant of drought.	Tolerates regular flooding.	Favoured by mowing and grazing.	Probably favoured by light applications of fertiliser.

Species name (Scientific name)	Soil type	Soil pH	Reaction to salinity
Rough meadow-grass (*Poa trivialis*)	Fertile mineral and organic soils.	Esp. >5.0	Intolerant.
Silverweed (*Potentilla anserina*)	Fertile mineral and organic soils.	Esp. >5.5	Occasional in saline soils.
Tormentil (*Potentilla erecta*)	Relatively infertile organic and mineral soils.	Esp. <6.0	Intolerant.
Creeping cinquefoil (*Potentilla reptans*)	Mineral and organic soils.	Esp. >4.5	Intolerant.
Selfheal (*Prunella vulgaris*)	Widespread, especially on moderately fertile mineral soil.	>5.0	Intolerant.
Meadow buttercup (*Ranunculus acris*)	Widespread on mineral and organic soils.	Esp. 5.5–7.0	Intolerant.
Bulbous buttercup (*Ranunculus bulbosus*)	Especially on mineral soil of intermediate infertility.	Esp. >5.0	Intolerant.
Lesser spearwort (*Ranunculus flammula*)	Mineral and organic soils of intermediate infertility.	Esp. 4.5–6.5	Intolerant.
Creeping buttercup (*Ranunculus repens*)	Very widespread, especially on fertile soils.	Esp. 5.0–8.0	Intolerant.
Yellow-rattle (*Rhinanthus minor*)	Widespread, especially on soils of lower fertility.	>5.0	Intolerant.
Common sorrel (*Rumex acetosa*)	Mineral and organic soils of intermediate infertility.	Esp. 5.0–7.0	Intolerant.
Great burnet (*Sanguisorba officinalis*)	Especially on mineral soil of intermediate fertility.	Esp. >5.0	Intolerant.
Marsh ragwort (*Senecio aquaticus*)	Mineral and organic soils.	Esp. 4.5–6.5	Intolerant.
Lesser stitchwort (*Stellaria graminea*)	Widespread, especially on soils of lower fertility.	Esp. <7.0	Intolerant.

Soil water-table	Reaction to flooding	Reaction to grazing and cutting	Reaction to fertiliser application
Damp sites – though intolerant of long dry periods, rapidly recolonises bare areas produced by drought.	Tolerates regular and prolonged flooding, but not in growing season.	Favoured by both mowing and grazing, especially where not very intense.	Favoured by all levels of fertiliser application.
Moist to damp sites, but tolerant of prolonged drought.	Tolerates regular (including tidal or prolonged) flooding.	Tolerant of (light) mowing and grazing.	Possibly favoured by light applications of fertiliser.
Wide tolerance.	Tolerates brief flooding.	Tolerant of mowing and grazing.	Probably suppressed by heavy rates of fertiliser.
Moist to damp sites, but tolerant of prolonged drought.	Can tolerate regular and prolonged flooding in winter.	Favoured by mowing and grazing.	Possibly suppressed by heavy rates of fertiliser.
Wide tolerance including drought.	Tolerant of regular flooding in winter.	Favoured by intense grazing (including aftermath).	Suppressed even by low rates of inorganic fertiliser.
Widespread, though commonest on moist soils, and tolerant of moderate drought.	Tolerant of regular flooding in winter.	Favoured by mowing and grazing.	Suppressed even by low rates of inorganic fertiliser.
Dry sites – tolerates prolonged drought.	Absent where waterlogging occurs.	Favoured by intense grazing (including aftermath).	Probably suppressed by higher rates of inorganic fertiliser.
Wet sites, intolerant of prolonged drought.	Common where flooding is regular (and prolonged) – occasionally an emergent aquatic.	Tolerates mowing and grazing.	Probably suppressed by higher rates of inorganic fertiliser.
Damp sites, but tolerant of long droughts.	Very tolerant of flooding – often abundant where water lies late in the spring.	Tolerates mowing and grazing.	Suppressed by higher rates of inorganic fertiliser.
Wide tolerance (different sub-spp. have different ranges).	Intolerant of prolonged floods.	Favoured by late mowing, and low-intensity grazing.	Probably suppressed by higher rates of inorganic fertiliser.
Wide tolerance, tolerant of prolonged drought.	Intolerant of long floods.	Favoured by mowing for hay with aftermath grazing.	Favoured by application of inorganic fertiliser.
Damp sites, but will survive prolonged drought.	Common where flooding is regular and prolonged in winter.	Favoured by mowing for hay with aftermath grazing.	Suppressed by higher rates of inorganic fertiliser.
Damp to wet sites, will not tolerate prolonged drought.	Tolerant of flooding – often abundant where water lies late in the spring.	Probably favoured by mowing for hay, avoided by stock.	Suppressed by higher rates of inorganic fertiliser.
Dry to moist sites, very tolerant of drought.	Intolerant of prolonged flooding.	Tolerant of cutting, and grazing of low intensity.	Suppressed by higher rates of inorganic fertiliser.

Species name (Scientific name)	Soil type	Soil pH	Reaction to salinity
Dandelion (*Taraxacum agg.*)	Very widespread. Includes 150 species with differing ranges and tolerances.	Esp. at high pH	Occasionally in saline soils.
Common meadow-rue (*Thalictrum flavum*)	Most common on organic soils of lower fertility.	Esp. >6.0	Intolerant.
Red clover (*Trifolium pratense*)	Widespread, especially on fertile soils.	Esp. 5.0–6.0	Intolerant.
White clover (*Trifolium repens*)	Mainly on fertile soils.	Esp. 5.0–8.0	Occasionally in saline soils.
Yellow oat-grass (*Trisetum flavescens*)	Especially on moderately infertile mineral soil.	Esp. >6.0	Intolerant.
Marsh valerian (*Valeriana dioica*)	Mostly on infertile organic soils.	Esp. >4.5	Intolerant.
Thyme-leaved speedwell (*Veronica serpyllifolia*)	Widespread on mineral and organic soils.	Wide pH range.	Intolerant.
Tufted vetch (*Vicia cracca*)	Widespread on fertile soils.	>4.5	Intolerant.

Soil water-table	Reaction to flooding	Reaction to grazing and cutting	Reaction to fertiliser application
Section *Erythrosperma* in dry sites; Section *Taraxacum* in moist sites; Section *Spectabilia* in damp sites; Section *Palustria* in damp–wet organic soils.	Very widespread, but generally intolerant of very prolonged flooding.	Favoured by (moderately intense) mowing and grazing.	Favoured by moderate rates of applied fertiliser.
Damp to wet sites, intolerant of prolonged drought.	Most frequent where flooding is regular.	Probably favoured by mowing for hay, may be avoided by stock.	Possibly suppressed by high rates of inorganic fertiliser.
Wide tolerance, most common on moist soils, but tolerant of short-term drought and waterlogging.	Normally absent where flooding is prolonged.	Favoured by mowing and grazing.	Strongly suppressed by (even moderate) applications of fertiliser.
Wide tolerance, but intolerant of severe drought	Wide range, but suppressed where flooding is regular and prolonged.	Strongly favoured by (quite intense) mowing and grazing.	Strongly suppressed by (even moderate) applications of fertiliser.
Wide tolerance, though tolerant of moderate droughts, and absent where waterlogging is prolonged.	Will tolerate regular, brief winter flooding.	Favoured by mowing and grazing.	Tolerant of a wide range of fertiliser application rates.
On damp to wet soils, intolerant of drought.	Tolerates regular flooding.	Favoured by annual mowing, will tolerate light grazing.	Probably suppressed by high rates of inorganic fertiliser.
Although common on dry soils (drought tolerant), frequent in sites with drainage impeded at depth.	Intolerant of (even short) waterlogging and flooding (though thrives in well-aerated stream-sides).	Probably favoured by relatively intense mowing, grazing and trampling.	Probably suppressed by high rates of inorganic fertiliser.
Moist sites, probably favoured by drought.	Intolerant of prolonged flooding.	Intolerant of heavy grazing, but frequent where an annual cut is followed by light aftermath grazing.	Suppressed by high rates of inorganic fertiliser.

Appendix 10
Habitat requirements of drainage channel aquatic and swamp plant species (drawn largely from Newbold and Palmer 1979, Newbold and Mountford in press)

Species name (Scientific name)	Trophic status/pH
Sweet-flag (*Acorus calamus*)	Meso/eutrophic to eutrophic pH >6.0.
Narrow-leaved water-plantain (*Alisma lanceolatum*)	Meso/eutrophic to eutrophic pH >5.5.
Water-plantain (*Alisma plantago-aquatica*)	Meso/eutrophic to eutrophic pH >5.5.
Fool's water-cress (*Apium nodiflorum*)	Meso/eutrophic to eutrophic pH 6.5-8.0.
Water fern (*Azolla filiculoides*)	Mesotrophic to eutrophic pH >5.0.
Lesser water-plantain (*Baldellia ranunculoides*)	Mesotrophic to meso-eutrophic pH >4.5.
Lesser water-parsnip (*Berula erecta*)	Mesotrophic to eutrophic pH >5.5.
Sea club-rush (*Bolboschoenus maritimus*)	Meso/eutrophic to eutrophic pH >6.0.
Flowering-rush (*Butomus umbellatus*)	Mesotrophic to eutrophic pH >6.0.
Intermediate water-starwort (*Callitriche hamulata*)	Oligotrophic to mesotrophic pH >4.0.
Blunt-fruited water-starwort (*Callitriche obtusangula*)	Mesotrophic to eutrophic pH >6.0.
Common water-starwort (*Callitriche stagnalis*)	Mesotrophic to eu/hypertrophic pH esp. 6.5–7.5.
Cyperus sedge (*Carex pseudocyperus*)	Mesotrophic to eutrophic pH >5.5.
Bottle sedge (*Carex rostrata*)	Oligotrophic to mesotrophic pH 3.5–6.0.
Rigid hornwort (*Ceratophyllum demersum*)	Mesotrophic to eu/hypertrophic pH >6.0.
Soft hornwort (*Ceratophyllum submersum*)	Mesotrophic to eutrophic pH >6.0.
Floating club-rush (*Eleogiton fluitans*)	Oligotrophic pH esp. 3.5–6.0.
Canadian waterweed (*Elodea canadensis*)	Oligo/mesotrophic to eutrophic pH esp. c7.0.
Nuttall's waterweed (*Elodea nuttallii*)	Mesotrophic to eu/hypertrophic pH >6.0.
Great willowherb (*Epilobium hirsutum*)	Esp. pH 6.0–8.0.
Water horsetail (*Equisetum fluviatile*)	Oligotrophic to eutrophic pH esp. 5.0–7.0.
Common marsh-bedstraw (*Galium palustre elongatum*)	Mesotrophic to eutrophic pH >5.0.
Opposite-leaved pondweed (*Groenlandia densa*)	Meso/eutrophic to eutrophic pH >6.0.

Note: the figures in this table do not give an indication of seasonal water regime preferences.

Water level above/below soil surface (cm)			Preferred Management
'Dry' limit	Preferred	'Wet' limit	
	−10+30		Maintenance of open deep water.
−30	−5+15	+30	Cleaning at intervals >3 years, maintenance of open shallow water.
−60	−5+15	+30	Cleaning at intervals >3 years, maintenance of open shallow water.
−20	+5+20	+60	Frequent cleaning – to maintain open, shallow water.
	Floating species.		Annual cleaning.
	+2+20		Marginal grazing, cleaning at intervals >5 years to maintain open, shallow water.
−5	+15+30	+60	Cleaning at intervals >3 years, maintenance of open, shallow water. Marginal grazing.
−20	+20	+60	Once established, requires only infrequent (>5 yearly) cleaning.
30	−10+20	+100	Maintenance of both open, deep water and marginal emergent zone, ie annual cleaning of central channel.
−2		+60	Annual cleaning.
	0	+60	Annual cleaning and marginal grazing.
−20		+40(+50)	Annual cleaning and marginal grazing.
−60	0–		Marginal grazing with minimal infrequent cleaning.
−15	+30+60	(+100)	Cleaning at intervals >3 years, maintenance of open, shallow water.
	Submerged floating.		Annual cleaning.
	Submerged floating.		Annual cleaning.
−5	+5+10	+20	Marginal grazing, cleaning at intervals >5 years to maintain open, shallow water.
+20	+50+150	+300	Annual cleaning.
	+30	+125	Annual cleaning – tolerant of pollution.
	−50–0	+10	Minimal management (including absence of grazing).
−3–10	+60	+100	Marginal grazing, cleaning at intervals >5 years to maintain open, shallow water.
−10		+40	Cleaning at intervals >5 years – maintain open, shallow water.
	+5+45		Marginal grazing, cleaning at intervals >5 years to maintain open, shallow water.

Species name (Scientific name)	Trophic status/pH
Mare's-tail (*Hippuris vulgaris*)	Mesotrophic to hypertrophic pH >6.0.
Water-violet (*Hottonia palustris*)	Mesotrophic to eutrophic pH esp. 5.0–6.5.
Frogbit (*Hydrocharis morsus-ranae*)	Mesotrophic to meso/eutrophic pH >5.5.
Fat duckweed (*Lemna gibba*)	Mesotrophic to eutrophic pH >6.0.
Common duckweed (*Lemna minor*)	Oligotrophic to eu/hypertrophic pH esp. >4.5.
Ivy-leaved duckweed (*Lemna trisulca*)	Mesotrophic to eutrophic pH >5.0.
Gypsywort (*Lycopus europaeus*)	Mesotrophic to eutrophic pH >5.0.
Purple-loosestrife (*Lythrum salicaria*)	Mesotrophic to eutrophic pH >5.0.
Water forget-me-not (*Myosotis scorpioides*)	Oligotrophic to eutrophic pH >5.0.
Spiked water-milfoil (*Myriophyllum spicatum*)	Mesotrophic to hypertrophic pH >5.5.
Whorled water-milfoil (*Myriophyllum verticillatum*)	Mesotrophic to eutrophic pH >5.0.
Yellow water-lily (*Nuphar lutea*)	Mesotrophic to eu/hypertrophic pH esp. 5.5–7.0.
White water-lily (*Nymphaea alba*)	Oligo/mesotrophic to meso/eutrophic pH >4.5.
Fringed water-lily (*Nymphoides peltata*)	Eutrophic pH >6.0.
Fine-leaved water-dropwort (*Oenanthe aquatica*)	Meso/eutrophic to eutrophic pH >5.5.
Reed canary-grass (*Phalaris arundinacea*)	Mesotrophic to eutrophic pH >5.0.
Common reed (*Phragmites australis*)	Oligotrophic to eu/hypertrophic pH >4.5.
Small pondweed (*Potamogeton berchtoldii*)	Mesotrophic to eutrophic pH >4.0.
Fen pondweed (*Potamogeton coloratus*)	Mesotrophic to eutrophic pH 6.0.
Curled pondweed (*Potamogeton crispus*)	Oligo/mesotrophic to eu/hypertrophic pH 5.5–7.5.
Flat-stalked pondweed (*Potamogeton friesii*)	Meso/eutrophic to eutrophic pH esp. >6.0.
Shining pondweed (*Potamogeton lucens*)	Meso/eutrophic to eutrophic pH esp. >6.0.
Broad-leaved pondweed (*Potamogeton natans*)	Oligo/mesotrophic to eutrophic pH esp. 5.5–7.0.
Fennel pondweed (*Potamogeton pectinatus*)	Mesotrophic to hypertrophic pH >5.5.
Perfoliate pondweed (*Potamogeton perfoliatus*)	Mesotrophic to eutrophic pH >5.5.
Lesser pondweed (*Potamogeton pusillus*)	Mesotrophic to eutrophic pH >5.5.
Hairlike pondweed (*Potamogeton trichoides*)	Mesotrophic to eutrophic pH >5.5.
Common water-crowfoot (*Ranunculus aquatilis*)	Mesotrophic to eutrophic pH 5.0-7.5.
Brackish water-crowfoot (*Ranunculus baudotii*)	Eutrophic pH >6.0.

Water level above/below soil surface (cm)			Preferred Management
'Dry' limit	Preferred	'Wet' limit	
−10	0+30	+100	Once established, can tolerate annual cleaning. Requires less frequent cleaning to encourage flowering/establishment.
−5	+30+60	+80	Marginal grazing, cleaning at intervals >5 years to maintain open, shallow water.
	Floating species.		Cleaning at >3-year intervals, and marginal grazing.
	Floating species.		Annual cleaning – tolerant of disturbance/pollution.
	Floating species.		Tolerant of a wide range of regimes, providing open water is maintained.
	Floating species.		Marginal grazing, and cleaning at >3-year intervals.
−90	−30+5	+10	Minimal management.
−40		+10	Marginal grazing, otherwise minimal management.
−20		+20	Regular cleaning, <3 years – maintenance of shallow water.
+10		+200	Annual cleaning – tolerant of disturbance.
+20		+200	Regular cleaning, <3 years – maintenance of open water.
−10–0	+30+200		Maintenance of open, deep water (possibly light annual cleaning).
	+30+250		Maintenance of open, deep water – cleaning every 1–3 years.
	+30+200		Annual cleaning – tolerant of disturbance.
−15		+100	Regular cleaning, <5 years – maintenance of shallow water.
−60	−40–0	+30	No marginal grazing, infrequent cleaning (>5 years).
−100	−20–0	+50	No marginal grazing, infrequent cleaning (>5 years).
	+20+100	+150	Regular cleaning, <5 years – maintenance of open water.
(+5)	+20+100	+150	Occasional cleaning, >5 years maintenance of open water. Marginal grazing.
(0)	+20+100	+150	Regular cleaning, <5 years – maintenance of open water.
	+10+75	+120	Regular cleaning, <5 years – maintenance of open water.
(+10)	+50+150	+200	Annual cleaning.
(+2)	+50+100	+125	Occasional cleaning >5 years maintenance of open, deep water.
	+20+100	+150	Annual cleaning – tolerant of pollution.
	+20+100	+150	Regular cleaning, <5 years – maintenance of open water.
	+20+100	+125	Regular cleaning, <5 years – maintenance of open water.
	+20+75	+100	Annual cleaning – probably tolerant of pollution.
0	+30+75	+100(150)	Marginal grazing, cleaning at intervals >5 years.
0	+20+50	+100	Marginal grazing, cleaning at intervals >5 years to maintain open, shallow water.

Species name (Scientific name)	Trophic status/pH
Fan-leaved water-crowfoot (*Ranunculus circinatus*)	Mesotrophic to eutrophic pH >6.0.
Greater spearwort (*Ranunculus lingua*)	Mesotrophic to eutrophic pH >5.5.
Celery-leaved buttercup (*Ranunculus sceleratus*)	Eutrophic pH >4.5.
Thread-leaved water-crowfoot (*Ranunculus trichophyllus*)	Oligo/mesotrophic to eutrophic pH >5.0.
Narrow-fruited water-cress (*Rorippa microphylla*)	Mesotrophic to eutrophic pH esp. 5.5–7.5.
Water-cress (*Rorippa nasturtium-aquaticum*)	Mesotrophic to eutrophic pH esp. >6.0.
Water dock (*Rumex hydrolapathum*)	Mesotrophic to eutrophic pH >5.5.
Beaked tasselweed (*Ruppia maritima*)	Brackish water pH >6.0.
Arrowhead (*Sagittaria sagittifolia*)	Meso/eutrophic to eutrophic pH >5.5.
Grey club-rush (*Schoenoplectus tabernaemontani*)	Mesotrophic to eutrophic pH >6.0.
Greater water-parsnip (*Sium latifolium*)	pH >5.5.
Bittersweet (*Solanum dulcamara*)	Probably meso/eutrophic to hypertrophic pH esp. 6.0–7.5.
Unbranched bur-reed (*Sparganium emersum*)	Mesotrophic to eutrophic pH widespread, but esp. 6.0–7.5.
Branched bur-reed (*Sparganium erectum*)	Mesotrophic to eutrophic pH widespread, but esp. 6.5–7.0.
Greater duckweed (*Spirodela polyrhiza*)	Mesotrophic to eutrophic pH >5.5.
Water-soldier (*Stratiotes aloides*)	Meso/eutrophic to eutrophic pH >6.0.
Lesser bulrush (*Typha angustifolia*)	Mesotrophic to eu/hypertrophic pH >5.5.
Bulrush (*Typha latifolia*)	Mesotrophic to eu/hypertrophic pH >5.5.
Greater bladderwort (*Utricularia vulgaris s.l.*)	Mesotrophic to meso/eutrophic pH >5.0.
Blue water-speedwell (*Veronica anagallis-aquatica*)	Oligotrophic to eutrophic pH >5.0.
Brooklime (*Veronica beccabunga*)	Oligo/mesotrophic to eutrophic pH 6.0–8.0.
Pink water-speedwell (*Veronica catenata*)	Oligotrophic to eutrophic pH >5.5.
Rootless duckweed (*Wolffia arrhiza*)	Eutrophic pH >6.0.
Horned pondweed (*Zannichellia palustris*)	Eutrophic to hypertrophic pH >6.0.

Water level above/below soil surface (cm)			Preferred Management
'Dry' limit	Preferred	'Wet' limit	
0	+25+75	+100(150)	Cleaning at intervals >3 years to maintain open water.
	−20−10	+50	Infrequent cleaning (>5 years).
−20	−5+20	+40	Regular cleaning (including spoil dumping) and marginal grazing (with trampling).
(−10)	+25+100	+150	Marginal grazing, cleaning at intervals >5 years to maintain open, shallow water.
−5		+20	Marginal grazing, cleaning at intervals >5 years to maintain open, shallow water.
+15		+30	Marginal grazing, cleaning at intervals >5 years to maintain open, shallow water.
	−10	+20	Infrequent cleaning (>10 years) and absence of grazing.
	+20+100	+150(200)	Annual or biennial cleaning – tolerant of tidal flooding.
0		+100(150)	Probably biennial cleaning – with marginal grazing.
0–5	+20+30	+60	Infrequent cleaning (>5 years) and low grazing pressure.
−30	−10+10	+40	Infrequent cleaning (>10 years) and absence of grazing.
		+30	No management other than maintenance of wet conditions.
	+20	+100	Where established – annual or biennial cleaning to maintain open central channel.
−30		+100(150)	Light marginal grazing and regular cleaning (<5 years).
	Floating species.		Annual cleaning.
	+20+75	+100	Cleaning at >3-year intervals, and marginal grazing.
	+10+100	+150	Infrequent cleaning and grazing, but maintenance of deep water.
−20	+10+75	+100	Infrequent cleaning and grazing, but maintenance of moderately deep water.
	+10+60	+100	Marginal grazing, cleaning at intervals >5 years to maintain open, shallow water.
	−5	+20	Cleaning >5-year intervals to maintain open, shallow water.
−25	0	+20	Marginal grazing/trampling and cleaning >5-year intervals.
−15		+40	Annual cleaning and marginal grazing/trampling.
	Floating species.		Annual cleaning – tolerant of pollution.
	+10	+150(200)	Frequent cleaning (<3 years).

Appendix 11
Products approved for use as herbicides in or near watercourses and lakes (adapted from Newbold *et al* 1989).

Chemical	Safety interval before irrigation	Approved products	MAFF No.	For control of:
2,4-D amine	3 weeks	Agricorn 2,4-D Atlas 2,4-D (Atlas CP Ltd) Atlas 2,4-D (Atlas Interlates) Dormone MSS 2,4-D Amine	07349 07699 03052 05412 01391	Floating and emergent water weeds and many broad leaf weeds on banks of waterway or drainage channel.
Dichlobenil	2 weeks	Casoron G (ICI) Casoron G (Zeneca) Casoron GSR (ICI) Casoron GSR (Zeneca) Casoron GSR (Miracle)	00448 06854 00451 06856 07925	Floating and submerged weeds.
Dichlobenil + Dalapon	non stated	Fydulan	06823	Weed and reed control near water.
Diquat	10 days	Reglone (ICI) Reglone (Zeneca)	04444 06703	Floating and submerged weeds and algae.
		Midstream (ICI) Midstream (Zeneca)	01348 06824	Submerged weeds in still or moving water.
Fosamine ammonium	nil	Krenite	01165	Deciduous trees and shrubs on banks beside water.
Glyphosate	nil	Barclay Gallup Amenity Clayton Swath Danagri Glyphosate 360 Glyfos Glyfos 480 Glyper (NuFarm) Glyper (Pan Brittanica) Glyphogen Mon 44068 Pro Mon 52276 MSS Glyfield Roundup (Monsanto) Roundup (Schering) Roundup Biactive Roundup Biactive Dry Roundup Pro Roundup Pro Biactive Spasor (Rhone-Poulenc EP) Spasor (Rhone-Poulenc Amenity) Spasor Biactive Stetson	06735 06715 06955 07019 08014 07677 07968 05784 06815 06949 08009 01828 03947 06941 06942 04146 06954 03436 07211 07651 06956	Emergent and floating weeds including reeds and water-lilies.
Maleic hydrazide	3 weeks	Regulox K	05405	Weeds and grass on river banks.
Terbutryn	7 days	Clarosan 1FG	03859	Floating and submerged weeds and algae.

Appendix 12
Glossary

Above Ordnance Datum   a measure of the height of the land surface relative to sea level.

aerobic respiration   respiration occurring in the presence of oxygen.

aftermath grazing   grazing after taking a crop of hay or silage.

anaerobic respiration   respiration occurring in the absence of oxygen.

batter   slope of a bank, expressed either as a ratio of horizontal distance to vertical distance (eg 1:3) or as the angle of slope (eg 65°).

berm   a horizontal ledge at the base of a bank or slope, that is at the level of normal flow and gives extra channel width in high flows.

biomass   a quantitative estimate of animal and/or plant matter.

brackish   water that is intermediate in salinity between fresh water and sea water.

bull beef systems   a group of young bulls reared for beef.

bund   a raised earth bank, eg for retaining water.

calves   young cattle under 6 months old.

capital works   initial capital outlay such as installing grazing infrastructure or engineering a RWLA (as opposed to maintenance works).

catchment   area from which water runs off to any given river, wetland or reservoir.

cation   a positively charged ion.

crome   a long-handled fork, with tines bent through 90°.

cull cows   female animals which have been removed from the main breeding, and/or milk-producing herd due to their age or unreliability.

culm   stem of grasses and sedges.

defoliation   the severing and removal of part or all the herbage by grazing animals or cutting machines.

detritus   material formed through the breakdown and decay of plants and animals.

dipwell   perforated tube inserted into substrate to allow monitoring of water-table levels.

drainable porosity   the volume of water that will drain from a saturated soil under the influence of gravity.

emergent plants   those plants that grow in water but have leaf structures that emerge above the surface, eg bulrush.

enhancement   small-scale environmental improvements.

eutrophic   nutrient enriched.

evapotranspiration   combined term for water lost from a soil or water surface (evaporation) and water lost from the surface of plants (transpiration).

fleet   coastal inlet or creek (chiefly south-eastern Britain).

floodplain   the low relief area of valley floor, adjacent to a river, that is periodically inundated by flood waters.

fog fever   an acute respiratory distress syndrome of cattle, which usually comes on within two weeks of introduction to lush pasture. Most common in suckler herds.

follower   suckler calf.

foot drain   small drainage channel in grasslands, designed to assist water distribution and flow.

forb   any herb other than a grass.

freeboard   distance between the water surface and top of the bank

gley   a soil that is permanently, or periodically, waterlogged and therefore anaerobic, characterised by blue-grey colours.

grip   see foot drain.

habitat   the local environment occupied by individuals of a particular species, population and community.

haemoglobin   the red pigment in blood responsible for the transport of oxygen around the body.

halocline   the boundary between two masses of water whose salinity differs.

halophyte   a plant which can grow in sites with a high concentration of salt, and which as well as having physiological adaptations, may often be recognised by its succulent and grey-green appearance

header ditch   a main ditch supplying water to a number of connecting ditches.

hydraulic conductivity   a measure of the potential water flow through a soil.

Hymac   a large-tracked digger, suitable for use on wet ground.

hypersaline   water or soil with an abnormally high salinity.

hypertrophic   water with an abnormally high nutrient loading.

invertebrates   animals without a backbone, eg insects, molluscs and earthworms.

larvae   early stage of life-cycle of invertebrates.

lekking   a social arrangement among animals in which a group of males assembles on a traditional breeding ground (lek) to display to visiting females.

litter   an accumulated layer of dead organic matter, mainly derived from plants.

liver fluke   a flatworm that can infect livestock, especially sheep.

Livestock Unit   an aggregated liveweight of animals equivalent to a standard cow of 550 kg.

macrophyte   large aquatic plant, as opposed to phytoplankton and other small algae.

meadow   grassland cut for hay or silage.

mesotrophic   freshwater bodies or soils containing moderate amounts of plant nutrients, which are therefore moderately productive.

micro-habitats   describes the conditions that individual or small groups of individual plants or animals live in.

migrant   an organism that moves from one region to another.

mire   a synonym of peatland, used to describe both bog and fen.

mole drains   narrow drainage tunnels made in sub-soil by cylindrical implement attached to a blade. When dragged through the soil the slit made by the blade closes, but the tunnel remains open.

monocultures   vegetation consisting of one species of plant.

niche   where an animal or plant lives within its community, which determines its activities and relationships with other organisms and its environment.

nurse crop   a crop that is planted to protect another crop by providing shade and preventing weed growth.

passerine   bird of the order Passeriformes, contains all perching or songbirds eg thrushes and finches.

pasture   permanent grassland that is regularly grazed by livestock.

penned   artificially held water level.

perennial   plant that normally lives for more than two seasons, and, after an initial period, produces flowers annually.

pH   a scale of 14 points indicating the degree of acidity or alkalinity of water or soil, with 7 as neutral.

photosynthesis   the use of energy from light to drive chemical reactions most notably the reduction of carbon dioxide to carbohydrates coupled with oxidation either of water to oxygen or of hydrogen sulphide to sulphur.

phytophagous   plant-eating, especially applies to invertebrates.

poaching   trampling by livestock causing land to break up into wet muddy patches.

pollarding   method of managing trees, particularly willows, by cutting the stem at head height or higher and letting it sprout. Recutting of these new branches takes place periodically thereafter.

rhizome   stem, usually underground, often horizontal, typically non-green and root-like in appearance, but bearing scale leaves and/or foliage leaves.

rhizosphere   zone of soil, in the immediate vicinity of an active root, influenced by the uptake and output of substances by the root and characterised by a microbial flora different from surrounded soil.

rosette   plant leaves growing flat and close to the ground.

saline   water or soil rich in dissolved salts.

set-stocking   the practice of allowing a fixed number of animals unrestricted access to a fixed area of land for a substantial part of a grazing season.

soke dyke   typically a drainage channel adjacent to a seawall, which effectively intercepts saline seepage.

splash-flooding   land flooded to at, or just above, ground level.

spoil   soil and/or vegetation removed during dredging or slubbing of drainage channels.

stolon   stem growing more or less flat on the ground, with long internodes, rooting at the nodes and/or tip and there producing new plantlets.

store cattle   are normally between one and two years old, and can be either bullocks/steers (castrated males) or cows. Store cattle may be sold on either in the autumn for fattening indoors or in the next spring for subsequent finishing on grass.

succession   the progressive development of one plant community into another, finally reaching the long-term stability of a 'climax community'.

suckler herds   consist of cows with calves at foot, reared for beef.

swamp   an area saturated with water for much of the time, but in which the soil surface is not deeply submerged. Often dominated by just one or two species of plant.

sward   above ground components of grassland.

tiller   an aerial shoot of a grass plant, arising from a leaf axil, normally at the base of an older tiller.

trapezoidal channel   most efficient drainage channel design, the profile forms a trapezium, with sloping sides and a flat bed.

turion   detachable winter bud formed by water plants, enabling them to survive the winter.

washland   extensive semi-natural area adjacent to a river created as a flood storage area.

waterfowl   wildfowl and waders, plus coot, moorhen and spotted crake.

water-table   level below which soil or rock is permanently saturated.

wet fences   drainage channels filled with water used for stock control.

wether   castrated male sheep.

wildfowl   ducks, geese and swans.

Appendix 13
Health and Safety

Information and Training

Training in pesticides use, the operation of knapsack sprayers and chainsaws may be obtained through:

Agricultural Training Board (ATB-Landbase), National Agricultural Centre, Stoneleigh, Kenilworth, Warwickshire CV8 2LG. Tel 01203 696996 for information on local ATB training centres.

National Proficiency Tests Council, National Agricultural Centre, Stoneleigh, Kenilworth, Warwickshire CV8 2LG. Tel 01203 696553. Write for information about the requirements for national testing and other organisations which may offer training courses.

British Trust for Conservation Volunteers (BTCV), 36 St Mary's Street, Wallingford OX10 0EU. Tel 01491 839766. Run training courses on a range of conservation techniques and equipment use, throughout the UK.

Information on the regulations governing pesticide use and other safety matters may be obtained from:

Health and Safety Executive (HSE), Pearson Building, 55 Upper Parliament Street, Nottingham NG1 6AU. Tel 0115 9712862 or HSE Infoline Tel 0541 545500.

Relevant Legislation and Regulations

Health and Safety at Work Act 1974

Management of Health, Safety and Welfare at Work Regulations 1992

Food and Environment Protection Act 1985

Control of Substances Hazardous to Health Regulations (COSHH) 1994

Control of Pesticides Regulations (COPR) 1986

Personal Protective Equipment at Work Regulations 1992

Provision and Use of Work Equipment Regulations 1992

Use of hazardous substances

The use of hazardous substances at work is mainly governed by COSHH and COPR.

The four stages for prevention of occupational health hazards and protection of workers are:

- the provision of instruction and information on occupational health hazards, precautions and personal hygiene
- removal or substitution of an 'unhealthy' process, eg where a potentially toxic chemical is being used, it may be possible to substitute a less toxic material that will do the same job
- segregation of processes so that only those immediately involved are in contact, eg arc welding may be carried out behind screens or enclosures away from casual passers-by
- personal protection – being the last resort in employee protection.

Additional safety information on pesticide use includes:

Working with Pesticides

Code of Practice for the Safe Use of Pesticides on Farms and Small Holdings

Guidelines for the Use of Herbicides on Weeds in or near Watercourses

The above are available through MAFF at the address in Appendix 3.

UK Pesticide Guide available from BCPC Publications Sales, Bear Farm, Binfield, Bracknell, Berks RG42 5QE. Tel 0118 934 2727.

Pesticides 1997 (and subsequent annuals) available from HMSO Books, PO Box 276, London SW8 5DT.

General Safety Precautions

Wet grasslands are potentially dangerous places in which to work, with soft, boggy, uneven ground, deep water and sharp vegetation. Operating equipment such as tractors, chainsaws and ATVs can be dangerous. Prior to undertaking any work on site the following should be considered:

- All persons intending to operate equipment or use tools must be trained.
- A risk assessment should have been carried out for each task by a person responsible for safety and all staff/volunteers be familiar with the assessment. This is a requirement of the Management of Health, Safety and Welfare at Work Regulations 1992.

- Under the same regulations, all staff/volunteers should be familiar with the hazards and risks and how to prevent/reduce them.

- All staff/volunteers should be provided with the required personal protective equipment including protection from foul weather.

- An agreed procedure for action in case of an emergency should be established prior to entering the work area.

- A first aid kit should be available on-site containing the minimum required items for the number of staff/volunteers present.

Working alone

Whenever possible, working alone should be avoided. If it is unavoidable, the following precautions should be considered:

- If possible, carry a mobile phone/CB radio/short-wave radio and maintain regular contact with base or home.

- Inform someone of your plans; where you are going, how long you expect to be. Try to give an indication of the time at which you expect to return.

- Avoid undertaking hazardous tasks such as operating machinery.

- Do not take risks.

Leptospirosis (Weil's disease)

Weil's disease is the most serious form of an illness called leptospirosis. In the UK it is most commonly associated with rats, which excrete the bacteria in their urine. The bacteria can survive in fresh water for about four weeks and people can become infected through contact with water or muddy soil contaminated by infected rat urine. The leptospira bacteria can enter the human body through cuts, grazes and sores and mucous membranes of the eyes, nose and mouth. Simple precautions to reduce the chances of contracting the disease are:

- Ensure cuts, scratches and skin abrasions are thoroughly cleansed and covered with a waterproof plaster.

- Avoid submerging hands or other parts of the body with cuts or abrasions in water.

- Avoid rubbing eyes, nose or mouth during work.

- Wear protective clothing where appropriate, eg waders and rubber gloves, and ensure these and other protective equipment are cleaned after use.

- After work and particularly before taking food or drink, wash hands thoroughly.

- For more information contact the Health and Safety Executive for a leaflet *Leptospirosis – are you at risk?*

Working on or near deep water

In addition to the standard safety precautions already outlined special consideration needs to be given to deep water:

- Avoid working on or near deep water if you are unable to swim.

- Ensure life jackets are available for all persons required to work on deep water.

- Persons operating boats should be trained.

- Be aware of the likelihood of flooding, eg tidal river, periods of prolonged heavy rainfall, and avoid working in areas with a high risk.

- Avoid steep or unstable banks adjacent to deep water.

- Do not enter the water if the river/ditch bottom is not visible.

Blue-green algae

Blue-green algae are natural inhabitants of many inland waters, estuaries and the sea.

In fresh waters, they are found in suspension and attached to rocks and other surfaces at the bottom of shallow waters and along edges of lakes and rivers.

For reasons that are not yet fully understood, bloom and scum forming blue-green algae in fresh water, brackish water and sea water are capable of producing toxins. These toxins have caused the death of wild animals, farm livestock and domestic pets in many countries, including farm animals and dogs in the UK in 1989. In humans, rashes have occurred following skin contact, and illnesses have occurred when blue-green algae have been swallowed.

Further information can be obtained from the Environment Agency.

Appendix 14
Acronyms used in the text

ADA	Association of Drainage Authorities
ADAS	Agricultural Development and Advisory Service
AOD	Above Ordnance Datum
AONB	Area of Outstanding Natural Beauty
ASSI	Area of Special Scientific Interest (Northern Ireland)
ATV	All-terrain vehicle
BA	Broads Authority
BASIS	British Agrochemicals Standards Inspection Scheme
BTCV	British Trust for Conservation Volunteers
BTO	British Trust for Ornithology
CAA	Civil Aviation Authority
CCW	Countryside Council for Wales
CMP	Catchment Management Plan
CMS	Countryside Management System
CoCo	Countryside Commission
COPR	Control of Pesticides Regulations 1986
COSHH	Control of Substances Hazardous to Health Regulations 1994
cSAC	Candidate Special Area of Conservation
CVS	Cover Value Score
DANI	Department of Agriculture Northern Ireland
DoE	Department of Environment
DoENI	Department of Environment Northern Ireland
EA	Environment Agency
EEC	European Economic Community
EN	English Nature
ESA	Environmentally Sensitive Area
EU	European Union
FEPA	Food and Environment Protection Act 1985
FYM	Farmyard Manure
GR	Grid reference
HSE	Health and Safety Executive
IBA	Important Bird Area
IDB	Internal Drainage Board
ITE	Institute of Terrestrial Ecology
JNCC	Joint Nature Conservation Committee
LA	Local Authority
LEAP	Local Environment Agency Plan
LDA	Land Drainage Act 1991
LSU	Livestock Unit
MAFF	Ministry of Agriculture, Fisheries and Food
MCPA	methyl-chloro-phenoxy acetic acid, a translocated hormone herbicide used to control broad-leaved weeds in grass and cereals
MOD	Ministry of Defence
MORECS	Meteorological Office Rainfall and Evapotranspiration Calculation System
MTR	Mean Trophic Rank
N	nitrogen
NCC	Nature Conservancy Council
NNR	National Nature Reserve
NPA	National Park Authority
NRA	National Rivers Authority
NSA	Nitrate Sensitive Area
NT	National Trust
NVC	National Vegetation Classification
OLD	Operation Likely to Damage
OS	Ordnance Survey
P	phosphorous
PDO	Potentially damaging operation
PPE	Personal protective equipment
PSD	Pesticide Safety Directorate
PTO	Power take-off
RDB	Red Data Book
RSPB	The Royal Society for the Protection of Birds
RWLA	Raised Water Level Area
SAC	Scottish Agricultural College
SCV	Species Cover Value
SEPA	Scottish Environmental Protection Agency
SNH	Scottish Natural Heritage
SOAEFD	Scottish Office Agriculture, Environment and Fisheries Department
SPA	Special Protection Area
SSSI	Site of Special Scientific Interest
STR	Species Trophic Rank
UK	United Kingdom of Great Britain and Northern Ireland
VAT	Value Added Tax
WES	Wildlife Enhancement Scheme
WLMP	Water Level Management Plan
WOAD	Welsh Office Agriculture Department
WWT	Wildfowl & Wetlands Trust

Appendix 15
Scientific names of species mentioned in the text

Vascular plants (after Stace 1991)

Alder	*Alnus glutinosa*
Alternate-flowered water-milfoil	*Myriophyllum alterniflorum*
Amphibious bistort	*Persicaria amphibia*
Annual meadow grass	*Poa annua*
Arrowhead	*Sagittaria sagittifolia*
Autumn hawkbit	*Leontodon autumnalis*
Barren brome	*Anisantha sterilis*
Beaked tasselweed	*Ruppia maritima*
Bindweed	*Calystegia* spp.
Bittersweet	*Solanum dulcamara*
Black poplar	*Populus nigra*
Blackthorn	*Prunus spinosa*
Bladder-sedge	*Carex vesicaria*
Blinks	*Montia fontana*
Blue water-speedwell	*Veronica anagallis-aquatica*
Blunt-flowered rush	*Juncus subnodulosus*
Blunt-fruited water-starwort	*Callitriche obtusangula*
Blunt-leaved pondweed	*Potamogeton obtusifolius*
Bogbean	*Menyanthes trifoliata*
Bog hair-grass	*Deschampsia setacea*
Bog pondweed	*Potamogeton polygonifolius*
Bog stitchwort	*Stellaria uliginosa*
Borrer's saltmarsh-grass	*Puccinellia fasciculata*
Bottle sedge	*Carex rostrata*
Brackish water-crowfoot	*Ranunculus baudotii*
Bramble	*Rubus* spp.
Branched bur-reed	*Sparganium erectum*
Bristle bent	*Agrostis curtisii*
Bristly oxtongue	*Picris echioides*
Broad-leaved pondweed	*Potamogeton natans*
Brooklime	*Veronica beccabunga*
Brown sedge	*Carex disticha*
Bulbous buttercup	*Ranunculus bulbosus*
Bulbous rush	*Juncus bulbosus*
Bulrush	*Typha latifolia*
Canadian waterweed	*Elodea canadensis*
Carnation sedge	*Carex panicea*
Cat's-ear	*Hypochaeris radicata*
Celery-leaved buttercup	*Ranunculus sceleratus*
Changing forget-me-not	*Myosotis discolor*
Clustered dock	*Rumex conglomeratus*
Cock's-foot	*Dactylis glomerata*
Common bent	*Agrostis capillaris*
Common bird's-foot-trefoil	*Lotus corniculatus*
Common club-rush	*Schoenoplectus lacustris*
Common couch	*Elytrigia repens*
Common duckweed	*Lemna minor*
Common knapweed	*Centaurea nigra*
Common marsh-bedstraw	*Galium palustre*
Common meadow-rue	*Thalictrum flavum*
Common mouse-ear	*Cerastium fontanum*
Common nettle	*Urtica dioica*
Common reed	*Phragmites australis*
Common sedge	*Carex nigra*
Common sorrel	*Rumex acetosa*
Common spike-rush	*Eleocharis palustris*
Common water-crowfoot	*Ranunculus aquatilis*
Common water-starwort	*Callitriche stagnalis*
Corky-fruited water-dropwort	*Oenanthe pimpinelloides*
Cornish heath	*Erica vagans*
Cowbane	*Cicuta virosa*
Creeping bent	*Agrostis stolonifera*
Creeping buttercup	*Ranunculus repens*
Creeping cinquefoil	*Potentilla reptans*
Creeping-jenny	*Lysimachia nummularia*

Creeping marshwort	*Apium repens*
Creeping thistle	*Cirsium arvense*
Crested dog's-tail	*Cynosurus cristatus*
Cuckooflower	*Cardamine pratensis*
Curled dock	*Rumex crispus*
Curled pondweed	*Potamogeton crispus*
Cut-leaved cranes-bill	*Geranium dissectum*
Cyperus sedge	*Carex pseudocyperus*
Daisy	*Bellis perennis*
Dandelion	*Taraxacum agg.*
Divided sedge	*Carex divisa*
Dogwood	*Cornus sanguinea*
Downy birch	*Betula pubescens*
Downy-fruited sedge	*Carex filiformis*
Dwarf mouse-ear	*Cerastium pumilum*
Elongated sedge	*Carex elongata*
Fairy flax	*Linum catharticum*
False fox-sedge	*Carex otrubae*
False oat-grass	*Arrhenatherum elatius*
Fan-leaved water-crowfoot	*Ranunculus circinatus*
Fat duckweed	*Lemna gibba*
Fen bedstraw	*Galium uliginosum*
Fennel pondweed	*Potamogeton pectinatus*
Fen pondweed	*Potamogeton coloratus*
Field maple	*Acer campestre*
Field wood-rush	*Luzula campestris*
Fine-leaved water-dropwort	*Oenanthe aquatica*
Flat-stalked pondweed	*Potamogeton friesii*
Floating club-rush	*Eleogiton fluitans*
Floating-leaved water-plantain	*Luronium natans*
Floating sweet-grass	*Glyceria fluitans*
Flowering-rush	*Butomus umbellatus*
Fool's water-cress	*Apium nodiflorum*
Fringed water-lily	*Nymphoides peltata*
Frogbit	*Hydrocharis morsus-ranae*
Glaucous sedge	*Carex flacca*
Golden dock	*Rumex maritimus*
Grass-wrack pondweed	*Potamogeton compressus*
Great burnet	*Sanguisorba officinalis*
Greater bird's-foot-trefoil	*Lotus pedunculatus*
Greater bladderwort	*Utricularia vulgaris s.l.*
Greater chickweed	*Stellaria neglecta*
Greater dodder	*Cuscuta europaea*
Greater duckweed	*Spirodela polyrhiza*
Greater spearwort	*Ranunculus lingua*
Greater water-parsnip	*Sium latifolium*
Greater yellow-rattle	*Rhinanthus angustifolius*
Great marsh-bedstraw	*Galium elongatum*
Great pond-sedge	*Carex riparia*
Great yellow-cress	*Rorippa amphibia*
Great willowherb	*Epilobium hirsutum*
Grey club-rush	*Schoenoplectus tabernaemontani*
Ground-ivy	*Glechoma hederacea*
Gypsywort	*Lycopus europaeus*
Hairlike pondweed	*Potamogeton trichoides*
Hairy buttercup	*Ranunculus sardous*
Hairy sedge	*Carex hirta*
Hard rush	*Juncus inflexus*
Hawthorn	*Crataegus monogyna*
Hazel	*Corylus avellana*
Heath lobelia	*Lobelia urens*
Hogweed	*Heracleum sphondylium*
Holly	*Ilex aquifolium*
Horned pondweed	*Zannichellia palustris*
Intermediate water-starwort	*Callitriche hamulata*
Ivy-leaved crowfoot	*Ranunculus hederaceus*
Ivy-leaved duck weed	*Lemna trisulca*
Jointed rush	*Juncus articulatus*
Least yellow water-lily	*Nuphar pumila*
Lesser bulrush	*Typha angustifolia*
Lesser marshwort	*Apium inundatum*

Lesser pond-sedge	*Carex acutiformis*
Lesser pondweed	*Potamogeton pusillus*
Lesser sea-spurrey	*Spergularia marina*
Lesser spearwort	*Ranunculus flammula*
Lesser stitchwort	*Stellaria graminea*
Lesser water-parsnip	*Berula erecta*
Lesser water-plantain	*Baldellia ranunculoides*
Loddon pondweed	*Potamogeton nodosus*
Long-stalked pondweed	*Potamogeton praelongus*
Mare's-tail	*Hippuris vulgaris*
Marsh foxtail	*Alopecurus geniculatus*
Marsh horsetail	*Equisetum palustre*
Marsh-mallow	*Althaea officinalis*
Marsh-marigold	*Caltha palustris*
Marsh pea	*Lathyrus palustris*
Marsh pennywort	*Hydrocotyle vulgaris*
Marsh ragwort	*Senecio aquaticus*
Marsh sow-thistle	*Sonchus palustris*
Marsh speedwell	*Veronica scutellata*
Marsh stitchwort	*Stellaria palustris*
Marsh thistle	*Cirsium palustre*
Marsh valerian	*Valeriana dioica*
Meadow barley	*Hordeum secalinum*
Meadow buttercup	*Ranunculus acris*
Meadow fescue	*Festuca pratensis*
Meadow foxtail	*Alopecurus pratensis*
Meadowsweet	*Filipendula ulmaria*
Meadow thistle	*Cirsium dissectum*
Meadow vetchling	*Lathyrus pratensis*
Milk-parsley	*Peucedanum palustre*
Narrow-fruited water-cress	*Rorippa microphylla*
Narrow-leaved water-dropwort	*Oenanthe silaifolia*
Narrow-leaved water-plantain	*Alisma lanceolatum*
Nodding bur-marigold	*Bidens cernua*
Nuttall's waterweed	*Elodea nuttallii*
Oak	*Quercus* spp.
Opposite-leaved pondweed	*Groenlandia densa*
Oval sedge	*Carex ovalis*
Oxeye daisy	*Leucanthemum vulgare*
Parsley water-dropwort	*Oenanthe lachenalii*
Pedunculate water-starwort	*Callitriche brutia*
Pennyroyal	*Mentha pulegium*
Pepper-saxifrage	*Silaum silaus*
Perennial rye-grass	*Lolium perenne*
Perfoliate pondweed	*Potamogeton perfoliatus*
Pillwort	*Pilularia globulifera*
Pink water-speedwell	*Veronica catenata*
Plicate sweet-grass	*Glyceria notata*
Pond water-crowfoot	*Ranunculus peltatus*
Prickly lettuce	*Lactuca serriola*
Prickly sow-thistle	*Sonchus asper*
Purple-loosestrife	*Lythrum salicaria*
Purple moor-grass	*Molinia caerulea*
Quaking-grass	*Briza media*
Ragged-robin	*Lychnis flos-cuculi*
Red clover	*Trifolium pratense*
Red fescue	*Festuca rubra s.l.*
Red pondweed	*Potamogeton alpinus*
Reed canary-grass	*Phalaris arundinacea*
Reed sweet-grass	*Glyceria maxima*
Ribbon-leaved water-plantain	*Alisma gramineum*
Ribwort plantain	*Plantago lanceolata*
Rigid hornwort	*Ceratophyllum demersum*
River water-crowfoot	*Ranunculus fluitans*
River water-dropwort	*Oenanthe fluviatilis*
Rootless duckweed	*Wolffia arrhiza*
Rough hawkbit	*Leontodon hispidus*
Rough meadow-grass	*Poa trivialis*
Round-leaved crowfoot	*Ranunculus omiophyllus*
Rowan	*Sorbus aucuparia*
Sallow	*Salix* spp.

Saltmarsh goosefoot	*Chenopodium chenopodioides*
Saltmarsh rush	*Juncus gerardii*
Saw-wort	*Serratula tinctoria*
Sea arrowgrass	*Triglochin maritimum*
Sea barley	*Hordeum marinum*
Sea clover	*Trifolium squamosum*
Sea club-rush	*Bolboschoenus maritimus*
Selfheal	*Prunella vulgaris*
Scented mayweed	*Matricaria recutita*
Shady horsetail	*Equisetum pratense*
Sharp-flowered rush	*Juncus acutiflorus*
Sharp-leaved pondweed	*Potamogeton acutifolius*
Shining pondweed	*Potamogeton lucens*
Silverweed	*Potentilla anserina*
Six-stamened waterwort	*Elatine hexandra*
Slender hare's-ear	*Bupleurum tenuissimum*
Slender-leaved pondweed	*Potamogeton filiformis*
Smaller cat's-tail	*Phleum bertolonii*
Small pondweed	*Potamogeton berchtoldii*
Small sweet-grass	*Glyceria declinata*
Smooth brome	*Bromus racemosus*
Smooth meadow-grass	*Poa pratensis s.l.*
Snake's-head fritillary	*Fritillaria meleagris*
Soft-brome	*Bromus hordeaceus*
Soft hornwort	*Ceratophyllum submersum*
Soft-rush	*Juncus effusus*
Spear-leaved orache	*Atriplex prostrata*
Spear thistle	*Cirsium vulgare*
Spiked water-milfoil	*Myriophyllum spicatum*
Spiral tasselweed	*Ruppia cirrhosa*
Spreading meadow-grass	*Poa humilis*
Stiff saltmarsh-grass	*Puccinellia rupestris*
Stream water-crowfoot	*Ranunculus penicillatus*
String sedge	*Carex chordorrhiza*
Sulphur clover	*Trifolium ochroleucon*
Sweet-flag	*Acorus calamus*
Sweet vernal grass	*Anthoxanthum odoratum*
Tall fescue	*Festuca arundinacea*
Tasteless water-pepper	*Persicaria laxiflora*
Thread-leaved water-crowfoot	*Ranunculus trichophyllus*
Thyme-leaved speedwell	*Veronica serpyllifolia*
Timothy	*Phleum pratense*
Toad rush	*Juncus bufonius*
Tormentil	*Potentilla erecta*
Trifid bur-marigold	*Bidens tripartita*
Tuberous thistle	*Cirsium tuberosum*
Tubular water-dropwort	*Oenanthe fistulosa*
Tufted hair-grass	*Deschampsia cespitosa*
Tufted vetch	*Vicia cracca*
Unbranched bur-reed	*Sparganium emersum*
Various-leaved pondweed	*Potamogeton gramineus*
Velvet bent	*Agrostis canina*
Water-cress	*Rorippa nasturtium-aquaticum*
Water dock	*Rumex hydrolapathum*
Water fern	*Azolla filiculoides*
Water forget-me-not	*Myosotis scorpioides*
Water horsetail	*Equisetum fluviatile*
Water mint	*Mentha aquatica*
Water-pepper	*Persicaria hydropiper*
Water-plantain	*Alisma plantago-aquatica*
Water-soldier	*Stratiotes aloides*
Water-violet	*Hottonia palustris*
Wavy St John's-wort	*Hypericum undulatum*
White clover	*Trifolium repens*
White water-lily	*Nymphaea alba*
Whorled water-milfoil	*Myriophyllum verticillatum*
Whorl-grass	*Catabrosa aquatica*
Wild angelica	*Angelica sylvestris*
Wild-oat	*Avena fatua*
Willow	*Salix* spp.
Yarrow	*Achillea millefolium*

Yellow centaury	*Cicendia filiformis*
Yellow iris	*Iris pseudacorus*
Yellow oat-grass	*Trisetum flavescens*
Yellow-rattle	*Rhinanthus minor*
Yellow water-lily	*Nuphar lutea*
Yorkshire-fog	*Holcus lanatus*

Invertebrates

Azure damselfly	*Coenagrion puella*
Bees	*(Hymenoptera)*
Beetles	*(Coleoptera)*
Blue-tailed damselfly	*Ischnura elegans*
Blowflies	*(Calliphoridae)*
Brimstone	*Gonepteryx rhamni*
Broad-bodied chaser	*Libellula depressa*
Brown-veined wainscot	*Archanara dissoluta*
Butterflies and moths	*(Lepidoptera)*
Bugs	*(Hemiptera)*
Caddisflies	*(Trichoptera)*
China mark	*Cataclysta lemnata*
Club-tailed dragonfly	*Gomphus vulgatissimus*
Common blue damselfly	*Enallagma cyathigerum*
Common darter	*Sympetrum striolatum*
Compressed river mussel	*Pseudanodonta complanata*
Craneflies	*(Tipulidae)*
Crawling water beetles	*(Haliplidae)*
Cream-bordered green pea	*Earias clorana*
Crescent striped	*Apamea oblonga*
Damselflies	*(Odonata: Zygoptera)*
Dotted fanfoot	*Macrochilo cribrumalis*
Dragonflies	*(Odonata: Anisoptera)*
Dung beetles	*(Scarabaeidae)*
Earthworms	*(Oligochaeta)*
Emerald damselfly	*Lestes sponsa*
Emperor dragonfly	*Anax imperator*
Essex skipper	*Thymelicus lineola*
Flame wainscot	*Senta flammea*
Flatworms	*(Platyhelminthes)*
Flies	*(Diptera)*
Four-spotted chaser	*Libellula quadrimaculata*
Goat moth	*Cossus cossus*
Grasshoppers	*(Orthoptera: Aerididae)*
Great silver water beetle	*Hydrophilus piceus*
Green-veined white	*Pieris napi*
Ground beetles	*(Carabidae)*
Hairy dragonfly	*Brachytron pratense*
Hoverflies	*(Syrphidae)*
Jenkin's spire snail	*Potamopyrgus antipodarum*
Large-mouthed valve snail	*Valvata macrostoma*
Large red damselfly	*Pyrrhosoma nymphula*
Large skipper	*Ochlodes venata*
Leaf beetles	*(Chrysomelidae)*
Leeches	*(Hirudinea)*
Lesser dung flies	*(Sphaeroceridae)*
Lesser silver water beetle	*Hydrochara caraboides*
Longhorn musk beetle	*Aromia moschata*
Lunar hornet moth	*Sesia bembeciformis*
Marsh carpet	*Perizoma sagittata*
Marsh fritillary	*Eurodryas aurinia*
Mayflies	*(Ephemeroptera)*
Meadow plant bug	*Leptopterna dolabrata*
Migrant hawker	*Aeshna mixta*
Millipedes	*(Diplopoda)*
Mosquitoes	*(Culicidae)*
Non-biting midges	*(Chironomidae)*
Norfolk hawker	*Aeshna isosceles*
Obscure wainscot	*Mythimna obsoleta*
Orange-tip	*Anthocaris cardamines*
Pearl-bordered fritillary	*Boloria euphrosyne*
Picture-wing flies	*(Tephritidae and Otitidae)*

Purple-bordered gold	*Idaea muricata*
Red-eyed damselfly	*Erythromma najas*
Reed dagger	*Simyra albovenosa*
Robberflies	*(Asilidae)*
Rosy wave	*Scopula emutaria*
Rove beetles	*(Staphylinidae)*
Ruddy darter	*Sympetrum sanguineum*
Scarce blue-tailed damselfly	*Ischnura pumilio*
Scarce chaser	*Libellula fulva*
Scarce emerald damselfly	*Lestes dryas*
Shaded pug	*Eupithecia subumbrata*
Shiny ramshorn snail	*Segmentina nitida*
Shore bugs	*(Saldidae)*
Shoreflies	*(Ephydridae)*
Silky wainscot	*Chilodes maritimus*
Silver hook	*Deltote uncula*
Small skipper	*Thymelicus sylvestris*
Snail-killing flies	*(Sciomyzidae)*
Snails	*(Mollusca: Gastropoda)*
Soldierflies	*(Stratiomyidae)*
Southern hawker	*Aeshna cyanea*
Springtails	*(Collembola)*
Twin-spotted wainscot	*Archanara geminipuncta*
Variable damselfly	*Coenagrion pulchellum*
Wandering snail	*Lymnaea peregra*
Wasps	*(Hymenoptera)*
Water boatmen	*(Corixidae)*
Water beetles	*(Dytiscidae)*
Water beetles	*(Hydrophilidae)*
Water ermine	*Spilosoma urticae*
Webb's wainscot	*Archanara sparganii*
Weevils	*(Curculionidae)*
Woodlice	*(Isopoda)*

Amphibians and reptiles

Common frog	*Rana temporaria*
Common toad	*Bufo bufo*
Grass snake	*Natrix natrix*
Marsh frog	*Rana ridibunda*
Newt	*Triturus* spp.

Fish

Bream	*Abramis brama*
Eel	*Anguilla anguilla*
Pike	*Esox lucius*
Roach	*Rutilus rutilus*
Rudd	*Scardinius erythropthalmus*
Sticklebacks	*(Gasterosteidae)*

Mammals

Badger	*Meles meles*
Fox	*Vulpes vulpes*
Mink	*Mustela vison*
Noctule	*Nyctalus noctula*
Otter	*Lutra lutra*
Pipistrelle	*Pipistrellus pipistrellus*
Stoat	*Mustela erminea*
Water vole	*Arvicola terrestris*

Birds

Avocet	*Recurvirostra avosetta*
Barnacle goose	*Branta leucopsis*
Barn owl	*Tyto alba*
Bean goose	*Anser fabalis*
Bearded tit	*Panurus biarmicus*
Bewick's swan	*Cygnus columbianus bewickii*
Bittern	*Botaurus stellaris*
Blackbird	*Turdus merula*

Blackcap	*Sylvia atricapilla*
Black-tailed godwit	*Limosa limosa*
Blue tit	*Parus caeruleus*
Carrion crow	*Corvus corone*
Coot	*Fulica atra*
Common gull	*Larus canus*
Cormorant	*Phalacrocorax carbo*
Corncrake	*Crex crex*
Curlew	*Numenius arquata*
Dunlin	*Calidris alpina*
European white-fronted goose	*Anser albifrons europaeus*
Fieldfare	*Turdus pilaris*
Gadwall	*Anas strepera*
Garganey	*Anas querquedula*
Golden eagle	*Aquila chrysaetos*
Goldeneye	*Bucephala clangula*
Golden plover	*Pluvialis apricaria*
Goldfinch	*Carduelis carduelis*
Grasshopper warbler	*Locustella naevia*
Great tit	*Parus major*
Greenland white-fronted goose	*Anser albifrons flavirostris*
Grey heron	*Ardea cinerea*
Grey partridge	*Perdix perdix*
Hen harrier	*Circus cyaneus*
Kestrel	*Falco tinnunculus*
Kingfisher	*Alcedo atthis*
Lapwing	*Vanellus vanellus*
Linnet	*Carduelis cannabina*
Little grebe	*Tachybaptus ruficollis*
Mallard	*Anas platyrhynchos*
Marsh harrier	*Circus aeruginosus*
Meadow pipit	*Anthus pratensis*
Merlin	*Falco columbarius*
Moorhen	*Gallinula chloropus*
Mute swan	*Cygnus olor*
Nightingale	*Luscinia megarhynchus*
Oystercatcher	*Haematopus ostralegus*
Peregrine	*Falco peregrinus*
Pink-footed goose	*Anser brachyrhynchus*
Pintail	*Anas acuta*
Pochard	*Aythya ferina*
Quail	*Coturnix coturnix*
Redwing	*Turdus iliacus*
Reed warbler	*Acrocephalus scirpaceus*
Ringed plover	*Charadrius hiaticula*
Robin	*Erithacus rubecula*
Redshank	*Tringa totanus*
Ruff	*Philomachus pugnax*
Sedge warbler	*Acrocephalus schoenobaenus*
Shelduck	*Tadorna tadorna*
Short-eared owl	*Asio flammeus*
Shoveler	*Anas clypeata*
Skylark	*Alauda arvensis*
Smew	*Mergus albellus*
Snipe	*Gallinago gallinago*
Song thrush	*Turdus philomelos*
Sparrowhawk	*Accipiter nisus*
Spotted crake	*Porzana porzana*
Starling	*Sturnus vulgaris*
Teal	*Anas crecca*
Tree sparrow	*Passer montanus*
Tufted duck	*Aythya fuligula*
Twite	*Carduelis flavirostris*
Water rail	*Rallus aquatica*
Wigeon	*Anas penelope*
Whimbrel	*Numenius phaeopus*
Whitethroat	*Sylvia communis*
White-fronted goose	*Anser albifrons*
Whooper swan	*Cygnus cygnus*
Woodcock	*Scolopax rusticola*
Yellow wagtail	*Motacilla flava flavissima*

References

ADAS (1993) Livestock Units Handbook, MAFF *Booklet 2267*. MAFF, Northumberland.

Alexander, M (Ed.) (1996) *A guide to the production of management plans for nature reserves and potential areas.* Countryside Council for Wales, Bangor.

Allport, G (1989) Norfolk's bean geese and their management. *RSPB Conservation Review* 3: 59–60.

Andrews, J and Rebane, M (1994) *Farming and Wildlife. A practical management handbook.* RSPB, Sandy.

Armstrong, A C, Caldow, R, Hodge, I D and Treweek, J (1995) Re-creating wetlands in Britain: the hydrological, ecological and socio-economic dimensions. In J Hughes and L Heathwaite (Eds) *Hydrology and Hydrochemistry of British Wetlands.* Wiley, Chichester.

Askew, R R (1988) *The dragonflies of Europe.* Harley Books, Colchester.

Ausden, M (1996) The effects of raised water levels on food supply for breeding waders on lowland wet grassland. *PhD thesis.* University of East Anglia.

Ausden, M and Treweek, J (1995) 'Grassland' In: W J Sutherland and D A Hill (Eds) *Managing Habitats for Conservation*, pp 197–229. Cambridge University Press, Cambridge.

Avery, M, Gibbons, D W, Porter, R, Tew, T, Tucker, G and Williams, G (1995) Revising the British Red Data List for birds: the biological basis of UK conservation priorities. *Ibis* 137 Supplement 1: s232–s239.

Bakker, J P (1989) *Nature management by grazing and cutting.* Kluwer Academic, Dordrecht.

Beardall, C (1996) Sensitive ditching work. *Farming and Conservation* 2(4): 18–21.

Beintema, A J (1982) Meadow birds in the Netherlands. In D A Scott (Ed) *Managing wetlands and their birds, a manual of wetland and waterfowl management.* IWRB, Slimbridge.

Beintema, A J (1986) Man-made polders in the Netherlands: a traditional habitat for shorebirds. *Colonial Waterbirds* 9(2): 196–202.

Beintema, A J, Thissen, J B, Tensen, D and Visser, G H (1991) Feeding ecology of charadriiform chicks in agricultural grassland. *Ardea* 79: 31–44

Bell, D and Chown, D J (1985) Foraging activities of carrion crows *Corvus corone* at West Sedgemoor, Somerset, 1985. Unpublished RSPB Report.

Bibby, C J, Burgess, N D and Hill, D A (1992). *Bird Census Techniques.* Academic Press, London.

Brooks, A (1981) *Waterways and Wetlands: a Practical Conservation Handbook.* BTCV, Wallingford.

Brooks, S J (1993) Review of a method to monitor adult dragonfly populations. *Journal of the British Dragonfly Society.* Vol 9, No.1:1–4.

Bullock, J M, Hodder, K H, Manchester, S J and Stevenson, M J (1995). *Review of information, policy and legislation on species translocations.* Contract report to the Joint Nature Conservation Committee. October 1995.

Burgess, N D, Evans, C E and Thomas, G J (1990) Vegetation changes on the Ouse Washes, England, and their conservation importance. *Biol. Conservation* 53: 173–189.

Cadbury, J and Lambton, S (1994) The importance of RSPB nature reserves for mammals. *RSPB Conservation Review* 8: 77–87.

Chelmick, D, Hammond, C, Moore, N and Stubbs, A (1980) *The conservation of dragonflies.* NCC, Peterborough.

Coles, B (1995) Wetland Management: a survey for English Heritage. *Wetland Archaeology Research Project Occasional Paper 9.* University of Exeter.

Collar, N J, Crosby, M J and Stattersfield, A J (1994) *Birds to Watch 2. The World List of Threatened Birds.* BirdLife International, Cambridge,

Corbet, P S, Longfield, C E and Moore, N W (1960) *Dragonflies.* Collins, London.

Corley, M F V and Hill, M O (1981) *Distribution of Bryophytes in the British Isles.* British Bryological Society, Cardiff.

Cramp, S and Simmons, K E L (1983) *The Birds of the Western Palearctic. Vol 3 Waders to gulls.* Oxford University Press, Oxford.

Cranswick, P A, Waters, R J, Evans, J and Pollitt, M S (1995) *The wetland bird survey 1993-94: wildfowl and wader counts.* BTO/WWT/RSPB/JNCC, Slimbridge.

Crofts, A and Jefferson, R G (Eds) (1994) *The Lowland Grassland Management Handbook.* English Nature/The Wildlife Trusts.

Dickson, R (1985) The lepidopterist's handbook. *The Amateur Entomologist* 13.

Doarks, C (1994) Changes in the aquatic vegetation in grazing marsh dykes in 'Broadland'. In Eurosite *The management of water levels and quality in and around conservation areas.* Proceedings of the 19th Eurosite workshop, Wimmeraux.

Doarks, C and Leach, S (1990) *A classification of grazing marsh dyke vegetation in Broadland.* England Field Unit Project Report 76.5. Nature Conservancy Council, Peterborough.

Drake, C M (1988a) Diptera from the Gwent Levels, South Wales. *Entomologist's Monthly Magazine* 124: 37–44.

Drake, C M (1988b) Water beetles of the Gwent Levels. *Balfour-Browne Club Newsletter* 43: 13–15.

Drake, C M (1988c) *A survey of the aquatic invertebrates of the Essex grazing marshes.* England Field Unit project no 50a. Nature Conservancy Council, Peterborough.

Drake, C M (in press a) The important habitats and characteristic rare invertebrates of lowland wet grassland in England. In: C B Joyce and P M Wade (Eds) *European floodplain and coastal wet grasslands: biodiversity, management and restoration.* John Wiley, Chichester.

Drake, C M (in press b) Factors influencing the species richness of aquatic invertebrates in grazing marsh ditches. In J Harpley *Nature Conservation and the Management of Drainage System Habitat.* John Wiley, Chichester.

Ellenberg, H (1988) *Vegetation Ecology of Central Europe: 4th Edition.* Cambridge University Press, Cambridge.

Evans, C (1991) The conservation importance and management of the ditch floras on RSPB reserves. *RSPB Conservation Review* 5: 65–71.

Fojt, W and Foster, A (1992) Reedbeds, their wildlife and requirements. Botanical and invertebrate aspects of reedbeds, their ecological requirements and conservation significance. In D Ward (Ed), *Reedbeds for wildlife.* pp 49–56. RSPB/University of Bristol.

Frederickson, L H and Reid, F A (1988) Considerations of community characteristics for sampling vegetation. In D H Cross (Ed.) *Waterfowl management handbook.* United States Department of the Interior Fish and Wildlife Service, Fish and Wildlife Leaflet 13.4.1, Washington.

Fuller, R (1982) *Bird habitats in Britain.* T and A D Poyser, Calton.

Fuller, R M (1987) The changing extent and conservation interest of lowland grasslands in England and Wales: a review of grassland surveys 1930–1984. *Biological Conservation* 40: 281–300.

Gibbons, D W, Reid, J W and Chapman, R A (1993) *Atlas of Breeding Birds in Britain and Ireland (1988–91).* T and A D Poyser, London.

Gibson, C W D (1996) *The effects of horse grazing on species-rich grassland.* English Nature Research Report No. 164. English Nature, Peterborough.

Gilman, K (1993) *Initial feasibility study of the creation and operation of a wetland reserve at Morfa-mawr, Malltraeth Marsh, Anglesey.* Unpublished report to CCW.

Gowing, D J G and Spoor, G (in press) The effect of water-table depth on the distribution of plant species in lowland wet grassland. In R Bailey, P José and B Sherwood. *UK Floodplains Symposium.* Samara, Tresaith.

Gowing, D J G, Spoor, G and Mountford, J O (in press) The influence of minor variations in hydrological regime on the composition of wet grassland plant communities. In C B Joyce and P M Wade (Eds) *European floodplain and coastal wet grasslands: biodiversity, management and restoration.* John Wiley, Chichester.

Green, R E (1986) The management of lowland wet grassland for breeding waders. *Chief Scientists Directorate No. 626.* Nature Conservancy Council, Peterborough.

Green, R E and Robins, M (1993) The decline in the ornithological importance of the Somerset Levels and Moors, England and changes in the management of water levels. *Biological Conservation* 66: 95–106.

Hall, M L (1981) *Butterfly Monitoring Scheme; instructions for independent recorders.* ITE, Cambridge.

Harold, R (1995) Creating wetlands at Holkham. *Enact* 3(1): 12-15.

Hawke, C J and José, P V (1995) *Reedbed management for commercial and wildlife interests.* RSPB, Sandy.

Haycock, N E, Burt, T P, Goulding, K W T and Pinay, G (1997) *Buffer zones: their processes and potential in water protection.* Proceedings of the International Conference on Buffer Zones, September 1996. Samara, Tresaith.

Hellawell, J M (1991) Development of a rationale for monitoring. In F B Goldsmith *Monitoring for Conservation and Ecology,* pp1–14. Chapman and Hall, London.

HMSO (1995) *Biodiversity* (2 vols). HMSO, London.

Jefferson, R G and Grice, P V (in press) *The conservation of lowland wet grassland in England.* English Nature, Peterborough.

Jefferson, R G and Robertson, H J (1996) Lowland grassland. Wildlife value and conservation status. *English Nature Research Report No. 169.* English Nature, Peterborough.

Jeffries, D (1996) Decline and recovery of the otter – a personal account. *British Wildlife* 7 (6): 352–364.

Johnson, M S and Bradshaw, A D (1979) Ecological principles for the restoration of disturbed and degraded land. *Applied Biology* 4: 141–200.

Kirby, P (1992) *Habitat management for invertebrates: a practical handbook.* RSPB, Sandy.

Lane, A (1992) *Practical Conservation. Grasslands, Heaths and Moors.* Hodder and Stoughton, London.

Large, A R G and Petts, G E (1992) *Buffer zones for conservation of rivers and bankside habitats.* National Rivers Authority R&D Project Record 340/5/Y. International Centre of Landscape Ecology, Dept. of Geography, Loughborough University of Technology.

Luff, M L (1965) The morphology and microclimate of *Dactylis glomerata* tussocks. *Journal of Ecology* 53: 771–787.

Luff, M L (1966) The abundance and diversity of the beetle fauna of grass tussocks. *Journal of Animal Ecology* 35: 189–208.

Madsen, M, Nielsen, B O, Holter, P, Paderson, O C, Jespersen, J B, vagn Jensen, K-M, Nansen, P and Grønvold, J (1990) Treating cattle with Ivermectin and effects on the fauna and decomposition of dung pats. *Journal of Applied Ecology* 27: 1–15.

MAFF (1974) Technical Bulletin Number 34, Climate and Drainage. HMSO, London.

MAFF (1994) *Water Level Management Plans: a procedural guide for operating authorities.* HMSO, London.

MAFF (1996) Water storage reservoirs – getting control over your water resource. *Booklet PB2512.* MAFF, London.

Marshall, E J P, Wade, P M and Clare, P (1978) Land drainage channels in England and Wales. *Geographical Journal* 144: 254–263.

McLaren, D P (1987) Chalk grassland: a review of management experience. *MSc Thesis,* Wye College, University of London.

Merritt, A (1994) *Wetlands, Industry and Wildlife. A manual of principles and practices.* The Wildfowl and Wetlands Trust, Slimbridge.

Merritt, R, Moore, N W and Eversham, B C (1996) *Atlas of the dragonflies of Britain and Ireland.* ITE Research Publication No 9. HMSO, London.

Moore, N W and Corbet, P S (1990) Guidelines for monitoring dragonfly populations. *Journal of the British Dragonfly Society* 6: 21–23.

Moore, P D and Chapman, S B (1986) *Methods in plant ecology.* Second edition. Blackwell, Oxford.

Mountford, J O (1994) Floristic change in English grazing marshes: the impact of 150 years of drainage and landuse change. *Watsonia* 20: 1–22.

Mountford, J O and Chapman, J M (1993) Water-regime requirements of British wetland vegetation: using the moisture classifications of Ellenberg and Londo. *Journal of Environmental Management* 38: 275–288.

Mountford, J O, Lakhani, K H and Holland, R J (1994a) The effects of nitrogen on species diversity and agricultural production on the Somerset Moors, Phase II: (a) after seven years of fertiliser application; (b) after cessation of fertiliser input for three years. *Final Report to the Institute of Grassland and Environmental Research.* Institute of Terrestrial Ecology, Huntingdon.

Mountford, J O, Tallowin, J R B, Kirkham, F W, and Lakhani, K H (1994b) Sensitivity, productivity and reversibility: a case study of the use of fertilisers on flower-rich hay meadows on the Somerset Levels. In: R J Haggar and S Peel (Eds) *Grassland management and Nature Conservation. BGS Occasional Symposium No 28:* 74–85.

Mountford, J O, Lakhani, K H and Holland, R J (1996) Reversion of grassland vegetation following the cessation of fertiliser application. *Journal of Vegetation Science* 7: 219–228.

Mountford, J O, Lakhani, K H and Rose, S C (in press) Pump drainage impacts on the aquatic macrophytes and bank vegetation of a drainage network. *Proceedings of Nature conservation and the management of drainage system habitat conference at Nottingham University, 1993.*

Newbold, C, Honnor, J and Buckley, K (1989) *Nature conservation and the management of drainage channels.* The Association of Drainage Authorities and the Nature Conservancy Council, Peterborough.

Newbold, C and Mountford, J O (1997) *Water level requirements of wetland plants and animals.* English Nature Freshwater Series No. 6. English Nature, Peterborough.

Newbold, C and Palmer, M (1979) Trophic adaptations of aquatic plants. *Chief Scientists Team Note No. 18.* Nature Conservancy Council, Peterborough.

Newson, M D (1991) Inventory of potential breeding wader sites. Unpublished RSPB Report.

Nix, J (1996) *Farm Management Pocketbook. Twenty-sixth Edition.* Farm Business Unit, School of Rural Economics, Wye College, London.

NRA (1995) *Pesticides in the aquatic environment.* National Rivers Authority.

O'Brien, M and Smith, K W (1992) Changes in the status of waders breeding on wet lowland grasslands in England and Wales between 1982 and 1989. *Bird Study* 39: 165–176.

Orford, R (1996) Reservoir design – for wildlife and landscape. *Farming & Conservation* – July 1996: 20–24.

Owen, M (1973) The management of grassland for wintering geese. *Wildfowl* 24: 123–130.

Owen, M (1983) New Grounds, Slimbridge. Management of summer grazing and winter disturbance on goose pasture. In D A Scott (Ed) *Managing wetlands and their birds, a manual of wetland and waterfowl management.* IWRB, Slimbridge.

Owen, M and Thomas, G J (1979) The feeding ecology and conservation of wigeon wintering at the Ouse Washes, England. *Wildfowl* 32: 73–88.

Palmer, M (1986) The impact of a change from permanent pasture to cereal farming on the flora and invertebrate fauna of watercourses in the Pevensey Levels, Sussex. In *Proceedings of the European Weed Research Society/Association of Applied Biologists 7th International Symposium on Aquatic Weeds,* 1986.

Palmer, M A, Bell, S L and Butterfield, I (1992) A botanical classification of standing waters in Britain: applications for conservation and monitoring. *Aquatic Conservation: Marine and Freshwater Ecosystems,* Vol 2: 125–143.

Perring, F H and Walters, S M (1962) *Atlas of the British Flora.* Nelson, London.

Piersma, T (1986) Breeding waders in Europe: a review of population size estimates and a bibliography of information sources. *Wader Study Group Bulletin 48, Supplement.*

Pollard, E and Yates, T J (1993) *Monitoring butterflies for ecology and conservation.* Chapman and Hall, London.

Pond Action (1994) *National Pond Survey Methods.* Oxford Brookes University.

Porter, K (1994) Seed harvesting – a hay meadow dilemma. *Enact* 2(1): 4–5.

Prosser, M V and Wallace, H L (1992) Vegetation changes at West Sedgemoor 1988 – 1992. Unpublished report to RSPB, Sandy.

Prosser, M V and Wallace, H L (1995) West Sedgemoor vegetation and hydrological monitoring 1993–94. Unpublished RSPB report.

Purseglove, J (1988) *Taming the Flood.* Oxford University Press, Oxford.

Ratcliffe, D A (1977) *A Nature Conservation Review* Vols. 1 and 2. Cambridge University Press, Cambridge.

Reed, T (1985) Estimates of British breeding wader populations. *Wader Study Group Bulletin* 45: 11–12.

Remane, A and Schleiper, C (1971) Brackish water as an area of colonisation of freshwater and marine organisms and specific habitat of brackish water organisms. *Die Binnegewasser Vol XXV. Biology of Brackish Water.*

Rhijn, J G van (1991) *The Ruff.* T and A D Poyser, London.

Rodwell, J S (1991) *British Plant Communities. Volume 2. Mires and Heaths.* Cambridge University Press, Cambridge.

Rodwell, J S (1992) *British Plant Communities. Volume 3. Grasslands and Montane Communities.* Cambridge University Press, Cambridge.

Rodwell, J S (1995) *British Plant Communities. Volume 4. Aquatic communities, swamps and tall-herb fens.* Cambridge University Press, Cambridge.

RSPB, NRA and RSNC (1994) *The New Rivers and Wildlife Handbook.* RSPB, Sandy.

SAC (1990) *Farm Management Handbook.* Scottish Agricultural College, Auchincruive.

Self, M (1997) Lowland wet grassland for waders. Unpublished RSPB report.

Self, M, O'Brien, M and Hirons, G (1994) Hydrological management for waterfowl on RSPB lowland wet grassland reserves. *RSPB Conservation Review* 8: 45–56.

Sheppard, D A (1991) Site survey methods. In R Fry and D Lonsdale (Eds) Habitat conservation for insects: a neglected green issue. *The Amateur Entomologist* 21: 205–208.

Sheppard, D A (1994) Grassland management for invertebrates. In A Crofts and R G Jefferson (Eds) *The lowland grassland management handbook*. English Nature/The Wildlife Trusts, Peterborough.

Shrubb, M and Lack, P C (1991) The numbers and distribution of lapwings *Vanellus vanellus* nesting in England and Wales in 1987. *Bird Study* 38: 20–37.

Simpson, N A (1993) A summary review of information on the autecology and control of six grassland weed species. *English Nature Research Report No. 44*. English Nature, Peterborough.

Simpson, N A and Jefferson, R G (1996) Use of farmyard manure on semi-natural (meadow) grassland. *English Nature Research Report No. 150*. English Nature, Lowlands Team, Peterborough.

Smedema, L K and Rycroft, D W (1983) *Land Drainage: Planning and Design of Agricultural Drainage Systems*. Batsford Academic and Educational, London.

Smith, K W (1983) The status and distribution of waders breeding on wet lowland grasslands in England and Wales. *Bird Study* 30: 177–192.

Smith, K W (1991) Breeding waders of damp lowland grassland in Britain and Ireland. *Wader Study Group Bulletin* 61 Supplement: 33–35.

Soutar, R G and Peterken, G F (1989) Regional lists of native trees and shrubs for use in afforestation schemes. *Arboricultural Journal* 13: 33–43.

Southwood, T R E (1961) The number of species of insects associated with various trees. *Journal of Animal Ecology* 30:1–8.

Spoor, G and Chapman, J M (1992) Comparison of the hydrological conditions of the Nene Washes and West Sedgemoor reserves in relation to their suitability for breeding waders. Unpublished report to the RSPB, Silsoe College, Silsoe.

Spoor, G, Gowing D and Gilbert, J (1996) *A quantitative approach to water level management planning on complex sites*. Proceedings of the 31st River and Coastal Engineers Conference. MAFF, London.

Stace, C (1991) *New Flora of the British Isles*. Cambridge University Press, Cambridge.

Stevenson, M J, Bullock, J M and Ward, L K (1995) Re-creating semi-natural communities: effect of sowing rate on establishment of calcareous grassland. *Restoration Ecology* 3(4): 279–289.

Stewart, A, Pearman, D A, and Preston, C D (1994) *Scarce plants in Britain*. JNCC, Peterborough.

Strachan, R (1996) Water vole sanctuaries. *Wildfowl and Wetlands* 116: 22–24.

Tansley, A E (1939) *The British Islands and their vegetation*. Cambridge University Press, Cambridge.

Taylor, C (1975) *Fields in the English Landscape*. Dent, London.

Thom, V (1986) *Birds in Scotland*. T and A D Poyser, Calton.

Thomas, G J (1980) The ecology of breeding waterfowl at the Ouse Washes, England. *Wildfowl* 31: 73–88.

Thomas, G J (1982) Autumn and winter feeding ecology of waterfowl around the Ouse Washes, England. *Journal of Ecology* 197: 131–172.

Thomas, G J, Allen, D A, and Grose, M P B (1981) The demography of the flora of the Ouse Washes, England. *Biological Conservation* 21: 197–229.

Thomas, G, José, P and Hirons, G (1995) Wet grassland in the millennium. *Enact* 3 (1): 4–6.

Thomas, J A (1989) Ecological lessons from the re-introduction of Lepidoptera. *The Entomologist* 108: 56–68.

Tickner, M B and Evans, C E (1991) The management of lowland wet grasslands on RSPB reserves. Unpublished, RSPB.

Treweek, J R, Caldow, R, Armstrong, A, Dwyer, J and Sheail, J (1991) *Wetland Restoration: techniques for an integrated approach*. ITE, Monks Wood.

Tyler, S (1992) A review of the status of breeding waders in Wales. *1991 Welsh Bird Report*: 74–83.

Tyler, S (1993) Yellow wagtail. In D W Gibbons, J W Reid and R A Chapman *Atlas of Breeding Birds in Britain and Ireland* (1988–91), pp 286–287. T and A D Poyser, London.

Ward, D E, Hirons, G J and Self, M J (1995) Planning for restoration of peat wetlands for birds. In B D Wheeler, S C Shaw, W J Fojt, and R A Robertson *Restoration of Temperate Wetlands*, pp 207–222. John Wiley and Sons, Chichester.

Wells, T C E (1983) The creation of species-rich grasslands. In A R Warren and F B Goldsmith (Eds) *Conservation in Perspective*, pp 215–232. Wiley, Chichester.

Wells, T, Bell, S and Frost, A (1981) *Creating attractive grasslands using native plant species*. Nature Conservancy Council, Shrewsbury.

Wells, T C E, Cox, R and Frost, A (1989) The establishment and management of wildflower meadows. *Focus on Nature Conservation*, No. 21. Nature Conservancy Council, Peterborough.

Wells, T C E, Frost, A and Bell, S (1986) Wild flower grasslands from crop-grown seed and hay-bales. *Focus on Nature Conservation*, No. 15. Nature Conservancy Council, Peterborough.

Williams, G and Bowers, J K (1987) Land drainage and birds in England and Wales. *RSPB Conservation Review* 1: 25–30.

Williams, G and Hall, M (1987) The loss to arable agriculture of coastal grazing marshes in south and east England, with special references to east Essex. *Biological Conservation* 39: 243–253.

Williams, G, Henderson, A, Goldsmith, L and Spreadborough, A (1983) The effects on birds of land drainage improvements in the North Kent Marshes. *Wildfowl* 34: 22–47.

Wolseley, P A, Palmer, M A and Williams, R (1984) *The aquatic flora of the Somerset Levels and Moors*. Nature Conservancy Council, Peterborough.

Wolton, R J (1992) *Management guidelines for Culm grassland*. English Nature, Okehampton, Devon.

Index

The alphabetical arrangement is letter by letter.
Numbers in *italics* refer to photographs.
Numbers in **bold** refer to case studies, figures
and tables.

Kent, grazing marsh losses **14**

lakeside wet grassland *7, 7*, **36**
lanes *see* droves and lanes
lapwing **66**, 68, 69, **71**, 72, *163*, **169**
levelling surveys *21*, **157**, **159**, **161**, **164-5**
lifting-gate sluices **86**, 87, *87*, *158*
lime, use on wet grasslands 42
litter layer, use by invertebrates 55
liver fluke 113
    life cycle **114**
livestock
    health products 116-17
    owning: advantages and disadvantages 111,
        112
    see also cattle; grazing; horses; sheep
livestock unit coefficients **106**, 106
Local Environment Agency Plans (LEAPs) 16,
    25, 26
location of site, management implications 20
Loch Gruinart **185-7**
Lower Derwent Valley **182-4**
lowland floodplains *see* floodplain grassland

Malltraeth Marsh **159-60**
mammals 11
management plans/planning **18**, 24
    considerations **18**; costs 24; legal and
        planning **23**, 205
    Malltraeth Marsh **159-60**
    strategies and options **28**
manure, farmyard 41-2, 128, 129
MATCH software package 136, **194**
meadows *see* flood meadow management
mechanical operations 117, 128
mire grasslands **8**, 33, *33*, 33-4, **210-11**
mole channels 89, 90
monitoring
    birds 145-6, 192-93
    drainage channel vegetation 137
    grassland vegetation 135-6
    invertebrates **140**, 140-4
    water levels 147
    West Sedgemoor **192-3**
moth, purple-bordered gold *184*
mowing
    conservation value 39
    effects on: plant growth 39, *40*; wildlife **129**
    equipment 103
    for hay/fodder *101*, 102; with aftermath
        grazing 104, **188-9**, **191**, **192**
    frequency 101
    practicalities, versus grazing 103
    removal of cuttings 102
    timing 101-2
    see also hay
mud *see* bare ground/mud

National Vegetation Classification 136
    floristic table for MG13 **136**
    of wet grassland **8**, **8**, 32-4, **34**, **35-6**
natural regeneration of grassland 118, **184**, **196**,
    196-7, **198**, **199**
Nene Washes *73*, 103, 111-12, **179-81**
nest protectors *169*
nest trampling 108
    calculating risk of **108**

nitrates *see* eutrophication
North Kent, grazing marsh losses **14**
North Meadow, Cricklade *32*, **188-9**
Northward Hill **195-7**
nurse crops, use in grassland establishment 120,
    199

ochre 91, 97
Old Hall Marshes **173-4**
organic fertilisers 41-2, 128, 129
otter 11
Ouse Washes 5, *5*, **154-6**
owls 75

parasites in livestock 113
    life cycles **114**
    treatment 116-17
passerines, breeding, census techniques 146
peat soils
    dessicated 83
    drainage channel density 132
    iron toxicity 91, 97
    poaching 55
    see also soils
pesticides
    use near watercourses 99
    see also herbicides; insecticides
phosphates *see* eutrophication
pipes, for sub-surface irrigation 89-90
pitfall traps, to collect invertebrates 142
plant plugs 119
plants
    and fertilisers and mowing **129**
    and grazing 39, **110**, **127-8**
    as indicators of water regime 37, **38**
    rare/scarce **9**, **46**; Insh Marshes **153**;
        Ouse Washes **154**; Pulborough Brooks **177**
    and salinity 91
    seasonal effects of flooding on **130**
    wet grassland communities 8, **8**; areas (ha) **9**;
        and hydrological management **194**
    see also aquatic/marginal plants; grasses;
        National Vegetation Classification;
        wet grassland *and under names of individual*
        species
plugs, plant 119
poaching 54-5, *104*, 104-5, 111
pollarded willows 62, 123, *124*, 125
ponds/pools
    digging on grassland 117
    rare/scarce plants **46**
    surveying invertebrates of 140-1
    temporary: value for invertebrates 56, 60
    see also flooding
pond-sedge, greater 34, *44*, 216
pondside wet grassland *see* lakeside wet
    grassland
poplar, black 124
Pulborough Brooks 13, **175-8**
pumps, water 88, **89**
    diesel *88*
    wind-powered **172**, *172*

quadrats 135-6

ragwort 113, 115
rails, census techniques **145**

rainfall, winter, and wildfowl at West
  Sedgemoor **192**
Raised Water Level Areas (RWLAs) **161-3**, **191**,
  193
raptors 10, 75
Ray, River, catchment **198-9**
redshank **72**, *72*
reed sweet-grass 34, 104, 218
refuge creation **190-1**
reintroduction of species 20, 118-19
reptiles 11
reservoirs 85, 87-8
restoration of wet grassland 118-22, **157-58**, **184**,
  195-7, **198-9**
  aftercare 122, **196**
  incentive schemes and grants 15-16, 202
rivers
  channelisation *12*
  maintenance authorities **93**, 203
  see also under name of individual rivers
rolling of grassland 117
roundworm, life cycle **114**
ruff 73

salinity 60, 91
scrub control 125, **153**
sedge-beds 33, 34
seeding
  Northward Hill **195**, **196**
  site preparation 119
  slot seeding 121
  sowing rates 120
  sowing times 120
seed sources
  hay bales 119-20, **198**, **199**
  seed banks 118
  seed harvesting 121, **188**, **189**
  seed mixtures 120; 'Cricklade Mixture' **189**;
    used at Loch Gruinart **186**; used at
    Northward Hill **195**; used in River Ray
    catchment **198**, **199**
seepages, management around 123
semi-natural grasslands 32, *32*
shading, effects of aquatic plants 49; effects on
  aquatic invertebrates 62
sheep
  grazing *105*, 105-6; labour requirements 111
  handling facilities 109, **180-1**
  health problems 112-13
  see also livestock
shepherding 111-12
  Nene Washes **180**, **181**
Sherborne Water Meadows **157-8**
shoveler *74*
shrubs *see* trees and shrubs
silage-making 102, 103, 158, **168**, **186**
silt soils *see* soils
Sites of Special Scientific Interest (SSSIs)
  management constraints 19
  Water Level Management Plans for 24-5
size of site, management implications 20
slot seeding 121, *121*
slubbing *see* maintenance *under* drainage
  channels
sluices **86**, 86-7, **87**, *87*, *158*
  Annaghroe Meadows *164*
  Earith (Ouse Washes) *156*

Holkham Marsh **168**
  and water distribution 82
  Wet Moor *163*
snake, grass 11
snipe 14, *72*, 72, **73**
soils
  and aquatic invertebrates 60
  and dam construction 86
  and foot drains 132
  hydraulic conductivity 83, **84**
  large-scale disturbance 117
  and plant communities **37**, *37*
  and salinity 91
  see also peat soils; water level management;
    water-tables
Somerset Levels and Moors *see* Southlake Moor;
  Westmoor; West Sedgemoor; Wet Moor
Southlake Moor *15*
spoil disposal 97, **176**
springs, management around 123
stocking densities 106-8
  determining factors **107**
  medium level rates **107**
storage of winter water *see* winter water storage
Strumpshaw Fen 96
submerged plants 45, 226-31
  see also aquatic/marginal plants
subsoiling 90
sub-surface irrigation 89-90, **90**
sulphur toxicity 91
surface flows, and water distribution 82
surface irrigation *see* foot drains
surveying *see* monitoring
swamp communities 8, 33, *33*, 34, 212-13
swan
  Bewick's *64*
  mute 73-4
  see also wildfowl

terraced irrigation **161-3**
terrestrial invertebrates
  effects of fertiliser use and mowing on **129**
  and flooding: summer 56; winter 55-6
  and grazing **63**, **110**, **127-8**
  habitats providing diversity 62-3
  monitoring methods 142, **142**
  seasonal effects of flooding on 130
  substrate requirements **54**, 54-5
  using bare mud **54**
  vegetation requirements 51-4, **52**
  and water regime 55
  see also beetles; dragonflies and damselflies
    and under names of individual species
tillering of grasses 39, **39**
tilting-weir sluices **86**, 87, *163*
topography, and water distribution 82
topping 102-3, *103*, *129*, **151**, **168**, **184**, **186**, **192**,
  195
trees and shrubs
  management 123-4, *124*, 125, **153**
  planting 124
  wildlife value 62-3, 123
trophic states of water **47**
  and drainage channel plants 47-8
  see also eutrophication
turfing 119
tussocks 51-2, 71

Other RSPB habitat management handbooks

*Reedbed Management for Commercial &
Wildlife Interests* by C J Hawke and P V José,
RSPB. 1996. ISBN 0 903138 81 6 £14.95

The New Rivers and Wildlife Handbook by
RSPB, NRA and RSNC. RSPB. 1994.
ISBN 0 903138 79 9 £19.95

*Farming and Wildlife – A Practical
Management Handbook* by John Andrews
and Michael Rebane. RSPB. 1994. ISBN
0903138 67 0 £21.95

Gravel Pit Restoration for Wildlife by John
Andrews. RSPB. 1990. ISBN 0 903138 60 3
£12